PROPHETS WITHOUT HONOR

PROPHETS WITHOUT HONOR

A Requiem for Moral Patriotism

William M. Strabala & Michael J. Palecek

Algora Publishing
New York

Library of Congress Cataloging-in-Publication Data 2002-006028

Strabala, William.
  Prophets without honor : a requiem for moral patriotism / by William
Strabala and Michael Palecek.
    p. cm.
  ISBN 1-892941-98-8 (alk. paper)
  1. Christianity and politics. 2. Christianity and justice. 3. Sociology, Christian. I. Palecek, Michael. II. Title.
  BR115.P7 S755 2002
  261.70973—dc21

                      2002006028

Front Cover: Mosaic adorning a chapel on Offutt Air Force Base near Bellevue and Omaha, Nebraska, Headquarters of the Strategic Air Command — dedicated to SAC personnel.

Printed in the United States

Table of Contents

Introduction   1
Historical Prologue: Prophetic Words Borrowed from Berrigan and
    Gorbachev   3
1. Prophets Hearing Voices from History   7
2. Political Prophecies: Divine Atomic Right to Rule   11
3. Slippery Footing: Bananas, Oil And Cold War Ice   17
4. Lionsden Prophecy: We The System   23
5. Prophecy Globalized: Trilateralism and Secret Teams   29
6. Good Land for Prophet-Making   39
    Schlesinger and McGovern Scope It Out   41
    Priests Venture In, Where "Food for Peace" Fears to Tread   42
    A Bit of Darrell Rupiper's Story   45
7. Lies to America, Lies to the Church: Rupiper and Vietnam   49
    Showing Up the Communists   49
    Showing Up the Viet Cong   52
8. Prophecies in Blood and Fire   57
    The Baltimore Four   59
    The Catonsville Nine   59
    Larry Rosebaugh's Story   62
9. A Ticket to 'Nam   73
    Albert   78
    Chuck   82
    The Nelsons   85
    Jerry   86
    Bill   87
    Artie   88
    A Mother   89

10. The Confirmation of Prophets 91
    Urban Renewal 92
    Rupiper and Grams' Last Words in Recife 94
    Kabat Takes a Turn 98
11. Through a Stained Glass Window, Darkly 103
    How to Get SAC'd 103
    Marylyn Felion 107
    Jean Petersen 110
    And the Nukes Go On 112
12. When Omaha Collides with Recife 113
    Mike Palecek 114
    Cruel, but All Too Usual 120
13. Heartburn in the Heartland 129
    Frank Cordaro 131
    Love Intervenes, Prophecy Triumphs 136
    Tom Cordaro and Angela Cordaro 138
    Bishop Dingman 140
14. Secret Memos and Smoking Guns 143
    Sowing the Seeds 149
    Reaping What was Sown 150
15. Of Hostages and Prophets: Rupiper in Iran 157
    Respect 159
    And Now, Disrespect 166
    A Prophecy, Like Life, Goes On 172
16. Iran-Contra: The Eichmann Corollary 179
    A Short, Modern History 180
    Oliver North and the South, the East and the West 181
    Which Laws for Which Citizens? 185
    Disclosure, If Not Closure 186
    A Whole Cast of Liars 188
    Plots and Subplots 195
17. Prophecies over the Death Squads 199
    Roy Bourgeois 201
    Linda Ventimiglia 205
    Rosebaugh and Bourgeois Keep the Prophets' Faith 206
    Another Round at Fort Benning 208
    The Plowshares Eight 210

18. Nuclear-Walled Jericho   217
    The Plowshares Eight   221
    The German Plowshares   223
    Silo Pruning Hooks   225
    When Good Friday was April Fool's Day   227
19. All For Oil: Desert Storm and Orphan Guts   231
    A Favor They Could Not Resist   232
    Other Organs of War   238
20. Post Mortem of the Conquest   241
    They Are Still Killing   244
21. The Church in Prophetic Crisis   253
22. The Prophetic Question   265
23. From Des Moines to Nuremberg to Rome and Back   271
    Michael Sprong   272
    Frank Cordaro   273
24. Medals for Heroes of Peace, Not War   277
    Charles "Angelo" Liteky   279
    Willa Elam and the Challenge of Making a Challenge   288
25. Prophecy Betrayed   295
    Carl Kabat: Nine Strikes, You're Out   295
    Paul Kabat   301
26. Prophecy of Plowshares in Space   307
27. Andromeda, Strained   311
28. At A Place Called Eden   319
29. Observing Prophecy in the Courtroom   325
    Carl and the Next Generation   325
30. Prophetic Aftershocks   333

AFTERWORD: IS THERE A WAY OUT?   337
    Prophetic Postscript: Towers of Babel   338
    Prophets, What Say You, Now?   344
APPENDIX: THE LIVES AND "CRIMES" OF THE PROPHETS   355

ACKNOWLEDGEMENTS

The authors wish to express their gratitude and appreciation to:

The mentors of co-author William M. Strabala, including the late Professor Leslie Moeller, University of Iowa School of Journalism, and the late Morton Margolin of the *Rocky Mountain News* — both for teaching this: What happens in our lives amounts to more than just events to be recounted, but the future to be understood and reported before mistakes of the past are repeated.

Kevin and Rich and Jean (friends imprisoned, at times, with co-author Mike Palecek), and all those who crossed the line to face the mental terror of what an increasing part of our lives must now confront and resolve in peace, and for its sake.

Rev. Jack Bremer and Norm Forer of the University of Kansas, for their background information and personal efforts in support of global betterment at a time of world crisis — a goal bonded by their vital involvement with at least one of the Prophets of this book.

Marylyn Felion and Mary Lou Pedersen, for their research assistance and involvement with the prophetic drive for human justice, with the wish that their vision, shared with the Prophets Without Honor, may come true.

Rosalind Strabala and Ruth Palecek, each for their spousal encouragement of their author-husbands.

Jim Cypher of The Cypher Literary Agency, Beacon, New York, for his essential professional assistance and advice.

Common people everywhere, who have the uncommon ability to create peace where there is war, supply justice where it is lacking, and foment freedom when it is needed.

To our loving parents.

To Philip and Daniel Berrigan, for setting the prophetic example.

To all those of every faith, gender, and color who have died or suffered at the hands of immoral governments — whether in war imposed or by revolution compelled — while promoting the cause of human freedom, racial justice and moral rectitude. Because these are gifts from creation, designed to be unwrapped only by mankind.

To the thousands of prophets, whether mentioned or not in this publication, who have risked it all to guide the world toward that ideal level of social justice and peace which gives grace to the machinery of our minds and spirits. Because these are the gifts discoverable only by humans capable of enhancing creation.

With a prayer for a change of mind on the part of those who persecute our prophets and thus rob the world of the humanity, justice and peace we collectively need in order to lay claim to being the intelligent part of the universe. Because the Creator gave us the task of perfecting this world with mind and spirit. REQUIESCANT IN PACE:

> To Rev. Paul Kabat, OMI, and to Sam Day
> To Archbishop Oscar Romero
> To Archbishop Juan Gerardi
> To Rev. Martin Luther King, Jr.
> To Archbishop Dom Helder Camara

To all our prophets departed, so that peace and freedom may live.

REFLECTIONS ON THE TITLE

A prophet is not without honor, save in his own country and in his own home.
— *Matthew, 13:57*

PROPHET: 1) A person who speaks by divine inspiration or as the interpreter through whom the will of a god is expressed. 2) A predictor, a soothsayer. 3) The chief spokesman of a cause or movement. 4) A leader espousing action against a perceived harm from the past, an evil in the present, or a portent in the future. 5) A political critic within a theocracy.
— *Dictionaries*

We know in part, and we prophesy in part. . . For now we see through a glass, darkly.
— *St. Paul, Corinthians 13:9-13*

The prophetic duty may at times be to call people to choose between their duty to God and their duty to country.
— *Harold Schmidt, pastor, First Lutheran Church, Omaha, 1985*

Then the king commanded, and they brought Daniel (the prophet) and they cast him into the den of lions. (Daniel said) 'My God has shut up the mouths of the lions' . . . Then was the king exceeding glad for him and he commanded that Daniel be taken out of the den . . . Then King Darius wrote to all the people, tribes and languages dwelling on the whole earth: 'Peace be multiplied unto you.'
— *Book of Daniel, Ch. 6*

They shall beat their swords into plowshares, and their spears into pruning hooks; nation shall not lift up sword against nation, neither shall they learn war any more.
— *Isaiah, 1:13 and the Plowshares Eight*

INTRODUCTION

This is an untold story, a back-door history of America, illustrated by the experiences of priests who put their lives on the line for their beliefs — priests who spent years of those lives in jail. They were penalized for challenging immoral government policies — policies that have brought little but war, exploitation and poverty to most of the world, but prosperity to America's reigning upper crust.

This book is about the foresight of prophets who have the simple human grace to recognize bad history in the making and to tell us how to avoid it for the future. These prophets have read what America's actions foreshadow — based on the bulk of what casts those shadows. The shadowy bulk that looms in their stories has to do with international intrigues whose effects are far from clear in the daily news. Their stories are about unfettered capitalistic economics, and the abuse that forwards its goals. Their stories explain how our society has become warped by political policies that are achieved by means that are flatly immoral by any secular scale of ethics.

This book explains why it was necessary for the prophets to raise their pennants of protest and why the government had to send them to jail. In the process, their stories expose the decay of the moral patriotism that our nation's founders bequeathed us.

This book, then, is about the political power of oil, and of those who control it to the point of corrupting decent human endeavor. Oil requires the application of politics, economic dominance, and military control, The book is thus about systems that negate the freedoms of speech and religious expression, torturing and killing those who defy whatever steals such freedoms.

Identified along the way are manipulated events that have brought us to the predicaments of our times: Domino theories; fear of Communism; national security; lies by presidents; trilateralism; globalization; exploitation; CIA treachery; FBI spying and murder; invisible, shadow government; war by proxy; corruption of power; and good old Uncle Sam-sponsored terrorism with all the terror of reprisals.

The book ends on a sad note of the prophecy fulfilled by the events of September 11, 2001. That is a date in history that might have been avoided, if only we had honored our prophets.

Governments do not have souls. When they make a mistake, they cannot make an act of contrition and change events that they should never have caused. They never feel the need to confess, and so they make things "right" by denial.

Patriots do have souls. Too often, they are nobly misguided souls. They cannot admit their government can be wrong. And so they never feel the need to make an act of contrition for the ethical errors of their government.

Prophets have too much soul. They can forgive what even the non-contrite deny, but they keep nagging them about the moral truth of peace and justice. That kind of government is called conscience.

That is why:

America is at war without ever having been truly at peace.
We are abolishing treaties that were intended to bring peace.
We don't have enemies, but we look for ways to create them.
We are creating weapons to defend ourselves against unidentified foes.
We maintain for future use atomic bombs that were too awesome to use in the past.
We destroy nations to save them from the results of prior predations.
We jail our priest-prophets for trying to prevent the crimes of war.
We use secret agencies to do all these things in the interest of national security.
We have half a world full of people who fully hate us.
We are so blinded, we have to ask why; and we have to ask what kind of country is this, and how the hell we got here.

These are the issues that this book explores; these are the questions it will attempt to answer.

There are people in this world who, by their deeds and thoughts, earn the title of prophet. In 1969, *before* he became a fugitive, hunted by a government enraged over his criticism of the very disorder that it had created and he had protested, Rev. Daniel Berrigan, S.J., spoke these prophetic words.

It is announced that a computerized center is being built in the Pentagon at a cost of some seven millions of dollars, to offer instant response to outbreaks of civil disorder anywhere in the land; that moreover, the government takes so serious a view of civil disorder that federal troops, with war experience in Vietnam, will have first responsibility to quell civil disorder.

We stretch out our hands to our brothers throughout the world. All of us, who act against the law, turn to the poor of the world, to the Vietnamese, to the victims, to the soldiers who kill and die for the wrong reasons because they were so ordered by the authorities of that public order which is, in effect, a massive institutionalized disorder.

We say killing is disorder; life and gentleness and community and unselfishness is the only order we recognize. For the sake of that order, we risk our liberty, our good name. The time is past when good men can remain silent, when obedience can segregate men from public risk, when the poor can die without defense.

Redeem the times! The times are inexpressibly evil. Christians pay conscious, indeed religious tribute, to Caesar and Mars by the approval of overkill tactics, by brinkmanship, by nuclear liturgies, by racism, by support of genocide.

And yet, in a time of death, the truth rules. In a time of death, some men — the resisters, those who work hardily for social change, those who preach and embrace the unpalatable truth — such men overcome death.

These words were spoken at the height of the Cold War, before the Gulf of Tonkin lie was promulgated; before the longest war in US history went into the records as a moral and military disaster; before the assassination by death squads of bishops, priests, nuns and thousands of peasants in Central America; before Iranians and radical Beirut Moslems felt compelled to take Americans hostage; before the Watergate burglary scandal; before the Iran-Contra drugs and guns scandal; before the Towers of Babel, called the World Trade Center, were leveled.

Berrigan's words were spoken before the US and the CIA kindled the Iran-Iraq War; before the need for Desert Storm; before the formation of the Rockefeller-ruled Trilateral Commission; before the establishment of computer-driven cyber-spy systems with names like *Carnivore* that now devour everyone's First Amendment flesh before it can live.

Berrigan's words of 1969 were buttressed on December 30, 2000, by those of no less an historic figure than Mikhail Gorbachev, who waited until after the quibbling of the Gore-Bush election had died down to criticize the US's imperial attitude toward the rest of the world. In an article published in the *International Herald Tribune*, entitled, "Mr. Bush, The World Doesn't Want to Be American," Gorbachev, who comes from an atheistic point of view compared to Berrigan, echoes his thoughts and those of his fellow prophets by saying:

It is time for America's electorate to be told the truth; that the present situation of the United States, with part of its population able to enjoy a life of extraordinary comfort and privilege, is not tenable as long as an enormous portion of the world lives in abject poverty, degradation and backwardness.

Berrigan's words, along with the protest actions of the prophets since that time, bespeak the very evils that even Gorbachev, once the archenemy of the US, insists are the world's enemy today. In 1969, America's hearing was blocked by the roar of the Vietnam War. In 2001, America was holding its political ears again as the sounds of terrorism exploded and bombs were dropped on Afghanistan — because American buildings had been smashed and lives had been taken in America.

Even during the years thought (by most) to be peaceful, those ears had similarly been closed to prophetic warnings against America's expanding militarism, at the very time when it was creating suffering and stirring hatred. America was then too busy in the Middle East comforting the righteous grief of European and Russian Jews to hear the cries of the rudely dislocated and never-compensated Palestinians who bore the post-war brunt of the Free World's solace for Israel. In 1982, Ariel Sharon, the "Butcher of Beirut," caused the massacre of 2,000 Palestinians at the Sabra refugee camps. Two decades later, Sharon was leading the state of Israel not toward peace, but toward reoccupation. Where does that leave the US on the issue of terrorism as supplier of the weapons of terror to Israel?

That, in part, explains why America was bombed by pirated airliners on September 11, 2001. That, in part, is why America is so hated, despite its efforts to feed the very people that its policies have starved politically. But the problems with the world today are much larger than the single issue of Israel and Palestine.

Given the 19th-century preconditions of European colonialism and the 20th-century evolution of US imperialism, here is a partial list of historical events that became the headwaters of the troubles that have flowed since, including the protests and prophecies covered in this book:

> 1908: Oil was first discovered in the Middle East, at Masjid-i-Salaman in Iran.
>
> 1917: The Bolshevik (communist) revolution, based on Marxism, erupted in Russia.
>
> 1927: Western oil companies discovered the rich Kirkuk Field in northern Iraq. This is the same area now under UN protection as a "no fly zone" following the 1990 Gulf War. With this 1927 Iraqi discovery, the world's major oil companies created on a map the "Red Line Agreement." Within that line, companies such as British Petroleum, Standard Oil, Texaco, Royal Dutch Shell, and Gulf Oil agreed not to act individually "either directly or indirectly in the production or manufacture of crude oil" in that area.
>
> 1946: The US offered to turn over its atomic bomb secrets to a United Nations trust and to destroy its store of nuclear weapons. The USSR vetoed the idea. (By July 25, 1946, the US proceeded with A-

bomb tests on Bikini Atoll, and by 1949, Russia exploded its own atomic bomb.)

1946: A state of Israel was created out of Palestine, incurring the wrath of Moslem Arabs.

1947: Truman signed the National Security Act, which established the CIA and the National Security Agency.

1941, 1951, 1953: Related events. Britain and WWII war ally Soviet Union used coups and assassinations to install their chosen leader in Iran, in order to control the production of oil.

1953: The Dulles brothers engineered a coup against freely elected Jacobo Arbenz in Guatemala to keep Rockefeller's United Fruit in control of the land. This formalized the Domino Theory against the feared advance of Communism worldwide, and set the bloody table for Iran-Contra many years later.

British historian Lord Acton pronounced, in 1887, the oft-cited words: "power corrupts, and absolute power corrupts absolutely." The events of recent history confirm that virtue and power don't mix.

What do you call the thousands of people who have been jailed over the past several decades in the US for protesting against the militaristic policies of the United States? You can't call them political prisoners, because, as President George H. W. Bush told the repressive Chinese regime at the time of the Tiananmen Square insurgency, "The US has no political prisoners."

That leaves no category except prisoners of peace, or prophets. In any case, we know there is a core group of such people who have set a prophetic example by their protests; that example now is being followed by thousands of others.

Here are the names, in alphabetical order, of some of the priest-prophets who suffered jail in trying to rally a whole nation: Daniel Berrigan, Philip Berrigan, Roy Bourgeois, Frank Cordaro, Carl Kabat, Paul Kabat, Charles J. "Angelo" Liteky, Michael Palecek, Larry Rosebaugh, and Darrell Rupiper. All of these men (except Palecek, who completed his degree but stopped short of being ordained) were or still are ordained Catholic priests. All but Paul Kabat are alive today. As of 2001, Philip Berrigan, Carl Kabat and Charlie Liteky are still in jail. By the time Kabat is released, he will have spent 16 years in jail. By 2002, Cordaro was back in jail for another protest.

Philip Berrigan and Charles Liteky left the priesthood to marry, and Philip also has been excommunicated by the Catholic Church. Liteky is the only Congressional Medal of Honor recipient to have been jailed. All of them continue to agitate for restoring moral integrity to a political system gone wrong. Many of them continue to risk jail for doing so. As both patriots and prophets they are, in their own country, Prophets Without Honor.

Like all prophets, these men have idealistic visions, and they hear, in the ears of their idealism, voices speaking to them from history, guiding them in what they say and do, and so they are not alone; nor is their prophecy exclusively masculine.

They are joined in their commitment and their actions by many women, and the voices they hear include that of the late Dorothy Day. She was co-founder of the *Catholic Worker* newspaper and organizer of a system of Catholic Worker communities that give aid and comfort to street people across the country. Her efforts began in the Great Depression. Her voice brought us many messages:

> If they come for the innocent without stepping over our bodies, cursed be our religion and our life.

> The point of the matter is this: We are paying for war, if we pay the tax. It is so important for us to hold to our stand even if the government lowers the boom. We have an absolute faith that we will keep going even if we lose everything. Our principle is what we are living for.

> We have all known the long loneliness and we have learned that the only solution is to love, and that love comes with community.

> Don't call me a saint. I don't want to be dismissed so easily.

> Where are the saints to try to change the social order? Not just to minister to its slaves, but to do away with slavery?

> The Church is the cross on which Christ is crucified. I think that, when I see the Church taking the side of the rich and powerful; when I see bishops living in luxury while the poor are thrown the crumbs of charity.

This kind of thought can also be heard in the lofty words of presidents, but the leaders' deeds never matched the rhetoric. LBJ spoke simultaneously of a Great Society that could afford both guns and butter and a nation that sought "no wider war." Nixon spoke of peace. The prophets saw only war, deceit and corruption, and so they bridged the gap between words and deeds — to the point of civil disobedience and jail.

Who are these Prophets Without Honor? A brief chronology of their lives is provided in the Appendix; the chapters to come review the substance of their lives and actions, and lead through the twists of history over the past 50 years to reveal the immorality of secret policies and actions to which the US government will never admit.

William VanEtten Casey, S.J., was first to place the placard of "prophet" around the necks of the Berrigan brothers when he wrote, in his book, *The Berrigans*, in 1971: "The Berrigans' gesture of pouring napalm on draft files and burning them, precisely because it is a symbolic gesture, fits not only the tradition of radical American politics, but also the prophetic tradition of symbolic acts." The then-newly-ordained Berrigans, by nature quick to identify and challenge anything wrong within the system, showed their affinity to the causes espoused by Rev. Martin Luther King, Jr. Having been born in poverty, they were quick to understand how the agendas of the rich nations and rich societies created whole classes of poor people of all colors on every continent.

What was needed, the Berrigans thought, was a way to establish that understanding in the mind of the American public. Like King, with his civil rights message, they wanted to be prototypes for spreading the anti-war, anti-nuclear, pro-human, pro-Christ message; to make the world resonate to such soulful themes as eliminating war because it was a source of poverty and prejudice. Like King, they thought to do so within a secular system that separated church from state, yet a system that, for political purpose, needed to hug the charisma of Christian philosophy. The Berrigans achieved success by resorting to radical forms of public notoriety. They were the first Catholic priests in US history to be arrested and jailed for political crimes: going to Hanoi without permission, and burning draft files in Catonsville, Maryland.

The '50s, '60s and '70s were times of special turmoil: social, racial, political, military and economic. New troubles piled on top of those in the '80s and '90s. In aggregate, the same problems still remain unsolved and threaten the third Christian millennium on earth and even nearby space. For the prophets discussed in this book, each historic intersection with history is burdened with moral issues. War over security stirs the moral issue of killing, creating conflict with peace and justice in society; the atomic bomb obliterates morality along with society; greed for oil creates issues of human exploitation and political power. All have social and moral connections with human poverty. How leaders of nations mishandled such intersections with moral issues explains the actions taken by the prophets who oppose them.

In the United States of the '50s, there was virtually no objection, on moral grounds, to the use of the atom bomb. People then seemed generally content to accept as right whatever axioms for action their governments or friendly neighbors presented. The fight against anything that seemed communistic was paramount and the politicians seemed to apply no moral restraints in that direction.

It was against such a backdrop of complacency that the prophets, starting with Rev. Martin Luther King, Jr., and then the Berrigan brothers, began their agitation for moral correction. They challenged the political, social, economic and military sectors of a misguided America, daring the nation to draw attention by jailing them, so that the world could see in them its own reflection . . . one that would show the loss of freedom and human dignity that occurs when a global military system has no conscience.

The Berrigans stirred the consciences of many other prophets and compelled like-minded people to take to the streets. Soon protests over civil rights and the immoral war in Vietnam stirred idealistic youth on the campuses of the world. The protests and expanding public turmoil spurred governmental reaction to the point of secret and illegal suppression and then outright killing — of students, by government troops at Kent State University, for example. Killings for similar reasons at Jackson State were given less prominence, most likely because its students were black and the US power-world was still white.

The prophets tended to think not in terms of black versus white, but right and wrong. They knew their government and parts of its society were wrong. As moral leaders, they had no choice but to act.

2. Political Prophecies —
Divine Atomic Right to Rule

From the technological and military side of world events, perhaps the advent of the atomic bomb has had the most enduring and moral impact. In close second place is war by proxy, such as that initially fought in Vietnam, when the nuclear powers realized that it would be impractical to use atomic bombs to get what they wanted. With the atomic age came prophecies from those on high, from those who had helped create the political power with which America, as a dominant part of the world system, may now be arrogantly taunting the have-not part of the world.

One prophecy came from President Harry Truman, who deplored the destruction caused by World War II as he assessed its aftermath in Berlin.

Another prophecy came from Leo Szilard and dozens of Los Alamos A-bomb scientists (including Einstein), who petitioned Truman not to use the bomb once it was determined that the Germans had not proceeded with its development. Szilard feared, correctly, that it would start an arms race with the Soviets.

President Dwight Eisenhower prophesied, in his farewell address in 1961, the rise of a "military-industrial complex."

As Truman was considering the use of the atom bomb against Japan, Szilard and numerous other scientists who had worked on it development petitioned Truman not to use it, but to run a demonstration of it, instead. But Szilard, a refugee from Hungary who was the real theoretical genius behind the bomb, was coming from a weak position; he had been restricted in his influence in the Manhattan Project. General Leslie Groves, the army's A-bomb ramrod, thought Szilard's political leanings were communistic, and he chose American physicist Robert Oppenheimer to head the Manhattan Project at Los Alamos. Groves either didn't know, or chose to overlook, the fact that Oppenheimer had been a member of the American Communist Party in his college days. Years later, after being formally forgiven, Oppenheimer would lecture against the nuclear arms race.

Truman, for all his outward crustiness, was not without moral sensitivity. In 1945 he toured the rubble of a devastated Berlin while en route to the Potsdam Conference. He noted, in a diary, the need for a lasting peace, and wrote: "I fear the machines [of war] are ahead of morals by some centuries." This was just days before he approved the use of atomic bombs against Japan. Was Truman being cruel and vindictive, or just pragmatic?

"The moral step [for dropping the atom bomb] had been taken with the firebombing of Tokyo," explains atomic physicist Hans Bethe. Truman's point was that, except for efficiency, there was no difference between killing 100,000 people with thousands of small bombs and killing that many people with a single huge one. Overlooked, and to some extent unknown at that time, were the lasting and hellish effects of radioactivity.

Truman's moral dilemma became the world's. It is a dilemma that has not gone away to this day. In fact, the moral issue was carried into earth's near-space when President George W. Bush moved to set aside the 1972 ABM treaty so that first-strike weapons, described as defensive, could be put into orbit around the earth for instant use.

The moral issue of missile-launched nuclear weapons put Carl Kabat behind bars, costing him 16 years of his life. (Most people outside the peace movement have never heard of him, even though he and the Berrigans started a movement called *Plowshares*, which has spawned nearly 100 protests worldwide.)

To his credit, in 1946 Truman offered, through Bernard Baruch, to place the secrets of the atomic bomb under control of the newly formed United Nations. (Hardly anyone remembers that, now.) In any case, the USSR vetoed the proposal and went on to explode its own atom bomb in 1949. The hydrogen bomb was soon to follow. The arms race predicted by Szilard began immediately after the Soviets rejected Truman's proposal at the UN.

For that reason, by 1947 Truman found it necessary to organize the CIA under the National Security Act. It was his alternative to the deceased General George Patton's proposed strategy to quash the communist menace by invading Russia. Much later, in its evolved form, the CIA became the nemesis of many of the priest-prophets as they conducted their missionary work in Third World nations where the agency's spies also operated. Truman's CIA was intended to be a non-military defensive gambit, placing the United States on a less violent path than that advocated by the Pentagon. Instead, it placed the United States in the same arena of world conquest by ideology and indirect militarism as the Soviet Union. The blustery General Patton-type of warrior was replaced by those of the CIA, the FBI and the National Security Agency, who planned for conquest and domination by illicit and sneaky means.

Could Truman have known that he was sowing the seeds of hatred of the United States? — hatred not of its freedoms, but of its abuse of power? The world reaction, judged by the history that followed WWII, was a kind of envy at a nuclear and economic level. That reaction was fed by ill-considered covert manipulations of emerging nations in the Americas, the Middle East and Asia, as the CIA installed its own agenda and agents in the leadership cadres.

It took Eisenhower to extract the US from Korea, where the so-called Domino Theory was first applied. At about the same time, Ike made a watershed prophecy that Carl Kabat years later was to adopt as the mantra for his nuclear dissent and resulting prison career.

Addressing the American Society of Newspaper Editors on April 16, 1953, Eisenhower said, in part:

> What can the world, or any nation in it, hope for if no turning is found on this dread road [of nuclear fear and force]? The worst to be feared and the best to be expected can be simply stated:
>
> The worst is atomic war. The best would be this: a life of perpetual fear and tension; a burden of arms draining the wealth and the labor of all peoples; a wasting of strength that defies the American system or the Soviet system or any system to achieve the abundance and happiness for the peoples of this earth.
>
> Every gun that is made, every warship launched, every rocket fired signifies, in the final sense, a theft from those who hunger and are not fed, those who are cold and are not clothed.

These very thoughts and words, long forgotten by most historians, are echoed even today by Kabat as he faces yet more prison for non-violent nuclear protest. Kabat also remembers another segment of Eisenhower's 1953 speech:

> This is not a way of life at all, in any true sense. Under the cloud of threatening war, it is humanity hanging from a cross of iron. . . . This is one of those times in the affairs of nations when the gravest choices must be made, if there is to be turning toward a just and lasting peace. . . . It is a moment . . . that calls upon them to answer the questions that stir the hearts of all sane men: is there no other way the world may live?

When Ike made the world aware of the moral and social issues of nuclear war, the message was regarded as noble rhetoric to which nobody paid any attention. Years later, when others such as Kabat did the same, they wound up in jail.

The United States' handling of its military power at this early stage set in motion everything that followed, including protests against government decisions. What followed was the love-hate relationship between the United States and the rest of the world, including nations that the US had rescued in the war, such as France. The Soviet Union did what it could to exploit this dichotomy but, at the same time, the US chose to play the game of dominance by following the Cold War rules dictated by the Soviets.

There was love for America's post-war compassion, yet hatred for how it used its power, and that is still the case today. With the atomic bomb in its pocket, the United States quickly came to be viewed as a political system forcing the rest of the free world to accept protection under a nuclear umbrella in exchange for a license to exploit foreign resources. Everything America seemed to stand for became suspect, and it still is.

None of this was directly Truman's fault. As Truman expressed it, the CIA was supposed to be "the quiet intelligence arm of the president," acting as a coordination center for intelligence already being gathered by other sources: army and navy, Office of Special Services (OSS) and the FBI. He was struggling to remedy the lingering aftershock of Japanese imperialism in Asia, German fascism in Europe, and communism in Russia; it was hard to predict exactly what his embryonic CIA would grow into.

The CIA was not empowered by the National Security Act of 1947 to be an autonomous intelligence-gathering agency or to establish clandestine operations. "Give-em-hell-Harry" Truman made that clear, years later. Truman complained publicly about the CIA's illicit assumption of power. He wrote an article that appeared in the *Washington Post* December 21, 1963:

> For some time I have been disturbed by the way the CIA has been diverted from its original assignment. It has become an operational and at times a policy-making arm of the government. . . I never had any thought that when I set up the CIA that it would be injected into peacetime cloak-and-dagger operations. Some of the complications and embarrassment that I think we have experienced are in part attributable to the fact that this quiet intelligence arm of the president has been so removed from its intended role that it is being

interpreted as a symbol of sinister and mysterious foreign intrigue and a subject for Cold War enemy propaganda.

As it turned out, one founding clause relating to the National Security Council and its errand-boy, the CIA, proved to be a loophole through which the CIA would expand its role beyond control. That clause stipulated that the CIA would "perform such other functions and duties related to intelligence affecting the national security as the NSC may from time to time direct."

Allen Dulles, the power-hungry director of the CIA, had interpreted Truman's verb "direct" to mean "approve." Under this approach, the CIA began to identify certain threats to national security and to propose certain plans to deal with them. The NSC wound up accepting the reports of threat and approving the courses of action as the CIA had planned them.

Militarily and economically, the United States thus replaced, on the totalitarian regime list, the European monarchies, the Russian czars, the Japanese emperor-gods, and the Nazi dictator, Hitler. Even though nobody liked absolute rulers, of whatever political stripe, and even though every system under absolute rulers has failed, America began supporting, with the help of the CIA, right wing dictators everywhere as its antidote to Communism. The failure of this new policy was illustrated best by the reaction by Cuba's Castro. Nevertheless, the policy continued unabated, and so do the protests against US political puppeteering.

The prophets, dealing with the effects of such policies in missionary lands, faced a larger question: Does the American public know, or even care, how its own society came to be so bent on dominance that it has cast aside its moral principles?

In fact, it was the power of the bomb itself, something that Dan Berrigan calls "Lord Nuke," which melted the moral reserves of the American public. Frank Cordaro blames the Church, which had, by his reckoning, given its blessing to the "just war" doctrine for centuries. America's military and political agencies capitalized on this moral paralysis in the public.

While no leader has used the atomic bomb since WWII, they all have behaved as if they would do so. Their bluff even had a name: MAD, or Mutually Assured Destruction. Not even the Church during the Holy Roman Empire had presumed to bless such an almighty power, even though it had granted kings the divine right to rule. Nevertheless, what emerged after Hiroshima and Nagasaki can only be called the divine atomic right to rule.

It is the prophets without honor who oppose by their protests such a nuclear divine right. As Frank Cordaro says, "all evils take their lead from the bomb."

General Omar Bradley today would understand Cordaro's statement, because it was Bradley who said, sometime after WWII was over: "We have grasped the mystery of the atom and rejected the Sermon on the Mount . . . Ours is a world of nuclear giants and ethical infants.

We know more about war than we do about peace; more about killing than about living."

Several emblematic images of the times illustrate why the prophets and domestic activists raised their voices in the past 50 years. Some feared an expansion of unseen government manipulation, but they did not realize that during the Truman and Eisenhower Administrations the United States had already planted both feet on slippery ground, bequeathing unsure footing to future administrations.

America had one foot in a pool of Middle East oil — slippery enough in itself, as Iran nationalized American assets there. It had the other poised on the political ice of Communism and the Cold War. Worse, its whole international path was lined with banana peels from Guatemala.

The first US slip on a banana came in 1953, when Allen Dulles was head of the CIA and John Foster Dulles was Secretary of State, and the Rockefeller-controlled United Fruit held almost all of the arable land in Guatemala, where it had established banana plantations to fill US fruit bowls and lunchboxes. The Dulles brothers in their law practice had United Fruit as a client and were pals of the Rockefellers. United Fruit paid field workers 50 cents a day. Their slave labor filled the holds of 50 ocean-going cargo ships bound for America. At that time, United Fruit owned Guatemala's railroad and port, and showed annual net profits of $65 million — more than twice the annual budget of Guatemala's entire government.

Noting the basic injustice of this exploitation, Guatemala's duly elected president, Jacobo Arbenz, appropriated, with compensation, 240,000 acres of his own country's land from United Fruit for distribution to the starving peasants. To America, Arbenz's socialistic move smelled like Communism. Putting their heads together, Secretary of State Dulles and CIA chief Dulles raised the anti-communist wolf-cry. In secret, they had the CIA hire a Marine lieutenant colonel, Phil Roettinger, to arm and train a rebel group — a forebear of the Reagan-era Contras. The CIA selected a little-known Guatemalan recruit, Castillo Armas, to be the country's next presidential dictator, and promised him all the guns needed to take back the plantations and maintain control. When the handful of rebels failed at their task and fled across the border, the CIA arranged to have several US planes buzz the capital and drop old iron bombs from World War II surplus. The tactic worked, triggering Arbenz's resignation and flight from Guatemala in 1954. The CIA then installed its man, Armas.

The 1953-54 rape of Guatemalan democracy and plundering of resources set the scene, in turn, for Armas's assassination by rebels in 1957. A series of coups and counter-coups ensued, dragging all of Central America into ongoing civil unrest and political wars. These wars killed hundreds of thousands and lasted for three decades.

In the end, CIA military meddling produced the Iran-Contra scandal, in defiance of US law and the Congress, for which no American participant ever was punished.

The CIA effort in Guatemala became a model for use worldwide wherever US policy needed to go underground. Eight years later, a similar tactic was apparently tried against Castro, but it was fumbled in the handoff between Eisenhower and Kennedy.

As far as US policies in Central America were concerned, efforts to nip Communism in the bud seemed most likely to be politically acceptable if carried out in secret — behind the smokescreen of lies or superficial deniability for any ethically questionable tactics. It seemed to be the only way to fight against similar tactics being used by the communist foe.

This was the Dulles "Domino Theory" at work — the fear that, if one country in a region fell under Communism, others would follow. By corollary, if the bad guys used dirty or secret tactics, then America should, too.

While the Dulles brothers were looking after their bananas, Premier-General Ali Rozmara was assassinated in Iran and Mohammed Mossadegh had taken power. He nationalized the country's oil assets, which mostly had been in British hands. Naturally, the events drew the interest of the Rockefellers and other American oil interests, because the Anglo-Iranian Oil Company, under the control of the British, had locked America out. Invoking the 1927 Red Line Agreement, which until then had been applied mostly to Iraq, America's seven major oil companies eventually barged their way into Iran's oil pool.

But not before the CIA pulled off its political coup.

Inspired by success in Guatemala, the CIA secretly set about overthrowing the Mossadegh regime in Iran and re-establishing the Pahlevi family to the throne. Britain had deposed the uncooperative old Shah during the war, but now that the oil assets that were in jeopardy, the Brits viewed post-war US intervention as a great favor.

As noted by a recent series of articles in the *New York Times*, there is no doubt that oil and fear of communist control over oil were at the core of the coup. This information was discovered in a secret history of the event written by "gentleman spy" Donald Wilber, a CIA recruit of those days:

Before the coup, the major US oil companies had few energy assets in Iran. Afterward, they had a 40% piece of the action (before kickbacks to the Shah).

The Mossadegh coup was code named TP-Ajax by the CIA. Recently uncovered documents indicate that CIA officers worked directly with royalist Iranian military officers and sent a stream of envoys to bolster the young shah, who was then described as "a vacillating coward."

To start the coup, the CIA directed a campaign of bombings by Iranians posing as members of the Communist Party. Agents planted articles, including ghost-written decrees by the shah, and editorial cartoons in newspapers to show the princeling in a good light. Popular support for the reluctant shah grew until Mossadegh capitulated and the CIA propped Shah Reza Pahlevi on the same Peacock Throne his father had filled before World War II.

Of course, oil was not the only interest the CIA had in control over Iran. It knew it would be needing a base (other than in Turkey and Pakistan) from which to fly its U2 spy plane missions over the southern part of the Soviet Union where the Russian space effort was concentrated.

It is an irony of Middle East history that Gen. H. Norman Schwartzkopf, Sr., directed the military phase of the 1953 coup against Mossadegh; and that, decades later, his son, General Norman Schwartzkopf,

Jr., led the Desert Storm assault against Iraq in the oil war over Kuwait.

In any case, to maintain the willy-nilly shah's grip on his own nation in 1953, the CIA endowed him with $5 million and set up SAVAK, Iran's brutal secret police, to shield him from counterattack. (The acronym stands for the Farsi words that translate into "Organization for National Security and Intelligence".) Then the US sold the shah billions of dollars worth of arms, paid for with oil money, to keep his position. As popular support for the overly-Westernized Shah waned over the years, SAVAK began its reign of terror by wholesale torture, kidnappings and killings among Islamic conservatives.

This set the scene for the US embassy takeover years later. It set the scenes for the Iran-Iraq war and the US agents' secret trading of guns and drugs in Central America. Later, it set the scene for the Desert Storm war, and finally, it triggered long-term hatred that led to the World Trade Center disaster.

Sparked by the success of two secret anti-communist terror campaigns of the Dulles brothers in 1953, the US government expanded its covert CIA operational policies to all of Asia and Central and South America. Some credit this policy of covert subversion with pushing Castro into the arms of the Soviet Union. When Castro learned that the Bay of Pigs operation had issued from CIA bases in Panama and Nicaragua, he began to export his revolution to South America and Africa, spearheaded by his right-hand man, Che Guevara.

As the US based its foreign policy on the slippery combination of bananas and oil, the world slipped and slid its way into revolution and counter-revolution in Central America, and the mess of post-colonial Vietnam. As a bonus, the US policy guaranteed the Middle East crises. Of course, the never-settled problems of the British and French exploitative colonial era had much to do with these predicaments.

The killing and injustice flowing from this chain of manipulated events is what the protest by the prophets has been all about. It's what the ignored Boland Amendment in 1982, banning interference in Guatemala, was all about. In fact, the 1953 Dulles banana revolution in Guatemala, using an obscure retired colonel, is what set the precedent for Iran-Contra and the exploits of Lt. Colonel Oliver North during the Reagan Administration. He too, was obscure until his made-in-the-White-House methods were unmasked. Sadly, North was punished less for his illegal actions than the prophets were for protesting them.

The Dulles brothers' penchant for using covert operations to counteract what they called the "Domino Theory" spread to Vietnam in the early days of the war when the US supposedly was involved only by way of "advisers." Actually, many of these were CIA mercenaries working under the name of Studies and Operations Group (SOG).

Once CIA was given a green light to conduct warfare behind the scenes, hire soldiers of fortune, train foreign agents, and overthrow governments, license was taken worldwide and illegal practices were applied even against domestic targets. The fever for secret manipulation on the international scene became a disease that eventually engulfed the Pentagon and the FBI as well as the CIA.

None of that was Truman's intent in 1947, but it was a result that some of the prophets experienced firsthand in places such as Recife, Brazil.

4. LIONSDEN PROPHECY: WE THE SYSTEM

As the nation's political pathology for spying progressed, it was copied by the FBI and was secretly known as COINTELPRO. Behind this shield, the FBI soon set up a secret network for domestic surveillance and subversion against such policy protesters as Dr. Martin Luther King, Jr., the Berrigan Brothers, and every civil rights group of the '60s, '70s and '80s.

When news of this domestic FBI spying was exposed in the mid-'70s, the entire covert network went into its underground and mimicked the CIA covert tactics internationally. While this hidden network's real name was never discovered, it has been dubbed LIONSDEN (LIaison Of Networked Systems for DENiability), for the purpose of discussing the system and how it operates even today.

It should be understood that LIONSDEN is not some theoretical conspiracy in which vast numbers of interconnected initiatives flow from a single master plan or mastermind. There is no master plan of intrigue under the guidance of an evil genius embracing all the various government agencies. Instead, LIONSDEN describes a phenomenon within the US government: a secretive style of doing business, what has become *conspiracy by outcome* among those agencies using undercover and immoral methods to achieve common policy goals at home and abroad.

LIONSDEN is a kind of automatically operating subsystem that drives how our economy, our military our politics and the whole society must proceed. To change one modality (by, for example, getting rid of all nuclear weapons) is to destroy the effectiveness of the whole. If LIONSDEN has a master, that master is all of America. We, the people, have become *We the System.*

It doesn't matter what we call the system because, as the FBI's rebellious and retired agent, M. Wesley Swearingen, says in his 1995 expose *FBI Secrets,* "The (COINTELPRO) program is still in operation today, but under a different code name. The operation is no longer placed on paper where it can be discovered under the release of documents under the Freedom of Information Act."

LIONSDEN could be Swearingen's ever-more-secret system; because it is more ambitious, more amorphous and more immoral than even the extra-legal COINTELPRO was. However, because the existence of LIONSDEN is by definition *deniable,* it can seem more fanciful than real. Even if LIONSDEN is impossible to prove, it can be diagnosed, like any malady through the symptoms it leaves behind. It is symptomatic of LIONSDEN when:

1. Leaders are caught in lies and denials about illegal or immoral actions. The Tonkin Gulf confrontation is one good example.

2. Leaders give their staff carte blanche instructions to take certain actions or achieve certain goals on the domestic political front in secrecy, and to spare them the details. The Watergate scandal is a good example.

3. Leaders signal that constitutionally-correct protests are to be suppressed by police and punished by the legal system. Examples include the Vietnam War protests by thousands of students and others; the anti-nuclear protests by priests such as the Berrigans; and the civil rights activities of Dr. Martin Luther King, Jr.

4. Leaders make use of secret organizations for foreign operations with instructions to develop their own financial means of support for actions barred by Congress. Iran-Contra comes to mind.

5. Leaders back secret paramilitary operations to achieve extra-legal goals. The fomenting of the Iran-Iraq war and the backing of the Contras in Central America are prime examples.

6. Leaders leave it to quasi-governmental and paramilitary advisory groups to plan economic and national security strategies behind closed doors. The FBI, CIA, Pentagon think tanks and Trilateral Commission have been involved in such matters for years.

7. Leaders prop up and use proxies in foreign nations to carry out

wars of suppression and campaigns of exploitation: Batista in Cuba, Armas in Guatemala, Shah Reza Pahlevi, Ngo Dinh Diem et. al.

8. Leaders succeed in getting the public to think that democracy is identical to free enterprise, capitalism, multinational business, globalization, American technical dominance, national security, atomic bombs, war, patriotism and Christianity.

Swearingen's revelations that suggest operations like LIONSDEN are buttressed from the military and political side by retired Air Force Colonel L. Fletcher Prouty. He filled key liaison roles between the Pentagon, the CIA and the National Security Agency during the '50s and '60s. Prouty describes in his writings what he calls "the secret team" which carried out CIA/Pentagon operations (illicitly, under the National Security Act of 1947). From within the government, Swearingen says, "emerges a portrait of a massive, deeply entrenched and increasingly ubiquitous institutional entity devoted to the curtailment of domestic political action and expression." He thus suggests an entity whose existence is unknown to outsiders and deniable by insiders, and whose conduct is beyond anyone's direct responsibility or control. It is a precursor of a shadow government that has been acknowledged only since the "War on Terrorism."

One of the figures central to an earlier LIONSDEN embodiment, not surprisingly, was the FBI's J. Edgar Hoover, who held conspiratorial hands with the CIA and the National Security Council. At the end of his book, Swearingen concluded: "The Hoover era will haunt the FBI for decades to come, no matter what historians and critics write, because J. Edgar Hoover and his sycophantic and praetorian associates embarked knowingly on a course to undermine the Constitution and justice system of the United States. . . Not until the FBI is forced to tell the truth will the citizens of the United State of America be safe from the national police force the FBI controls and the COINTELPRO it secretly continues to operate."

Swearingen's and Prouty's revelations support the notion that a LIONSDEN-like phenomenon exists and has been growing in the government ever since Nixon's attorney, John Dean, described it as a "cancer on the presidency." With the passage of the USA Patriot Act in 2001, the interagency spiral of LIONSDEN can only tighten as America pursues it war on terrorism.

In his expose, Swearingen divulges names (some of them in code) of FBI people or hired assassins who murdered black activists in the Weathermen and Black Panther movements. They neutralized Elmer "Geronimo" Platt of the Black Panthers by framing him for the murder of

Caroline Olsen, after husband Kenneth Olsen had been guided by the Los Angeles Police Department to pick Pratt out of an FBI photo lineup. Other FBI-orchestrated murders of black activists, according to Swearingen, included John Salvage and Sylvester Bell, both of Los Angeles; and Alprentice Carpentner and John Huggins on the UCLA campus in 1969. Some of these murders, according to Swearingen, were carried out by black hit men recruited and trained by the FBI, who were subsequently placed in the government witness protection program. His point is, if America has done such lawless things at home, what even worse things has it done in LIONSDEN secrecy abroad?

Where was J. Edgar Hoover while all of this was going on? He was behind the scenes, covering his tracks. The FBI's murders might have been brought to light in 1977, except for the sudden and suspicious death of William C. Sullivan, the FBI's No. 3 man. Swearingen suggests that Sullivan, on his way to join a hunting group in 1977, knew too much. His fatal accident happened to occur just days before Sullivan was to testify before a Congressional committee about FBI extralegal secrets.

All of these inter-related events coalesced at a time when the US extraction from the Vietnam War was the topic of the day. It was a time when killing the enemy, under any pretext, was coming to be seen as ethical behavior.

Over time, the LIONSDEN system has become a comfortable governmental universe for controlling whole nations, and it behaves just like the universe described by Stephen Crane in *War is Kind*:

"A man said to the universe, 'Sir, I exist.'

"'However,' replied the universe, 'that fact has not created in me a sense of obligation.'"

That is the kind of governmental universe that has produced Iran-Contra, the Tehran hostage crisis, the Iran-Iraq war, Desert Storm, and the invasions of Panama, the Bahamas, Somalia and the Balkan states. Although these American military adventures were disguised as anti-communistic, patriotic and humanistic forays, in effect they were just as deadly as the evils they were intended to prevent, and prevented not communism but peace and justice.

In 1973, just as Carl Kabat was leaving his priestly mission in Recife, Brazil, President Nixon sent Nelson Rockefeller on a fence-mending assignment to the Latin countries, where, as they say in the movies, the natives were restless. Kabat issued a kind of prophecy. He recalls thinking that Rockefeller never would ask for humanitarian aid; instead, he would instead ask for military aid. That's exactly what happened.

Carl, who has spent nearly 16 years in jail for non-violent protests, insists he is not a prophet, just someone faithful to his missionary calling. That calling has to do not merely with helping the poor, but trying to stop whatever it is that makes and keeps people poor. For Fr. Carl Kabat, the cause of poverty and suppression of freedom is Rockefeller-style militarism, just as US supremacy through nuclear weapons is globalized terrorism on an atomic scale.

Globalization, the political vehicle for plundering the resources of the world for the benefit of First World economies, has evolved since the earliest days of oil in America. The Rockefeller dynasty still plays a leading role in this process, although from behind the scenes now. Because militarism is one of the pillars of globalization, and because military force increases instead of decreases poverty, globalization has become, in some starving corners of the world, as contemptible as its founder.

From 1955 to 1964, Col. L. Fletcher Prouty, USAF Ret., was working out of the Pentagon. His assignments included intelligence liaison with officials such as John Foster Dulles and Allen W. Dulles and the Joint Chiefs of Staff. In other words, he was the liaison officer between the White House, the CIA and the US Air Force for Clandestine Operations under National Security Council Directives.

As he reports in his book, *Secret Team,* Prouty describes a kind of "high cabal" operating under anonymity. Its objective was to make the world what it is today under an undeclared doctrine of one world order. "The Secret Team," Prouty says, "consists of security-cleared individuals in and out of government who receive secret intelligence data gathered by the CIA and the National Security Agency (NSA) and who react to those data with paramilitary plans and activities such as training and advising. . . . The power of the Secret Team," Prouty says, "derives from its vast intragovernmental undercover infrastructure and its direct relationship with great private industries, mutual funds and investment houses, universities and the news media."

Prouty adds that the Secret Team has very close connections with the power structure in the US and scores of other countries. He says it is able, "when it chooses," to topple, create or influence governments almost anywhere in the world. A key part of such power is the ability to obtain and secretly dispense weapons from the US military in support of such interference with the sovereignty of foreign nations and the freedoms of their people (for example, the mining of Nicaragua's harbors during the Iran-Contra mess and the killing of 12,000 people there by US-backed Contras.)

Projecting beyond his book of 25 years ago, Prouty claims what he describes is extant and operative today:

> The Secret Team (now) is a bewildering collection of semi-permanent or temporarily assembled action committees and networks that respond pretty much ad hoc to specific troubles and to intelligence inputs from various parts of the world, sometimes in ways that duplicate the activities of regular American missions, sometimes in ways that undermine those activities, and very often in ways that interfere with and muddle them.

He notes that the printing of the "Pentagon Papers" by *The New York Times* in 1971 exposed the CIA-Pentagon Secret Team concept and showed how it had "gained so much control over the vital foreign and political activities" of government functions. That is why the government tried unsuccessfully to prohibit publication of the papers that were passed along by Daniel Ellsberg, a conscience-stricken member of a Secret Team think tank. (Those think tanks still flourish today and have as members former high-level officials such as Zbigniew Brzezinski and Henry Kissinger.)

Prouty says part of the CIA's Secret Team *modus operandi* was to put its men in genuine military disguise. "It is often quite difficult to tell exactly who many of these men are, because some may wear a uniform and the rank of general and really be with the CIA," Prouty says. Thus, the government itself condoned the impersonation of military officers by the CIA when it suited their purpose; and the Pentagon winked at it.

Even more illuminating is his explanation of how the Secret Team was able to insinuate itself into the seat of government and then export policy programs subversive to the sovereignty of foreign nations — in competition, it is assumed, with the Soviet Union. The CIA Secret Team knew that, once intelligence was delivered, the civilian executives at the National Security Council would ask them what might be the wisest military response. While this tended to short-circuit the ability of the Secretary of State and the Defense Secretary to advise on military matters in detail, it put the CIA in a very powerful position.

That is how, during the Vietnam War, General Victor H. Krulak (who headed the Secret Team in the office of the Special Assistant for Counterinsurgency and Special Activities of the Joint Chiefs) was able to draft for Defense Secretary Robert McNamara a report on his tour of Vietnam even before McNamara had returned from that pre-planned "fact finding" tour. The Secret Team delivered that report — with recommendations for attacking North Vietnam — to McNamara in Hawaii, on his way home to advise the President: the CIA set the policy for US incursions into Laos and Cambodia.

According to Prouty, all the CIA had to do to get approval for any plan was to say "anti-communist," or "national security". Such assessments would coincide with reports from the FBI to the same effect, because J. Edgar Hoover saw communists and national security threats everywhere. Inevitably, this would elicit from the Security Council the need for action. That action, of course, was the one predicted, desired and premeditated by the CIA/Pentagon brass. Such methods and procedures circumvent normal channels, confusing the chain of responsibility and creating the danger of malfeasance and misfeasance within the executive branch. In effect, they constitute a betrayal of public interest and trust.

While the CIA-Pentagon Secret Team concept was in full bloom and serving the Vietnam War effort, Nelson Rockefeller and his Wall Street brothers, David and Laurence, were busy with plans of their own that had a LIONSDEN twist.

The Rockefellers were the grandsons of the robber baron John D. Rockefeller, whose Standard Oil corporation had held a monopoly on US oil refining for years. Accordingly, controlling the politics that could affect their economic empire was something that seemed almost genetic in the family. John D. Rockefeller once had an oil monopoly; the monopoly now sought by his grandsons was grander: that of behind-the-scenes power.

The grand cabal was hatched at a meeting in July, 1972, at the Rockefeller estate in Pocantico Hills north of New York City. At this time, the US was bombing Hanoi and NY Governor Rockefeller was being criticized for the massacre of dozens of inmates at Attica state prison. In the nation's capital, the Watergate scandal was unfolding with the indictment of G. Gordon Liddy, a CIA operative, and a string of other associates. There were rumors of an oil embargo, as OPEC began to set its own prices. (The Oil Producing and Exporting Countries in the Middle East included Saudi Arabia, Yemen, United Arab Emirates, Abu Dhabi, Kuwait, Libya, Iran and Iraq.)

In this uncontrollable mix of economics and politics, the Rockefellers might easily have seen their fortunes and their future going down the drain with the rest of the oil-dependent world — Japan being the most vulnerable by dint of its total lack of domestic oil resources. The Rockefeller-run Chase Manhattan Bank was heavily committed both in Iran and Japan, and could not afford to lose its economic leverage.

In concert with the ideas of Zbigniew Brzezinski of Columbia University, David Rockefeller succeeded in forming, with his brothers, Nelson and Laurence, the Trilateral Commission. From the start, this required a little political cross-dressing, because it used then-Democratic Governor of Georgia Jimmy Carter as its stalking horse. The Trilateral Commission's self-assigned charter was to plan and advise the US government on the world's economic, political and national security affairs.

The Trilateral Commission takes its name from its three members: the United States and Canada as one entity; Western Europe with its emerging Common Market as another; and Japan as the third. Japan and Europe joined this Free World troika because each was being cut in for a share of the winnings at a time when the US held most of the cards.

However, the driving force would come from the Rockefellers and their Chase Manhattan bank. The administrative clout came from Brzezinski and from then-governor Jimmy Carter, who seemed to be made of the kind of clay that could be molded for use in a Rockefeller-controlled White House. Indeed, Carter was selected for his trilateral role because he was honest, naive and malleable — alloys of character most commonly found in simple people, even those as bright as Carter. The Commission, if it was to sneak up on the world, needed someone relatively unknown but open to guidance as a future presidential candidate, because Nelson Rockefeller was too visible for political comfort. Besides, he had a losing image in presidential bids. (However, as a footnote on timing, he formed the Commission just months before Agnew and Nixon resigned and President Ford named him Vice President.)

Of course, the Trilateral Commission was not fabricated by the Rockefeller brothers from scratch. At the time, the Council on Foreign Relations (originally formed by President Wilson), was doing the very things that the Rockefellers wanted to take over, and it served as the Trilateral Commission's predecessor and operational model. The Council of Foreign Relations had already received funding from the Rockefeller Foundation.

Nelson Rockefeller had insinuated himself into the workings of government across several decades and administrations. Roosevelt had appointed him coordinator of inter-American affairs and Assistant Secretary of State for American republic affairs. Truman had named him chair of the International Development Advisory Board. In these capacities, Nelson Rockefeller had even wielded an influence on the formation of the Organization of American States in 1948. One big aim of the OAS was to provide a mechanism for the settlement of disputes and for military and economic cooperation between the US and the 20 Latin American nations. Under that military arrangement, the School of the Americas was formed in the early '50s to train counter-insurgency forces. Some of them came to be known as the death squads of Central America.

Rockefeller also was appointed by Eisenhower to head an advisory committee on government organization. Recommendations of this committee ultimately established the Department of Health, Education and Welfare, and the US Information Agency, and thereafter reorganized the Departments of Agriculture, Defense and Justice. For years, Nelson's political clout had made a good amalgam for the Rockefeller family power base in banking and Wall Street; not to mention saving the Rockefeller investments in the banana republics and extending Standard Oil (now Exxon) tentacles into the oil-rich sheikdoms of the Middle East.

The Trilateral Commission was expected to consolidate and strengthen those economic interests, using the levers of power available through the United States government (regardless of party politics). What was good for the Rockefellers, apparently, was thought to be good for the world.

Under Roosevelt, the Council of Foreign Relations evolved from an advisory into an operational and controlling role within the State Department. In this capacity, some politicians said the CFR had more power than Congress because of the leverage it gave the president with the movers and shakers of the world. Its membership has always included ex-presidents and would-be presidents, such as Thomas E. Dewey, Eisenhower and Nixon as well as Adlai Stevenson, John F. Kennedy, Hubert Humphrey and George McGovern.

The CFR's own mission statement says: "The council's membership of over 3,800 American citizens includes the country's leaders in business, academia, the media, civil society and government. . . It is dedicated to strengthening America's role in and understanding of the world by better comprehending global trends and contributing ideas to US foreign policy. . . The council does not take institutional positions; however, independent task forces do advocate certain policies as a result of their work."

Recognizing the opportunity to become the power behind the White House throne, and keeping in mind the enforcement power of the CIA-Pentagon oligarchy, the Trilateral Commission became at first a silent partner with the CFR under this mission statement: "To foster closer cooperation among the principal democratic industrialized areas with shared leadership responsibilities in the wider international system."

But eventually, using the LIONSDEN paradigm, the Trilateral Commission took over most of CFR's functions, including those pertaining to the OAS and its hemispheric security. In fact, the Trilateral Commission and the CFR have nearly identical board membership and directors. Today, the Council of Foreign Relations is primarily a "Who's Who" of corporate and university VIPs who are also directors and members of the Trilateral Commission. Functionally, the two are melded into a LIONSDEN system. This entrenchment affords the Trilateral Commission unlimited power and privileges over the world economy throughout the US, Japan, Canada, and Western Europe.

Such behind-the-scenes power over the rest of the world creates in the public mind an uncomfortable feeling that such a "shadow government" might be responsible for shadowy things. Certainly, for the US to put policies into effect at the suggestion of the Trilateral Commission creates some interesting constitutional problems. Words from the Trilateral Commission's own documents testify to its quasi-subversive influence and image:

> The effective operation of a democratic political system usually requires some measure of apathy and non-involvement on the part of some individuals and groups. Secrecy and deception are inescapable attributes of... government.
>
> The vulnerability of democratic government in the United States comes... from the internal dynamics of democracy itself in a highly educated, mobilized, and participant society.

These very words suggest that "globalization" is leading to the globalization of economies, societies, and war-making power — globalization in every region of the world under the banner of US-puppet democracies.

Of course, any sort of globalization requires control. A true democratic form of government, however, is not conducive to control across diverse cultures and distances. What the Trilateral Commission needs for a US-run plan for globalization is a chain of controlled democracies, like the ones in Central America that President Reagan tried to control by means of the Iran-Contra effort.

This kind of neo-colonial control-by-system requires the eradication of personal and economic freedom within client states; it requires "democratic" dictatorships that can be as benevolent or malevolent as needed, while appearing to operate as US-style democracies; it requires the force of arms and the connivance of secret agencies to do what is not publicly acceptable.

Trilateralism and globalization are tools LIONSDEN uses to knot together the National Security Council, the CIA, the Secret Team, the FBI, the Pentagon, the White House, the School of the Americas death squads, Wall Street interests, and the State Department, the last of which supposedly directs foreign policy goals. Because membership of the Trilateral Commission includes presidents, Cabinet members, Wall Street moguls, political party bigwigs, members of the House and Senate, Fortune 500 executives, leading educators and even media figures, there is no doubt that it constitutes a shadow government operating beyond the bounds of democracy. Where this leaves US citizens and government officials over matters military and economic seems iffy. Where it leaves the citizens of other countries is as obvious as the poverty, the drug and gun deals, the despots and the wars they have suffered as a result.

Although, considered in isolation, the Trilateral Commission mechanics is transparent enough to seem innocent, the effects of its work include exploitation, suppression of human rights, war and murder (all of it deniable by the FBI, the CIA, the National Security Agency, the Pentagon and the White House). Either the executive branch of government has abrogated its Constitutional duties to the Trilateral Commission, or that commission has usurped them. Given the fact that control of key governmental roles lies naked to the Trilateral Commission, that group seems to constitute an unofficial hierarchy of unconstitutional power. It includes several foreign nationals, all operating in violation of the US Code, Title 50, Section on War And National Defense #783, which reads:

> It shall be unlawful for any person knowingly to combine, conspire, or agree with any other person to perform any act which would substantially contribute to the establishment within the United States of a totalitarian dictatorship, the direction and control of which is to be vested in, or exercised by or under the domination of control of, any foreign government.

The Rockefellers are "persons" under this law. The matters they control are central to the powers of the constitutional government. The formation and operation of the commission is an act that contributes to the establishment within the United States a totalitarian system under the control of several foreign governments. Control over economic, political and military policies would seem to be quite total.

Even if clever wording from legal eagles makes the Trilateral Commission sound squeaky clean, it clearly has garnered the power of a dictatorial, global, supra-governmental body capable of impinging upon the rights and freedoms of people worldwide, with license to loot. This puts the United States at odds with the intent of its own laws and policies, with a shadow government opposed to the will of the people of the United States and their power of self-determination under the Constitution. This is the point at which politics and morality of government become glued or unglued.

Without putting their fingers on it, the prophets have been protesting for years what the Trilateral Commission is, does and represents. They may not have known enough to blame the CIA and its Secret Team and their LIONSDEN methods for the effects on people of other nations, but they recognized immorality well enough to protest against the government and leaders that inflicted war, oppression and poverty — even if it was done by remote control.

The concern of the prophets is as much for the moral side of the equation as for the patriotic side, because each affects the quality of the other. They protest the corruption of moral systems by economic and political aggressors. They protest the assault by secular systems on the moral systems of human spirit, freedom, peace and justice.

As Darrell Rupiper says of his experience in Brazil years ago, "The strings were pulled by those in Washington for the sake of the multinationals. They don't know the world — " Rupiper says, "those who think they run it. And so they must kill and abuse others to hide their ignorance, while those who do not resist the killing process become, in the end, the most victimized. That's the condition of the world today."

The prophets are not alone in their criticism. In 1980, Eqbal Ahmad, a fellow for the Institute for Policy Studies in Washington, reported the existence of three levels of government in the US:

1) The one familiar to the general public.

2) The "shadow government" of special interests including leading banks, the arms industry, the oil trusts, the huge construction cartels such as that formed by Howard Hughes, plus individual eminences like

Kissinger, the Rockefellers and J.J. McCloy, the secret architect of America's foreign policy establishment.

3) The "invisible government of intelligence operatives of the CIA, defense intelligence, national security agencies and so on."

What happens to the society and to government when its invisible constituents take over?

The prophets know. The fruits of government abuse that they have witnessed on many occasions are death and poverty. They sense that a government that puts itself in the shadows and makes itself invisible to the people it governs amounts to government by neoplasm.

Neither the shadow government nor the invisible government can be traced to the Constitution of the United States of America. Yet it was they who shaped the Nixon Doctrine, according to Ahmad, and popularized its use in international affairs. The Nixon Doctrine became the clevis connecting US policy for military and economic dominance to LIONSDEN-style agencies: the CIA, FBI, Pentagon, White House, and National Security Agency — and, through them, to the Trilateral Commission, which arose later.

Basically, the Nixon Doctrine, under the guidance of Henry Kissinger, recognized that the US public could no longer, with popular success, manage limited wars by direct intervention in places like Vietnam. That's why it called for the training and use of troops indigenous to the country or region where it was necessary to subdue resistance to US objectives. "Only if the buffer [client nation] proves insufficient does the great power become involved," says the Nixon Doctrine (as described by Ahmad), "and then in terms that make victory more attainable and the whole enterprise more palatable to the American public."

This was nothing but war by proxy. Plausible deniability and, thereby, public approval, was the main goal. That mix made use of the violent side of the School of the Americas, as well as the formal and informal forces noted above — all for the sake of national security and the anti-communist effort.

The Nixon Doctrine was applied by establishing a network of "regional spheres of influence" among key countries within various regions of the world. In the case of the Middle East, for example, the spheres of influence where the US had puppet regimes were Israel and Iran (in the days of the Shah). When trouble arose in any sphere of influence, the US had only to use and support the indigenous armies of threatened allies from behind the scenes with massive and direct technical support, including arms and CIA advisors. Thus, the Shah, using his army and the CIA-trained

SAVAK, could be enlisted for the lead role in suppressing local or regional opposition in the oil rich region of the Middle East.

Nixon's sphere-of-influence policy was politically reinforced by Carter and Brzezinski when the Trilateral Commission was established. The Nixon Doctrine has evolved into the notion of operating in the Middle East by means of worldwide coalitions, as was done in Desert Storm and, now, Enduring Freedom.

The prophets had no clear view of these unseen governing bodies that in fact became the hidden reasons for their protests. They sensed a festering immorality of means and purpose, as events such as the Vietnam War ballooned. This caused them to oppose all US policies that were carried out by military arms and suppression within the Third World. Their opposition applies in every such case. That is why the prophets chose as their targets of protest nuclear weapons, various military establishments, and the politics and machinery of war.

The poor are the people defended most staunchly by the prophets, because the prophets believe that it is they who are ultimately victimized by the military and economic power. Indeed, militarism first creates the entire class of the poor, as Carl Kabat and all his friends have noted consistently in their careers of prophecy.

6. Good Land for Prophet-Making

There is a point of land on the northeast shoulder of Brazil that juts out into the Atlantic Ocean with all the geographic truculence of a linebacker's dislocated pads. Perched like a challenging chip on this shoulder is a festering collage of *favellas*, mud flats, fetid dumps, squalid boat docks, and hilly tangles of tropical growth, all encircling a few eclectic neighborhoods that look like the remnants of a middle-class suburb from the Great Depression. At the center are a few showcase high rises and neon-lit malls, like glossy downtown mushrooms transplanted from New Orleans. For the sake of simple description, it is called a city. Its name is Recife, Portuguese for "reef."

This is the star of the state of Pernambuco, which, for all of its physique, cannot shoulder its human burden. It has become the burden of the prophets who lived and worked there — and of some who still do. The geography seems fertile enough, bearing now (as it did forty years ago) a land greened and sweetened by sugar cane fields. But under the cloak of coastal verdure, then as now, the land is infected with mud villages poxing nearly to death its bony and dusty interior. All of this is just miles from the Atlantic shore surging with refreshing but undrinkable water and fish as sickened by pollution as the people who eat them.

But mostly, the pollution of the people and their souls comes not from what they have, but from what they lack: a reason for living.

If the land had a wish, it probably would be this: to get rid of these pestilential poor and their swarms of flies feeding on death. But, enslaved by Fortune 500 companies under conditions worse than any in the American South two centuries ago, these trapped people cannot be swatted out of existence nor can they fly from the conditions of this open-air dungeon.

Life Magazine photographer Gordon Parks, having completed a photo essay on Brazil's living conditions in the '60's, said his journey there showed him the worst poverty he had ever seen. As a black youth growing up on a Kansas farm with fourteen siblings, Parks knew poverty. And he learned even more about it during his world travels and documentaries. In Brazil, he was so moved by the pathetic conditions that he adopted a son, Flavio DaSilva, who had tuberculosis. Parks tried, in vain, to save him with love.

It was to this land then, that prophets such as Rupiper, Kabat and Rosebaugh came. There were others, but the actions of these three attracted the attention of those paid to keep watch. The prophets came to this place on the winds of secret but deceptive promises from the LBJ White House to Catholic Church authorities.

This is a land owned by porcelain-faced, fashionable people who live a sugary existence in the far-off high rises of Sao Paulo, Rio de Janiero, Brasilia and even New York. This is the land of opportunity for the multinational corporations, the godchildren of Chase Manhattan Bank. It is for them that the dictators dance like puppets and behave like brutes toward any fellow countrymen who would resist for the sake of human rights and personal freedom. The multinational corporations come from the US to establish a balance of payments in international trade. They work to keep Third World nations in debt to the International Monetary Fund, the World Bank, and to US multinationals.

At the time of the 1964 military coup in Brazil, for example, US companies owned half of the meat industry, half of the iron and rolled-metal industry, 56% of the textile industry, 72% of the electric power industry, 80% of the cigarette manufacture, 80% of the pharmaceutical production, 98% of the automobile industry, and all of the oil and gasoline distribution.

These figures are based on the research of Prof. Muller of the American University, and were included in his book, *The Earth Managers*. Such dominance by North American companies establishes the smothering profile of an exploitative infrastructure that even today surrounds the people throughout Central and Southern America. It still bleeds them to the point of hopeless surrender or death by military and political oppression. Economic and political self-determination have never been among the options granted by their *gringo* masters, all modeled after the Dulles and Rockefeller brothers. For such cause, the prophets still cry out — along with the people they suffered with and cared for.

Schlesinger and McGovern Scope It Out

At least two years before any modern missionary or prophet set foot here in Brazil, the political apostle of John Kennedy, Arthur M. Schlesinger, Jr., surveyed the area as a scout for the *Food for Peace* program. This was 1961. With him was Sen. George McGovern. Schlesinger described the trip in his book, *A Thousand Days*. The Schlesinger-McGovern team, accompanied by a cameraman, flew to Recife in Brazil's desolate northeast. There they met Celso Furtado, a young economist who at that time was head of SUDENE, the federal commission for the development of the northeast. The foursome first drove through the humid area along the coast, devoted largely to sugar cultivation, then headed toward the semi-arid land in the interior.

Schlesinger reports he had never seen such an area of despair. He described it as "one bleak, stagnant village after another, dark mud huts, children with spindle legs and swollen bellies, practically no old people." Furtado told Schlesinger that life expectancy, for those who survived their first year, was 29 years.

In one village they entered a hut where a baby was dying, apparently of measles, in its mother's arms. The rest of the family of seven sat on the dirt floor, some eating with their hands. The food seemed to be beans and farina. Schlesinger noted that when the group entered, the family didn't even stir, except for a naked baby, perhaps 18 months old. The toddler held out his arms as if expecting to be taken up. But because he was covered with scabs and pock marks, none of the visitors touched the boy. The cameraman, who had come along to record evidence of need sufficient to convince Congressmen, kept flashing pictures of the depressing scene.

Schlesinger goes on to say that Furtado was realistic in his assessment of what might be done to help. His view was this: There was no present hope of doing anything in the semi-arid zone, and so it was best to concentrate on the sugar lands. Furtado believed an emergency food program would do no good, because it would disturb the existing dietary balance that kept the people marginally alive.

"Real development," Furtado told Schlesinger and McGovern, "means giving people the possibility of being happy in their work. These people hate their work." He said in any case they were too weak to work very long. If they were given food with no change in their way of life, they would only work less, Furtado concluded. Nothing else would change.

As the group was driving away, Furtado discussed that status of women as an indicator of the area's state of development. He told Schlesinger that in the poor areas women no longer had the grace or form of a woman; they were more like beasts of burden.

The Schlesinger team spent nine hours in the hinterlands before returning, tired and depressed, to Recife. With a touch of irony, he noted that as the four of them got out of the car, an enameled Brazilian girl come out of the hotel. Furtado, seeing that she was dressed seductively in high heels and a chic Paris dress, commented dryly, "We are obviously back in a developed country."

Schlesinger took time to reflect on the day's affairs as he prepared his report. He had learned that Furtado had come from a ranch in the interior. He knew that during the '50s the US embassy had regarded him with mistrust as a Marxist, if not a communist. In Schlesinger's view, Furtado seemed to regard himself as being in a personal race to solve the problem of the northeast — in competition with an "agitator", Francisco Juliao, who was organizing peasant agrarian unions and urging them to seize the land.

Schlesinger concluded that he and McGovern were appalled by the scope of the problem and were intent upon carrying the cause of northeast Brazil back to Washington.

As it turned out, Recife found no shoulder to cry upon in Washington. President Kennedy and most of his programs had been swamped by larger events, such as the Berlin Wall, the Bay of Pigs affair, organized crime hearings, and the Cuban Missile Crisis. If there was any lingering hope of remedy, it was assassinated with Kennedy in 1963. Worse, almost simultaneously there was a military coup in Brazil. The mood and the opportunity for effective reform had died in violence at both ends of the Recife episode.

Priests Venture In, Where "Food for Peace" Fears to Tread

Therein lies another tale that forms the core of the prophets' story: two years later, when the advance party of Oblate missionary priests came to give moral muscle to this corner of Brazil, their assessment was no different from Schlesinger's.

There was nothing but mud huts supported by sticks, sickness, malnutrition, and an infant death rate that exceeded 50%. Living and working conditions were beyond description. There seemed to be no hope, even from religious faith, because hope breeds desire to better the political and social setting. When that hope is continually frustrated, as the prophets would learn, it breeds only protest — which is met with suppression — and finally resignation to a fate crafted by rich parasites.

Thus Recife was a field fertile only for the growing of prophets who later were to languish in prisons while an American president told the world that "we have no political prisoners." No fewer than six Oblate priests became political road-kill as either a direct or indirect result of Recife. Their names, in no special order, are Darrell Rupiper, Peter Grams, Larry Rosebaugh, Giles Wagner, Boniface Wittenbrink, and Carl Kabat. All were kicked out of Brazil for political reasons. Among them, three are still priests who have been jailed for US political crimes, two are dead of natural causes, and one is married.

When it came to Brazil, Kennedy's successor, Lyndon B. Johnson, had a notion of reform similar to what Schlesinger and McGovern had hoped to propose. It was soon smothered by the politics of the communist witch hunt, the Vietnam War, and LBJ's sloganeering over guns-and-butter diplomacy. On LBJ's hidden list was an opportunistic plan to make use of the anti-communist position of the Catholic Church. Foreign missionaries seemed to him to make ideal bait when trolling for communists. (How he set this up with the Recife priests will be detailed further on).

For their part, prophets are too ingenuous to have enemies or to be spies, because they think that, communist or not, we are all children of God. True prophets consider political distinctions to be meaningless; that's why they readily become the enemies of the politicians who regard such distinctions as real and inimical to the United States. Then, prophets doing their spiritual thing in foreign lands become political targets, liable to be jailed as subversives in a state that has been made answerable to the US.

Of course, the load of suffering could be lifted from ordinary people if resources now spent on armaments were spent on human needs such as agrarian reform and jobs with living wages — the very things that Kennedy and Schlesinger and McGovern originally had in mind. What is seen only by the prophets in the lives of their poor parishioners is the unsigned debt that all of them bear as a burden of their country's obligations to US companies or the World Bank. Debt forgiveness is indispensable because the fundamental situation will not otherwise change. Debt forgiveness is like the forgiveness of sins — sins that for the most part have not been committed by their parishioners.

For all their good intentions, prophets are not always practical. Not all understand the economic details and the dislocations of land reform. They may not fully appreciate that the world's economic systems might collapse when resources are taken from the rich and given to the poor, that agricultural markets and economies worldwide can be destroyed by giving away foodstuffs. There is the balance of payments to worry about, exchange rates, and borrowed money to be repaid with interest. These are the worries of the Trilateral Commission, laid upon the poor of the world for perfection of entitlement by those who make such rules.

Prophets need no systematic vision of these details, for they have a larger view. They are like Samson who pulled at the pillars and deliberately brought down the roof upon himself to make his captors understand their mutual plight. In the end — as is the case with all prophets — while they may gain recognition for their vision, they are prophets without honor in their own land. And if they be too insistent, they are jailed with the lions as punishment and consumed for public satisfaction.

In 1961, not even Schlesinger would have been so pessimistic about some of the same harsh realities that the prophets and he and his own boss were to encounter. At that time, JFK's programs, such as Food for Peace and the Alliance for Progress and the Peace Corps, were not entirely altruistic. Kennedy, as Schlesinger pointed out in his book, *A Thousand Days*, was determined that what had happened with Castro in Cuba would not be repeated. There was always the bogeyman of Communism to deal with. Nevertheless, when Kennedy found out from his brother-in-law, Sargent Shriver, who directed the Peace Corps, that the CIA was infiltrating the ranks of "volunteers," he was reported to be livid over the subversion of his noble program.

There seems to be a final irony in Brazil. Neither the prophets nor Arthur Schlesinger knows what happened to Celso Furtado. Probably nobody cares now about the dying people that Celso, the prophets of Recife, and even Juliao once cared about — each in his own way. "I suppose," says Father Carl Kabat, "that the bony children I once gave bread to in Recife are dead now." He sighs a sigh of resignation. He knows such dying is always easiest in a land that is already dead, for there is no spirit left alive to resist.

Keeping that spirit alive is what Kabat and Rosebaugh and Rupiper struggled to do in Recife as they defied men who wore black suits but were not priests. However, it was Rupiper's style of ministry that irked them most.

Father Darrell Rupiper, a member of the Catholic Oblate order, began his priestly career as a missionary in Recife. (His efforts abroad eventually would lead him as far as Tehran and the hostage crisis.) "Rup," as his friends call him, used as his philosophical mantra the words of Edmund Burke: "The only thing necessary for the triumph of evil is for good men to do nothing." His own personal take on this idea is that no god can lighten a load that a mortal will not first try to lift. It was this approach to fighting social injustice and to promoting peace, coupled with strong sermons about human rights and God-given dignity, that got Rupiper kicked out of Brazil in 1968. He was charged with being a threat, by his words, to that nation's security.

Rupiper had been sent to Brazil in 1965 by his religious superiors in the US after they had made a deal with the LBJ White House for "schools and hospitals." (See the next chapter for details.) Here are some recent recollections of Father Rupiper, OMI, relating to the government's covert operations in two hemispheres. They include the accusation that government agents killed an Iranian friend of his in Omaha in 1980.

A Bit of Darrell Rupiper's Story

As a farm boy, on my first train trip from Omaha to St. Louis, I had the strong experience of not knowing that the world was so big. I had no idea of the things in store for me.

Years later, when I left the States from Miami to go to Brazil, I cried because I was leaving this country that I loved so much and knew so little about.

When I was forced to leave Brazil — having been accused of being a communist, of inciting people to revolution, and being an internal security risk — I cried again. I had learned more than I ever wanted to know about the terrible repressive, aggressive, super-power behavior of this country, what its policies inflicted on people. . . They were simple people like me who had no idea how big the world was or how or why it was creating so much misery for them. They understood the world of God but not the world of man, now being run by my own country with no regard for human dignity.

I realized that noble visions have no power unless people with power have noble visions. Our country was founded by men with noble visions of patriotism and morality who fought to gain power for their ideals. Our country has since lost its vision and has only raw power by which to claim righteousness. I felt like I had just witnessed the requiem for moral patriotism.

When I left Brazil, Archbishop Dom Helder Camara (four times nominated for the Nobel Peace Prize) pleaded with me to go back and tell the American people what their government is doing to "our people". He said, "Unless the American people come to know, there will never be any progress in Brazil or anywhere in Latin America." In the case of Iran (later), we heard the same message.

So I think now of protesting constantly against my own government many times, of having spent time in jails and prisons in Brazil and the States, six times. I think of having fallen in the hands of the dreaded military in Brazil and of having become the subject of an international incident both in Brazil and in Iran.

I think about Iran [where he made two independent visits to the US hostages in 1979-80], and being hounded by my government in both cases; becoming an object of hatred during the Iranian episode; being regarded as an outcast renegade by many local people and even some of my own relatives.

All of this because I believe in the One who has a special love for the poor and voiceless.

It was no secret to the Brazilian people that the US played a huge role in their economy — and in their subsequent hunger and dire poverty. Not that the Brazilian "big boys" didn't play a part. But by and large, the strings were pulled by those in Washington for the sake of the multinationals. It was no secret that the Peace Corps was infiltrated with CIA agents. Nor a secret that USAID agents taught torture methods. Nor the fact that the Brazilian military (after the 1965 takeover) had received their training and "toys" from the US.

The man who was torturing (others) while I was in their prison bragged that he had received his training from the International Police Academy in Washington. He connected it to National Security Agency. Anyway, his name was Luis Miranda, an ironic name, given the Miranda rights thing. But this Miranda used his US credentials to scare me, as if the screams in the dark of night weren't enough. So did the general when he wasn't pretending to be a good guy.

Then there was a known teacher of torture methods, supposedly connected with USAID, but really with the CIA. Here was a US citizen, plying his obscene trade in Brazil. He was known to demonstrate his skills by kidnapping homeless people and then using them alive to show his death-squad students the best way of extracting confessions by torture. When he moved from Brazil to Uruguay to spread his methods, he was killed by rebels. They hated him. His name, I think, was Dan Mitrione. But it's been a long time.

Someone told me he even had a slogan, something about the right amount of pain in the right place to get the right effect. I'm glad he didn't get his hands on me or Pete. I heard that when his body was brought back home to Indiana, Richard Nixon sent a big red-white-and-blue floral wreath as if to honor him for his sadism.

Nixon had his own form of honor down there. The clubs that police used in Brazil were called "pau de Nixon," meaning Nixon sticks or clubs. No wonder South Americans spit at him on his vice presidential goodwill tour.

About a week after Peter Grams and I were arrested (December 13, 1968) our bishop, Dom Helder Camara, was finally allowed into the prison to see if we were being tortured. He told us that a telegram had arrived from Washington saying that unless these two priests were released immediately, all military aid would be cut off. For Washington, it was vital that the media not be stirred up to look into US behavior and secret meddling in the south.

Dom Helder begged us to stay in prison, if we could stand it, so that public attention might be focused on the US meddling and military abuse of citizens. He thought this might stop the flow of arms. I wanted to stay, but I knew from the reaction of Pete Grams that he was about to go crazy. When we were alone, he covered his ears and shook his head to shut out the sounds of other prisoners being tortured.

Besides, we had been told by the general that we would be offered no defense, that we would be declared guilty and would then have to spend two years in prison. And then we would be kicked out as traitors to Brazil and the US. I knew it would break Pete.

I offered to stay if Pete could be released, but the general who ran that part of Brazil wouldn't deal. Either we both stayed and faced the grim future, or we both had to leave immediately. So we agreed to leave, even though I wanted to honor Dom Helder's request.

But his point about Washington's getting its way remains. After the whole thing was over, I remember receiving a copy of the perfunctory hearings about the case in Washington. There were so many lies in it and so many lines blacked out that I could barely recognize they were speaking about us or our case.

While most people are enraged by the unzipped White House, I learned that the same people are blind to the real sins of this nation. Everyone becomes expendable if it can be done in a way that no one will find out. Death threats, blackmail, character bashing, lies are not given a second thought by those who are the architects of money-grabbing or power-grabbing schemes disguised behind international robbery.

During the Iranian debacle, I received a letter addressed to "TRAITOR PRIEST" in Omaha. My mail was messed with in a big way, my telephone also. One day I was talking to CBS in New York, and because we were talking about some heavy stuff, the phone went dead.

The Young Americans for Freedom (YAF) were having a heyday against me. On the top of their letterhead was a picture of Reagan and a quote from him saying, "Now I need you more than ever." For what? For the kind of burglary that Nixon had promoted, that's what.

A rivalry between two YAF members for chairmanship of the organization ended up in the courts when it was revealed that one of the rivals had broken into my Omaha house and gone through my things looking for evidence that he thought might incriminate me in some way. I guess his vigilante method was his way of trying to be a government citizen-hero. It reflects on the White House thinking of the times and what I felt was continuing CIA tactics.

About Iran? After my return, I was fearful for my life because of our government in those days. And I do not doubt that an Iranian friend of mine studying in the Lincoln-Omaha area was killed as a warning to me to keep my mouth shut. It didn't work, and I continued to speak out, saying that if I am killed, please investigate because I have been threatened by our government.

There is something prophetic about the 1961 visit to Recife by Schlesinger and McGovern, because in 1964 Recife was once again to become a point of interest for the White House; this time, the LBJ White House.

Recife had also become a point of interest for the Oblates of Mary Immaculate (OMI) in their Central Province of the United States. The Oblates, a group of Catholic missionaries, were founded in France at the time of the French Revolution to specialize in serving the poor. Among the Oblates' number were three young priests who would become prophets without honor: Rupiper, Carl Kabat and Larry Rosebaugh.

The Oblates had thrived in Canada and, by the '60s, had grown to several hundred members in America, thanks to an aggressive recruiting campaign within the parochial school system and the establishment of major seminaries by the Oblates in the US. Given the growth in their ranks, the Oblate administration in Rome was calling for priests to staff a mission being planned for Brazil. The focal point was Recife. "Since we will one day be a large and numerous province," wrote Father William Coovert, OMI, "we need a vast mission field in order to be able to staff it with the personnel we one day hope to have."

Showing Up the Communists

It was springtime, 1964, when Coovert, the Oblate provincial, traveled from his St. Paul headquarters to Brazil to review preparations for the planned cadre of missionaries. About this time, the government of Brazil underwent a coup, and Coovert suddenly found that his exposure to the political and social situation there caused him to be in demand by various government agencies, including the Peace Corps and the White House.

"The timing is perfect," Coovert said in a letter. "They (the US government) have been waiting for a chance to get into Brazil to show up the Communists."

At about the same time that Father Rupiper and his Oblate priest colleagues were being ordained and readied for their mission in Recife, the Vietnam War was heating up.

While LBJ was worried about the instability in Saigon, he also had to watch his back door in South America. The CIA had just successfully engineered the overthrow of Joao Goulart in favor of a military regime. But with Castro and Che Guevara exporting their brand of communist rebellion from Cuba as retaliation for CIA thrusts from Panama and Nicaragua, LBJ needed some independent grassroots intelligence about the area.

The coincidence of the coup with Fr. Coovert's visit was too fortuitous to pass up. Recognizing the Church's long-standing opposition to Communism, LBJ invited Coovert to the White House — probably at the instigation of Vice President Hubert Humphrey, who knew that Coovert was a fellow-Minnesotan. LBJ wanted up-close information from an independent source, and to get it, he began to make wide-ranging promises of a quid-pro-quo nature.

Coovert, who had dozens of Oblate priests at his command, was flattered and obliging. He then reported to his priest associates that the White House discussion had centered around the political situation in Brazil, particularly Recife, where the Oblates were planning to build their mission. Perhaps because of the 1961 expedition to Recife by Schlesinger and McGovern, Johnson recognized the potential for a spy plan. Judging by Coovert's reaction, LBJ offered a behind-the-scenes aid package for the area.

"I am sure we will get Peace Corps, housing, industry, schools and hospitals for Recife," Coovert wrote to his Oblate superiors in Rome, "plus a good income to run our own house." Divulging details of the meeting with LBJ and Vice President Hubert Humphrey, Coovert added, "We got two gigantic programs through Washington. One for food and one for buildings." At that time, the headquarters for the Oblate Central Province was in St. Paul, Minnesota, Humphrey's political turf.

The offer did not come without strings. LBJ was not about to let a group of idealistic priests become loose political cannons. Within six months of the White House meeting, without any review by his provincial board, Coovert formed in 1965 the Oblate International Association (OIA), and patched it into the Recife operation. This was a 26-man committee "to provide experts in business, education, social and political fields" as the Oblate priests established their missions. The purpose of the OIA, Coovert said, "is to provide professional advice and direction for overseas projects of the Oblate Fathers. In addition to serving the interests of the Church, their aid as missionaries would aid US efforts to stem the threat of Communism in South America."

The OIA was supposed to assist the Oblate priests by "introducing American companies, or existing Brazilian companies, as a means of expanding employment opportunities in Recife," Coovert said. Once jobs and incomes were secured, the plans were to provide housing for these new employees. The long-range goal of the joint government/OIA/Oblate venture, as Coovert explained it, was "to arrest the hopeless spiral of ever worsening conditions in Recife and provide an atmosphere in which the honest and more energetic of these poor can begin to live a life of hope and dignity."

Obviously, in addition to serving the interests of the Church, Coovert's intent was to have his missionaries indirectly assist US efforts to stem the tide of Communism in South America. What he did not know was that some of the appointees to the OIA came through the CIA door. The missionary priests who were sent to Brazil had no anti-communist master plan that matched the one constructed by LBJ and Fr. Coovert. They had no contact with anyone from the OIA, to their knowledge. The priests in the field were responding merely to a call from the Oblate order's superiors in the US and Rome to perform priestly duties in one of the poorest areas in the world.

The depth of Fr. Coovert's naivety was revealed when he visited the Recife mission shortly after its start. As Rupiper recalls, fishing was Coovert's hobby. While on tour of the Recife area, he saw some of the barefooted villagers fishing and remarked how wonderful that they could have such a hobby.

"I told him they were fishing for their next meal," Rupiper says. "I think he thought I was kidding."

LBJ's unconstitutional plan, oddly mixing Church and State goals, failed because none of the missionary priests had received instructions to behave like secret agents in cassocks. When priests like Rupiper and Grams preached too strongly about hope and human dignity to the impoverished laboring class, they were arrested by military police who were armed by America to carry out its policies. LBJ's hidden manipulation didn't work because, as Rupiper notes in his recollections, "the reality down there changed me."

"I knew nothing of Communism," Rupiper says to this day. "Nor any communists. I only tried to snatch my parishioners from the jowls of starvation," he says with an ironic twist of words. "The American-backed, gun-toting officials, trained by the CIA, just couldn't accept the fact that Jesus was not a communist, I guess."

If any money ever flowed from the LBJ White House to Recife, as promised to Father Coovert, it went through government channels as foreign aid into the pockets of corrupt officials. As a result, local officials made false promises of new developments in order to clear the cities of unwanted slum-dwellers.

The subsequent refusal of the priests to identify McCarthy-type targets among their impoverished parishioners under questioning from visiting locally-hired government agents radicalized the community of Oblate priests and led several of them, including Kabat, to a lifetime of peaceful protest and dissent — much of it spent in US maximum security prisons.

Showing Up the Viet Cong

These events would seem to be somewhat puny compared to others that were unfolding in the headlines of the times; but the Recife events were such that, coupled with LBJ's lies about Vietnam, they would create prophets of protest from among the priests sent to Recife. Their protests would make ripples that still lap at the shores of war and peace in the world.

It was in July 1964 when the news came that the Viet Cong had won their biggest battle, in the Mekong Delta of Vietnam. This development worried President Johnson. He wanted a quick, decisive end to the war and needed some means to show Hanoi America's strength and resolve in the face of the South Vietnamese army's ineptitude. To do this, he secretly authorized what came to be known as Operation 34-A. It was the "Big Lie" for which then-Secretary of Defense Robert McNamara was to apologize, in tears, 30 years later.

34-A was a CIA-concocted plan for preemptive raids on the North Vietnamese coast, coordinated by CIA advisers using South Vietnamese commando units. Targets included fuel storage depots on two North Vietnamese islands in the Gulf of Tonkin. The action, as described in Noam

Chomsky's book, *Deterring Democracy*, was carried out the night and early morning of July 30-31, 1964. Following the raid, the destroyer *Maddox*, loaded with electronic surveillance equipment, moved in close to scan the scene. This was known as a DE SOTO patrol.

Seeing the ship, the North Vietnamese assumed the US attack was continuing, so they attacked the *Maddox* with three patrol boats on August 2. Clearly, they assumed the *Maddox* had everything to do with the raid, even though it had never left international waters. In the exchange, and with air cover from the nearby carrier, *Ticonderoga*, one patrol boat was sunk and another damaged. The provocative raid was kept from the public's attention, but Sen. J. William Fulbright said the next day in conversation with George Ball that he thought the covert US action was intended to provoke Hanoi into a response that would give the US an excuse to make air strikes against the North. Fulbright was right, but nobody gave him the satisfaction of saying so.

When Hanoi made no public announcement of the skirmish, LBJ assumed the Reds had got his "get-tough" message and were content to say nothing. The thinking in the White House was that Hanoi had mistakenly attacked the *Maddox*. Even so, Johnson gave orders that destroyer patrols would be conducted at a greater distance from the coast by two ships working together, but that any future attacks would be met with the intent of destroying the attackers.

Hanoi was not quiescent, however. In fact, the North Vietnamese regarded the *Maddox* as part of the US belligerency. This was learned from intercepts of the North Vietnamese communications by the *Maddox* following the skirmish. Even at 60 miles offshore, all US ships were now considered to be hostile to the North. This was reported by the skipper of the *Maddox* to Washington. The message also indicated that torpedo boats were preparing to attack in the open sea. LBJ determined, after consultation with advisers, that if such an attack came, a Congressional resolution supporting a counterattack would be in order. And so the original US provocation was playing into the master plan: a way to attack North Vietnam and blame it on them.

On August 4, McNamara told the President he had received a message from the *Maddox* and the *Turner Joy* that radar showed the two ships were about to be attacked.

"I want not only the patrol boats destroyed," LBJ is quoted as saying, "but I want everything in that harbor destroyed. I want to give them a real dose" (quoted in *Flawed Giant* by Robert Dallek).

Johnson then arranged for the TV networks to give him time in the evening to announce his response to the North Vietnamese attack. Planning the attack then proceeded in the White House basement war room. As these plans were progressing, another message came in from the *Maddox*. It seems there had been no attack. Freaky weather effects and wave actions had affected radar readings. Tense sonar-men only thought they had seen torpedo traces (as declassified files would show many years later).

LBJ called Admiral Sharp, commander of the Pacific naval forces, to clarify the situation. Sharp said, "The latest dope we have is a sort of ambush attempt by the PTs." In response to a direct question from McNamara, Sharp told the White House that "there is a slight possibility" that there was no attack. He later confirmed that "there was indeed" an attack (*Deterring Democracy*, Noam Chomsky.)

LBJ grilled CIA chief John McCone, a member of the National Security Council, about why the North Vietnamese would carry out such an attack in international waters, risking war with the whole US Navy. McCone was said to reply: "The North Vietnamese are reacting defensively to our attack on their off-shore islands. They are responding out of pride and on the basis of their own defense considerations. The attack is a signal to us that the North Vietnamese have the will and determination to continue the war. They are raising the ante." What he failed to mention was that the North Vietnamese navy didn't amount to much, and so they had little to lose that couldn't be replaced quickly by the Chinese or the Soviets.

By 11 PM that evening, LBJ falsely announced to the world that North Vietnam had made an "unprovoked" attack on the destroyers. He proceeded with the announcement, despite doubts, because he had committed to the TV airtime in advance. He called for Congressional support for a military response as well as for resolution for a more general policy of engagement. Two days later, LBJ got his Gulf of Tonkin Resolution from Congress. The rest, as they say, is history. But the American public didn't know about the phantom attack, the US provocations, and the Tonkin Gulf lie until years later.

Also forgotten in the turmoil was the prior Indochina peace provision, after the defeat of the French: that there were to be elections in North and South Vietnam to determine the future of the divided Vietnamese nation. The election delay, backed by the US, had become permanent policy in quiet defiance of the peace treaty with the French. The option for war under the domino theory was substituted, because the US feared a communist outcome in such elections.

To resist any North-South election, the CIA under Allen Dulles had installed Ngo Dinh Diem, one of its "assets" in Saigon, as premier of South Vietnam. In 1963, Kennedy (just before his assassination) allowed the CIA to snuff Diem in a coup for failure to achieve its objectives. It was a permission that JFK regretted, as presidential tapes were to show, much later.

The news files tell the rest of the story as LBJ took over in the White House.

CONGRESS APPROVES GULF OF TONKIN RESOLUTION; WIDER WAR LOOMS

Washington, Aug. 7, 1964 — The Senate and House of Representatives voted almost unanimously Friday give President Johnson greater authority to strike back against the communists in North Vietnam.

Responding to the President's appeals for support following attacks on US ships by North Vietnamese patrol boats, Congress approved what is being called the Gulf of Tonkin Resolution.

Many of the Congressmen who approved the resolution expressed their misgivings about the widening involvement of the American military in the war.

Earlier this week, President Johnson announced on a special TV broadcast that he had ordered air strikes against the PT boats and communist coastal facilities following torpedo attacks on the American destroyer Maddox which were on routine patrol in international waters. He called the North Vietnamese actions "open aggression on the high seas."

Secretary of State Dean Rusk said of the earlier US response, "The other side got a sting out of this. If they do it again, they'll get another sting."

The war headlines grew increasingly ominous for the Johnson Administration as LBJ finished out Kennedy's term. The GI death toll in Vietnam for all of 1964 totaled 136, with 1,022 American soldiers listed as wounded. In 1961-62, there had been 32 Americans killed, and in 1963 the number had been 76.

On January 20, 1965, Lyndon Baines Johnson began his first elected term of office as President. Speaking without coat or hat in chilly Potomac weather, LBJ's inaugural words outlined his plans for a greater America: a "Great Society" which could afford both guns and butter. America, he said, "seeks no dominion over our fellow man, but man's dominion over tyranny and misery."

At another point, he noted that "we are all passengers on a dot of earth. . . How incredible it is that in this fragile existence we should hate and destroy one another."

His eloquent and sensitive words were quickly carried away by the headlines describing America's efforts to destroy others and make everyone a passenger on the Vietnam escalator of war.

US AIRCRAFT STRIKE NORTH VIETNAM

Washington, Feb. 11, 1965 — The Johnson Administration Thursday ordered air strikes against targets in North Vietnam in retaliation for guerrilla attacks directed by Hanoi against military installations in South Vietnam.

The White House said the air strikes were in response "to provocations ordered and directed by the Hanoi regime." The President added, "we seek no wider war."

In the ensuing years, the war in fact was widened by Johnson. The original plan to simply use military advisers in Vietnam was not working, so the previous coup leader, Lt. Gen. Nguyen Khanh, who also was commander-in-chief of the South Vietnamese armed forces, was overthrown in yet another coup. Without any reliable leadership, the US had to get further involved or back out. Johnson opted for more involvement.

As the war in Vietnam intensified, the Oblate priests were struggling to help the poor in Brazil. They saw no aid for schools and hospitals being funneled in from the LBJ Administration. They knew that any such funds had by now been redirected to the war effort or the pockets of the Brazilian regime. There were plenty of guns, but no butter.

The priests became bitter about all things military, because now they understood how warfare anywhere drains away resources that otherwise could be applied to solve human problems. In this sense, the Vietnam War became the flash point for the priests in Recife and in America. Its ripple effects were to be evident through the end of the 20th century.

Theirs was an effort that was to merge with similar discontent growing at home. Back in America, the young people's attitude about the Vietnam War is summed up by this message that was pasted on the carrying cases of guitars: "Join the Army. Travel to distant lands. Meet strange people with exotic customs. And kill them."

Philip and Daniel Berrigan did not wake up one morning and decide to stage an anti-war protest. Rather, the Berrigans had spent most of their thinking lives concerned with the symptoms that brought on the Vietnam War and continued to flow from it: poverty and economic and social injustice.

Daniel had spent twelve years studying to be a Jesuit priest, and Philip had spent eight years in reaching the priesthood within an order known as the Society of St. Joseph (Josephites). The Josephite priests worked mainly among blacks, at a time when it was proper to call members of that minority Negroes, (when they weren't being called intentionally ugly names).

The Berrigans had known poverty from the Great Depression. They had seen it on a family farm in the Iron Range of northern Minnesota. They had seen it at their farm near Syracuse, New York. Later, they saw it in New York City, in Washington, New Orleans and in all the black ghettos. They discovered the ties between militarism, poverty and racism. Just as the Vietnam War expanded gradually, so did their urge to do something about its gross immorality. They wanted to set an example, to do something lasting that others might emulate.

That "something" had to capture public attention and it had to be as nonviolent as the war was violent. It took months of discussion among like-minded intellectual friends. It took exposure to, and involvement in, the civil rights movement in Birmingham and Selma, when James Farmer of the Congress Of Racial Equality and Dr. Martin Luther King summoned the help of clergymen of all faiths.

The urge to do something convinced them to join the Freedom Riders in Alabama and Mississippi. But they were quickly ordered by the Catholic Bishop, Richard O. Gerow of the Jackson diocese, not to interfere on his lily-white diocesan turf. Gerow successfully pressured the Berrigans, through their religious superiors, to withdraw from participation with the Freedom Riders. Ironically, Gerow's conservative pontificate occurred while the Kabat brothers, Paul and Carl, along with Rosebaugh and Rupiper were seminarians at Pass Christian, Mississippi. In fact, as bishop, he ordained both Paul and Carl Kabat. Gerow's portrait was on heroic display in the seminary dining hall where the future prophets ate. In this way, the Oblate prophets, like the Berrigans who preceded them, had experienced mutual contact with a reactionary bishop who did nothing about voter poll taxes in a state where civil rights of the poor undereducated blacks were at stake.

In some nobly twisted sense of justice, the Kabat brothers, Rosebaugh and Rupiper, while trained under Gerow's framed visage, were later to form their own resistance to anti-protest edicts of the Gerow kind. As with the Berrigans, their dissent was directed at the racial, political, economic and military policies that had drawn the tacit blessings of the conservative elements within the Church.

Gerow's success in limiting Catholic participation in the Freedom Riders, was a temporary victory for moral restraint. Philip Berrigan himself visited the Oblate seminary in Mississippi while Rupiper, Rosebaugh, Wittenbrink and Grams were in their formative stages. He became a hero whom they did, indeed, later emulate.

The Berrigans knew that if their search for a special attention-building action were to succeed, it had to be powerful enough to build a mood of empathy within the student power-base on campuses across the country. It needed organizing and publicity. It needed to be something that would percolate into society. It required defiance in the face of political arrogance. It meant a struggle with the institutional Church and with the nation's Hooverian warlords. It would take, they knew, the courage of personal conviction, raw-gut planning, internal strength and mobilization to action. During this period of agonizing reflection, the Berrigan brothers came to realize that the United States would become a just nation only when its bloated power declined to a point where it could no longer abuse its preeminent position.

As Philip Berrigan puts it in his book, *Fighting the Lamb's War*: "Imperial states are about ripping people apart, chewing them to pieces; that's what the government was doing in Southeast Asia, and that's what it was doing at home."

The Baltimore Four

The Berrigans took their first step October 22, 1967. Dan Berrigan was arrested in a march against the Pentagon. He was still in jail when his brother, Philip, and three others poured a mixture of their own blood on draft files in Baltimore. They became known as the "Baltimore Four." A compiled news dispatch explains:

> PROTESTORS POUR BLOOD ON DRAFT FILES
> Baltimore, Md., Oct. 27, 1967 — Philip Berrigan, a Roman Catholic priest of the Josephite order, and three of his accomplices splattered their own pre-bottled blood Monday on Selective Service files here.
> They said it was to protest the Vietnam War. The men entered the Baltimore Customs House and asked to see their draft files. When the file drawers were opened, the men produced containers of blood from their briefcases and poured it over the files.
> Berrigan said the blood symbolized that which was being shed by both Americans and Vietnamese people as well as the blood of Christ. While waiting at the office for the FBI to arrest them, Berrigan issued a call to others "to move with us from dissent to resistance."

The four, Tom Lewis, David Eberhardt, Jim Mengel and Philip Berrigan were released on bail pending sentencing. At the time, as Philip Berrigan recalls, "Vietnam was burning. Watts, Newark and Detroit were burning."

Because Vietnam was burning, Dan Berrigan took advantage of an invitation extended through a Quaker peace group to visit Hanoi to further the release of three captive American pilots. The delegation did gain the pilots' release, but the government, prompted by super-patriot J. Edgar Hoover, portrayed Dan Berrigan as a traitor. The opportunity for peace negotiations, opened by Berrigan's visit, was summarily spurned by the US.

The Catonsville Nine

Dan Berrigan had scarcely returned to the US when he joined his brother and seven others in another draft protest action. Philip, who was free on bail while awaiting sentencing for his Baltimore protest, led the raid on the draft files at Catonsville, Md. The date was May 17, 1968. Together with the Berrigans, David Darst, John Hogan, Thomas Lewis, Marjorie Melville, Thomas Melville, Georgia Mische and Mary Moylan removed files from the Selective Service office and burned them with homemade napalm, using a Green Beret recipe of gasoline and soap. They became known as the "Catonsville Nine." Before they were brought to trial and sentenced, however, Philip was sentenced to six years in prison for the Baltimore action.

As Philip Berrigan later explained in his autobiography,

> We just wanted the judge and jury to see that our government was dousing Vietnamese children with the same terrible stuff we poured over those draft files. We were cooking Vietnamese in white phosphorus, poisoning their food and water with herbicides, burning down their homes, violating international treaties, and showing contempt for God's law.

The actions of "The Catonsville Nine" set off a national furor. There were draft card burning protests in the streets, and student riots on campuses. Eventually it led to a nationwide manhunt by the FBI when Dan Berrigan, out on bail, decided not to surrender to federal agents to serve his jail term. Dan Berrigan's decision to become a persecuted fugitive of international fame was ideally suited to building sympathy for the cause within the public mind.

In his autobiography Dan Berrigan calls draft cards "hunting licenses for human beings." In both the Baltimore and Catonsville instances, the prophets were motivated by government policy that they perceived as immoral. In opposing these policies, the Berrigan brothers were not acting on a moral code of their own invention. Both highly trained theologians, they were well aware of the teachings of Pope John XXIII in the encyclical, "*Pacem in Terris*" (Peace on Earth). The encyclical, in parts quoted by Philip Berrigan, says that freedom from war, and peace without fear, are impossible without the recognition of human rights, and their possession by all men. Berrigan asserts that, to achieve this condition, the pope implies that action by nonviolent agents of peace may be required. "Justice demands that the arms race should cease," the encyclical says, referring to the prophecy of Isaiah about turning swords into plowshares. Pope John's words further suggest, Philip Berrigan says, that because of the arms race, two-thirds of mankind languishes in hunger and the misery of militarism.

Consequently, the Berrigans and their colleagues claimed a moral basis for protest based on the teachings of the Church and the Bible. The

Berrigans, in setting a symbolic prophetic example, were not alone. The "Milwaukee Fourteen" was just one of the groups inspired by their example. It is very likely that they were inspired as well by the following news story:

US BOMBERS DROP NAPALM NEAR CAMBODIA; CIVILIANS IMPERILED

Saigon, April 15, 1965 — American bombers dropped 1,000 tons of explosives and searing napalm on a suspected Viet Cong stronghold near the Cambodian border of South Vietnam.

Military experts said the napalm is a highly flammable gel with a gasoline base capable of searing through jungle foliage, and ground fortifications.

Military officials said civilians have been warned to vacate the area. It is not clear by what means the warnings were issued or whether the warnings came before or after the bombing assault.

Larry Rosebaugh was an Oblate seminary friend of Darrell Rupiper and the Kabat brothers. Dorothy Day's radical style of spirituality was an early influence. In fact, he prizes among his few possessions a pencil sketch he drew of Dorothy Day. Larry's natural penchant for direct action to seek remedy for social ills was enhanced by his acquaintance with the Berrigans.

Rosebaugh's assignment after ordination in 1962 had taken him to teaching assignments in Duluth, St. Paul and Chicago Catholic high schools and weekend parish work. Unhappy with the comforts of parish life, he asked to be assigned to the streets of Milwaukee. There he helped to form the "Casa Maria" (Mary's House) as a Catholic Worker refuge for street people.

Then the Vietnam War came along. He felt that war and its killing were violations of God's commandment, and he knew that some of the young men he had taught in high school were being sent to Vietnam to kill or be killed. Inspired by the Berrigans, Larry helped to lead a group of 14 people in burning draft files in Milwaukee. The group became known as the "Milwaukee Fourteen." They included Don Cotton, Michael Cullen, Fr. Robert Cunane, James Forest, Jerry Gardner, Bob Graf, Rev. Jon Higgenbotham, Fr. James Harney, Fr. Alfred Janicke, Doug Marvy, Fr. Anthony Mullaney, Fred J. Ojile, and Bro. K. Bash O'Leary.

Rosebaugh is bashful about telling his story because he fears it might sound self-serving. And so his story came to be written by one of Larry's seminary friends, by then a newspaper reporter, a few days after visiting with him behind bars. The story developed during a visit in the Waupun State Prison near Milwaukee. The year was 1970. The leaves were turning bright, and the Vietnam War was turning dark. Leading this prison visit was Rupiper, who had been named Chaplain of the Catholic students' Newman Club at Champaign, Illinois, after being kicked out of Brazil.

Larry Rosebaugh's Story

A PRIEST SENTENCED TO LIFE — of Resistance

WAUPUN, WIS., 1970 — A two-year sentence has turned into a "life term" for a priest bound by vows of poverty, chastity and obedience. He is now bound by bars at the Waupun State Prison near Milwaukee, Wisconsin.

That's because he feels the corrupt system which led him to burn draft files has "delivered him into resistance." A whole lifetime of it. But the lifetime's not easy.

From his cell, Father Larry "Frog" Rosebaugh admits: "I am such a fragile man. I break easily. I am close to the edge, tight on the rope of life. Yet I have grown to love that existence."

Almost no one in Milwaukee remembers Larry's name nor his actions as part of the "Milwaukee Fourteen." On September 24, 1968, fourteen men, including five priests and a protestant minister, removed approximately 10,000 1-A draft files from Milwaukee's Selective Service Board and burned them with homemade napalm in a square dedicated to America's war dead. Then they calmly waited to be arrested.

Larry's friends do remember the courage of his convictions. The judge and jury may remember the difficulty they had in distinguishing between the law and the action, versus the man, the times and his motives. Attorney William Kunstler represented Larry and the others at their trial, but was unable to persuade the judge to allow an argument of conscience. Perhaps the cleaning woman remembers the bouquet of flowers she received from the arrested Fourteen — as an apology for having frightened her when they used her keys to enter the building containing the draft files. Possibly someone remembers that no one was hurt, that there was no violence or bloodshed, and that the only property damaged was paper.

The action, and what it stood for in 1968, has faded. And so, futility is one of the things that Larry (he doesn't care for the title "Father") finds most difficult as he languishes in maximum security, serving the final days of his two-year sentence.

"No. I wouldn't do it again," he says quickly, when asked.

It sounded like a stunning reversal, as if his spirit had been broken. Here's a man who once hiked 42 miles around the Bay of St. Louis, Mississippi, in 11 and a half hours, just as a lark. Here's a guy who operated Casa Maria, a no-praying-for-your-meals shelter for men who were the social dregs of Milwaukee. Here's a guy who had the guts to submit voluntarily to arrest, trial, humiliation and inevitable punishment by the system for the sake of protesting a war he thought to be immoral.

This is the same man who, once imprisoned, managed to get a story to the outside world about racial abuse in the Fox Lake, Wisconsin, prison. At the time, he was two months away from parole review. When the story was published in the newspapers, it embarrassed and enraged the warden. Larry's punishment? He was sent to the maximum security prison at Waupun, where he suffered through 30 days of solitary confinement. His parole review was put off.

Then, while at Waupun, he refused to be "rehabilitated" by working in the prison laundry or the license plate shop for 35 cents a day. How could anyone presume to rehabilitate a man of God who, years before, during a seminary work period, had cut his hand while working with sheet metal on a drill press — a man who, spurting blood, blurted no vulgarities but feared instead that a damaged hand might be an obstacle to ordination?

Then Larry explained "why he wouldn't do it again":

"I mean, I wouldn't do it the same way. Maybe I would have done it sooner or with more public attention. It might seem that being in jail puts my cause in jail with me, but it's the best witness anyone can give to the correctness of a cause and to what is wrong with our system."

Hearing this explanation, it was plain that Father Larry's spirit was far from broken. He may be masking that spirit in a guerrilla kind of way, but I sensed it was stronger now, even as his body had grown thin from his life in a cell. At 5'10" and a skinny 155 lbs, he doesn't look like a dissenter in his sloppy-fitting prison khakis. His manners are subdued, the way the warden likes them, but his voice carries with it an inner conviction that is evident only to those who know how to read the spirit dwelling in his flashing blue eyes.

Shortly before Larry deliberately broke the laws of the United

States in his 1968 act of civil disobedience, he wrote: "Can I become a poor man in such a climate? Wear the skin of another man's existence? These questions each man must ask himself, wherever he is. If not, he must move on (to a lesser existence)."

The story about Larry, written by his seminary friend after the prison visit in 1970, continues:

While Larry is in prison, the Vietnam War continues. Human beings on both sides, but especially the poor of several Asian countries, are killing and being killed. Larry, along with other in the "Milwaukee Fourteen," reasoned:

"We had to trace the roots of the Vietnamese struggle and suffering, and admit that all too many of those roots converge in the soil of American values and priorities.

"Millions had to die at America's hands, while in the process, millions of America's sons were torn from family, friends, health, sanity and often life itself. Victim and executioner have been trapped in the same dragnet of death."

That is why Larry and the 13 others concluded in their action statement:

"Today we destroy Selective Service files because men need to be reminded that property is not sacred. Property belongs to the human scene only if man does. . . . Indeed, our nation has seen, with such isolated exceptions as the Boston Tea Party, devotion to property take ever greater precedence over devotion to life."

After helping to burn property he thought "had no right to exist," Larry found the answer to his question about whether he could wear the skin of another man's existence, as he wrote from prison:

"I can finally be fed myself by the poor man, burn draft files, and see my life being enriched by those who have the least."

Even so, while in prison, Larry still suffers the consequences of his action, as he knows he must, under a penal system that seeks to "rehabilitate" convicts — which, by definition, now includes people like Larry who would rather rehabilitate the system.

He remains convinced that the penal system, which he has come to know on its grimmest terms, needs rehabilitation as badly as the entire system he is convicted of transgressing. His prison experience teaches him that his prison of bars "is not much different" from the world itself.

"Each holds its occupants captive — one by cruelty, the other by effect of the cage," as he points out. And so it has always been logical for Larry to find a just cause for his crusading spirit in either place.

The basis for his judgment of the prison system and the source for his Quixotic impulse to right any wrong can be found in the opening portion of the apologia issued by the "Milwaukee Fourteen":

> Generation after generation, religious values have summoned men to undertake the works of mercy and peace. In time of crisis, their values have further required men to cry out in protest against institutions and systems destructive of man and his immense potential.

Every priest-prophet who has endured prison echoes the same refrain and has immense sympathy for anyone imprisoned just because of the inhuman conditions that prison, by definition, imposes. They know that the need for prisons flows not from the evil of the inmates but from the society which creates the need by its systemic evils.

"It's not so bad accepting a sentence for something you believe in," Larry says from prison. "It's accepting the added conditions you are sentenced to that is hard."

Part of what he has been sentenced to is the rehabilitation program. He is learning how terribly wrong, inhuman and unjust is the treatment of prisoners, especially among racial minorities, in the name of that program. And that is the agony of his resistance to it. What he seeks to reform in society imposes its own torture of change on him.

The irony of Larry's self-aggravated sentence is this: He is spending his time in a maximum security prison among men who have committed the most heinous of crimes. By contrast, the crime that put him in maximum security was not the burning of the draft files, but rather his voiced objections to racial injustice in prisons while serving there for something equally wrong within the system outside.

"Face it," he says. "I'm a political prisoner. There is no worse crime." Then he adds, "At least I have a chance to read and to think and to improve my mind. I couldn't do that in the prison laundry or shop.

"They've got a lot of the wrong people behind bars," Larry insists, "and they're doing all the wrong things to them." When he told that to prison officials, he says they simply reply that only the professional penologists know the proper treatment of prisoners.

"You don't know anything about handling prisoners," one associate warden told Larry.

"But I'm not stupid," Larry says he responded. That response earned him a 30-day dose of solitary.

"During the first two weeks I nearly went crazy. And they didn't even give me the bread-and-water treatment. They don't do that anymore. They don't have to. They didn't even shut the wooden door over my cell to cut off the light," he recalls. "It's the being alone that gets you. The lack of communication. And the fear.

"I guess I had the sense to ask for some paper and pencils and a Bible. That helped. I must have written a hundred sheets. Mostly I asked myself what I am doing here. But it's quiet. There's nothing. It's empty. Alone. Fear.

"You think the same thoughts so many times it drives you crazy. You think about not giving in. You fear you will. And you have to communicate. Time goes on endlessly.

"Don't give in. Don't give in. Write. Think. Quiet. Nothing. Alone. Fear. Just the fear of it kills you.

"Finally, after about two weeks, I couldn't stand it any longer. I panicked. I thought I was going crazy. I thought I was crazy to stay there any longer. I knew I was going to be behind bars no matter what I did. . . whether I worked in the shop or not.

"So I sent a note with the guard, telling the warden I'd go back to work if he'd let me out of solitary. After the guard left, I really got frightened. I was afraid they had finally done something to me that would change me forever.

"A couple hours later I sent the warden another note, before I had gotten any reply on the first one. I told him I was changing my mind, that I wouldn't go back to work after all. The guard seemed disgusted and commented that the warden probably wouldn't pay attention to any third or fourth note. But I told him to take the second one anyway.

"Then I knew peace. Then the final two weeks in solitary weren't so bad. I knew I had won. In fact, this place now is sort of like the seminary. I think the seminary training helped me get by here. I don't mind it much at all now."

For many of the other inmates who haven't known the rigors of old-fashioned religious discipline, Waupun is no seminary even if the iron bars are reminiscent of the grilles of a medieval monastery.

"A lot of the other guys have had it worse than I have," Larry says. "They (the guards) don't leave the wooden doors open in solitary for them. There's no light for them. No books or paper. And when they go out of their minds, the guards chain them down. I don't know who administers the tranquilizers."

In any case, Father Larry Rosebaugh, who did not kill, but protested killing, was treated as if he did kill.

Father Rosebaugh, who did not rape, but who instead honors the vow of chastity, was treated as if he did rape.

Father Rosebaugh, who did not rob or mug or assault, but who merely protested the mugging of the world without violence or bloodshed, found himself confronted by a cruel and blind maximum security prison that no longer was carrying out his original sentence — which he accepted maturely as a consequence of his morally justified actions. Instead, the prison was punishing him for trying to make prisons, such as Waupun and Fox Lake, a little more human for white and black inmates alike because they are all God's children.

He likes to think he was doing the same thing for the world when he was arrested in Milwaukee.

As the "Milwaukee Fourteen" statement puts it:

> For a growing number of us, the problem is no longer that of grasping what is happening. We know it by heart. Ours is rather a problem of courage. We wish to offer our lives and future to blockade, absorb and transform the violence and madness which our society has come to personify.

Later, Larry Rosebaugh was to write a lengthy article published by *The Catholic Radical* newspaper, entitled "The Day of the Priest Is Over." Upon reading it, a friend was heard to remark, "If that is the case, then the day of the layman and his world are over too." But the day of the priest was not over for Larry Rosebaugh, because his stay at Waupun marked the beginning of the day of the prophet.

Larry Rosebaugh's prison experience was not to be his last. By quirk of fate, events in his life would involve the White House with Recife, Brazil, and jailed missionaries as they had in the past. This relationship started with the 1961 exploratory visit by Schlesinger and McGovern to Recife just before the Oblate missionaries settled in there. The Recife connection repeated itself with the LBJ invitation to Father Coovert as the Oblate priests began their work there in 1964, and it resurfaced in June 1977 with the visit of Rosalyn Carter, the nation's First Lady.

After Waupun, it turned out that Rosebaugh was assigned to Recife, where he wound up in jail for feeding what Larry called "the street kids." This involved making the rounds of trash bins to salvage half-rotted vegetables for making soup. This was at a time when homeless urchins were often rounded up and jailed or summarily killed as thieving pests. For his humanitarian efforts, Rosebaugh and a non-Catholic friend were jailed.

The visit of the First Lady, who was on a human rights study, came just after Rosebaugh's release from the Recife prison, along with Mennonite missionary Thomas Capuano. They had been accused, but never tried, for theft of the cart they used to gather the spoiled vegetables to feed the street kids.

Pictures of Mrs. Carter in news magazines show her flanked by the two ragged, unshaven and skinny missionaries. She promised, according to articles in both *Newsweek* and *Time* in June 1977, that she had "a personal message to take back to Jimmy."

"We told her of the horrible treatment in the jail," Rosebaugh recalls. "Men starving on a ration of three spoonsful of grain and water a day; men beaten with nail-studded ropes; some had all their fingertips beaten; one man was placed in a tank of water and then forced to nearly drown himself to avoid bullets as guards shot all around him."

Before leaving, Mrs. Carter demanded of her Brazilian hosts that the Recife jail be closed, Rosebaugh says. She promised pressure from the Carter administration if it did not happen, because this was part of the military regime that the US was supporting with CIA-funneled military aid. According to *Newsweek*, Mrs. Carter described the Recife jail in which Rosebaugh and Capuano who had been held as "squalid."

"I have listened to their experiences," Mrs. Carter was quoted as saying, "and I sympathize with them."

Rosalyn Carter had no way of knowing that Schlesinger had brought back a similar human rights message to JFK about Recife way back in 1961. She had no way of knowing that LBJ had made and reneged on certain promises to the Oblate missionaries in 1964 concerning ways to improve human conditions at Recife.

After the First Lady's departure, Larry and his Mennonite associate were kicked out of Brazil, just as Oblate priests Kabat, Wittenbrink, Grams, Rupiper, and Wagner had been years before. Whether any jail reform was ever made is doubtful.

News reports in that same week show that President Jimmy Carter was wrestling with his own Democratic organization in Congress over issues such as balancing the budget; lower farm price supports; a drive to stop federal financing for the construction of dams and irrigation projects in the West; alternate energy sources; health, labor and welfare issues; and the struggle with inflation. Also, Carter's energy policies came under attack from the redoubtable Sen. Robert Byrd, a Democrat from West Virginia.

Somewhere in this brew of conflicting events, Rosalyn's global human rights message apparently got lost. Within just about two years, Jimmy hosted a formal state dinner of praise for the Shah of Iran, whose police force was brutalizing the Iranian people under CIA tutelage. Carter discovered too late that the limb he was perched on was being sawed off behind him by his own policymakers. He saw the Shah deposed; saw the US embassy in Tehran occupied by Iranian radicals; and saw his military plan to rescue the American hostages go down in dust in the Iranian desert.

In any case, by 1977, Recife's Oblate history had once again touched that of the White House. In this way, the prophetic circle from JFK to LBJ to Jimmy Carter via the Oblate missionaries in Recife was complete; but, as before, the importance of the message was lost as presidential ears were tuned to the LIONSDEN frequency. History was forced once again to take the path of violence, and the prophets continued to witness a chain of hurtful policies, such as Iran-Contra. In all the years that followed, Rosebaugh, who thought he had sent a message in 1977 with a very special emissary that would make a difference, kept sending that message by his actions.

Those actions had begun in 1967 when Larry took his ministry to the streets of Milwaukee (just months before he organized the Milwaukee Fourteen). Rosebaugh says, "My entry into the rain and cold of the streets back then was a slow and prayerful one. There came a calming down inside, a realization as to who was calling me along this path. Then I came to the area lived in by persons who had hit the bottom.

"One of their 'hotels' appeared to be a gutted-out factory building. What a shock as I opened the door to my room: whiskey bottles lined the floor, and a container of cottage cheese was left spoiling on the chair. The greatest shock came when I looked at the sheet that covered my bed. The dirt didn't upset me as much as the small, jumping insects all over the bed along with the crawling roaches. To be under the sheets was better than resting on top because insects were dropping from the ceiling."

While living with the homeless in Milwaukee, Father Larry became an outspoken critic of how the US government was treating the poor. He also protested its involvement in the Vietnam War. And that is how he came to burn military draft files on the streets of Milwaukee and be sent to prison.

Upon his release, Father Larry was drawn to the foreign missions, where people were suffering, as he had been, for political reasons. He was assigned to the mission at Recife. Once there, he became interested in the work of Dom Helder Camara, the archbishop. Dom Helder was, by this time, gaining international attention as a champion of the poor and he had been nominated for the Nobel Peace Prize. Dom Helder lived in a simple room in the back of his cathedral, instead of in the archbishop's palace. He personally handed food to beggars who came to his door. For this, he was give the reputation of being a communist.

One day, a man named Jorge came to Dom Helder, looking for food. His only possession was a bag filled with clay. He was eating the clay in order to keep the worms inside his stomach still. Jorge died in Dom Helder's arms. As a result of Jorge's death, Dom Helder asked his friend, Father Ed Figueroa, OMI, if he knew of anyone who would be willing to minister directly to the homeless. Father Ed called Father Larry, who jumped at the challenge. For the next six years, Father Larry was homeless in Recife.

Because of his daring ministry, Father Larry met with opposition from the US-supported Brazilian military. Friends feared for his life. Police considered him a communist, and traditionalists within the Catholic Church thought it was inappropriate for him, as a priest of the Catholic faithful, to be living with society's castaways.

"I remember one time when Father Larry was reciting the Our Father with a group of prostitutes, beggars and street children," says Father Ed, who operates an orphanage. "A middle class man came up to me complaining that a priest should not be praying with such people. I told that man that he might be able to recite the Lord's Prayer, but Father Larry was *living* it."

Rosebaugh's superior and longtime friend, Fr. Jim Kohmetscher, says, "Father Larry is different. He takes the challenge of being one with the poor literally." Kohmetscher, who himself has ministered since 1963 to those who are miserable in Brazil, concludes: "Father Larry is very much a prophet. He makes you think."

A publication of the Oblate Fathers describes the saga of Larry Rosebaugh's ministry in Recife:

For six years, Fr. Larry Rosebaugh, OMI, lived in extreme poverty. His home was the streets of Recife, Brazil, with its beggars, drunkards, rats and roaches. He pushed a cart to collect leftover food and wood. His bed was a piece of cardboard and some plastic. It was the happiest six years of his life, he says.

"Around 7 PM, I would gather the leftover vegetables from the streets — tomatoes, sweet potatoes, carrots, onions and whatever we could find. They were somewhat spoiled, but it didn't matter because I would place them in a large pot in which we boiled our soup. As we began to prepare the vegetables, the kids abandoned to the street, women who earned their daily bread as prostitutes, men and women down and out and just plain hungry, would gather and wait for the soup.

"Sharing our soup, I began to learn the stories surrounding the lives of my friends. Sometimes I cried to myself. I was tired and my clothes got a bit greasy, as clothes lived and slept in will do. But I was experiencing a certain satisfaction. Smiles greeted me frequently, and kids with no parents shared a corner of my ragged blanket at night."

Father Larry's work with the poor, collectively classified as communists, put him in conflict with the Brazilian government. In May 1977, he was arrested without cause and was thrown into jail. His release came only when the Brazilians learned of Rosalyn Carter's pending human rights visit.

"There were 37 men in the cell," Larry recalls, "all nude. The heat was stifling. Bodies were jammed together like sardines. One person was obliged to curl his body around the hole in the sawed-off toilet seat, with atrocious odors exuding. I found myself standing most of the night because the heat from the rotting human waste under the floor was more than I could bear. In the morning, another man was brought into the cell, his body covered with wounds inflicted by a barbed rope used by the police."

It was at this point that Rosalyn Carter's visit gained Larry a moment of positive attention in the popular press (as recounted above). That bit of fame, however, had no effect where reform in South and Central America was concerned. It did, however, cause the Brazilian dictatorship to kick him out.

In 1980, Rosebaugh was so angered by the assassination of Archbishop Oscar Romero in El Salvador that he took his protest to the grounds of Fort Benning, where the death squad that killed Romero had been trained. That action, an incursion onto the base, brought him two more years in jail. Upon release, he turned his efforts of salvation to El Salvador and later to Guatemala.

The sinister results of Iran-Contra became evident in Central America, and Larry's dreams of a finer world never came to fruition. Neither did those of Jimmy or Rosalyn Carter; LIONSDEN machinations ground their White House vision as grist under its millstone.

Rosebaugh saw massacres of poor people in El Salvador and Nicaragua at the hands of US-armed squads that Washington called freedom fighters (Contras). He witnessed the brutal repression of peasants who sought nothing but freedom from the tyranny that was still being imposed by political, economic and military proxy from the US

"In Guatemala, Larry's life consisted of rising at dawn," a friend explains, "then meditation and prayer before setting out on his trek at jungle's edge around his parish.

"Walking is something he has to do in his parish, which consists of 42 missions spread through the jungles. It takes him up to twelve hours of slogging through the mud and mosquitoes to reach some of them."

With little to call his own, Larry has this to say: "I can put everything I have in a bag and start walking down the road to the next intersection with the Lord and his people."

Somewhere in that tote bag, taking up no visible room, are the memories of the burning of draft files; time spent in jail; time spent helping people to become human again; protests against death squads trained at School of the Americas; and bitter memories of governments that kill — and tell the American people it is for their own security and well-being.

The real weight Larry bears, although he won't say so, is not the burden of all the lives that his efforts could not save, but all the lives his prophetic message has not yet reached . . . the lives of the world's leaders, who make violence their policy and code of morality.

9. A Ticket to 'Nam

In his inaugural address in 1965, President Johnson referred to the people of the world as passengers on a dot called earth. But soon, many of them were to become passengers traversing that dot to a place called Vietnam. LBJ spoke as if he were not on board for that trip, but simply waving goodbye at the departure gate as the world headed off to a Titanic doom.

If there was any aspect of the Vietnam War that churned the guts even of those who supported it, it was the LBJ-McNamara war escalation process: the gradual expansion of war efforts as each preceding step fell short of the envisioned level of conquest. He asked for more men, more money, more helicopters, more bombs; and got only more casualties for a cause that not even the South Vietnamese believed in.

Due to French stalling after Dien Bien Phu, the North-South elections that were called for in the Indochina settlement had never taken place. The delay was due to the domino-theory protocol that had been established by John Foster Dulles and his brother at the CIA, Allen W. Dulles. Their policies were inherited, like it or not, by Dean Rusk and Robert McNamara.

What worried the young people of America, who were designated by their draft boards as cannon fodder, was the draft card. All young men had to register for the Selective Service under penalty of law; they had to have the cards in their possession under penalty of law; and it was against the law to destroy them. They had to take the ride to Vietnam or go to jail and carry the brand of criminal.

At some point, many of these ticket holders would be selected as special passengers. The final destination, of course, was the Vietnam War. That is why thousands of young men burned their draft cards and opposed the war. Whether for moral or practical reasons, they wanted neither to kill nor be killed, especially for a lost cause more closely connected to faded French colonialism than to any real American interest.

Even after the Berrigans burned draft files and Dan led the law on a moral cross-country chase, even after his release from prison, the Catholic Church and most of its faithful were not persuaded that the war was evil.

Excuses are one thing, and reasons are another; it is not difficult to explain the position of the Church at large, its lack of sympathy with the moral minority even as that minority objects to war as murder. The Church, in concert with the political establishment, has become what Dan Berrigan describes as "the Pantheon of Power," self-endowed with the arrogance of every omnipotent god ever worshipped by mankind, especially Mars. While Dan did not feel the need to expound upon his pantheon concept, the prophets did, and the Plowshares Movement (with its call to beat swords into plowshares) expanded.

Within the arsenal of the Catholic Church was the power, divinely assumed, to forgive sin through the ears of its priest-confessors. Among the forgivable sins that defy the Ten Commandments is that of murder — as long as the one who does it confesses, is contrite, and asks forgiveness. The confessor is by conscience prohibited from giving up the penitent to the law, but is morally obliged to urge the sinner to give himself up voluntarily if true forgiveness is to be consummated.

Over the centuries, this moral ambivalence has become a social reflex, and one of convenient expectation by states where the Catholic Church thrives. There may be no sinner confessing, but there is a confessor-presence all too ready and willing to forgive whatever transpires within the governmental and military milieu. That's because the confessor-concession of the Church must survive for its own sake. Today's status quo is not unlike the medieval period of indulgences-for-hire to which the rebel priest, Martin Luther, objected. The shocking conclusion, in simplest form today, is that the Church philosophically allows war because most people believe the Church holds and bestows the power of God to forgive war, as with all sins. That is called the "just war" indulgence, and it seems to prosper on the concept that we are all sinners in need of forgiveness. This is the thin moral glue that binds Church and State like two sides of the same coin.

That's how the people, who stand in the moral purview of the Church on one leg, and in the political purview of the state on the other leg, have come to presume the forgiveness of sin in the matter of war. For that purpose, the state has always kept at its elbow such public confessors as Cardinal Spellman and Cardinal Cushing — just as previous eras and empires have had their Medicis and Richelieus.

In the end, the Church's power to forgive is what made the Berrigans' moral witness against war fall on mostly deaf ears, especially in the Sunday pews; because every war holds the sons of the fatherland as servants indentured to war and death; because the parents of those young men, equally indentured, can never be convinced that their automatically-absolved government is or was wrong — otherwise, their sons would be simply hired murderers.

In any case, the murderers in war have a God-given, Church-delivered right to be forgiven in advance, as a kind of plenary indulgence of war. War becomes acceptable in the world because murder is forgivable in the Church; the more so when the political welfare of the Church-State society is at stake. However, there is no forgiveness for those who challenge the propriety of that stake.

To draw attention to the moral distinction inherent in this dichotomy, the Berrigans and other prophets burned draft files. They tried to show the parents of this land, struggling to understand and to do the right thing, that it was the system, not their righteous sons, that was causing the murder. Sad to say, most people were unable to follow the prophets in focusing their blame on this distinction, and those few who did were faulted, scorned and jailed.

The war and the draft continued.

The draft card became a hated symbol for the production of cookie-cutter, GI-Joe citizens. At that time, the Selective Service System was headed by Gen. Lewis B. Hershey. His views were outlined as part of an internal memorandum released in 1965 to all local Selective Service Boards. According to the memo, Hershey apparently viewed his role as little more than that of any procurer on the street:

> While the best-known purpose of the Selective Service System is the procurement of manpower for the armed forces, a variety of related processes take place outside delivery of manpower to the active armed forces. Many of these may be put under the heading of "channeling manpower." Many young men would not have pursued a higher education if there had not been a program of student

deferment. Many young scientists, engineers, tool and die makers and other possessors of rare skills would not remain in their jobs in the defense effort if it were not for the program of occupational deferment. Even though the salary of a teacher has historically been meager, many young men remain in that job seeking the reward of deferment. . . .

Delivery of manpower, the process of providing a few thousand men with transportation to an induction center, is not much of an administrative challenge. It is in dealing with the other millions of registrants that the system is heavily occupied, developing more effective human beings in the national interest. . . .

Throughout his career as a student, the pressure, the threat of loss of deferment continues. It continues with equal intensity after graduation. His local board requires periodic reports to find out what he's up to. He is impelled to pursue his skill rather than embark on some less important enterprise, and he is encouraged to apply his skill in an essential activity in the national interest.

The psychology of granting wide choice under pressure to take action is the American or indirect way of achieving what is done by direction in foreign countries where choice is not allowed.

Clearly, this is military double talk saying that any regime in Washington has the power, under threat of impressment into a murder gang, to make citizens into productive taxpayers. If not, they're cannon fodder — and forced to do things they might not otherwise do, such as killing foreigners. In effect, the United States was holding an M-1 rile to the heads of every young man who chose not to become a soldier, forcing him to look for a way to dodge conscription. One such dodge was college.

In late 1971, the military's coercive tactics eased somewhat when the Pentagon began its program for the all-volunteer army. While registration for the draft at age 18 for all males is still a requirement, if the draft is used at all, selections are made by lottery. This avoids the appearance of selection by racial prejudice or deferment by privilege or political favor.

Martin Luther King, Jr., another prophet of these times, was quick to realize the civil rights inequities in the Selective Service operations. The better-educated and more advantaged white youths had a chance to gain college deferments and avoid Vietnam, but this was rarely true for the minorities. And, as King correctly pointed out, minorities carried a disproportionate burden of injury and death in the battlefields of Vietnam, even under the all-volunteer army. Why? Because the armed services offered a paycheck, room and board; and black youths, being short on education and employment skills, had few other options.

Sadly, King's protests served to make him an even bigger target for those who found his goal of racial equality threatening. Greatest of these critics was the FBI's own J. Edgar Hoover. In the end, King too, became a victim of the war. So did nearly every American and Vietnamese, as the headlines and stories below show.

15,000 PICKETERS AT WHITE HOUSE PROTEST VIET WAR

Washington, April 17, 1965 — Demanding a withdrawal of American troops from Vietnam, 15,000 students from across the nation marched with picket signs outside the White House Saturday.

President Johnson neither saw nor heard them. Warned in advance, he had flown to his Texas ranch.

The students, organized by the left-leaning Students for a Democratic Society, were left with little to do but parade to the Washington Monument and then to Capitol Hill. They did so peacefully, observers reported.

KY NAMED PREMIER IN SOUTH VIETNAM

Saigon, June 19, 1965 — Air Marshal Nguyen Cao Ky Saturday was named South Vietnam's Premier. In accepting the new post, Ky vowed to mobilize all able-bodied men in the war against the Viet Cong.

Appointed by the 10-man Military National Leadership Committee headed by Gen. Nguyen Van Thieu, the move signals the strengthening of the stranglehold which the military has over the Saigon government ever since a 1963 coup triggered the death of former President Ngo Dinh Diem. While militant Buddhists prefer a long-promised civilian government, observers reported they seemed to accept the appointment.

The scarf-wearing Ky received some of his training in the United States. As commander of the South Vietnamese Air Force, Ky has led air strikes against North Vietnam.

650 GIs KILLED IN NAM; PRESENCE NUMBERS 108,000

Saigon, Sept. 8, 1965 — With 26 Americans killed and 44 wounded this week in the Vietnam War, the US Military Command in Saigon reports that the number of Americans killed since 1961 in South Vietnam totals about 650.

The report noted that the number of US troops in Vietnam will soon reach President Johnson's goal of 125,000.

South Vietnamese casualties were 180 men killed to the Viet Cong's 420 — a "kill ratio" reported to be in the government's favor, but lower than usual.

Albert

Behind such headlines were stories that never got told completely: the stories of families whose sons were killed, crippled or disgraced by the manner in which the Vietnamese war was conducted.

The story of Albert, a farm boy from Iowa, is one among thousands that never made the headlines, because it is so common to the families of those injured by the Vietnam War. Here is the story that might have been written if some newspaper reporter could have talked to him in Fitzsimons Army Medical Hospital, Aurora, Colorado, just five days after his leg was blown off in 1969.

DECORATED FARMBOY RETURNS MINUS LEG, SPIRIT

Everywhere, Iowa, 1970 — Two years ago, Albert was cultivating corn from a John Deere tractor on his father's farm near this town which his great-great grandfather pioneered in 1840.

With the help of an artificial leg, Albert could drive that tractor even now, if he wanted to. But he is too bitter, too consumed with an assumed hippie lifestyle. His father is disgusted with him, his long hair and his behavior. After years of being close to his father, the bitter feeling is mutual now. Albert was not even present for his father's funeral. Years before that event, Albert had this to say:

"All he cares about is money," Albert says. "Buying and selling farms. Everybody, even Uncle Sugar, wants me to be something I can't be. I guess Uncle Sugar wanted me dead. But I guess I'll just live off of old Uncle Sugar. Know how much my leg is worth?" He knocks on his plastic leg as if for luck without answering his own questions.

It takes a few beers and several deep hits on a joint to get Albert talking about 'Nam. You learn that he was drafted into the army after a teenage have-to marriage that didn't work out. His son was two years old when he left for 'Nam. In the course of action, Albert took bullets on two different occasions. Neither wound was serious enough to send him Stateside, but enough to earn him a bronze star and two purple hearts. Then he tells you that once in the field, he decided that an M-79 rifle grenade launcher was his preferred weapon, because you didn't have to take time to aim carefully. You just pointed and reacted.

"Hell, if the drug lords in Costa Rica need a soldier, I'd make a good one," he says. "You can settle everything right away with a grenade launcher. It's noisy and messy, but those are the only two things wrong with war, I guess."

He laughs at his own sarcasm.

Is this the same kid who was taught by nuns and attended Mass every Sunday with his family, brought up on the traditional Catholic ethics?

Then Albert tells you about sending home his shattered squad members in body bags.

"You'd wedge their dog tags between their front teeth, and give a kick to make sure it stayed," he says, sucking on a beer. "At first it seemed really cold and cruel, except you knew they were dead, and you didn't want them to get misidentified. After a while, you quit caring. You had to, just to survive."

Drugs, lots of pot, was another means of survival, he explains.

"It's the only way to get over being scared. You get relaxed; then your senses heighten. Man, you can shoot straight, quick and steady under pressure. You ain't scared anymore. But you can get paranoid, too.

"And when the Slopes kill somebody in your squad, you get reckless and angry and you're ready to kill anything that moves. So that's why I carried the pot for my squad. To keep them under control."

Soberly, Albert recalls performing mercy killings on more than one "gook." The slang testifies that his sense of racial propriety was also blown away in Vietnam.

"This gook was wounded. He begged me. His guts were hanging out. I learned the Viet words for 'kill me.' So I did it. More than once. Why let him suffer? Shit, he would kill me, wounded or not. It didn't matter. Nothing mattered. It upped McNamara's body count. None of it seemed real. To this day, it seems like a dream. It was like swatting flies on the farm."

Albert tosses his head to arrange the straggly hair covering his bony face.

"Anyway, after being released from the field hospital after my first wound, and a little 'holiday' with the girls in Saigon, they sent me back. After nine months in 'Nam, I got field-promoted to E-5 because I had lost every member of my original squad. Tag, you're it.

"Their replacements were just kids, and scared. At 22, I was the old man. I carried their pot just to keep them from getting too paranoid. Let them have some at night. They didn't know what to look for. After two purple hearts, I thought I did. So I would take point.

"You know what I did with them damn medals? I threw them into the river (Iowa River) on grandad's old place. My uncle farms it now.

"Anyway, I was in this rice paddy, and there was this hootch. It looked like a trap. It was too far away for an M-79 shot. I needed to get closer. I made my way along the dikes of the paddy so I could see what I was stepping on. After nine months and lots of marching, I had a great set of thighs, despite two bullets. But I also had something like jungle rot in my toes.

"I remember seeing the trip wire just as I hit it. I remember loudness in my ears and me laughing inside because the wire was stolen GI. Tougher to see. Then tumbling with the dirt, like inside a vacuum sweeper. I came down upright. I thought I would land on my feet, but there was nothing to support me, so I fell over. I felt and heard some bones crunching. But I never lost consciousness.

"My squad came running. I hollered to stay back, but they didn't. The first thing I did was look for my rifle; then I felt to see if my balls were blown off. Because if they were gone, I was going to finish the job with my rifle. I guess I was lucky to be long-legged and hanging tight. But I got rid of the jungle rot."

You can't forget the hard irony in his laughter. You want to tell him to get back to his life, to get back on the tractor. After all, he was much better off than some of the other men at Fitzsimons Hospital. At least he had use of what was left of his legs. But his next words ruin the opportunity.

"Tell you what, buddy," he says, patting his plastic leg. "This is an instant sympathy-getter. Yes, sir, it works with the ladies. Works every time."

There is more hard irony in Albert's laughter. Somehow you know that putting him back on the tractor would be the equivalent of a slow mercy killing.

His father disowned him for his hippie lifestyle, and his hero's medals are at the bottom of the muddy river that flows into the drain of the country, the legendary Mississippi — the river which, in flood, enriched his grandfather's bottomland. This is the river where his father and uncles fished — mostly for catfish and carp during the Great Depression just to keep food on the table.

Suddenly Albert makes you realize these are things are gone for him, just like his leg. This one-legged Albert can't go back to what he was; and he's got no way to make himself go forward, even on a John Deere.

LBJ SENDS 50,000 MORE TROOPS TO VIETNAM

Washington, DC, July 28, 1965 — At a nationally televised news conference Wednesday, President Lyndon Johnson announced he was sending 50,000 more troops to South Vietnam "immediately," to boost strength there to 125,000. Monthly draft calls will be raised from the current 17,000 to 35,000.

LBJ said the US is involved in Vietnam because "we have learned at a terrible and brutal cost that retreat does not bring safety and weakness does not bring peace." At the same time, the President called on the United Nations to work harder on Vietnamese peace efforts, and said the US is willing to discuss peace proposals with the North.

FBI ARRESTS DRAFT CARD BURNER

Montpelier, Vermont, Oct. 18, 1965 — David Miller, a member of the pacifist group formed by publisher Dorothy Day of the *Catholic Worker*, was arrested in Vermont Monday under charges of burning his draft card at an anti-Vietnam rally in New York last Friday.

Miller, described by friends as a "quiet college student" is the first person to be arrested under a new federal law signed by President Johnson. If convicted, Miller could be sentenced to five years in prison and fined $10,000. [Note: he received a 2 and a half year sentence.]

"I think the draft is wrong," Miller told reporters. "I am opposed especially to this war."

Thousands of demonstrators marched against the Vietnam war on Saturday in New York and around the country. Many of them appeared to be mothers and fathers and professional people as well as students.

2ND MAN IMMOLATES SELF

United Nations, New York, Nov. 9, 1965 — Roger Allen LaPorte, a former seminarian and member of the Catholic Worker movement, burned himself to death Tuesday outside the UN Building.

Before striking the match to ignite his gasoline-soaked clothes, the victim told passersby it was his protest "against war, all war."

A week ago, Norman Morrison, a 32-year-old Quaker from Baltimore, immolated himself in similar fashion in front of a Pentagon entrance. His self-sacrifice was made all the more dramatic by the rescue from his arms of the man's 2-year-old daughter as he set himself ablaze.

Terrified onlookers snatched her away just as the flames ignited. Morrison's wife said later her husband was very upset "over the great loss of life and human suffering" caused by the war.

The practice of self-immolation over the war began in Vietnam in 1963 among Buddhist monks in Saigon.

Chuck

Albert's cousin Chuck was among the thousands scorned as "draft dodgers." In fact, they were war resisters for whom simple conscientious objection status did not go far enough.

Chuck started life with high ideals. He went through prep school for seminarians and had hoped to be a priest in the Missionary Oblates of Mary Immaculate. Deciding the celibate life was not for him, at age 20, he opted for liberal arts studies at the University of Iowa and then Iowa State University at Ames.

However, his moral anguish over the Vietnam War was not assuaged by the fact that, as a college student, he could defer being drafted. Chuck was revolted by "the compulsory killing" that it forced on young men "who either knew or strongly suspected that they and the American people were being deceived about Vietnam."

"There was no truly honorable option for those who could not accept the notion of 'my country, right or wrong,'" he says. "That seemed to be the mental and moral currency of the time. Of course, you could refuse the draft and go to jail, but that was the equivalent of the punishment for a deserter. There was similar public contempt for those who left the country. Those who left did so in disgust or anger, some in sadness, and more in horror over what was happening to America the Beautiful."

Chuck searched for guidance. His novice master in the seminary had advised him, upon leaving the seminary, "to stay out of Vietnam."

"I thought little of it at the time," Chuck recalls, "because, like many others in 1965, I assumed that the conflict would be decided one way or another in a year or two. I hadn't really formed a moral opinion beyond my objection to killing. At the university I consciously searched for answers via philosophy, political science and psychology. But answers were few and far between, never satisfying and always tentative or conditional.

"The Vietnamese were fed up with foreign domination and were obviously not wanting the US as a substitute for the French colonialists. An estimated 80 percent of the South Vietnamese were considered to be in sympathy with the North because they had beaten the French. And so the US advisory role had to be escalated.

"Outside the classroom, some bumper stickers read, 'Drop the bomb,' and 'Nuke 'em,' while other graffiti proclaimed, 'Fighting for peace is like fucking for chastity.' Then came 1968. It was an 'annus horribilis.'

"Vietnam was a full scale war based on a flimsy Tonkin Gulf near-incident. The same year Martin Luther King, Jr., was killed for opposing the war and civil injustice. That was in April, I think. Bobby Kennedy, another war opponent, was assassinated in June. Depression, already my constant companion, deepened when my draft board prematurely ended my student deferment. I got the mistake corrected, but the unfairness of the draft kept eating at me. So did the war. There was no moral justification for it, or for supporting it. Increasingly, suicide presented itself as an honorable answer and a solution of merit in a world that seemed crazy and out of control.

"I felt pressured to take a stand and prove that I was neither unpatriotic nor a coward. Late in 1968, I returned my draft card with its II-S deferment to the draft board, saying I was doing so in lieu of committing suicide. I think I sent a copy to my Congressman, whose name I have forgotten, or maybe the draft board sent him a copy."

That letter, dated December 18, 1968, said in part:

"I'm sending you my draft card with this letter in lieu of committing suicide before the end of this year, as I had been planning. . . . This is in no way to be construed as a letter requesting an appeal, a hearing or a personal appearance with you. . . nor do I want 'conscientious objector' forms, or any sort of conscientious objector status.

"Do whatever you must under the law. I must accept whatever follows. What I will have tonight — to go on living — springs solely from this act of open defiance. The military and nuclear wealth of nations has become god. It is not to be trusted, least of all for national security. I hereby reject it and the security it is said to, but does not in fact, provide. There is no security in a munitions factory."

As Chuck recalls events from more than 30 years ago, the veins of his temples stand out, enhancing the cerebral size of his large head.

"The respite this letter gave me was brief," he says quietly.

Imagine the shock of Church's parents upon receiving an urgent telephone call from the office of their congressman, asking with a sense of urgency whether Chuck was still alive, and saying that he said he had a letter from Chuck threatening suicide. His parents' shock went through several stages, as they called their son's apartment in Ames and heard his sullen voice.

He had, indeed, taken a bottle of non-prescription sleeping pills.

"I swallowed a whole bottle of Sominex," he recalls. "I didn't expect to wake up. But when I did, my eyes were so dilated I could hardly see. So I checked into a hospital, got some counseling, and then returned to classes. I guess I felt better inside, having made the effort. It proved I wasn't afraid to die, just of having to kill or support killing.

"Then, in May, just as I was about to graduate, the Ohio National Guard killed four students at Kent State. And there was Jackson State. By this time, I had read Fulbright's *Arrogance of Power*. Then the newly authorized draft lottery placed me in the top 25 percent of those birth dates to be used for call-up. This made it virtually certain that I would be drafted. It was then that I decided to go to Canada, which had passed a law welcoming war resisters.

"When I told my cousin, Albert, he said that was doing it the hard way. He suggested that just before my pre-induction physical, I should drink a whole pot of coffee. He said that would send my blood pressure so high I could win a rejection. Even that seemed cowardly, yet here was Albert, a one-legged war hero, giving advice like that. Anyway, he offered to give me a ride into Canada.

"Before I left, my father, who wasn't pleased with my decision, asked me to check with a lawyer and a priest first. The lawyer told me what I already knew about the legal repercussions. But the advice I got from the priest was the worst and most depressing.

"He said if I got an induction notice, I should show up for it, and if I got in the army and was sent to Vietnam, 'I should set a good Christian example!' That blew me away!

"Is this how Fr. McEleney was advising dozens of young men on campus in the same position as me? To go to war and be good Christians while killing? He broke my religion with just a few stupid words. While trying to talk me out of going to Canada, he actually talked me into it.

"I told my cousin that I was leaving on the bus the next day. Instead, he insisted on driving me to Canada. He told me, 'I've never seen a peaceful part of the world, and it's time I did.'" Not long after driving Chuck to

Canada, Albert joined an anti-war protest at the Rock Island Arsenal in Illinois.

Chuck remained in Quebec for several years, learned to speak French, and gained a "landed immigrant" status. He worked as a caregiver in nursing homes. He might have been there to this day but for a heartbreak affair with a girlfriend from Trinidad.

Chuck's brother helped him return to the States after amnesty was granted to those who had gone to Canada. Ironically, Chuck's brother at that time was a regional field representative for the advertising agency handling the new promotional campaign for the All-Volunteer Army program.

Chuck never realized the potential of his near-genius mental abilities (96th percentile). He is now dealing blackjack in a riverboat casino. He thinks often of his cousin, Albert, who subsists on a government veteran's pension as a bike-riding recluse near an Amish community in Iowa. Although Albert is not a Mennonite, he appreciates their old-fashioned, peaceful ways. He is known to have raised both wolves and exotic pigeon breeds in his rural home, because of his love for living things.

Chuck lives a quiet bachelor life, satisfied that he did the right thing morally in declining the ride to Vietnam.

The Nelsons

Somewhere in the Pentagon's military files on Vietnam is a detailed notation about the death of one of its one-star generals in a helicopter shoot-down. Less well noted would be the death of the Chief Warrant Officer, Scott Nelson, who piloted that aircraft. Here is his family story, recounted by one of his friends:

"I especially remember Scott because I arranged a blind date with him for my sister while Scott was on leave before shipping out to Vietnam. His mother, Ruth Nelson, was my secretary at IBM in Boulder, Colorado.

"Scott wasn't enthusiastic about going off to war, but like many other young men faced with few options, he felt this would be the best way he could do it. He knew pilot skills would be in high demand when he mustered out. But here's the cute and human part: the morning after Scott's date with my sister, his mother proudly reported to me Scott's comments that he was pleased to have finally met a nice 'old fashioned' girl. We both laughed, making our own assumptions about his comment.

"Whether romance would have blossomed, we will never know. Six weeks later, Scott's helicopter, with the General aboard, was ambushed in a wall of groundfire. I went to the funeral, when Scott's body was returned, and watched a broken-hearted father and mother place a Bible in the casket as it was closed before burial.

"Within a year, Scott's father, Stanley, was dead of the kind of heart disease you can get only from burying your child. Ruth hung on a bit longer, but never quite regained her perky personality. Her only son was dead."

Obviously, the Nelson family story was repeated thousands of times within white, black, yellow and brown families across the country. As those families suffered, Secretary of State John Foster Dulles's theory of Asian countries falling like dominoes to the communist menace was used to induce the American public to continue to sacrifice their sons and daughters.

Jerry

You don't have to be directly under fire in Vietnam (or any war) to go crazy from its emotional and psychological effects.

Jerry was a big raw-boned, blond-headed youth from the Polish section of Chicago. He was an Air Force Policeman (AP) in 1963 when he snapped. One of his best friends was killed in action over Vietnam. While some tough-guy types can carry the load of such emotional trauma, Jerry's sensitive side won out. He was discharged on medical-psychological grounds from the Air Force in 1965, and still survives mostly on a government disability pension, certified by the VA.

Jerry may have a John Wayne swagger and a hidden tear in his eye, but that internal conflict has not stopped him, as a barroom bouncer, from knocking the chip off the shoulder of many a bully.

"He's the kind of guy with a soft heart and a gristly fist," says a friend who has been through more than one scrape with Jerry as his sidekick. "Loyal as heaven, tougher than hell. The kind of guy you'd want to cover your back, even if neither of you were looking for trouble. If you're his friend and somebody crosses you, that's their lookout. Then, after the dust clears, a week later, he'll show you a new painting he's done that has no relationship to anything except some beautiful things churning like blended flowers in his mind."

A recovered alcoholic, Jerry has abandoned his rougher side in favor of using his Hasselblad camera and his easel. At age 57, at the turn of the millennium, Jerry lives in the foothills of the Rocky Mountains above Denver in his log cabin near Pine Junction, Colorado. The seclusion allows him to paint the demons of Vietnam out of his life and those of his friends.

"Most demons of Vietnam," he will tell you, "resided in places other than Hanoi."

Bill

If you were a black teenager and a high school dropout in the Vietnam era, you were given an express ticket to Vietnam. That was the case for Bill Scott, now a real estate salesman in Denver. An article in the *Denver Rocky Mountain News* tells the rest.

At 15 in Gilmore, Arkansas, Bill dropped out of school to work in the cotton fields to help his family. His life seemed headed toward something type-cast in a grade B movie. So he moved to Chicago, where he lived with his brother's family while working two jobs. He sent what he could to his kin in Arkansas.

Before long, he was a grunt, walking point in Vietnam for his infantry unit. He won that distinction because his predecessor got killed doing the job. Somehow, he survived — although on two occasions he was almost killed by shrapnel, some of which he still carries in his back.

The worst thing about coming back to America, he says after many years, was having "to convince people that I was civilized. As a teenager, being an infantryman, you are doing things and involved in things that are not civilized," Bill says.

That's why, today, he enjoys dressing in a tie and white shirt with cufflinks and selling real estate. As a child, he thought it was marvelous that privileged white folks dressed in white shirts even when it wasn't Sunday.

But it wasn't as easy at that. Upon his army release at Fort Carson, Colorado, Bill moved to Denver, where he hocked his two Purple Heart medals for $40 each to make the rent on an apartment. Even so, civilian life for him "was like Christmas. I was just happy to see people who had haircuts and clothes with color."

Mr. Scott is not bitter about the war, although he won't debate it and he wouldn't discuss it with his sons. "Those racial and social issues of whether it was right or wrong are for other people to sort out," he says. "There's a lot to talk about; but they needed to focus on education."

Having grown up fatherless in a family of twelve, and having survived the shrapnel of two shells in Vietnam, Bill Scott says he's just happy to be alive. But he knows that there were many like him, black and white, who will never have a chance to wear a white shirt and tie every day.

Artie

His name is Artie Guerrero. Not Arthur, not Art, but Artie. Everybody calls him Artie, because he smiles and jokes and schmoozes just like you'd expect somebody named Artie would do. That's how you get along in life when prejudice for Latinos and blacks is always just around the corner, as it was for Artie at 26th and Arapahoe` in Denver.

Maybe Artie's schmooze explains how he got to be a newspaper advertising salesman, but it doesn't explain how he became permanently crippled by Vietnam. It was nearly a year after Artie returned from the war to his job in Denver, when he first noticed increasing difficulty in walking. The limp, in a way, came from the weight of his Purple Heart and other medals.

His right leg, which had taken a bullet through the flesh, just wouldn't do what he wanted it to. No one made the connection between that injury and the more serious one received from shrapnel and a bullet through the shoulder muscle. The doctors at the VA hospital finally began to think of multiple sclerosis, unrelated to the injuries.

Artie's platoon of Army Rangers was in a fierce firefight at An Khe. It was an ambush. He saw one of his buddies shot through the head. Another was knocked down, screaming for help. Going after him, Artie didn't feel the bullet go through the flesh of his leg, but he heard an explosion and felt a searing pain leap through the muscle that connects the shoulder to the neck.

A year later he was back on the job in Denver. The pain had slowly subsided in the gnarled scar on his shoulder, but Artie's leg was suddenly not functioning — even though he seemed to have recuperated from his wounds.

His increased disability took him from his job, but his employer loyally maintained his base salary. The Veterans' Administration insisted his malady was not related to the war wounds. That made Artie mad. A gregarious, good-looking man, Artie kept smiling, even on crutches. But the anger and impatience that he had not experienced since Vietnam were written between the lines on his graying forehead.

After private consultation, the true diagnosis came in: the bullet through his neck and shoulder muscle had formed scar tissue that was pinching and destroying a nerve center serving the leg. It was stress-induced sclerosis, a disease of the central nervous system.

The only consolation for Artie is in the knowledge that he was trying to save his buddy. His despair is the knowledge that he failed, because of a bullet triggered by events on a war ride that many veterans do not understand to this day — no matter how proudly they served, Artie still believes he was right to be in Vietnam.

Now retired, Artie is reminded of his buddy's death with every monthly disability check from Uncle Sam. The reminders linger like salt in a sore that will never quite heal inside. But he smiles because he is helping others, from his wheelchair, as President of the Crippled Veterans of Vietnam.

A Mother

Cleo Lucero of Salida, Colorado, has a framed picture of a young man in military uniform. It is her son, Anthony, as he was at age 25. "He would be 60 now," she says with a mother's aged, broken voice. Her story was told on the pages of the *Denver Rocky Mountain News.*

She displays his medals, a Silver Star and Bronze Star for bravery and a Purple Heart, awarded for his actions with the 101st Airborne. The metal trinkets are cold on her wrinkled, trembling fingers. She recalls that Anthony spent four years in the army, then came home to be a miner in the mountains of Colorado. But he patriotically re-enlisted for duty in Vietnam.

Cleo puts the picture and the medals away. All she has left now are the memories they evoke, and they make her cry.

Anthony and Artie and Scott and Jerry and Bill and Albert and Chuck and thousands of mothers and fathers were all passengers on this trip. So were millions of others, in two lands distant from each other in geography and culture. Some participated in the war and brought back scars. Others, no matter where they were, have their own scars deep within.

The prophets of the times heard about these personal wounds and witnessed the tragedies recurring like endless TV reruns, among the poor — even in lands far away from Vietnam. They knew and felt they were on the same ride with everyone else in the world, and set out to throw a monkey wrench into the works the only way they could: By protest.

They knew, as events unfolded, that when everyone without privilege arrived at the end of the line, there would be no glory: just death in a ditch and a name on a wall in Washington, or life lived in a nightmare of medals, caskets, and psychosis. For the survivors, there would be just pain and anguish made the more severe for lack of justification.

The prophets learned, in the blood and bones of their parishioners, that no system of power on earth leaves anyone alone to decide his future. The prophets tried to wake up the public to this fact. But the power of priests to shock the public's conscience ended up jailed with all the other bodies on this forced journey.

In the late '60s, politicians and police were nearly overwhelmed by the tide of protests over civil rights and activism against the Vietnam War on the streets of America. Perhaps that's why suppression of human rights (under US imperialism) in places like Brazil was ignored. It was to Brazil that a group of missionary priests had gone at this time, with the intent of rectifying human rights abuses. With them, they took the dubious promises of help from the Commie-hunting Johnson Administration. They spent years coping with poverty and death in the *favellas* of Recife. Trying to relieve the misery of the people, they were labeled leftists by the CIA-inspired dictator, Gen. Humberto Branco.

Among these idealistic "men of god" were Rev. James Kohmetscher; Rev. Edward Figueroa; Rev. Darrell Rupiper; Rev. Peter Grams; Rev. Giles Wagner, now dead; Rev. Boniface Wittenbrink, now married; Rev. Bruce Heit; Rev. Roger Bergkamp; Rev. Ken Steiner, now married; and, later, Rev. Larry Rosebaugh and Rev. Carl Kabat — all of the Oblate order of Catholic priests, designated OMI.

When these priests went to Recife, no one told them of the goal to help fight Communism, an effort that their superior, Father Coovert, had envisioned as a friendly and benign collusion with the US government (as mentioned above). The priests were so busy trying to help feed and house the poor families in order to then provide spiritual comfort that political orientation was not even in their frame of reference. Their notion of Communism probably had more to do with the Soviet Union and its postwar occupation of Eastern Europe than with exploited peasants in Brazil.

All of them had but one moral imperative, established by their religious group: "to serve the poorest of the poor. . . Whatever their work, Oblates will collaborate, according to their vocation and by every means compatible with the Gospel, in changing all that is a cause of oppression and poverty."

The exhortation comes from the founder of the Oblate order, St. Eugene DeMazenod of France, whose missionary zeal was sparked by the French Revolution. DeMazenod also said he wanted "no smoldering wicks" among the candle flames of his associates. No wicks were smoldering in Recife, but those that flamed in the US thereafter were snuffed out, by intent of the courts.

Although companies such as General Electric had a large presence in the Recife area, the pay was abysmal, according to Carl Kabat. Unemployment was at depression levels, and union activism was considered *per se* communistic.

"They (GE) didn't have to pay a living wage," Carl Kabat recalls. "They could fire you for no reason. To keep anyone from earning higher pay, they would fire some workers one day and hire some back the next day for less money. They could hire anyone in your place. There were ten people waiting for any job. All paid slave wages."

Those who were "lucky" had employment in the nearby sugar cane fields owned by rich absentee land barons in Rio De Janiero. At least, they could gnaw on raw cane like the rats did, and extract some sugar energy. Unfortunately, most of them soon lost their front teeth from decay, according to Rupiper. He says infant mortality by age one was in excess of 50 percent.

Under these conditions, the priests found it was impossible to work at improving the daily lot of the people without being suspected of fomenting social unrest or rebellion. They had no way to change the lives of people who were preoccupied with survival, combing the refuse of the garbage dump and searching through the polluted muck of the seashore for shellfish. The rat was a common dietary supplement.

Urban Renewal

How some of these people were reduced to such squalor makes an incredible tale, as Rupiper recalls:

"One day, the mayor (of Recife) handed out a few *cruzieros* to one poor slum dweller. That fellow was supposed to convince a number of his neighbors in Recife that he had received a new home on the outskirts of the city. He was paid to tell them that if they boarded government trucks, they would also be taken to the site of their new homes, that very day.

"When the trucks arrived, even those who didn't want to go were forced to do so, at the point of bayonets. The mayor's men then delivered them all to a point near the Oblate mission. There was no turning back for the displaced. As soon as they left, bulldozers demolished their former slum. Some of them had even torn boards from their old hovels to use for fencing around their new promised homes. What they found was a brush-covered hillside overlooking the town dump.

"The headlines in the newspapers the next day read: 'MAYOR TAKES SWIFT ACTION'."

Rupiper sighs as he recalls the scene:

"So I had an instant parish of 2,000 homeless poor, each with nothing but unmarked hillside plots of brush. It was not even the mayor's land to give or sell, anyway. If there was money from America to finance such a project, the mayor just stuffed it in his pocket.

"Later, surveyors came and laid out the hillside in 10-by-12-foot plots, for which the new 'owners' were expected to pay rent. Rent collectors came regularly to extort what they could and threaten the rest. It was like the TV cartoons we used to see about the villain with the mortgage and the poor widow. Except in this case it had become real. Almost surreal.

"The mayor did this to spruce up the city for the sake of foreign tourism. The newspaper applauded the mayor for his swift action in giving the poor people new homes. There were no homes, of course, except what the people could build of sticks and mud and junk from the dump.

"One woman gave birth the night she was moved. She delivered her own baby and cut the umbilical with her machete as she was trying to clear the brush from the hillside of her non-existent home. She came to us crying and angry and worried about how she would shelter her new baby.

"So we priests began to talk to them about this inhumane treatment and about how Jesus would have reacted. On a practical level, our reaction was to help them dig a well, at the foot of the hill. It took quite a few days.

"When we got it dug and had water, we asked the government for tile or blocks to line it. We were told to abandon it and let the government dig a well. They clearly wanted no exhibitions of self-help and independence," Rupiper says. "We never got our tile, and the well eventually caved in."

"Such was the place where Father Coovert envisioned a 'City of God' with the help promised by the LBJ Administration. It never came. If it did, it disappeared into pockets of government officials. The people never saw it.

"We tried to get the people to church, but very few came. To attend any meeting made you suspect. So I began publishing our sermons in a weekly bulletin and handed it out to them. Father Peter Grams was working with me on this. The parishioners took the bulletins to work and shared them with others.

"Gradually, more of them began to come to church, even the men. But by this time, the bulletins had caught the attention of the chief of police," Rupiper says.

"So he called me and Peter Grams into police headquarters. He had a copy of every bulletin I had ever written. And because he couldn't believe I had mastered Portuguese so quickly, he asked me who had written them.

"I did," I told him.

"But who edited them?"

"Nobody but me," I insisted. "He didn't believe me, and asked me who I was protecting. He wanted to know names of those attending Mass and distributing the bulletins. He wanted to know who the communists were. I wouldn't tell him anything. I didn't understand his concern. I didn't know any communists. I only knew people who were suffering and trying to improve their life conditions. The homilies simply talked about human dignity in the eyes of God. And how God loved them even if others did not. I suppose that didn't make the officials look good. So I became a target."

Rupiper and Grams' Last Words in Recife

From the States, the Oblate provincial of the missionaries had been offering to build modern schools and hospitals, presumably from funds with LBJ's government strings attached. But the Vietnam war now took precedence. It really didn't matter, because the Recife missionaries thought the LBJ package would have sent the wrong message: it would have identified them in the eyes of their poor parishioners with their government oppressors.

The priests feared that the military government would be the first to take false credit for such improvements, and the word of God that the missionaries preached would then dry up for lack of ears to hear. There were "men in suits" who circled like vultures around the mission. Rumors were that they occasionally made suspect people disappear at night.

"By this time, I was constantly followed," Rupiper says. "Every Sunday, a man in a suit and tie would attend Mass and take notes. Then one day two men came and told me to stop preaching or change my message. I told one of them I would, if he could tell me one thing from my sermon which was not true."

"The man stared at me and said, 'This is not a day for truth'. I began to get a little scared then, just from his eyes and tone of voice.

"He wanted to know which people were communists. There was a big fear, among the military, of communists. I didn't know who, if any of my people were communists, and I was not about to compromise any of my friends and parishioners by answering anything. The surveillance continued. I once asked the man taking notes during my sermons if he was connected to the chief of police. He admitted that he was.

"Then there was a time when a woman with whom I worked closely in the parish invited me out to dinner for my birthday. It was common for the police or CIA to try to put a priest in the company of a woman over a cocktail and snap a picture to make it look like a sex scandal, to discredit us. So I asked her if she would mind inviting another friend as well, because it was standard practice for us priests to stay in groups — and tell the others where we were at all times, in such cases. We had to protect ourselves. Three of us went to dinner, and that was it," Rupiper says.

"This oversimplifies my five-year ministry in Recife. But I sensed when the end was approaching. I was preaching a sermon one evening, when I distinctly heard an inner voice say, 'This is the last time you will be preaching to my people.' Simple as that," Rupiper recalls.

"I was so badly shaken I stopped my sermon in mid-sentence. I cried with heavy sobs. My parishioners were puzzled. Even now I hesitate to say so out loud, but I am as sure now as I was then that it was the voice of God."

Rupiper's dark eyes search to see if his words will be believed by his interviewer or whether he might be judged delusionary. His own certainty tickled a personal grin of satisfaction from him.

"I finished the liturgy, and when the people had left, a gang of several dozen military men surrounded us and took me and Pete Grams to jail. There, the same inner voice told me I was on the right side.

"After four or five hours of intense questioning by the chief of police. . . his name was Moacyr Sales. . . I was put in a closet on a chair facing the corner. I heard Sales tell the guard, as he left, 'If they move or talk, shoot them.'

"The guard wore a pearl-handled pistol. It seemed huge. He tried to get friendly and even asked me to come to work for the government. His hand stayed eagerly near the pistol. I just kept my mouth shut and tried not to move. When I had a chance to read his eyes, I think he admired my strength, because he knew I was not about to cave in.

"Throughout the ordeal, it was maybe ten days, I felt amazingly strong. I knew God was with us. I wasn't sure He would keep us from harm, but I knew He was there. I remember feeling sorry for our brother Oblates who had no notion of what might be happening to us.

"They separated Grams and me, so I was worried about him. There were interrogations, always about what communists we knew. And during the night, there were screams from other prisoners being tortured. Finally, our archbishop, Dom Helder Camara, got some attention from Washington.

"Although the archbishop suggested we could do more good by staying, he worked for our release. His point was that maybe with us in jail, the US would cut off aid and the flow of guns. For that outcome, I was willing to stay, but I think he knew it was asking too much. The screams were getting to me, but they were driving Pete crazy with fear (judging from his eyes and gestures, when I saw him).

"I suggested that I would stay if they would let Pete Grams go. The general in charge of the northeast section of Brazil — I've forgotten his name — sent back word that it was both of us, or neither. We were released on condition that we leave Brazil immediately. It was Christmas Day; but it didn't seem like it."

The two priests returned to the St. Louis area by way of Miami. Grams stayed with his parents who lived there, and Rupiper recuperated at the house of the Oblate Fathers in Belleville, Illinois, across the Mississippi River from St. Louis.

Upon their return, the following article (excerpted) appeared in the *St. Louis Post-Dispatch* Sunday, Dec. 28, 1968:

FR. GRAMS TELLS STORY OF OUSTER BY BRAZIL

Two American priests were resting in St. Louis this weekend after being ordered out of Brazil on Christmas Day. Their expulsion stemmed in part from things they published in their parish bulletin, which had a circulation of 200.

"On December 13, a Friday, the army closed the National Congress and declared an act in which they took away freedom of speech, freedom to meet, habeas corpus, and the right to an attorney," said the Rev. Peter Grams of St. Louis. "On Saturday, the lead article in our bulletin criticized this."

Sunday morning, Father Grams and the Rev. Darrell Rupiper of Carroll, Iowa, the parish priest, continued their criticism in their sermons at Christ the Redeemer Parish in Jordao, a suburb of Recife on the Brazilian coast. That night they were arrested.

"We were forced to leave because we told the truth," said Fr. Rupiper. "I do not regret the things that we have suffered because of speaking the truth. The truth must be spoken.

"They said we were agitating the people," he continued. "They said we — I — was agitating the people because I had criticized the government and their policies."

Those ten days in the Recife police cell with an armed guard nearby were indicative of the terror tactics used to keep opposition to the established order in Brazil at bay, the priests said. Even at that, the men said they were given privileged treatment compared to what is meted out to most Brazilians.

"I know personally a student who was taken, and brutally beaten in the lower regions," said Father Rupiper. "After being released, he was sent to a hospital. He was considered an agitator. He was asking only for school system reform."

The first three days, the men were not allowed to speak with each other. They underwent questioning in individual interviews. Monday night, the American consul came to the jail and arranged for the priests to have beds to sleep in.

"We found that we were the first prisoners in the history of that police department to get beds," said Father Grams.

"The questioning was not brutal. They asked us what we thought of the government. But we heard screams in the room above. Maybe those screams in the dark were part of the interrogation process."

There was no ventilation in that room (it is summer in Brazil). Finally they were given a choice. They could leave the country voluntarily or face a military court on a charge of subversive agitation.

"We were told that if we decided to face trial, the questioning would continue 30 days, after which we would await our turn for a military court with a two-year backlog of cases. And they told us we would be found guilty," said Father Rupiper.

A few hours before the two priests left Recife, another Oblate father, the Rev. Giles Wagner of Pierce City, Mo., had fled from Recife because he feared he might also be arrested. Father Wagner had written an article in the same parish bulletin on conscientious objection to entering the Brazilian armed forces.

The release of Grams and Rupiper was not without its price in human life. About six months later, Rupiper got word that Father Henrique, Archbishop Dom Helder Camara's aide, was kidnapped, brutalized and hanged by a death squad of President de Costa e Silva.

"It was a warning to the Bishop," Rupiper says. "It was revenge for his intercession on our behalf. Anyone who speaks out on social justice in Brazil is labeled as a subversive agitator. All types of fear tactics are used to maintain the people in their slavery to the state. Their strongest fear is that of being labeled a communist because they know that can bring torture and death.

"It is like Archbishop Dom Helder once said, 'When I feed the poor, they call me a saint. When I ask why the poor have no food, I'm called a communist.'"

Some time after his return to the US, Grams left the Catholic priesthood. Rupiper was assigned as Chaplain to the University of Illinois at Champaign, where he put his Brazilian experience to work trying to inspire moral idealism among the students. Since 1995, Rupiper has been in charge of the novice phase of priest formation for the Oblate Fathers in Illinois.

For him, this assignment is a return to the place where, 40 years ago, he received his own priestly formation from a white-haired German priest who had served in World War I on the side of the Kaiser. The old priest humorously claimed, as comic relief in some of his homilies, that the only airplane his unit shot down was one of the Kaiser's.

This novice-master's frequent remark, Rupiper recalls, was, "'Brudders, ve are not made of concrete und shteel.' It was his constant reminder that, no matter how dedicated and consecrated to a cause, we are human and frail, after all."

Kabat Takes a Turn

Carl Kabat, who had nearly three years of prior service in the Philippine missions, was one of the priests who replaced Rupiper and Grams in Brazil. He was to learn quickly that in Brazil, as in the Philippines under Marcos, US-backed dictators are violent and corrupt. Their only obligation is to rule with US-supplied weapons and pretend that any suppression they authorized was directed against a communist enemy. Siphoning off the country's US-bolstered resources is the reward for doing US bidding.

Under these political conditions, Kabat experienced every day the begging of the children in his parish of poverty. Each morning they would come and clap their hands outside Kabat's hovel.

"Father, give us some bread," they would say, as if reciting the line from the Lord's prayer.

"So you give and you give until you have to hide a few scraps for yourself," Kabat recalls.

After nearly five years in Brazil, Kabat had become so dedicated to his Recife parishioners that his missionary associates feared he was endangering both himself and their own continued presence there. He left for his own good and that of the mission in 1973. He was replaced by Fr. Larry Rosebaugh, the strong, silent rebel of Milwaukee, then just two years out of Waupun Federal Penitentiary for burning draft files. Before Kabat left Recife, he had built in his own mind the notion of what was going on in the political world, and what he had to do to protect his poverty-stricken parishioners.

> "About the time I left," Kabat recalls, "Nixon was sending down (Nelson) Rockefeller to find out what was wrong. To myself, I said, 'Gee, Rockefeller could buy half of those countries he's investigating. So why wouldn't Nixon send down somebody like my mom or dad?' Because it was certain what Rockefeller would say when he came back: 'Send more guns.' And they did.
>
> "Maybe if Nixon had sent an ordinary person down there, he would have said, 'Boy, these people are starving. Boy, these people need jobs. Boy, they need schools, so let's send them funds. . . send them implements. . . let's send them things that will help them. Let's help them find a way to share their land so that maybe they could have small farms and live on them and raise crops and make a living.'
>
> "But, instead, Rockefeller came back and said to send more guns."

With this kind of mission in mind, Kabat had helped build a rickety kind of pavilion for public meetings and school sessions. By adding an old Victrola and a few scratchy vinyl records on weekends, he sponsored weekly dances for the young folks, to help raise their morale.

"I can recall in Recife, just shortly before I left, I had one section that was about 400 mud and stick houses. They had no water, no roads, no lights, no schools, no nothing. They would go down to this big stream where they would wash clothes. The stream was filled with their own urine and whatever else. That was also their drinking water. They should have been allowed to have fresh, clean water.

"So I asked those folks what they were wanting. They said schools for the youngsters, so maybe they could find a better way to live.

"So I was trying to build this hall, school, whatever else you call it. In the process, I knew that the younger single adults, from about 13 to 21, had really nothing to occupy themselves in the evening, to be happy about.

"We started having dances, and we used an old record player that was run by batteries. We had some kerosene lights and cans with wicks, so that the kids could come and enjoy themselves and have some recreation. But during one of these dances I was having there, these men walked in, wearing ties and suits, and they were acting very official and trying to break up this party. I told them to get lost."

The next day, Kabat's colleagues urged him to leave, because they feared he would be arrested and the mission would be closed.

"Later, after I left Brazil, I heard there was a court thing at which I was supposed to appear to answer questions in regard to the dance activities.

"So I would say this about my vision of what it is to be a priest: He should be someone who would be a spokesperson for not only the local people, but for the international family — whether it be about arms, war, starvation, the economy, jobs, labor unions, how to farm or whatever. . . to say that such things are necessary, that the kingdom of God requires such earthly things."

When Carl Kabat returned to the United States, he stayed and worked with his brother Paul, also an Oblate priest, who was stationed at Bemidiji, Minnesota. There, Fr. Paul was not only Newman Club chaplain for students, but he also administrered to the life-broken leftovers of American Indians and society's remains from the rusting Iron Range. Bemidji was part of the mining region that for decades had supplied the country with taconite for its steel mills.

As early as 1968, Paul Kabat had engaged in protests at Offutt Air

Force Base near Omaha, where the Strategic Air Command staged its flying headquarters-bombers in case of nuclear war. (Paul Kabat died of a stroke, defrocked of his priesthood, in the spring of 1999.)

In the meantime, due to his experiences first in the Philippines and later at Recife, Carl Kabat had evolved into a prophet in search of a way not only to deliver his message but to achieve some positive results.

"I knew, as soon as I returned to the US, that I no longer could make life in America fit the Third World," he says, "Either I had changed or this country had changed."

Carl recalls visiting his parents and casually opening the refrigerator. "It was so well-stocked, I started to cry," Kabat says, "because where I had been, my parishioners didn't even have refrigerators — but the army had guns."

Kabat's message became one of opposition to war and instruments of war, especially nuclear weapons. He was convinced that nuclear weapons, even if never used, were immoral because they helped to keep so much of the world in poverty and fear. He figured that nuclear weapons ate up assets that might have been used for much more humane and higher moral purposes, just as President Eisenhower had suggested. And so he began a series of protests with like-minded friends, especially Philip Berrigan. The protests would keep him in jail most of his life.

In simply trying to help extricate poor people their predicament, Kabat had become convinced that the US government, with its military-industrial complex, was a danger to moral decency and to its own democracy. At the same time, he remained a patriot to the cause of God-given human freedom. He simply wanted more of it shared with the rest of the world.

Pursuing that conviction, in 1980 Kabat joined with the Berrigans and others in taking symbolic actions against nuclear facilities under a program the prophets called "Plowshares."

The name is a reference to the text in Isaiah that speaks of beating swords into plowshares and giving up the use of war. "Plowshares" became a worldwide movement. It exists to this day with perhaps a hundred protests internationally to its credit.

Father Carl's view of the world was an epiphany personalized by all the prophets without honor. It flowed from an unsettling discovery, a discovery not unlike that made by the character Yossarian in the novel *Catch-22*.

Like Yossarian, Kabat concludes that the entire world system is snared in the military web of its own making. The world, and each person in it, has become a bloodied victim caught by its own petard: Security now flows from mutually assured destruction and the only way to have peace is to first make war.

Kabat's Catch-22 world has discovered that you have to be crazy to use nuclear weapons. But you also must have nuclear weapons to protect yourself from the crazy people who have them. The United States is the only nation that ever used the atomic bomb, but it is not crazy — even as it hides behind its crazy power. To prove its sanity, the US used less-crazy conventional warfare in Vietnam, where its Catch-22 predicament evolved this insane military logic to explain its actions: "We had to destroy the village to save it."

• When Kabat's world asks, how this free-speech system can also have the power to jail peaceful, non-violent protesters to the excesses of its own system, the catch-22 answer is: "Because it has become immoral."

When asked what has made it immoral, the catch-22 answer is: "Because it has the power to be immoral."

Other catch-22 corollaries are evident in every corner of the world:

"We're going to give you democracy and peace, even if we have to kill you to do it."

"We're going to give you the freedom of our system, even if we have to force you to accept it."

"We're going to develop your economy, even if we have to steal your resources to do it."

In this way, the nation's Catch-22 citizens are mentally disconnected from their economy and military, as Maryknoll prophet Roy Bourgeois once discovered at an Exxon shareholder meeting in Chicago. He asked the chairman of the board, "Is there a direct relationship between the poverty in El Salvador and the profits you get from exploitation?"

Angry Exxon shareholders booed and hissed him down, and the chairman felt no need to answer the question.

How to Get SAC'd

After Rupiper's return to the US from Recife, he served as a chaplain at the University of Illinois Newman Center for Catholic students, where the campus anti-war "vibrations" resonated with his own experience. Then he was assigned to the Oblate House of Studies in Omaha.

Before long he established, with the help of Catholic and other local volunteers, a shelter for street people. This was not a "preaching and singing in exchange for a warm place to eat, sleep and defecate" operation. Those who wished to could attend Sunday services; Rupiper would say Mass and talk about social justice and human dignity. This format was the basis for his ministry for several years. Meanwhile, he developed a growing sense of opposition to the nuclear presence of the nearby Strategic Air Command. (His revulsion to SAC eventually led him to Tehran, to visit the US hostages — a story explored in a later chapter.)

By now, Reagan was in office and the ground was being prepared for the Iran-Contra scandal.

The Strategic Air Command (SAC, now called STRATCOM) was (and still is) located at Offutt Air Force Base, in Bellevue, Nebraska, near Omaha. It was from SAC that all nuclear targets worldwide were determined. In the early 1980s it was customary for the military command to open the grounds to the public, in a carnival atmosphere, once a year. The object was to put on display the military muscle of the US, the more to gain the admiration and ongoing support of the public for the nuclear strike capability that this base offered to the nation.

It was from here that the B-47 Strato fortresses, the B-58 Hustlers and later the B-52s carried into the air their nuclear weapons or their elusive flying command posts — ready to assault foreigners whose only transgression was to live in the wrong country. Certain foreign governments were classified as the politically evil enemy; thereby, Rupiper understood that the children of whole nations, and along with them all Americans, were put at risk. The flying nuclear command posts were part of what McNamara and the Pentagon called *Project Looking Glass.* That project meant that there was always a command post in the air capable of ordering a nuclear war in case the enemy staged a sneak attack on America.

The problem, in the view of missionaries like Rupiper, was that it was no longer clear who was retaliating against whom and for what; but it was clear that retaliation on either side was as immoral as mass murder by the Nazis. Equally clear was the fact that the US military had no such moral qualms and had crossed its own white line in trying to anesthetize America's moral conscience.

On June 13, 1983, 250,000 red-white-and-blue citizens from the heartland assembled at an "open house" hosted by Offutt. This was the military's chance to show off, to win friends and influence people. The nation's everyday kind of people ogled the bombers and watched the air show, where special effects from the movies were played out, live. It was a feel-good kind of event filled with innocent human curiosity and genuine patriotism. A few less-secular minded people, such as Rupiper and layman Tom Cordaro, also visited the base chapel.

Inside the chapel, Cordaro and Rupiper saw, to their horror, a stained glass window depicting in a cubistic and surrealistic form the truncated mushroom cloud of an exploding atomic bomb — the very hellish end product of this military base. The window, financed by private funds, had been placed there as a salute to the US Air Force wing that had dropped the bombs on Hiroshima and Nagasaki.

Officially, the Air Force says (on a boastful postcard portrayal sold at its SAC museum) that the window "is dedicated to the SAC personnel." An examination of that window suggests a certain sardonic effect, whether intended or not, by the artist commissioned to do the work. The clever design reveals many intriguing effects. If you turn the postcard picture upside down, the image of an atomic mushroom cloud emerges in shattered form as it fractures everything around it; the world blown upside down. Rightside up, it shows the figure of a pilot in camouflage flight suit. A white woman and two children (watching either proudly or apprehensively) lurk in the background. One child has a dark complexion but the other characters are white. Above are the blood-red lightning bolts emanating from a Zeus-like mailed fist, which also crushes in its grip a shield and olive branch. This is the intimidating logo of Strategic Air Command. In the bottom foreground, the crushed image of a helmeted warrior seems to lie.

At upper right artistic eye can make out what appears to be the nose and needle-like wings of an aircraft followed by a fat contrail. The bomb-dropping pilot stands in the central portion of the window and is shown in a light reminiscent of artwork depicting Christ's ascension into heaven. Certainly an atomic bomb has the power to immediately dispatch body and soul into the heavens, as dust returns to dust with considerable outside help.

All these images are dominated by the stem of a mushroom cloud in the background. The streaks of color and their slashing arcs across the stained glass window as a whole bring to mind the ricochet lines from photographic plates produced by subatomic particles in atom-smashing experiments.

When you hold two postcard pictures of the window edge to edge, the lines of the mosaic patterns match and extend the single picture into a larger picture with repetitive images, repeatable like infinite fractals. Artistically, the stained glass window is an awesome symbolic rendering of the physical moment of total atomic destruction; the instant reversal of creation on earth. It is ironic and cruel that it should also portray at its mushroom base a helmeted warrior and children who might be both perpetrators and victims of such destruction.

To Rupiper and Cordaro, this window in the SAC chapel became a new kind of "looking glass", mockingly bringing to mind the words of St. Paul in his first epistle to the Corinthians: "We know in part and we prophesy in part; now we see through a glass darkly."

Rupiper and Tom Cordaro viewed the window, and SAC's *Looking Glass* operation, as literal and symbolic embodiments of man-made death and destruction. They felt it was an effort to beatify war, by those who were profoundly insensitive to anything holy, including the sanctity of life. To find such an incongruous image enshrined in a place dedicated to what is sacred and non-violent was shockingly oxymoronic.

Rupiper and Tom Cordaro didn't know whether to laugh or cry. Instead, they decided to get even.

Every year thereafter, on the August anniversary of Hiroshima, Cordaro and Rupiper helped mobilize another kind of "open house" at SAC, one to memorialize the ultimate insanity of having nuclear weapons.

In later years, Tom's priest-brother, Frank, would do the same at Christmastime to commemorate the Feast Day of the Innocents, which honors the children killed by Herod after the birth of Christ. It was their symbolic way of throwing a rock through the mushroom cloud of the window, so that the warming grace of the real sun might shine through, unfiltered by the blood-red tinges of war.

The Cordaros and Rupiper, along with members of the concerned public, began crossing the white line that officially barred entry to the base. On many of those occasions, they were arrested, and were issued "ban and bar" letters which said they could not come back without risking trial and jail. They came back again and again and were tried and jailed as many times.

Whenever base officials choose not to accept "open house" guests, they enforce the line with Air Police. Like bullies who draw lines in the dirt, the military challenges anyone to step over that line. Many have done so, peacefully. Many have suffered in jail for their boldness. Even when Rupiper asked in writing for an official audience with the base commander to discuss matters of peace, war and morality, he was met only with tight-jawed military SWAT teams. Since retiring, one of SAC's former commanders, Gen. George Lee Butler, has joined the ranks of several dozen star-rank officers who now advocate the abolition of nuclear weapons. Years ago, crossing that white line was a violation of a law that the base commander pompously promulgated:

"This white line is the demarcation line between Offutt Air Force Base and civilian territory. If you cross the demarcation line without the express permission of the installation commander, you have violated Title 18 of the US Code, which means you are trespassing on a federal installation. At that time, when you cross that demarcation line, you will be placed in custody."

Deliberate trespass was not just the exclusive undertaking of bold men. Among the hundreds taken into custody over the years were dozens of remarkable women — remarkable for their soft-spoken but resolute demeanor, giving witness to the overall justice of the protest. Archetypes of this kind of protesting women were Sister Joyce Horbach, a white-haired Franciscan nun from Dubuque, Iowa; Sister Marylyn Felion, who served briefly in Nicaragua; and a 69-year-old great-grandmother named Jean Petersen.

Sister Joyce is the aunt of Darrell Rupiper. Now in her eighties, she still has a warm smile, fueled by the fire for peace that glows in her eyes. Her style is as warming as it is disarming, probably because she spent all of her adult years teaching elementary school children to read and to add two plus two. What she sees in today's world are people who cannot add up the complex factors within modern society and reach a non-violent answer. The judge didn't agree with her kind of social arithmetic and on two separate occasions gave her jail terms of 10 and 30 days.

Marylyn Felion

Marylyn Felion is a retired nun who taught school for many years in Omaha within the Sisters of Mercy, an order better known, perhaps, for their hospital work. Today, in her mid-sixties, Marylyn's facial features seem as pleasant and unspoiled as the conscience she wishes the world would adopt. That conscience says no person or state should kill another. For her beliefs and actions, she received jail terms of 30 and 75 days. The stiffer sentence came after her sit-in at the chancery office of Archbishop Daniel Sheehan in Omaha. For his part, Sheehan not only prosecuted the nun to the full extent of the law, but declined to grant her the sanctuary or forgiveness of the Church against her punishment.

Marylyn later "married" a black deathrow inmate named Robert Williams, who had committed murder and rape. Therein lies a story within a story about freedom and love and systematic abuse. The story is about two people, one white and female, one black and male, each of whom was physically abused by their parents as children. Each contained the seething seeds of rage, which brought them together. Each reacted differently to the predicament of life, but later found in each other a unity of spirit.

The rage in Williams surfaced on the occasion of a bitter divorce. It brought Williams to the point of a binge, during which he raped and killed two women friends who had tried to take away his pistol and calm his anger. By most social standards, Williams' behavior had always been erratic. Court psychiatrists said it was because of the beatings he took as a child from his drunken father — with his mother's approval. This, of course, was no excuse for his own brutal actions.

In Marylyn's case, her rage was self-contained. Her travail surfaced in her maturity in the form of depression and suicidal tendencies. Her childhood difficulties stemmed from abuse by her stepmother. It seems her stepmother raised her along the classic storyline of Cinderella, mothering her natural children with favoritism while abusing her stepchild. But, Marylyn never knew she was a stepchild until her teenage years. As a source of solace, she turned to the convent life, much as angry men are said to turn to the French Foreign Legion.

And so, one day a white woman brimming with sympathy for all things peaceful met a black man worthy of that sympathy. There was to be no judge, no priest to consecrate the union they made verbally, with prison bars between them, ten days before Marylyn's chosen man, Robert Williams, was executed. There was no time for a honeymoon or conjugal consummation. He gave her a small cross, which she still wears around her neck. Days later, she placed in his coffin a turquoise ring she had worn for many years. She couldn't give it to him while he was alive, because of prison rules.

"We both had physical scars from beatings as children," Marylyn says. "We knew, despite what either of us had done to deserve our fates, that we had something in common." She is content to be a "widow" leading the life of a nun without benefit of community, even as her daily actions benefit the community of mankind at large.

Williams never claimed to be innocent and Marylyn does not defend him. Her intent was to put him at peace with himself, society, and his maker, while sublimating her own tribulations. His execution had been set aside, at one point, by the Supreme Court decision that said capital punishment was cruel and inhuman. His execution in the end was brought on by a Supreme Court reversal, allowing states to resume capital punishment.

Long before she met Williams, Marylyn had developed her sympathetic proclivities as she taught class after class of school children. Eventually, psychological pressures from her childhood years brought her to a kind of nervous breakdown and she was released, at her request, from her vows and her convent life. A treatment period of six years followed.

Eventually, Marylyn's urge to help other people led her back into action. Thus, in 1985, she found herself in Nicaragua with the Witness for Peace program at the height of the Iran-Contra activity. Witness for Peace positioned people in key countries to observe and record atrocities committed by death squads trained at the School of the Americas. Part of the witness training, Marylyn explains, was to identify a worst personal fear. Marylyn's worst fear was that she might have to observe the actual killing of a person by the Contras, and not be able to prevent it.

Fate delivered her from her worst nightmare. The day before she was to be sent into the warring sections within Nicaragua to live among the peasants, Marylyn was afflicted with amoebic dysentery. Before she was shipped back to the United States, she almost died of toxic shock syndrome. However, her fear about having to witness a death was now one step closer to reality, in a different guise:

"Once the Supreme Court reinstated the death penalty," Marylyn says, "I became associated with any and every group that opposed capital punishment. Even so, I could not bring myself to visit any of the people who were being executed. This was while I was living in the Omaha area."

It was then that she heard about the case of Robert Williams. He came within hours of execution before a stay in the prison at Lincoln, Nebraska.

"So I wrote this poor man to say how glad I was that he was still alive," Marylyn says. "We corresponded for two years and I began to understand that, indeed, he was guilty of the crimes. I also learned of the rage from childhood that drove him, for so many years, to his final terrible actions. And I thought of my own parallel experience.

"Finally, when the Supreme Court turned down his final appeal, I knew the end was near. I needed to see him on an unrestricted basis, just to give him comfort. I remembered from my own childhood how much I needed comfort after being beaten and had nowhere to turn. I projected this to Robert.

"Robert said the only way I could visit him on an unscheduled basis was to establish 'ministerial status.' This was a problem. How is a nun to do that in a male-priest-only religion such as the Catholic Church? So I asked a favor of the Sisters of Mercy. My former mother superior gladly gave me the title of 'spiritual advisor', and so I became the official spiritual advisor for the welfare of Robert Williams."

Every-day visits at the Lincoln jail were soon to follow. Eventually, the friendship warmed into what might be called Platonic love.

Before Robert Edward Williams was executed, Marylyn Felion had become an established artist. Even though she had never seriously taken up brush and palette, Marylyn's watercolor portrait of her jailhouse husband as *"Black Jesus"* won an award from the *National Catholic Reporter* and was among the works displayed at the *"Jesus 2000"* art show in Chicago.

Robert was executed December 2, 1997, and Marylyn considers herself a widow even though their marital union was never consummated. She says, in a resigned yet upbeat tone of voice, "That will happen in the life to come."

In this life, meanwhile, she has joined the effort to eliminate the death penalty.

Jean Petersen

Jean Petersen has always been feisty when her back is against the wall. She is the kind of landlady that everybody would pay extra to have. Frail and unarmed, she barred a contingent of FBI agents seeking to invade her house in order to arrest Marylyn Felion, her boarder. Delicate arms braced against the door jamb, she challenged the men in the dark suits and sunglasses to show their credentials and arrest warrants.

By Jean's account, the FBI men said they didn't need any credentials because they were in pursuit of a felon. (The trespassing case in point was a misdemeanor.) They flashed only their weapons.

Jean countered that, for all she knew, they could be terrorists and she would allow them to enter her house only over her dead body. Another boarder, a husky male, backed her up by standing in the doorway.

What do you do when confronted by cops who don't show badges? You call cops who will, Petersen reasoned. So she called the local police, who then convinced the FBI that they should behave in a legal and proper manner, show their IDs and warrants, and proceed. Otherwise, *they* would be arrested on the basis of Petersen's complaint.

As all this was happening, Marylyn was peeking down the staircase, relishing the show of force between a determined old woman and the Feds. When the bulls quit jostling each other, Marylyn gave herself up, over Jean's objections.

Jean Petersen is like that. Everything was reasoned and peaceful when she crossed the white line at Offutt and was arrested. But because of her advanced years and frail health, the judge refused to give her jail time. So she continued to cross the white line, and the military police continued to arrest her, gently.

According to a report in the *Omaha World Herald*, Petersen said she was "offended" by the fact that Federal Judge Richard C. Peck had refused to send her to jail. She felt as if she should be treated the same as her fellow-protesters.

Finally, on January 29, 1984, Petersen received a one-day sentence for her political intemperance after entering a guilty plea. Asked whether she would repeat her protest action at the base, Petersen was quoted as saying, "I don't know why not." Two months later she did, in a white gown adorned with lettering speaking of the ashes of war. She called it a "SAC Cloth." A soldier wearing a beret tenderly escorted her off base like a grandson guiding an elderly grandmother. It was snowing. Jean was smirking. The MP was not. He seemed to know that she was not his prisoner. His face, snapped in a news photo, seemed to betray a reluctance that said, "I am just following orders."

In one protest, Rupiper was arrested without even crossing the white line. He was handing out leaflets from the median of the approach road to the base. The highway patrol arrested him and Tom Cordaro, citing an auto traffic law that prohibited cars from stopping and standing on the highway. How this vehicular law applies to people on foot along our nation's local driveways is questionable, and such concerted actions make apparent (and render suspect) the arbitrary fraternity between the civilian and military police, when they choose to stretch the law and use if for harassment.

During the '80s, thousands of protesters gathered at the SAC gates, and hundreds crossed the line and were arrested, including the Kabat brothers and the minor children of an American Indian family. Scores were sentenced. Some did hard time in prison. A few, like co-author Mike Palecek, were driven to the point of insanity, in jail, both because of their temperament and their treatment.

Why did they do it?

The answer is not just the mushroom cloud in the stained glass window, but what that cloud stood for. The stained glass window in the SAC air base chapel is a moral contradiction. It is a threat by the military to drop more bombs and indiscriminately kill more people, as if in the name of God and peace, at the same time.

Ordinary people crossed and recrossed the line at Offutt, never exhibiting one instance of violence. This created a problem, because the military is trained to deal with violence, not with peace or its symbolic acts. Likewise, the courts are geared to deal with those who break the law with social malice, not with those who have higher or peaceful intent. There is, in the law, precious little precedent for judge and jury to deal with a righteous spirit in conflict with the letter of a law that may be immoral in its consequences.

Attorney William Kunstler's defense of the "Catonsville Nine" (the Berrigans et. al.) and the "Milwaukee Fourteen" (Rosebaugh et. al) is memorialized in a booklet, *Delivered into Resistance*. He quotes Harvard University Law School Professor Paul A. Freund, saying: "A jury should be allowed to acquit people who act in a measured way for reasons of conscience." No judge since the revolutionary colonial times of John Peter Zenger (a printer who broke a British law against freedom of the press), has ever allowed a jury to vote on the issue of conscience. The Zenger case was a central point of Kunstler's defense, but in dozens of cases that were to follow, Judges were inflexible. The patriotism of Zenger in colonial days didn't apply to the "unpatriotic" protests of priests in the middle of the Cold War.

One judge was heard to rebuke Fr. Rupiper at his 1979 hearing in Chicago: "Don't deny it. I saw you do it on television. And don't preach to me out of the Bible. I have my own, right here in my desk drawer."

Without recusing himself from the case, the judge then passed sentence, in violation of the constitutional guarantee of impartial court proceedings and fair trial.

And the Nukes Go On

It is impossible to understand what was happening in Omaha and elsewhere, over the issue of nuclear weapons, without understanding that the United States military, its politicians and its citizens would do or believe nearly anything to slay the dragon of Communism, especially after Premier Nikita Khrushchev pounded his shoe on the podium at the United Nations in 1961.

For the US, only the atomic bomb could slay that dragon. Of course, the Soviet Union was the reciprocal party in this kind of thinking. The prophets could do little about USSR policy, so they focused on the US.

The development of better and bigger "nukes" proceeded, especially under Reagan. His military expansion added about $400 billion to the nation's deficit. Without regard to the national debt and the effects of such financial encumbrances on the world economic system, Star Wars was invented both in Hollywood and Washington. This happened at the time when Reagan opposed the nuclear weapons freeze of the Kennedy-Hatfield proposal in Congress, in 1982. Reagan was more interested in trickle-down economics.

Then the prophets without honor began to realize that keeping the nation on a military footing *does* create such a thing as trickle-down economics: and the prophets and their parishioners in Third World countries knew it as global poverty.

12. When Omaha Collides with Recife

In 1979, when Darrell Rupiper and Carl Kabat heard that there was a government-sponsored arms bazaar in Chicago selling military weapons to Third World nations, they went to protest. By coincidence, Michael Palecek, still a seminary student, was drawn to the same event. Then the plot thickened.

When Kabat and Rupiper recognized several attendees as the generals who had kicked them out of Brazil, they went prostrate in front of the entryway to object. They were arrested for blocking the entry and were jailed in Chicago's Metropolitan Detention Center. In this way, Recife and Omaha collided-- in Chicago. Palecek, who had never met Rupiper or Kabat, was deeply influenced by the Chicago protest and arrests.

Upon release, Rupiper and Kabat vowed privately to expand their protests. Rupiper focused on Offutt Air Force Base. He rallied many of the people who worked with him, at the hastily organized Nuclear Freeze Office set up by *Nebraskans for Peace*. These included Tom Cordaro and his brother Frank, another of the prophets, not yet ordained.

By this time, Carl Kabat had made friends with the Berrigan brothers, and along with others they formed plans to engage in a Holy Week protest in the nation's capital. At this point, Mike Palecek relates his participation in events that eventually were to drag him through several prisons, and to the brink of insanity.

Mike Palecek

"In Chicago, I was just a naive kid. Our group had marched around the hotel entrance and lobby singing peace songs. As a member of the crowd there, I saw that two priests had been arrested. At some point, the two of them blocked the entry to the arms bazaar or crossed some police line.

"So there was some confrontation, and Rupiper and Kabat got arrested. I went back to St. Paul by train, determined to be a peacenik," Mike says, recalling his heady adventure. He then relates how he came to know the Berrigan brothers.

"Dan Berrigan came to St. Paul in 1979 to speak at Macalester College as part of a symposium on Vietnam. I was a seminarian at St. Thomas, just a few blocks away. I wanted to hear Berrigan speak because I had just returned from the Chicago protest, the first I had ever observed up close.

"So I attended the Berrigan symposium. After he spoke, I asked him to come to St. Thomas seminary to speak. He agreed, and did so. Then he invited the seminarians to come to Washington for Holy Week protests at the White House and the Pentagon. I was overwhelmed. This was Dan Berrigan. In my mind, he was a hero. But, anyway, two of us from Minnesota joined him in Washington."

Because he acted as an observer, Palecek's story sounds like that of a reporter as the group entered the White House:

"We took the bus to the White House and waited in groups to go through on the tour. This was the first time I had seen the White House, so I was just milling around looking at old furniture and trying not to look like someone who should be apprehended.

"And so our group acted like any normal tour group does in the White House, gawking at the furnishings, marveling in awe at the sense of history. Most of us were in ordinary street clothes, disguising the fact that several of us were priests and nuns. But there was one priest in clerical suit. It was Holy Week, and Easter was just a few days away.

"When the tour was over and the crowd was dispersing outside on the portico, the priest produced a small container of blood and poured it on the steps or maybe on a pillar. This was Carl Kabat. Others in the group unfurled banners."

Tourists stood aghast, Palecek remembers. Uniformed guards rushed over and placed Kabat in a headlock. He did not struggle, so the handcuffs went on easily. Other guards snatched away the banners and ushered their owners off the White House grounds. Among the group were Philip and Dan Berrigan, Sister Anne Montgomery, Sister Elizabeth McAlister (who had become Philip Berrigan's wife), Lou DiBenedetto, Father Richard McSorley, and Art Laffin.

For his role in spilling blood on the White House steps, Kabat was booked and released, to be tried and sentenced later.

After regrouping at St. Stephen's Church in northwest Washington, the protesters proceeded to the Pentagon, Palecek and his seminary friend still tagging along as sympathetic observers.

There, in the public commons area that forms the inside mall, the group performed a bit of protest theater, singing anti-war songs and finally pouring blood and sprinkling ashes around the pillars and doors. Carl Kabat, who had rejoined the group, was again arrested.

For his protests at the White House and the Pentagon, Kabat spent eleven months in jail, two for the White House blood spilling and nine for the Pentagon action.

"After these two experiences," Mike says, "my desire to join their effort was unshakeable. But I'm getting ahead of my Berrigan story.

"To show you how naive I was, once I got back to St. Paul, I was surprised to find out that there were those in the Church who did not agree with me. I was totally convinced that the message of Berrigans, Rupiper and Kabat about the poor and about war was on the mark.

"My parish priest, Fr. Walter Nabity, advised me to stay away from the protesters. Stung and confused by his criticism of them, I wrote to Dan Berrigan. Here's what he wrote back:

Sept. 21, 1979

Mike:

I was happy to hear from you. I'm sorry, though, that things have become so unclear in your thoughts since we met and you came East for the protests.

I think your parish priest is full of baloney. Please don't hesitate to tell him so, if you want to. He reminds me of all the cutout-clerics I've met over the years who went on to get their degrees while innocent children died in Vietnam and many of us went to prison.

I don't envy him his degrees from Harvard and Columbia. I've lectured in both places and find them rich centers of moral retardation. As for people getting paid to protest, it's here that the baloney goes rancid. Our payment was years in prison to protest the killing; his payment was something else again.

I hope someday he picks up the New Testament and gets some light on the life, imprisonment and death of Jesus. Also on some texts like, "love one another, as I have loved you."

Well, enough of that. If I am angry, it's at his defamation of those I love. He sounds as though any outrage in the world would find him indifferent among his books and degrees. I just wonder what sort of advice someone like that is capable of giving to someone like you.

As far as his cult talk goes, I think your seminary is closer to the cult reality than Jonah House. There, you and other young people seem to be being brainwashed — cleansed of all traces of the gospel and of Christ, in order to prepare for a safe and pallid clerical future, in which *you* can go on to advise other young folks against becoming Christians and witnesses. How's that for turning things around?

Any place (like Harvard, Columbia or St. Thomas) that is neglecting to give young people a vision of life, faith, a human future, doesn't deserve to go on. I hope you leave there. I hope you find a community that is not lost in fantasy and immaturity with its mutterings of Communism and cults.

That's all so much useless bullshit. It has absolutely nothing to do with Christ or our Church. In fact, it's like a so-called religious branch of the State Department or the Pentagon, peddling the kind of religion that will allow murder to be legitimized, nukes to be created, the innocent and poor wiped out.

I thought, when I came to your seminary, Mike, something better might be in the air. (Usually I avoid such places.) Evidently, I was wrong. But for Christ's sake, don't condemn yourself to such a future.

Come back and see us when you want to. You'll always be welcome. Meantime, we go on with the work of non-violence, responsibility, hope.

— Daniel

Thus encouraged, Mike continued with his personal epiphany.

"I volunteered at the Minneapolis *Catholic Worker*, began giving away my clothes and albums, and eventually left the seminary to join the New York City *Catholic Worker*, on the lower East Side.

"I went through some trauma with my girlfriend back in Nebraska. At that point, I thought I was through with the peace movement. So I went back to school in Norfolk, Nebraska, to get a teaching certificate. Then Ruth and I (now Mike's wife) got back together.

"About this time, 1980, three nuns were murdered in El Salvador, and somewhere in that context, I read about protests at Offutt Air Force Base and Fr. Darrell Rupiper. I remembered I was with him in Chicago at the arms bazaar protest. So I began driving the two hours from Norfolk to Omaha, going to meetings, writing letters. But that wasn't enough.

"I had a $10,500 job as a history and religion teacher at St. John's high school in Bancroft, Iowa. But I was in over my head. My father died on a Friday morning, and Ruth and I were married Saturday night. I quit my job and moved to central Iowa. Then it was black earth, the *Des Moines Register*, Reagan elected; it all crowded in.

"It couldn't have been much fun for Ruth. I spent most of my time locked in a spare bedroom listening to the tapes of Dan Berrigan's talk at the seminary and reading every peace book and newsletter I could find. I got depressed; but it felt like shyness."

During this period, Mike quit his teaching job and worked at a group home for retarded adults. After considerable reflection, Mike decided to get arrested. And he did, by trespassing at the Offutt Air Force Base, and then later in the military recruiter's office in Norfolk, Nebraska. His ensuing peace efforts and rash of arrests over the years would give him more than he bargained for, and an FBI rap sheet at least 19 pages thick.

Mike Palecek's connection with the prophets had begun with his seminary days in 1979. It ended, for all practical purposes, after his release from jail (for the fifth time) in 1988.

In those ten years, he demonstrated several times against the use of nuclear weapons at the Strategic Air Command base near Omaha, and met and gathered at protests run by the Berrigan brothers, Darrell Rupiper, and numerous other peace agitators, many of them nuns, many of them non-Catholics. Mike took on not only the political and military regimes of the United States, but his own Catholic Church. He picketed even the Bishop of the Omaha diocese, by holding up a placard in front of the congregation during the bishop's homily on Easter Sunday. Mike's intention was to get the bishop to denounce the nuclear arms race and the presence of nuclear bombs at the SAC base near Omaha. His sign asked a simple question: "The Omaha Catholic Church Supports SAC: Why?"

At about the same time, two of Mike's friends, Marylyn Felion and Kevin McGuire, did a sit-in at the bishop's chancery. They were arrested and served time in jail, at the bishop's insistence.

On May 3, 1983, the Catholic bishops of the United States had ratified a pastoral letter denouncing nuclear war and calling upon Catholics to help rid the world of nuclear weapons. The bishops' message said in part: "We must summon the moral courage and technical means to say no to an arms race which robs the poor and the vulnerable." Yet, when Mike took refuge in the cathedral after a protest action and begged the bishop for the ancient protection of "sanctuary," the bishop refused to grant it, even as the FBI waited outside to pounce. Pretending to be a church janitor, Mike hid his face from view as he carried sacks of trash out the back door of the church and made his escape in a car left for him by his wife. He was in hiding and on the run for ten days, before surrendering.

On one of his prison stints, Mike fasted for seventeen days, accepting nothing but water, while he waited for a letter from the bishop denouncing nuclear weapons, especially at the SAC base. In part, Mike fasted as a protest over what he felt was his abandonment by the Church. Palecek felt he had summoned that moral courage to say no, just as the pastoral letter counseled. But when he asked for Church sanctuary against imprisonment, the Church had turned him away. The Church in its resolution had also said the manufacture and possession of strategic nuclear weapons "are acceptable" if "minimal" and the US and USSR are moving toward disarmament.

Mike grew skinny before the bishop's non-epistle arrived. The letter conceded nothing new about the bishop's (and Church's) position on nuclear arms. Despondent, Mike quit his fast. He was then transferred to Chicago's Metropolitan Corrections Center, where many members of the street gangs of Chicago were jailed.

Like the Church, the prison system showed Mike no mercy. Since Mike had once been (for two months) a corrections officer in a work-release program at a state hospital, he was placed in a prison section normally reserved for cop-convicts. He was, in prison parlance, "wearing a cop jacket," but he wasn't given any special protection from the non-cop inmates who bared their canines.

"At lunch one day, a prisoner bent down and whispered softly the word 'die.' And die I was sure I would, one way or another, because I couldn't even eat. I smelled my own fear, like iron simmering when it's pulled from the embers. I chain-smoked for something to stay busy with. The ashes covered the front of my clothes. I was unable to care enough to brush them away. I thought of Carl Kabat. I really wondered how in hell he and the others were able to stand so much of this."

Eventually, as the tension mounted, Mike took the first step. He started a fight with a prisoner who seemed to be threatening. Mike wound up in solitary confinement "for his own protection."

Letters of concern to the warden about Mike's treatment from friends such as Dan Berrigan brought no change. Mike was not even reconsidered for a "Level One" classification, which means those least likely to escape and therefore entitled to better treatment before release.

The only offense Mike ever committed was repeatedly to cross a line drawn across the road at Offutt Air Base, in protest over the threat of nuclear war.

Mike did part of his time in prison even after he was married and had his first child. Somehow, his wife Ruth suffered through the period with him. Small wonder that before Mike was reunited with them, he went "stir crazy." To this day, Mike is on medication to stabilize his emotional and mental equilibrium. The measure of his personal distress certainly can be seen in his face and eyes.

When you first talk with Mike, you hear words that should be in italics for all their soft shades of sadness, but in bold face for all their conviction. You see fragile childlike eyes brimming with eager affection for whatever lives and moves around him. In his face, you see — no, you sense — contours of benediction. Some people call it "charisma," others call it "ingenuousness." Still others speak of an aura, or karma. And you ask yourself, where is this man's nerve?

After all, he didn't serve all that much time: ten days in the Sarpy County Jail; thirty days in Douglas County Jail; fifty days in Lancaster County Jail; six months in federal prison and six months in Pottawatamie County Jail.

. Perhaps Mike's anguish is the process that Hemingway had in mind in his novel, *The Old Man and the Sea*. By the time the saga was over, the old Cuban fisherman's prize catch was chomped to nothing by the sharks as he struggled to row back to shore.

Here, you remind yourself, here is a man who righteously has defied the system and has been broken. Whatever was hard as bone within his mind and spirit now has formed unseen velvet scabs that protect, while projecting from beneath, the vulnerable soul. At times, that soul, that mind, can sound confused — as if it wants to cry or rage at what is wrong.

Cruel, but All Too Usual

So what is Mike's real story? What happens when the world breaks you and you go crazy in prison? Mike tells it in his own words, in no special hurry:

"It's not much, really," Mike says. "Just enough to make a vegetable out of me." He laughs.

"You learn to shit in public and sleep with a rolled-up cloth over your eyes. I think I was doing thirty days for protesting the slaughter of nuns in El Salvador when I began to go crazy.

"Kevin McGuire and I began to fast. It was one of several times we tried. It was after our El Salvador sit-in at a Nebraska congressman's office. He called the cops.

"I was placed in a silent room, where seconds crawl past you like worms on the sidewalk. Then I was taken to the maximum-security floor with the murderers and rapists. I was afraid to come out to the floor, and stayed in my room. I remember repeating Bible phrases to stay alive, or at least to stay occupied.

"Reaching for an item was like stretching across the Grand Canyon. Finally, my release date came, and the hallucinations stopped," Mike says.

However, he still hung on to his memories. Such as the time, a year earlier, when the Church betrayed Kevin over the sanctuary issue. At that time, Kevin was supposed to go to court over a SAC trespass. Mike suggested that Kevin try for church sanctuary. This put the FBI on his trail. When it was all over, the parish priest tricked Kevin into going out a side door and locked it behind him.

"With his wife and new baby, Kevin walked from the church to his home, where the FBI was waiting. They pounced on him like they must have pounced on Jesus. Kevin went to prison. He's out now. Long ago. Burned out like me on the protest thing, but he's working in the *Catholic Worker* soup kitchen in Omaha.

"There was another time I want to tell you about," Mike says. "I don't remember whether it was before or after I went nuts."

Mike wrote down some of his disjointed recollections. Whether they are schizophrenic, hallucinatory, or paranoid, they are real experiences that show just how much of himself Mike put on the line and how much the system sadistically extracted.

"I'm riding downtown with hands cuffed, my wrists pressed together like a toddler stuck in the motion of trying to catch his first plastic ball. The door is locked, with the lock knob removed. My door can only be opened by a responsible adult from the outside.

"The scene from my window is like something from a novel about things and times I no longer had a connection to. The marshals talked about office women, football scores and a hunting trip. For a moment, it was me and some high school buddies out for a cruise down Main. But these guys didn't want to shoot baskets; they wanted to have careers, bass-fishing boats and racquetball lockers.

"Those things demanded they shoot me if I tried to run to find my wife and son. And it wouldn't have been any different if these two were from my old gang of pals. My friends would have shot me, too. Just doing their job, who could blame them?

"One marshal turns his head to where I could see his left eye and half of his straight nose. He asks how my wife is. Why would he care? Why did he want to know? I look out my window.

"How did I get to this place? If they really knew me, would they take me to prison? What if we stopped and picked up my fourth grade teacher, Mrs. Widhalm? She could tell the marshals how, when she asked the class to use a word in a sentence, I always made up a sentence about baseball. I was famous for it.

"What if my high school baseball coach, Mr. Bruening, could be here and tell them how, when I was catching batting practice, a foul ball ricocheted and hit me just above the eye. I didn't want to get stitches. I wanted to go back and keep practicing. I watched the drops of blood turn the green grass red.

"Doesn't blood count? Doesn't any of that stuff mean anything? What was jail for, then? I did trap those sparrows in the snow with mousetraps, but I didn't think anyone knew about that.

"The marshals park the car on the east side of the federal building in their reserved space. They lead me to the elevator for the ride to the ninth floor. In the marshals' holding cell behind the courtroom, an FBI agent questions me. Then I'm led into the courtroom in my oversized insulated jean jacket. I never did grow into it.

"My wannabe hippie lawyer is there. He is pissed about the sanctuary thing. I nod and try to smile through my closed mouth, lips compressed. My moustache moves slightly up and down, giving an indication of a smile. I wiggle my toes, tap my heels. These old white shoes of mine that I get to wear today feel like balloons on my feet. . . the Saturday shoes intended for comfort. But they don't allow me to smile. My head still feels vacant as a gym after the game.

"Ruth is seated bravely in the front row. My head is shaking; my lower lip is numb. It has been that way for a few days. It means I am depressed; that much I know.

"I feel light-headed, out of body. The judge enters the large room, opulent with the silent thick carpet and chairs so stuffy. It's so no one notices you when you either sit down or get up. We rise. He sits. We sit. Like in church. I'm off rhythm. *Kyrie Eleison.*

"A nameplate says this is the courtroom of US District Judge Lyle Strom. The judge, in his late '50s with glasses, black robe and salt-and-pepper hair, begins his day with a stern flick of the gavel, too quick to see, like a squatted bullfrog slurping flies. The room turns into a blue lake. It is the home of this frog that keeps his implacable steely eyes staring ahead and seems not to move his body.

"Then the room returns, silent with gaveled order. I shouldn't be surprised, but I am. It seems strange and hard to be here. I tug on the sleeves of my jacket. It has red flannel lining and is overly warm. But it is a hand too long on each sleeve, and its ill fit makes me feel crazy.

"Then my eyes meet Ruth's, glazed with nervous confusion. They were trying hard to understand, looking for a way to convey hope, searching for some sign of strength in my manner — and finding none.

"The judge had allowed a psychiatrist to see me in jail, but she wasn't there, having submitted her report to the court. What it says, I don't know, but I imagine (it would say) that I'm nuts.

"During our last visit, I wasn't able to talk to Ruth. Well, just one word at a time, force it out, struggle to get the next word going.

"I think she watched me with her eyes wide open, like she was seeing a Stephen King movie played out and she doesn't like the scary part. Ruth and I had spent hundreds of hours sitting with our toes touching, on the sofa, fetching sodas for each other from the kitchen. Now she could not help me. I was beyond her grasp. My suffering was my own. It was like walking in to tell my grandmother I had murdered the neighbor's baby.

"I think I told her that I give up. I miss my wife and son too much to do this. I no longer gave a shit about nuclear weapons or the ghetto. I mean, the guys in the prison module are part of the reason I'm sitting here. But they would just as soon kill me or drive me crazy just for something to do.

"My shrink's report tells the judge the patient-inmate has weeping spells that come and go beyond his control; that patient-inmate is suffering from post-traumatic stress disorder possibly from a previous prison experience. (This may be reference to Palecek's solitary confinement at the federal prison in La Tuna, Texas, for refusal to eat.)

"The judge says I can talk with Ruth and the lawyer over in the corner of the courtroom. I have the option of moving to the mental hospital in the federal prison at Springfield, Missouri, or the federal medical center at Rochester, Minnesota, or to stay in the county jail.

"It's too hard. I can't think. I want to go to sleep. My head bobs as if on rollers. My eyes look at the gallery, the judge, the marshals, my cozy shoes. I tug at my jacket, lick my lips, wipe my face slowly with my palm — from my forehead down my nose, lips and chin, with fingers sticking straight up — the way crazy people do when they want to make it look like they're thinking things over, when really they don't know where they are. That's me. I want to laugh and jump up and down and pull at my hair. I slide back into some kind of catatonia. A short trip.

"Somebody decides I'll stay here, and hope for some way to be released early. I weakly shake their hands. The bastard lawyer, the wimpy, long-hair-gonna-go-home-now bastard, he mutters about having had to spend his Thanksgiving with his in-laws.

"I push away from the table and fall into line with my marshal convoy. I force myself to look and wave at Ruth. I see the courtroom as in a TV docudrama, my head on a swivel. I wonder whose life this is. My feet and hands are no longer there. Anywhere as if they had left the building.

"She's staring, then waving, as our friends begin to gather around her and decide who will ride with whom going home. I wonder if in some countries somebody would have tackled the marshals and taken me home with them.

"I turn toward the back courtroom door, the loser's exit, and wonder how someone goes about committing suicide. Who could a guy ask?

"I'm led to the elevator, past the black woman at the desk and through the building exit to the unmarked Dodge and back to my cell, where I have my cigarettes. Or did.

"'I wasn't made for this', I tell my cellmate. He gives me one of my cigarettes. We smoke.

"I tell him about the time we played Papillion High. When Tom Ballantyne, our split end, rushed out of the huddle and came back with a twenty-dollar bill. It was that kind of year. That twenty dollars was the highlight of our season.

"I tell him how I cried when my dad bought me an old lady's station wagon as my first car. That night, I sneaked outside and tore the mudflaps off. I never said thanks to Dad. Kind of took the car under silent protest.

Just asked where the keys were.

"Well, that car became a legend, a famous party barge. The clutch went out after I graduated. I miss it," I tell my cellmate. "I never amounted to much after I lost that car."

One morning not long after, Mike heard a key turn in the lock. The guard yelled "roll 'em up." The marshals were there, and Mike was on his way to Chicago Metropolitan Correctional, where Kabat and Rupiper had spent time. Mike recalls his farewell.

"I turned to my cellmate and said, 'This can't be me. Yesterday I was playing kickball on the asphalt.' His response? He asked me for my unspent allotted quarters for the phone. Then I fell in step with the marshals and headed for the airport."

The account Mike gives of his few weeks in the Chicago slammer is a continuation of his nightmare. After a fight and solitary and paranoia about being killed by the Spanish-speaking inmates, Mike serves out his time. He is once again home with his wife Ruth and son, Sam.

While Mike was going through the mental hell he describes, his friends on the outside, distressed by his condition, wrote an appeal for his freedom:

LETTER TO THE EDITOR

Today Federal District Judge Lyle E. Strom sentenced Mike Palecek to six months in federal prison and a $1,000 fine for crimes against the state, that is, us. The people. Palecek's crime spree, two counts of trespass, took place last spring when he walked across a white line at Strategic Air Command Headquarters, Offutt Air Force Base, Bellevue, Nebraska, to protest the arms race that impoverishes millions today and threatens annihilation of hundreds of millions in a very uncertain tomorrow.

If Palecek's sentence is "justice," then we may as well call nuclear terror "peace on earth."

Mike Palecek does not aspire to be a martyr. He does not want to be in prison. He is reminding all of us that the arms race is killing us in spirit if not yet in fact, just as surely as it is intended to holocaust our "enemies."

Mike Palecek is simply a Catholic who is trying to live out the clear intention of our God for justice and peace, trying to respond to the mission and the best impulses of our Church, which embraces all of humanity. Has he read too closely the gospels we all know?

Perhaps he shares too strongly the conviction of Pope John Paul II, who said in his encyclical: "War and military preparations are the major enemy of the integral development of people." The Holy Father calls the responsibility for this development as the urgent moral obligation of every Catholic so that there may be justice in all things towards all people with caring respect for human dignity.

Is Mike thereby the enemy of the people? How do you rehabilitate a man from such a noble cause? Should we break him of his faith in God's vision for us all? Do we really want to crush his hope of a better world of justice and peace, in our brutal prison system? Must we spend thousands of dollars of public money to punish him for his concern for God's people and for God's creation? Isn't it time that we ask Judge Strom that Mike's sentence be reduced to time served or vacated entirely?

Let us ponder the thoughtful words of the Old Testament prophet, Gamaliel, who said in a case being contested: ". . . in this case, I tell you, do not take any action against these men. Leave them alone. If what they have planned and done is of human origin, it will disappear. But if it comes from God, you cannot possibly defeat them. You could find yourself fighting against God."

It was written and signed by several of the prophets with whom Mike had cast his lot, including Rupiper.

Even then, Mike was not willing to abandon the world to the nuclear weapons at SAC. Once again he crossed the line. Once again he was sentenced and sent to the county jail.

"It wasn't really a tough jail," Mike says. "The judge allowed me to have weekly contact visits with Ruth and my son Sam. After each visit, I would hurry back to the cell so I could look out the window at their car, three floors below.

"But gradually I fell apart again. I felt the pressure on my chest and did not sleep for days. I had to force myself to eat, to comb my hair, to take a shower.

"A psychiatrist prescribed Xanax, and I stopped making 90-degree turns around the corners, and I was able to smile again.

"While I was in jail this last time, I had written to the judge and asked other people to write to the judge telling him I would never cross the line at Offutt again. Just, please, let me go home. He said he could not do that, because of the sentencing guidelines.

"The FBI would not let up. They asked the US Attorney to bring felony charges against me for breaking bail. The attorney refused to do that. I think he knew I was already toast. I asked him for an interview so he could see what shape I was in, but he refused. So I served out my time.

"The groveling before the authorities, the public hearing in front of my friends and enemies to seek freedom, the crying sessions in the jail on visits with my psychiatrist . . . what can I say? They were total humiliation.

"While I was in Council Bluffs, Bill Farmer, an Omaha artist, brought slides of a show he was doing in clay of various depictions of the suffering Christ. I could understand exactly what those pieces meant.

"When Darrell Rupiper came to visit, he said that, yes, maybe I would regret all this later, but that I had to survive. 'They broke you,' he said. 'Get better and make them break you again.'

"It took me ten years to go back to the gate at Offutt, and eleven years to cross the line again. It was the day after the US bombing of Iraq in 1999. The entrance had changed, and they didn't even recognize me as a repeat offender.

"All those years between Council Bluffs and 1999, I dreamed of returning to Offutt, and prison, as a hero, the comeback kid. As I walked up the drive again with my thou-shalt-not-kill sign, I did not feel any glory. Just scared. A very familiar scared."

During his ten years of freedom, Palecek had worked as a writer for several small Midwestern weeklies and even as editor of the *Byron Review* in Minnesota. He won several state press awards for his work. There are no other honors for Mike except what he now finds at home. Still, Mike Palecek inwardly feels an anguish and fear similar to that of Damocles, as if the entire world were now dining in the hall of a tyrant king, beneath a nuclear sword dangling by a single thread.

Pawing through the cardboard boxes of his belongings, Mike says, "I keep finding things I didn't know I had." Then, like the lion in the *Wizard of Oz*, he adds wistfully, "Maybe I'll find my courage somewhere in one of these old boxes."

Anyone who talks to Mike knows he does not lack courage, but lives in fear of his own paranoia about the nation that he loves. . . That nobody will believe him and that he might fail because nobody is following his lead. Mike sums it up this way, "To know the truth about America (today). That's all I need to have really lived." He thinks if others know that same truth, they, too, shall have lived.

Mike Palecek still has the courage to say no when even Church and country are wrong. He finds his comfort in the lines of Hemingway's *A Farewell to Arms:*

If people bring so much courage to this world that the world has to kill them to break them, of course it kills them. The world breaks every one and afterward many are strong at the broken places. But those that will not break, it kills. It kills the very good and the very gentle and the very brave impartially. If you are none of these you can be sure it will kill you too, but there will be no special hurry.

Mike believes he is strong, at many broken places.

So does Sister Marylyn Felion. Like Mike and Kevin, she challenged the Catholic Church, sought sanctuary from the institution that invented the word and the concept, and was turned over by Church officials to the FBI.

All of them, by conscience, indicted their Church as accomplice to the killings by the military system because the Church never took the moral step of separating itself from the killing that the US military represented, while Marylyn and Mike and Kevin did.

As Archbishop Daniel Sheehan of Omaha told Felion, on chancery stationery, September 13, 1989, "I see no point in (your) discussing any of these issues with me."

At issue was the archbishop's failure to denounce nuclear war as symbolized by the SAC presence in his diocese, despite the denunciation of nuclear war in the 1983 pastoral letter of the Catholic bishops of the United States. Archbishop Sheehan drew a hand-washing conclusion: activists such as Felion sought only "to embarrass the Church," and him personally. Cast aside was the symbolism of Felion's actions, representing the tens of thousands of victims among the Catholic and other faithful, in distant lands, whose deaths by American terrorism seemed not to embarrass or disturb the Church.

The patriotism of the American public swelled as a response to the continuing challenge from the perceived threat of the Soviet communistic empire during the '70s and into the '80s, just as nuclear and space weapons technology advanced. Nowhere did that pride in America's nuclear dominance swell more than in its geographic center, the heartland of America, isolated from the more urgent realities tugging at the frazzled sleeves of the world.

Underground nuclear missile silos proliferated throughout the Midwest: in Kansas, Nebraska, Missouri, the Dakotas, Colorado and Wyoming. Nebraska was home to the Strategic Air Command for directing nuclear war, if necessary, from the air. Colorado also had its Rocky Flats A-bomb factory and NORAD. For largely patriotic reasons, the rustic people in these areas did not seem to mind being the bull's eye of the Soviets as long as the US was training similar crosshairs on the commies.

Space age missiles, whether tipped with nuclear warheads or not, were accepted in the heartland because the missile had shown America's political enemies just how superior the nation and its salt-of-the-earth heartland could be. There were precedents:

1. Years before, then Vice President Nixon had won his "kitchen debate" with Khrushchev. And the heartland had cheered.
2. Kennedy won his game of missile poker with the Soviets, over Cuba. And the heartland cheered.
3. Neil Armstrong and his astronaut buddies had planted the American flag on the moon. And the heartland loved it.

But the SAC base meant heartburn, too, as it drew protesters against nuclear war, many of them from the heartland.

In 1983, a Nebraska farmer named Virgil Tworek-Hofstetter stepped across a white line at Offutt Air Force Base and was arrested. He spoke to the media:

"My belief," said Tworek-Hofstetter, "is that nuclear weapons are wrong. They are not justifiable. They are carried by planes here and we are accomplices in that. I'm here to be neither a victim nor an accomplice to these actions. As a citizen, as a human being, I have no moral excuse not to protest." Virgil Tworek-Hofstetter was arrested willingly because, like his prophet-friends, he resented every trained military killer, who presumed to draw a white line to demarcate where morality begins and ends in the world.

Tworek-Hofstetter is reminiscent of the words of Henry David Thoreau, who wrote in his dissent over the war against Mexico, "Under a government which imprisons any unjustly, the true place for the just man is also in prison." That is where Virgil, like the others in this book, wound up.

In 1985, Rev. Harold Schmidt, a Lutheran pastor, wrote to the *Omaha World-Herald* about the protests at the SAC base led by Rupiper: "Patriotism at its best is the criticism of the present in the hope of the future, a restless pilgrimage toward what might be. As we love our land enough to criticize it, as we are patriotic by keeping it ever under God's judgment, so we will continue to call it to repentance and change even as we praise and thank God for its freedom, its greatness, its opportunities. In that sense, the prophetic duty may at times be to call people to choose between their duty to God and their duty to country."

In such spirit, the Cordaro brothers and Rupiper continued give the heartland of America heartburn over their protests.

Frank Cordaro, even before he finished his studies for the priesthood, had established three hospitality centers in Des Moines for the homeless, one especially for battered women. He was co-founder of the Catholic Worker Community there, working with dedicated nuns and Catholic laity that included his brother, Tom, and their mother, Angela Cordaro.

At about the same time, in Omaha, 120 miles west of Des Moines, Darrell Rupiper had also established a hospitality center for the homeless. And working through the Oblate Center for Studies, he had organized a cadre of conscientious protesters against war, which by this time meant nuclear war.

Physically, the two priests could not be much different. Cordaro is a stocky, heavily-muscled man, a former football player. Rupiper is a small-framed, soft-spoken but wiry person. Both were equally tough-minded in their stand: "Thou Shalt Not Kill."

In the early '80s, both priests led protests at Offutt Air Force Base. In Cordaro's case, the protests, even through 1999, have mostly been linked to the August 6 anniversary of the atomic bomb dropped on Hiroshima. However, Fr. Cordaro's first protest came in 1978 at Dow Chemical's Rocky Flats nuclear weapons plant, where he joined dozens of protesters in blocking the railroad tracks. Protesters were eventually arrested and removed, after a five-day standoff. Participants from Colorado included Mag Herman, Ken Seaman and Bill Sulzman, a priest who had been fired by the Denver archdiocese for his anti-war activism. (Herman and Seaman would later be arrested at the Atomic Energy Commission's Nevada test site, and Sulzman was arrested with Carl Kabat for trespass at a Colorado nuclear missile silo in 2000.)

After the Rocky Flats experience, Frank Cordaro had the support of his brother, Tom, who is not a priest but a devout family man. They and some of their followers helped fill the ranks of many of Rupiper's protests at the SAC base (and vice-versa). Rupiper was arrested and jailed half a dozen times for crossing the white line at SAC — that white line that was invisible on "open house" days but that otherwise marked the out-of-bounds. At his rallies, Rupiper was joined by crowds of hundreds, many of whom were also arrested and jailed. Rallies by the Cordaro brothers have been also been attended by hundreds from the Iowa-Nebraska area.

Within a few years, Rupiper was reassigned and left Omaha. But the Cordaro brothers continued with the cause.

Frank Cordaro is a country priest who administers God's Communion and consolation to sincere farm folks in the style in which he thinks Christ would do it: through rebellion and resistance to what is wrong. A story is told that Fr. Frank once granted "sanctuary" to a parishioner's manure spreader to keep it from being taken in foreclosure. In his style, much like Mike Palecek, Cordaro mixes discussion of the financial difficulties of family farming with protests about the Catholic Church's support for the war establishment. It is a style that brought, from the Catholic Church, threats of excommunication for Cordaro.

Frank Cordaro

The front page picture in *The Washington Post* on Friday, November 30, 1979, shows a bewildered Jimmy Carter standing behind his podium, watching a bespectacled man sprinkling ashes from his raised hand just a few feet away.

This is Frank Cordaro, years before his ordination, looking more like a bearded rabbi than a Catholic priest-to-be. A security man is about to lead Cordaro away.

At the time, Cordaro had completed all of his philosophy and theology courses in the seminary, and was about to be ordained a deacon — the final step before priesthood. He had earned his master's degree in divinity already, and his doctorate was about to be completed. But he was eager for social action, and so he had temporarily abandoned his studies to establish the Catholic Worker House in Des Moines. Here is how he tells it:

"Somehow I got my name on a list to go to Washington to listen to a pep talk on the SALT II treaty. I was surprised, because I had already done some spilling of blood at the Pentagon and I had been arrested at Rocky Flats. But I got clearance.

"I begged the money to fly out there. I spent the night at Jonah House in Baltimore with Phil Berrigan and Liz McAlister, trying to figure out what I should do when I got to the White House. I wanted to make a symbolic action and say what I could. So I took some ashes out of their fireplace, put them in a plastic bag, and tucked it down inside my pants.

"After the White House tour, I make sure I get a good seat for the briefing. I take third row, center aisle, maybe 15 feet away from the podium. I'm very nervous, of course, because I know what I'm going to do.

"While I'm sitting there, in comes Bishop Thomas Gumbleton. He was the only bishop in the country who wrote against the treaty, not because it gave the Russians too much, but because it allowed for the development and employment of first-strike nuclear weapons. When I saw Gumbleton, I feel such confirmation.

"But being nervous, I get up and walked over to him. I quietly ask him if he would say a prayer for me. 'Why, yes, I will,' he said, obviously at a loss to understand the nature of my request.

"I'm thinking the President will be the first one to speak. Instead it is Zbig Brzezinski, Carter's answer to Henry Kissinger. I amuse myself by thinking that they like to have someone who talks funny in their Cabinet. So Zbig drones on for nearly an hour. Then there's this general, who sounds like he's from Texas. The gist of his statement is

'President Carter, *he* don't trust the Russians; Mr. Brzezinski, *he* don't trust the Russians; and me, *I* don't trust the Russians.'

"And I'm thinking, what's the point of all this? If we don't have trust as a component of security, we're bankrupt. I'm thinking mooning them would have been appropriate, except you don't *do* that in the White House.

"Finally, the President is announced. We all stand and clap.

I'm thinking, hey, this is the White House. This is the President of the United States. Three major networks are covering this. Maybe he's right and I'm wrong. Maybe I shouldn't do this. But then I go into what I call 'willful doing.' This is a play. I've got a role to play, and so does he.

"As everyone is sitting down, I know I have to hit the center aisle. So I get up and grab the ashes out of my pants. My back is to the crowd. From behind me, it could have looked like I was pulling a weapon.

"Also, I'm Italian American, and I had a black beard. The country was just nine days into the Iranian crisis, and to some who were there, I might have looked like an Iranian. So when I took that step toward the President, I felt the whole crowd just stop. Their hearts stopped.

"I immediately turned around because I didn't want to personally confront the President. Then, a number of things happen simultaneously. The crowd recovers, and seeing that I am an opportunist, start to boo me and shout things like 'sit down, you bum.'

"My voice goes high because I'm so nervous. 'Friends! SALT II is a lie, and Jimmy Carter is lying to us. These ashes represent the dead from the first strike.'

"I tried to shake out the ashes. But remember, they've been tucked inside my pants all morning in this plastic bag, so by the time I got them out, the body moisture had condensed inside the bag, and the ashes came out in wet clumps. Some folks were laughing. Then I realized that the funny part was my strange movements to keep my unbelted pants from falling down.

"Quick as can be, this Secret Service guy comes and grabs me by the arm. 'Now, young man, you're all right. Just come out here. . . ' I think he thought I was some kind of loony.

"Of course, no one heard me. No one heard a word I said, but it was all on the TV. They picked up everything. Later on, a woman from Iowa got up and said, 'Mr. President, I like that young man you had dragged out of here. We're concerned how anyone in the peace movement can support a treaty that allows for first-strike weapons.' So the media people got hold of her, and got my name, where I'm from and the statement I was making.

"First, the Secret Service wanted to know if I was crazy. Second, they wanted to know if I had planned to harm the President. Third, they checked my record. When they realized what I was trying to do, they just wanted to keep me out of the media. And they didn't want to press any charges, because I was an invited guest.

"About all I did was to be rude, and rudeness is not necessarily illegal. The enforcement guys were asking themselves how the hell they let me through. One of them said, 'I guess you know this means you'll never get invited to the White House again.'

"That night, it made all three major networks. Walter Cronkite mentioned my name, and it was on all the front pages. The prophet Isaiah never got that kind of exposure. Of course, when I got back to the Jonah House people, they're all saying, 'Man, you could have got shot.'

"I was still thinking about how silly I looked trying to keep my pants from falling down and shaking those wet clumps of ash. It gave me a flashback to my Pentagon protest two years before when I got arrested.

"There I was with a group of picketers getting ready to pour blood on one of the pillars in the commons plaza there, when out of one of the Pentagon doors comes my old eighth grade teacher, Coach Amadao. He is now an officer in the Air Force.

"He comes over to talk to me. You should have seen the Pentagon cops. They were really taken in by this — two guys from Iowa meeting on the Pentagon steps. One's an Air Force officer on business in the Pentagon; the other's a protester. We talked for a few minutes. He asked me three different times whether I knew what I was doing.

"He didn't say I was dumb; he didn't say I was stupid. He just wanted to know. And I could say with a great deal of conviction that, yeah, I did.

"When he left, we all let go of our protest signs and did the blood spilling on the pillars. No sooner did I get the blood on the pillars than my hands were handcuffed. We were all screaming, 'The Pentagon is a temple of death.' Our voices reverberated among those huge pillars.

"Then out of nowhere came these storm troopers, maybe 70 strong. Blue jump suits, big American flag, large clubs, combat helmets. All but two of them were black. They took us to a bus.

"As soon as we got on the bus, the two black guys who had me took off their helmets and sat down. They said, 'We're real glad that guys like you keep comin' here because these people (in the Pentagon) are nuts. And they WILL use nuclear weapons. You're just . right on, man.'"

Since that time, Cordaro has concentrated his protest efforts at SAC (STRATCOM, as it's now known). His first arrest there came in 1980 after a group altered a SAC billboard that proclaimed "PEACE IS OUR PROFESSION." The word PEACE was changed to WAR, and the sign was then splattered with Cordaro's blood.

These events were the start of a priestly protest-and-prison career for Cordaro, mostly for "crossing the line" at Offutt. However, in 1998, his "criminal" actions culminated in the pouring of blood on a B-52 at an air show at Andrews Air Force Base, near Baltimore, and beating on its bomb-bay doors with a carpenter's hammer. He called it "Gods of Metal Plowshares," with the B-52 symbolizing the "God of Metal."

Cordaro's protest was an outgrowth from the first "Plowshares" action taken by Carl Kabat, the Berrigan brothers and five others at a General Electric missile plant in 1980. After several years of jail and appeals, GE became enmeshed in a contract scandal over the missile program and dropped its charges against the "Plowshares Eight."

Independent "Plowshare" actions soon proliferated under the direction of others.

The Plowshares movement spread to Europe when new US missiles were set up there. A headline on October 29, 1983, blared: MILLIONS IN EUROPE PROTEST US MISSILES. Underneath was a story out of the Hague which said:

> Princess Irene of the Dutch royal family broke with tradition today when she joined a peaceful rally of some 500,000 persons at the Hague to protest NATO's deployment of intermediate range missiles. The deployment begins in England and West Germany next month.
>
> Royalty customarily keeps silent on sensitive political issues. "The weapons we have built," the Princess said, "have now put us on the edge of the abyss and we cannot afford one more mistake."
>
> Last week saw similarly heavy protest demonstrations in West Germany, Britain, Stockholm, Rome, Paris and Brussels.

Love Intervenes, Prophecy Triumphs

Between 1979 and 1998, Cordaro protested dozens of times, suffering arrest and serving prison time totaling more than three years. Like the other prophets, Cordaro's urge to protest came after exposure to the plight of the poor. In his case, that exposure came during a summer internship at St. Augustine's Catholic Church in the South Bronx and a summer at the Davenport, Iowa, Catholic Worker House. These experiences caused him to start a similar operation in Des Moines.

At first, Cordaro intended to interrupt his priestly studies only until he got the Des Moines *Catholic Worker* house up and running. But love intervened. As he puts it, "I fell in love with a woman — something that the Catholic Church did not approve of, for those seeking ordination." Eventually, when love faded, he finished his divinity studies and was ordained in 1985. He then returned to his moral crusade against nuclear war and, indeed, all killing.

Cordaro put his finger on the core issue of the immorality of international militarism when he said in a newspaper interview, "Every war is just a preparation for the next one."

Cordaro is aware that every president of the United States since FDR has gone to war by dropping US bombs on a foreign nation. (Besides World War II, the US has been directly engaged in war actions in more than a dozen countries including Korea, Vietnam, Cambodia, Laos, Libya, Lebanon, Iraq, Panama, Grenada, Ethiopia, several Balkan nations, and Afghanistan.)

To Cordaro, "the bomb" has come to symbolize what is wrong with the world's society under the tutelage of the United States. In the back of his mind tumbles the thought that these undeclared wars waged by the US may be simply a way of getting rid of old ordnance and testing weapons systems.

"The atomic bomb is the major form of evil in our times," he says in every Catholic journal that will print his words. "All other evils and oppressions (racism, sexism, materialism, militarism and violence in all its forms) take their lead from the bomb. The bomb has its own internal rhythm, manifested in the arms race. Our future with the bomb is a world with less and less human freedom. In nations that continue to seek security in the bomb, the human spirit will be outlawed to protect the bomb (and those nations that make it)."

His thoughts are seconded by other prophets, including those who, like Carl Kabat, have seen the human misery created in Central America by the process of protecting US interests with the threat of the bomb. These same prophets have witnessed death directed by made-in-the-USA dictatorships — all of them designed to protect the bomb and thus fatally delay other solutions for ending human misery.

Cordaro is quick to point out that even the Catholic Church, whose members live within both Third World and First World nations, has "bellied up" to the militaristic demands from the First World for killing.

"It's a critical flaw in Catholicism and the larger Christianity," Cordaro says. "It's what I call the 17th-century heresy: the acceptance of state-sanctioned violence. Its roots go back to sometime between Constantine, the first Christian emperor, and Augustine, the theologian. The Church simply bellied up to this key component of the (State's) need to be able to kill and run the affairs of Caesar. It (that pragmatism) just kind of washed out Jesus's pacifism and Christian non-violence (from both Church and State)"

Ironically, Cordaro's criticism is inspired by the 1983 pastoral letter of the US bishops' conference on the subject of nuclear arms, which they call "immoral." It says, at its core, that nuclear weapons are immoral— but acceptable (because of pre-existing political exigencies) only if those possessing atomic weapons are *actively involved in reducing and eliminating them* (author's emphasis) from arsenals. Cordaro and the other prophets, Catholic and non-Catholic alike, were inspired to carry out the charge laid down in that document. That clause encouraged them to intensify their protest efforts. But the part of the message that provided an excuse for nuclear nations provided an excuse for the courts, as well.

Even today, not many bishops are willing to let their priests carry out the resistance to war that the bishops' words seem to exhort. In the cases of layman Kevin McGuire, father of three, and Marylyn Felion, the Church betrayed them and turned them over to the FBI; it did the same to Mike Palecek, father of two children.

The Catholic Church more recently raised the stakes against protesters when it threatened to excommunicate Cordaro. He calls the excommunication threat "absurd," and he takes the Church's own moral dichotomy in stride:

I'm comfortable identifying my relationship with the Roman Catholic Church as my family. There's some things I have real trouble with — the institutional structural stuff — but the Church is more than that. The Church is more than the bishops and the hierarchical structure. It's more than the dogma. Those aren't the things that are attractive about the Church for me. It's a living, breathing human and spiritual family. It's just that the family members at large cannot go on breathing and living with all the wars and the godless finality of nuclear weapons.

In the meantime, Fr. Cordaro is equally at ease in helping his farm-parishioners protest national and political policies that lead to foreclosures on family farms. While many of the same people disagree politically with their priest over disarmament, they receive comfort from his spiritual and moral support in secular matters. They they know he is sympathetic to their difficulties, such as how they can feed their families from the depressed prices they receive for the food they grow for the rest of the country.

Cordaro has also become a champion of all prison inmates, no matter what crime they might have committed.

"Many of them acknowledge their crimes. They know why *they* are in prison," Cordaro says. "But they just can't believe the federal government is sending anybody up for six months for doing what *I'm* doing. They think it's so minor. I think (when they know about me) it has a positive effect on inmates. Their whole scene is degrading to begin with. It helps them to see that the government jails even priests who don't do anything but step across lines and try to speak for peace. It helps them to see they are not the problem. The prison system itself, the society that sentences them, is the greatest violator of human rights. The system becomes the real criminal (which is not to excuse what they have done)."

Tom Cordaro and Angela Cordaro

Having served several terms in federal prisons, Father Cordaro's brother, Tom, knows all about how the government deprives inmates like him of even their limited prison rights. Being held incommunicado by the legal system is a violation of everyone's constitutional rights, whether a prisoner or not. Being held incommunicado for weeks and months on end is exactly what happened to Tom Cordaro. He calls what happened to him, "Floating Siberia." The technique is simple: For any reason, real or imagined, prisoners can be placed on what is called "disciplinary transfer." That means they are in a lockdown situation and moved from place to place. This is used primarily for murderers, rapists, robbers and "troublemakers."

"It has the effect," Tom Cordaro says, "of making you disappear. When you get to the new place, you may not have the ability or right to make a phone call, to write a letter or contact anyone on the outside. And when you finally get a stamp to mail a letter, you may be moved again before your friends can get a letter back to you. It's a way of keeping prisoners in this no-man's land. . . the Floating Siberia.

"In fact," Tom Cordaro says, "the last time I was in the federal system, I started in Omaha. Then I went to Sandstone, Minnesota; then Leavenworth, Terre Haute, and Chicago, and finally, from Chicago back to Sandstone, which was my original intended destination. This was on a 50-day sentence. So they keep you in transit to keep you out of touch. It's like twisting the knife or rubbing salt in a wound.

"But the one letter that I was able to get out to my mother during this period helped. The letter got into the hands of the *National Catholic Reporter* and the publicity organized the whole damned country. They were swamped with letters, just overwhelmed. They got so frightened that when I got to Terre Haute, they decided to put me in a camp. A lot of the public would not have known about this Floating Siberia, otherwise."

Tom Cordaro, who worked for the national office of *Pax Christi*, brushes aside the sobriquet of prophet and as of 1999 is the "Peace and Justice" relations man at St. Margaret's Parish in Naperville, Illinois. Tom ought to know about prophets, because he once published an ecumenical national newspaper called *Voice of the Prophet* designed to acquaint students on more than a hundred secular campuses with social-political issues of the day.

"The prophets of this world," he says, "are the poor. They tell us, by comparison, just who we are, in ways very plain to see."

Angela Cordaro, widowed mother of six and supporter of her two "radical" sons, also has been arrested for crossing the arbitrary property line at Offutt Air Force Base. She was placed on probation. She says, "I am very ashamed of my country. I'm ashamed. I . . . you know this flag deal that (George W.) Bush is pushing out here . . . I can remember parades where the hair on my arms would stand up straight when my flag went by. I haven't . . . I haven't had that feeling for a long, long time.

Mrs. Cordaro may not be at peace with her leaders, but her priest-son Frank has made his peace with his bishop, settling their differences over his style of protest. Father Frank operates more behind the scenes now, through his *Catholic Worker* efforts, advising others on what actions to take without using his pulpit to promote public confrontation. And so, he stays involved where the social action is and acts as a "substitute" priest at parishes in need of weekly mass and sacraments.

His involvement continues. In August 2001, he was arrested again at Offutt Air Force Base. He and three others were caught praying on the wrong side of the entrance to the base. Cordaro's trial was postponed due to a heart attack, from which he is recovering.

Bishop Dingman

The Cordaro family has not been alone in dueling with the Pentagon. Father Frank had a true friend and mentor in Maurice Dingman, the bishop of the Des Moines diocese, who had sponsored him through the seminary and had ordained him. Bishop Dingman was in the process of mobilizing other US bishops to protest against nuclear arms when he suffered a stroke in 1986; he died in 1992.

In one of his last public statements, at a parish rally in Glenwood, Iowa, Bishop Dingman told a resistance-retreat crowd of 600 people: "This meeting is in keeping with the peace message that we Catholic bishops of the United States wrote in May 1983. Part of that document speaks about a non-violent approach. We haven't really done much about that up to this point."

He then led the group to the gates of Offutt Air Force Base. With his toes on the white line, Bishop Dingman, as reported in the *Omaha World-Herald* on February 15, 1985, had this to say about America's war-making proclivities:

> We tremble as we stand at the gates of SAC, this place that could unleash on the world a nuclear holocaust. Today we pray for release from the captivity of our trust in weapons and the arms race, which are brutalizing us.
>
> It seems to me that we can win a war without any weapons, that we can really preserve our freedoms and our peace if we can engage in a new kind of approach. We don't have to use weapons. We can use our minds and our wills and use a moral means.

Dingman's jaw tightened, the Omaha newspaper reported, as he watched first of several groups of protesters cross the white line drawn on the road at the base gate. Sending the cadres of protesters across the white line, in orderly fashion, was Father (then Deacon) Frank Cordaro.

As Bishop Dingman watched the last of 226 protesters cross the white line to be arrested, he said, "We have to bring to the attention of our decision-makers that we have to get rid of these weapons. It is a great danger to our future."

In another time and another place, but under similar circumstances, Rev. Daniel Berrigan, S.J., warned the world that "We are captives of our future."

"Those are the words of a prophet," Cordaro says, "fallen by the wayside that Christ talked about."

Sowing the Seeds

Fifty two people were taken hostage at the US embassy in Tehran on November 4, 1979, but the crisis began long before that date.

More accurately, the Iranians' action was a hand-me-down from the Red Line Agreement of 1927 among Western oil interests, as they drew property lines across the oil field maps of the Middle East.

The embassy takeover also was a delayed reaction to the ouster of Premier Mossadegh, in 1953, when the Shah Mohammed Reza Pahlevi was restored to the Peacock Throne by US and British intrigue. It was, finally, a way to get even for the brutal terrorism served up to the Ayatollah Khomeini and his followers in June 1963 when they tried to overthrow the Shah. Here is one press report:

TEHRAN, IRAN, June 6, 1963

— More than 30 Moslem religious leaders were arrested in Iran as riots spread from Tehran to other cities. One of those arrested was the Ayatollah Khomeini. Iranian security officials (SAVAK) say Khomeini and others were trying to topple the regime of Shah Mohammed Reza Pahlevi. The fighting in Tehran became so intense that the Shah and his family took refuge at the summer palace at Saadabad.

Shiite mobs were allegedly recruited and paid by the religious leaders, who are opposed to the Shah's land reforms and new rights for women. Three unveiled women were killed by one mob, according to reports on the streets.

Under pressure from Western influences, the Shah has been urging Moslem women to unveil their faces and even wear attire fashionable in Paris or New York in defiance of Moslem law on such matters.

The fate of the Ayatollah remains unknown at this time. In the past, SAVAK, the Shah's security force, has been accused of torturing and killing opponents of the regime. Knowledgeable sources say that a more likely fate for the Ayatollah is exile.

Years later, after the Western nations had endured the 1973 OPEC oil embargo, Mideast oil once again was on the mind of the US president:

CARTER SAYS US MUST TREAT OIL CRISIS LIKE WAR
WASHINGTON, D.C., April 18, 1977 — In a televised speech to the nation this evening, President Jimmy Carter warned that the US must respond "to the moral equivalent of war" to the nation's dwindling oil supplies.

War of a very real kind, with little morality, developed under the intentions of the United States. Years after the Ayatollah Khomeini had been forced into exile by the Shah of Iran, this news article hit the media. It bannered the onset of the Mideast oil wars:

PARIS, FRANCE, October 6, 1978 — The French government today granted refuge to the Ayatollah Khomeini after he was ordered expelled from political asylum in Iraq, where he has been since his rebellion against the Shah of Iran in 1963.

The Baghdad regime ordered him out of the country as a gesture of peace to Iran. The Ayatollah has been agitating against the regime of the Shah from a base in Iraq.

Khomeini had nowhere to go until Iranian imams prevailed on French President Giscard d'Estaing. The move shocked most of France's Western allies.

Khomeini made no concessions in accepting French asylum, saying: "No satisfying solution to the Iranian political problem is possible without the disappearance of the Pahlevi dynasty."

The march of headlines prior to the takeover of the US embassy in Tehran hinted at that possibility:

November 6, 1978 — SHAH PUTS ARMY IN CHARGE OF IRAN
December, 1978 — MILLIONS MARCH AGAINST SHAH IN IRAN
January 30, 1978 — SHAH FLEES IRAN
February 1979 — KHOMEINI TAKES OVER IN IRAN
May 26, 1979 — KHOMEINI BLAMES US FOR ATTEMPT ON AIDE
October 22, 1979 — SHAH IS BROUGHT TO NEW YORK HOSPITAL

Of course, the final headline in that series was on November 4, 1979, when Iranian students loyal to Khomeini seized the US embassy and took all its occupants hostage. It happened one year to the day after the Shah's forces had shot and killed rioting students at the University of Tehran. Iran, like the US, suffered its own Kent State crisis. But the US leaders did not see the corollary.

However, the real trigger for the embassy invasion in Tehran was the admission into the United States of the Shah, ostensibly for treatment of cancer. By the 6th of November, the moderate government of Prime Minister Bazargan was dissolved, leaving the Ayatollah in complete command.

"This is not a struggle between the United States and Iran," the religious leader told his nation, "This is a struggle between Iran and blasphemy." He urged the students to stand firm, saying, "Why should we be afraid? We consider martyrdom a great honor."

The students added a few themes of their own: "Khomeini struggles; Carter trembles"; "Carter is supporting this nasty criminal under the pretext of sickness." This banner was placed above the heads of 10 US embassy hostages, four white women and six black men, all of whom they voluntarily released on the 20th of November.

It is believed the women were released because of certain Moslem taboos about contact with women. The blacks were released because they were considered an already-oppressed minority in the US However, at least one black hostage, Charles Jones, continued to be held because he was thought to be a CIA agent, along with two other women.

After tentative diplomatic exchanges, the Carter Administration ordered all Iranian assets in the US frozen — and all communication, to boot.

The immediate question asked by the American public, which was taken wholly unawares by all this drama, was, Why? Why all this Iranian rage? Why this drastic action? Their ignorance was due to deliberate governmental disinformation. The US government was not about to give the public a true list of the causes. But if the public had had such a list, it would have read — in reverse chronological order:

- The United States had frozen billions of dollars in Iranian assets.
- The US, a non-Moslem country, was sheltering the Shah.
- The US had made, or sponsored, an attempt on the life of one of the Ayatollah's aides, Ayatollah Hashemi Rafsanjani, the previous May.
- They had orchestrated the banishment of Khomeini in 1963 for protesting the Shah's corruption of Moslem traditions and culture.
- SAVAK, the Shah's secret police who were established by the CIA, had terrorized and murdered Iranian citizens for years.
- The Shah had presided over the establishment of the "Seven Sisters" oil agreement under ARAMCO.
- The Shah had been selling Iranian oil to the West for years, pocketing millions of dollars in kickbacks and accepting bribes for permitting drug trafficking — promoted by the CIA in order to fund its illicit programs.
- The United States and CIA had played a major role in overthrowing Premier Mossadegh, who had nationalized Iran's oil industry.
- The Red Line Agreement of 1927 gave non-Iranian companies control of Iran's oil.

Historical antecedents aside, the Iranian student hostage-takers wanted just two things: 1) the extradition of the Shah back to Tehran; 2) an acknowledgment from the US that it had wrongly installed and supported the Pahlevi regime, with terrorism. A return of the Shah would have amounted to such an admission.

In addition, there was one other hidden irritant that not even Khomeini could talk about publicly: The crown jewels, the basis of Iran's *rial* monetary system, had been stolen by the Shah when he left the country.

Uncertain of the fiscal and monetary consequences of discussing that event in public, the Ayatollah was seething. He was no economist, but he had to run the country as if he were. And although the Iranian economy was now basically driven by oil, disclosing the loss of the jewels, symbolic as it was, could have very real consequences in the foreign exchange market. The economic well-being of the Ayatollah's Moslem faithful, and his country, hung in the balance. Having alienated the country's best oil customer for the sake of his theocracy, he had to make sure that the theocracy would endure.

Here is how the Ayatollah perceived insult heaped on injury: the hated Shah and his American allies had killed, tortured and persecuted his people under the bloody fist of the CIA-trained SAVAK; they had plundered Iran's oil assets; they had corrupted Islam among his people; they had stolen the crown jewels; and now, on the pretext of the Shah's illness, the "Satan" had sheltered the Shah in New York — placing the jewels in the vaults of the Rockefellers' Chase Manhattan Bank, the correspondent of Tehran's Bank Melli.

It was not until after the Shah's death that the theft of the crown jewels came to light.

The headlines in two successive issues of an obscure Denver weekly newspaper, the *Rocky Mountain Journal*, explain it best:

ARE THE CROWN JEWELS MISSING?
JEWELS BASIS FOR CURRENCY
DID SHAH SCUTTLE IRANIAN CURRENCY?
AMERICAN "PIGEON" TELLS OF IRAN IN THE FINAL DAYS OF SHAH'S RULE

The substance of these articles was this: that the Shah of Iran in his final day of power took with him the crown jewels of Iran, which were the basis of the country's currency, the *rial*.

The sense of pillage that the theft of the crown jewels caused contributed to the takeover of the US Embassy and the prolonged holding of the hostages. It was, after all, a question as much of symbols as of economic reality.

In turn, the seizing of hostages led to the seizing of Iran's cash assets in US and European banks. The actions and counter-actions led to a frenzy of follow-on events, including perceived threats against the hostages, the illicit visit of Rupiper with the hostages, and the war between Iran and Iraq.

One outstanding episode in that frenzy was the unsuccessful hostage rescue attempt by the Carter Administration and the illegal actions by the

Reagan Administration to ransom, in secret, the hostages for money and guns. When that illegal plan later came to light, it unmasked the Iran-Contra scandal that violated US policy on Central America as set in laws passed by Congress.

The story of the Shah's theft, published in a newspaper that was hardly nationally known in 1980, did not cause much of a stir. The Iranians already knew what had happened, and the American public had other concerns. The US was planning its raid to rescue the hostages, and the administration was not eager to confirm the news.

The major regional media (*Rocky Mountain News, Denver Post* and Associated Press) picked up only a few carefully edited paragraphs of the weekly's story. The world thereby was deprived of an understanding of the underlying cause of Iran's continuing hatred for the US — and it was thereby doomed to another decade of political intrigues and death for thousands.

Following are some excerpts from the *Rocky Mountain Journal* article of February 20, 1980 about the crown jewels:

> Iran's deposed Shah apparently removed at least some of his country's crown jewels the backing for that nation's currency, just before he vacated the Peacock Throne — a move that could have serious economic ramifications, the Rocky Mountain Journal has learned.
>
> Reports reaching the Journal that the Shah may have taken the priceless jewels — an act similar to stealing the gold in Fort Knox — were confirmed last week by Ali Khorram, the San Francisco-based consul general for the Islamic Republic of Iran. He said, "I am sure the Shah did take some of them (the jewels) with him."
>
> Speaking through his personal secretary, Juanita Deness, Khorram added that he would "assume" the crown jewels would be one of the areas of inquiry to be undertaken by the United Nation's commission in its promised probe of alleged "crimes" leveled by the Iranian government against Shah Mohammed Reza Pahlevi.
>
> The Journal was tipped to the possibility of the disappearance of the jewels several weeks ago by an American who spent two years in Tehran and whose work brought close contact with top officials of the Shah's regime.
>
> Beyond the financial impact of the jewels, however, lies another story told to the Journal by the American informant. The original

source of the informant's story was Iranian Premier Gholam Reza Azhari in late 1978, just as the Shah was making plans to flee Iran.

Azhari revealed a long-range plan for the eventual return of the Shah's son, Crown Prince Reza, now 19, to the Peacock throne. This was to be accomplished by fomenting a schism between two rival ayatollahs, Ruhollah Khomeini and Shariemadari. The private conversation with the American informant took place as Azhari, then chief of staff of Iran's armed forces, was about to be named as premier of a newly formed military government. That government was to last a mere two months (from November 1978 to January 1979) when the Shah replaced Azhari with Shanpour Bakhtiar and a civilian government in an unsuccessful eleventh-hour stab to maintain control of the throne.

Azhari charged that ARAMCO had conspired to dump the Shah "because the Shah would not go along with the price increases OPEC (the Organization of Petroleum Exporting Countries) wanted," the source said. (ARAMCO is the Arabian-American Oil Co., consisting of Exxon, Texaco, Shell, SOCAL, Gulf, Mobil and British Petroleum. Along with the Arabian Oil Company, this combine of companies acts as the marketing arm for most of the oil exported from the Middle East.)

"Azhari said that when the Shah was gone, the Ayatollah Khomeini would come in. Then the plan was to get rid of Khomeini in favor of the Shah's son (then 18). He would come back to the country when he was 21 because at that age the people would respect him as an adult," the informant told the *Journal*.

"Azhari said there was an ayatollah (Shariemadari) in the north, near Iraq, who did not like Khomeini and who was going to be their instrument in getting rid of Khomeini.

"The interesting thing," the *Journal's* informant said, "was when he (Azhari) told me that whenever the Shah leaves the country you, (America) will get your peace treaty signed between Israel and Egypt. That prediction came true."

The informant's conversation with Azhari, referenced in this article, took place in December 1978. By January 1979, the Shah had fled Iran to Egypt, and the Ayatollah Khomeini returned from his year-long exile in Paris. In March 1979, the peace treaty between Egypt and Israel was signed.

In July of that year, the last of the US-backed Somoza family dictators was ousted in Nicaragua, signaling events that would lead to Iran-Contra.

In September 1979 the Shah of Iran was brought to New York for treatment of cancer after a sojourn from Egypt to the Bahamas to Mexico. That same month, the Soviets invaded Afghanistan, an event that would begin to change the world, moving it another big step forward toward September 11, 2001.

Reaping What was Sown

In November 1979, an angry mob of Iranian students invaded the US embassy in Tehran and took hostages. In December 1979, an unauthorized delegation of 49 Americans, including Father Rupiper, visited the hostages. Rupiper and two others returned for Easter in April 1980. Just days after their visit, a helicopter raid to free the hostages failed. The Shah eventually died in exile, in Egypt, in August 1980.

The following month, the CIA's war erupted between Iran and Iraq, just as the *Journal's* informant was told by Azhari it would, once Egypt and Israel had buried the hatchet. For the next few years, Saddam Hussein, armed to the teeth by the US, remained a friend fighting Iran on behalf of his ally. Then he found out the US was sending arms to Iran. Saddam didn't know about the Iran-Contra deal, but he did know he had been double-crossed. He took the war with Iran to a stalemate and then began plotting revenge against the US.

While the theft of the crown jewels had hardened Iran's resolve in 1979, the match that had lit the fuse in Tehran was the United States' admission of the Shah. Indeed, the Shah had contracted cancer and needed medical attention; but New York was not the world's only center of medical excellence.

New York was, however, home to the Rockefeller's Chase Manhattan Bank, the US correspondent bank for Bank Melli in Tehran, where the crown jewels were supposed to reside. The Shah, sick or not, needed to make a "deposit" if his heir to the Peacock Throne were ever to use these symbols to reclaim that throne.

Everyone in the Carter Administration knew the danger of a blow-up in Iran if the Shah were allowed into the US. An embassy takeover was a known danger. Ways of working around this problem were intimately discussed by State Department officials far in advance.

Here is an "EYES ONLY" letter, dated August 2, 1979, three months before the Tehran Embassy takeover. A copy of this letter was given to Rupiper by an Iranian friend long after its origination; it is from Henry

Precht, director of the Office of Iranian Affairs, to L. Bruce Laingen, chargé d'affaires of the US embassy in Tehran. It is a kind of "smoking gun," where fault for the takeover is concerned. It reads:

> Dear Bruce:
>
> I was finally able to see your cable dealing with the same subject as the enclosed piece. I liked your thoughts very much and believe — with a few details of difference — we are in accord. My paper was prepared at Newsome's request with strict instructions not to cut anyone else in except those shown as clearing and Peter. So please protect me absolutely.
>
> Sincerely,
> Henry Precht

[The first page of the attached memorandum is missing. Page 2 picks up:]

> We should begin to prepare the Iranians by telling them of the intense pressures for the Shah to come here — pressures which we are resisting despite our traditional open-door policy.
>
> If the constitutional process does not proceed and the Iranian instability seriously increases, and if there is no prospect for Iran to settle down, there may be an argument for going ahead and admitting the Shah anyway to get the inevitable step behind us. But it will be necessary first to review how dangerous the situation is.
>
> In either of these scenarios we should aim for a positive change in our position on the Shah by January, 1980. [Here, there is a marginal notation by Laingen: "why so early?"] If this plan is adopted it probably would not be advisable to disseminate it beyond a close circle in the Executive Branch; perhaps a few key individuals outside might be informed so as to reduce pressures for a change. We would have to discuss the issues with Members of Congress to indicate that we were addressing the issue and hope to resolve it successfully. This would reduce pressures which could lead, for example, to a Congressional resolution calling on the administration to admit the Shah. However, this would increase the likelihood of leaks and our having to deal with the provisional government before we are ready.
>
> Conditions: It would help substantially in explaining our position to the Iranians if the Shah were to renounce his family's claim to the throne. We believe the likelihood of his doing so is extremely remote, but the idea could be explored privately by trusted intermediaries so

that if the Shah refused, he would have no possibility of blaming the USG [US government] for a course he rejected.

Should the Shah refuse to renounce his claim, we should leave no doubt in the Iranian mind as to our attitude. We should make it quite clear publicly that we consider any claim to the throne by his family rendered invalid by the Iranian constitutional process, and we should make it clear privately to the Shah and his friends that we would not tolerate any counter-revolutionary acts here which might violate US law, or our customary policies regarding political activities of persons admitted for temporary visits.

Security: We have the impression that the threat to US embassy personnel is less now than it was in the spring; presumably the threat will diminish somewhat further by the end of this year. Nevertheless, the danger of hostages being taken in Iran will persist.

We should make no move towards admitting the Shah until we have obtained and tested a new and substantially more effective guard force for the embassy. Secondly, when the decision is made to admit the Shah, we should quietly assign additional American security guards to the embassy to provide protection for key personnel until the danger period is considered over.

Before proceeding further we should have more detailed work on the legal, security and Congressional relations issues. [Laingen here scribbles a note: "How this done?"]

This letter and memorandum:

1) Shows that the US knew that the Shah was going to be bounced out months before it happened, and that a takeover of the embassy would occur if the Shah came to the US; but it vastly underestimates the immediacy of such a reaction.

2) It suggests getting the Shah to renounce his family's claim to the throne as a conciliatory gesture to Iran, to avoid a totally hostile takeover. But there was no follow through. In other words, it indicates that at least part of the official opinion in Washington favored dumping the Shah in recognition of the mood of the Iranian people. (American public was never told this.) But it assumes that the Shah would never agree, and that inevitably the Shah would have to be let into the US.

3) It shows reluctance to share information with the Congress and with the White House because of fears about the results of a potential public disclosure. This probably proved fatal, bringing on exactly what was feared.

4) It shows State Department officials' obsession with protecting their flanks. This explains how such debacles as the embassy takeover were allowed to happen despite knowledge of what was coming. Whether these suspicions were properly conveyed to the President is unknown. If they were, then Jimmy Carter made poor and even arrogant decisions in the White House.

5) It shows that State was willing to promote discussions about a post-Shah government before the Shah had capitulated, and that it did not want to stage a counter-revolution to re-establish the Shah. Why this attitude was never conveyed to the Ayatollah after the Shah left seems stupid and fatal.

A search for the figures most closely connected to this memo, conducted years later, led to informational dead-ends. Besides Precht, Michael J. Howland, Bruce Laingen, Victor Tomseth, Donald Cooke, Charles Jones, Jr., Richard H. Morefield, and Phillip Ward were involved. All held some sort of official embassy positions at the time of the takeover. All of them refused follow-up contact with the clerics who had visited them in 1980. Phone and Internet inquiries made 20 years later produce responses such as "action canceled", or "this site unavailable."

In any case, the above memo amounts to a smoking gun held by Jimmy Carter and Ronald Reagan, on behalf of the United States of America. Reagan's election-team cabal was working behind Carter's back at the time the memo was written, to win credit for the hostage release on inauguration day.

The question becomes, who pulled the trigger? Who fired the gun that resulted in the ascension of Ayatollah Ruhollah Khomeini, instead of the more moderate forces, in Iran?

The answer: Zbigniew Brzezinski, the alpha-male advisor to the National Security Council under Carter and co-progenitor of the Trilateral Commission. His war-mongering stance, leading to chaos in Iran, is outlined by William H. Sullivan, former ambassador to Iran, in an article in *Foreign Review*, Fall 1980. Sullivan's fulmination against Brzezinski shows that both of them had an intimate knowledge of Laingen's memo to Henry Precht, who had charge of the Iranian desk of the State Department. It shows that:

1) Sullivan agreed the Shah should not be allowed to enter the US, a recommendation that Brzezinski overruled. Why? Brzezinski thought a military confrontation with rebel elements, using loyal remnants of the Iranian army (then leaderless) might win the day.

2) Sullivan warned the White House that letting the Shah into the

US might produce a riot or takeover at the US Embassy in Tehran.

3) Sullivan tried to arrange, through the Shah, a peaceful transition government that might have prevented the embassy takeover by the Iranian students.

4) Sullivan told the White House the Shah would rather abdicate than ask his army, at this point, to "kill his own people." (This indicates that the Shah wanted to cut the puppet strings connecting the CIA and SAVAK, after 25 years of being induced by the US to terrorize his people; but this change of heart came only after the Shah had extracted somewhere between $2.5 billion and $25 billion in Iranian assets.)

5) Sullivan's warnings and memos were junked by the National Security Council so that Brzezinski's plans to put down the Iranian uprising by force might be implemented.

6) Even as Sullivan tried to coordinate a transition of power from the Shah to the transitional government and then to the exiled Ayatollah Khomeini in Paris, Brzezinski asked Sullivan on an unsecured telephone line whether Sullivan could arrange a military coup against the emerging revolution.

As Sullivan, frustrated by months of having his delicate negotiations ignored, puts it in his white paper on the matter, "I regret that the reply I made (to Brzezinski) is unprintable."

Sullivan's accounting dovetails neatly with the account of events in Iran as reported in the Denver newspaper article, the source of which was a person teaching in the American School in Tehran, whose identity in 1980 was given only as "the pigeon."

It seems the pigeon, as a teacher of the offspring of highly-placed Iranian officials, had the confidence of Gen. Gholam Azhari. The General had been installed by the Shah on November 5, 1978, as head of a provisional military government assigned to put down the rioting in Tehran.

While Sullivan was telling Washington that Azhari might be the last chance for the Shah to control the revolutionary dynamics, Azhari was telling his little son's teacher that there was a counter-revolutionary plan to restore the Shah's son to the Peacock Throne once the Shah left and the dust had settled.

The key part to settling that dust involved inciting a civil war among Ayatollahs Khomeini, Khameini and Shariemadari. This was to be accompanied by a war between Iran and Iraq, which the US by this time was arming heavily, even with chemical weapons, through arm's-length deals.

Such was the background of events that subsequently drove the recent history of Iran, Iraq, Kuwait, White House politics and even Central America, once Iran seized the US embassy in Tehran.

All of these events and others would conspire to involve one of the prophets from Recife, Brazil, Darrell Rupiper. When he went to Tehran, he already had in his possession the Precht memo showing the US's obtuseness. Rupiper didn't recognize, at the time, that the memo would become the possible motive for the killing of his Iranian friend in Omaha — which he took as a warning from the CIA that he should stay out of Iran and keep his mouth shut.

Walter Cronkite used to sign off his television newscast by saying, "What kind of day was it? A day like all days, filled with the events which alter and illuminate our times." Perhaps neither he nor his audience understood exactly how the days altered, and how little they illuminated, the times in which the heroes of this book were living and the people for whom they spoke. For these were the same days that affected everyone, princes, paupers and prophets alike, in their corners of unreported darkness.

Later, Cronkite took to saying, "And that's the way it is." The prophets might have added, "but doesn't have to be."

The US government, with all its military power, was unable to react directly against Iran and the Ayatollah Khomeini for several reasons. Brzezinski however, was looking for a covert counter-revolutionary path. In the meantime, he ruled out non-military options, by forbidding official-channel contacts with the Ayatollah prior to the imam's return from his exile in Paris. This thwarted Ambassador William Sullivan in his search for ways to support a peaceful transition away from the Shah before hostilities broke out. The Carter Administration position was that there could be no benefit in communicating with the Iranians. The US was not talking to Iran (except through insults in the mass media); Washington doesn't negotiate with "terrorists". It called the Iranian students terrorists and said that anyone who talked with them was a traitor.

The somewhat specious arguments against direct action included that:

1. Any military action against Tehran would likely result in the slaughter of the hostages. (Contacts by Rupiper and others later indicated that the devout Moslem students did not want war with the US and would not kill their captives outright.) They did not do so, even after the abortive assault by Carter. But, with communication cut off, no one could have known.

2. Oil-producing Moslem countries would construe any direct massive attack as an attack upon the Islamic world, creating allies for Iran and drawing in the Soviet Union on the basis of political opportunism.

3. Any large-scale military action would put Israel at risk — America's best client state in the Middle East. Islamic Arabs would eagerly seize any excuse to drive Israel out of Palestine.

• The fallacy of this position was proven by Norm Forer, the Kansas University professor who sent Rupiper and others to Iran. In effect, the US policy against communicating with the Iranians turned 52 hostages into pawns and made impossible their extraction by any practical means. The only way out for them was by way of back-door deals, and that's exactly what happened.

Even before Reagan was elected, his backers (including ex-CIA chief George Bush and soon-to-be CIA chief William Casey) paid $40 million to Iranian President Bani-Sadr, in a Paris hotel, in October 1980. The main condition was that Iran delay the release of the hostages until after Reagan's inauguration. In this way, Reagan borrowed a page from Nixon's Vietnamese pre-election tactics against LBJ at a time when the incumbent non-candidate was trying to negotiate peace with Hanoi.

This Reagan scheme, later quietly called, in CIA circles, "The October Surprise," was designed to assure that Carter could not gain release of the hostages — just in case he found any way of doing so before the election.

With that deal, never revealed to the hostages or their families, came the secret promise of future gun deliveries to Iran. The US was undertaking to restore a balance of military power in the oil-rich Persian Gulf — a balance which the US had upset during its military dalliance with Iraq. These events, of course, subsequently led to the Iran-Contra scandal, which also involved hostage taking in Beirut at one of the critical points in the struggle between Israel and the Palestine Liberation Organization (PLO).

Meanwhile, back home, at about the time the Iranian students were storming the embassy, Rupiper and Kabat were being arrested for protesting the arms bazaar in Chicago. Rupiper had no notion of going to Iran. However, while the students on the campus of Tehran University busied themselves with their new importance as captors, in 1979, there were movements afoot on at least two campuses in the US that would break the stony wall of hatred and silence, if only for a short time, between the US and Iran. Those who made the effort would draw the wrath of the CIA, the US State Department and the Carter Administration; personal sanctions would follow, including murder committed as a warning signal.

Rev. Darrell Rupiper would be at the heart of this breakthrough. But when it all was over, this man, who himself had been a prisoner several times, would know what it means to be a Prophet Without Honor in his own land — even among those he had sought to comfort and set free.

Respect

Rupiper's role evolved in this way: a professor of industrial relations at the University of Kansas, Norm Forer, and Methodist pastor Jack Bremer, had formed an ad hoc group known as the American-Iranian Crisis Resolution Committee.

At the time of the hostage crisis a large contingent of Iranian students happened to be registered at the Lawrence campus — they had been sent to colleges that were thought to be docile enough to coexist with the Iranians. As the confrontation between the Shah and the Iranian dissidents in Tehran grew from 1978 to 1979, Forer and Bremer were engaged by their own campus administration to try to stave off any hostilities between American and Iranian students on campus. They also sought to head off fights among factions of the Iranians themselves, who sometimes had differing views of the regime of the Shah and the Ayatollah, who was still in exile. This work started as a process of student focus groups.

The effort had barely begun when the students in Tehran captured the US Embassy. The crisis group shifted into high gear. From years of labor union experience, Forer knew the power of negotiating. "You have to get the parties talking and keep them talking," Forer says.

Out of the nucleus of student discussions and panels emerged the idea of exchanging visits between students from Tehran, who by now were holding hostages, and students from American campuses, especially at Lawrence. Gradually, that idea was refined: a group of Americans, representative of its grassroots, were to visit Tehran and open person-to-person talks with some of the captors. Then a group of Iranians would visit the campus at Lawrence and hold face-to-face meetings with their counterparts.

Both professors had contacts within the US government, who had contacts with the US State Department. With a little string-pulling and arm-twisting, the first phase was set up: the trip for 49 or 50 to be taken in December 1979. A reluctant State Department approved the passports, but there was to be no publicity originated by the group.

"A friend of mine in the Justice Department convinced State that this might be an informal way to open two locked doors," Forer explains. "Our story was that once the informal part was done, then the heavy-duty officials could walk through those doors, sit down and talk, with both sides saving face. No pre-conditions except the willingness to talk and air grievances.

"Behind the scenes, some brave souls in State bought the idea, but without any official sanction."

Amazingly, the funding for airline tickets came from the students in Tehran, which Forer says shows something about their interest in breaking the impasse, and their fear of triggering war.

"Sure," the voluble Forer says, "they could get some propaganda windfall, so what? I'll tell you what: the Iranians were afraid there would be a war, an invasion by the US. They weren't afraid of dying, as I learned from the Iranians on the Lawrence campus. They were afraid of what suffering and misery might ensue to the survivors. They had a conscience, these people. They were afraid that the Americans didn't care a bit about causing suffering because they had inflicted so much terror under the regime of the Shah and the fist of SAVAK. I had some personal experience.

"Before the overthrow of the Shah, there were two or three SAVAK agents on campus (Lawrence, Kansas) tracking the movements, the actions, the thoughts of Iranian students. As I got involved with the Iranian students, I received a mysterious phone call from one agent. I recognized him from his high-pitched squeaky kind of voice. One of the students had previously warned me about him. He had called my family first, then me, with veiled threats.

"I am known for being somewhat long-winded and circuitous in my discourse," Forer says. "Not this time. I told him if he ever called me at home again I would cut him a new asshole."

It was not all bluster. Forer is a tough-minded Russian Jew who had emigrated to the US years before. Usually soft-spoken and soft-mannered, he cut his American teeth as a labor negotiator in the New York area. While in Russia, he was known as a member of an opposition underground Jewish labor group. In his years of travel and teaching, Forer had developed personal relationships with Mossadegh and with other moderate Iranians such as Bani-Sadr and Sadegh Ghotzbadeh, who were not on the side of the Shah.

In fact, he had made a secret trip to Iran in 1977 to learn more about the growing movement there against the Shah. Forer's SAVAK caller, of course, knew all of this and knew that any threat by Forer to ream a new orifice in his large bowel could be made to happen, at least figuratively.

"I am not a violent man," Forer says, excusing his verbiage. "I just wanted to scare him off. That's all SAVAK understands. But there was a time when I told my friends that if I ever died under mysterious circumstances, it would be the doing of SAVAK or connections they might have with CIA."

Apparently the threat worked, and Forer was not bothered after that, especially after the Shah lost power. So he and Bremer (who later moved to Northwestern University, before retiring) proceeded with their plans for the Tehran trip of 49. As he explains,

"The tough part was in selecting those who should go. Naturally, all the big names of the protest movement wanted on board. But I didn't want a lot of conflicting egos. I wanted grassroots. I polled some of the peace groups for recruits. I also wanted a cross-section of Americans: men, women, Jews, Catholics, Protestants, blacks, whites, other minorities.

"*Nebraskans for Peace* recommended Father Rupiper. It was an excellent choice. He had a large following among students and peace activists through his ministry in Omaha. He had guts, but no ego. He stood up against the brass at SAC, and he took his time in jail for his cause. He wasn't a bomb-thrower. I needed people like that, cool under pressure, who weren't identified as US stooges. Grassroots America. Religious. Somebody the other side could trust.

"Rup understood that this was not a negotiation. This trip was simply to show the other side that not all of America was hostile to them. That Americans could listen without trying to force a point of view.

"Part of our problem was William Sloane Coffin (Yale Chaplain and noted dissenter over Vietnam). He had been over there earlier with me and a few others as a precursor. We were trying to set up details for future visits and informal negotiation. We had the quiet help of a few thinkers in the State Department. But Coffin proved to be a grandstander. His premature efforts nearly blew the whole program that we were shaping at the time.

"Once he got to Tehran, Coffin tried to throw his weight and reputation around. He came off as if he were on the side of the US government instead of taking a neutral position. He demanded to see all the captives at the same time. For their own security reasons, the student-captors refused. They didn't like Coffin's attitude, and the overall reaction among them cast a shadow over the larger plan that called for the Iranian student-captors to visit Kansas.

"After our group's December visit, the Iranians decided against sending a delegation to Lawrence," Forer says. "So there went our plan to exchange roles. By this time, the State Department was against it, because if the Iranian students came over here, it would look like tacit recognition of the Iranian action. Just when it seemed like the whole deal would blow up, the Iranians made a counter-suggestion.

"If they could pick three people from the delegation of 49, and if we could send them back to Tehran, there might be a release of hostages, but not so close in time as to create the appearance of linkage.

"My God! It was a breakthrough. The State Department was against it, because their policy was not to negotiate with terrorists. But in this case, there was not any negotiation with any official. It was people to people. There was no *quid pro quo*. When certain of my friends in the Justice Department convinced the State Department of that point, the deal was on.

"So guess who the Iranians selected from the group of 49? A Protestant minister, Jack Bremer, who had helped organize the first visit, and a Catholic priest, Darrell Rupiper. To have a show of diversity, we invited a black Methodist minister, Warren Thompson of Kansas City. With my coordinating role (at home), there was a Jew in the mix. And we were talking with militant Moslems. It was a miniature United Nations."

Forer took out a second mortgage on his home to finance the trip for the delegation of three, which took place the first week in April 1980. It was just before Easter.

Rupiper, now in his '60s, talks about the trip:

"There were a few ground rules. First of all, we were there as guests of the Iranian people. It was understood we were not to smuggle out any communications or messages. (This would later cause him grief.) And we were not to offer hope of release to anyone.

"This was basically a goodwill mission. We were trying to open a few doors that the Iranians were willing to unlock. We weren't trying to kiss ass, nor did we expect any special favors for our side. I tried to be neutral. I knew we needed to listen.

"We knew they had valid reasons for their actions, and we intended to let them know our side had valid complaints for redress. Plus we wanted to do what we could to boost the morale of the hostages. We were as close as you can get to a visit from home. The Church says it is a work of mercy to visit the imprisoned.

"We met with the hostages in small groups, mostly two at a time. We would talk with them. Ask them if they were being mistreated in any way, because there was a lot of publicity about torture and mistreatment. They all said that was not the case. In fact, many of them said they had received books for reading, including the Bible, or birthday cakes on their birthday. They even played chess with their captors.

"Then I or one of the others would invite them to pray with us. Or read from the Bible. Most of them did. For the Catholics who wished, I would hear their confessions in private."

It was during his individual conversations with the hostages that Rupiper thought one of the hostages was having a tough time, emotionally and mentally. And so on April 8, Rupiper, according to the journal of Jack Bremer, offered to stay, himself, in place of the troubled hostage, whom Rupiper perceived as being "very nervous."

The entry in Bremer's personal log tells the story, never revealed to the media because the trio (Thompson, Bremer and Rupiper) thought it might sound contrived:

Bremer's Journal, April 8, 1980

Later Fr. Rupiper called me to his room (11 a.m.?) and told me of a special experience of opening the Bible randomly and reading the first verses of Galatians, in which Christ gave himself to free the world from evil powers: *Grace to you and peace from God our Father and the Lord Jesus Christ, who gave himself for our sins and set us free from the present evil age, according to the will of our God and Father to whom be the glory forever and ever. Amen* —Galatians, 1:3-5.

Also, a friend in Omaha had given him a verse on a folded piece of paper and asked him to open the paper and read the message while he was in Iran, so he (Rupiper) would know he was not alone. (It was John 16:32 — *The hour is coming, indeed it has come, when you will be scattered, each one to his home, and you will leave me alone. Yet I am not alone, because the Father is with me.*)

Darrell felt these verses were God's messages to him: that he should try to exchange himself for one of the hostages.

We met with Hussein, Mohammed and Moshe (the Iranian counterparts) to discuss this experience. Darrell told them the exchange would be a witness to our faith in their care for the hostages and of our faithfulness to Christ.

Earlier Rupiper had told me that he would like to borrow my Bible and also for me to meet personally with his parents to explain what had happened, in case he was accepted as a substitute for a hostage — one who is not enduring well and should be released. The hardest thing (Darrell said) would be on his family, whom he thought would understand and accept it.

Darrell told the Iranians: "I would want no privileges the others do not have, nor reveal any knowledge of political developments."

Hussein said that they praised Darrell's sacrifice and treasured our new friendship. Hussein said: "We need not say that you are good. God knows that. We have a similar way of opening the Koran and finding God's will. . . But the way things are. . . something somewhat different is needed."

Darrell and I had agreed earlier that it was important to be ready to accept a "no" as well as a "yes" to his offer. In either case, God's will would be done.

Mohammed and Moshe gave replies also, with assistance from Hussein. Moshe seemed to be the most authoritative. They said, "This is a very interesting experience for us."

Mohammed said that the act of taking hostages is not (one of) taking a nation hostage, to demand things of a nation; it is a state of war between forces of evil and good. "We see you (Rupiper) as a member of the American nation. But we saw them (the embassy staff) not as members of the American nation but as individuals who were plotting against us."

Moshe said, "Your offer (to exchange yourself for a hostage) is perfecting you, by putting yourself in the place of those who are suffering. This is a wonderful thing to do, freeing the captives, moving toward the perfection of God, holy and divine. But it would mean taking (you) a leader, representing the true American people. By taking you, it would confuse the identity of the Embassy as a center of evil activity."

[Jack here inserts a personal comment that he feels God is at work among the five talking at the table.] Then Moshe concludes by saying, "It is a good experience for us. To see this spirit of sacrifice in Christianity. God has already rewarded you inside for your intention."

That was how the Iranian hostage-holders said "no" to Fr. Rupiper's offer to exchange himself for one of the hostages. None of the parties said anything further about the offer, and the discussions and hostage interviews continued after that point, Rupiper explains.

"One of the complaints of the hostages was that they were receiving mail from all over the world, but not from their loved ones. The hostages themselves said they thought their own government was interfering with the mail. Before leaving for Iran, we had heard the same thing from relatives of those who were being held hostage.

"When we challenged the students about the mail, they reported that they delivered all mail to the hostages as soon as they received it, and mailed all letters promptly without any tampering on their part. They said that in some cases it looked as if the incoming mail had been tampered with before they received it. They did not know by whom.

"I guess I doubted their word," Rupiper recalls, "but I didn't say so to their face because I had no proof. For all I knew, the CIA or the State Department or the Iranian government could have intercepted the same mail. But, again, I had no proof. So there was nothing I could do. I kept trying not to draw conclusions on either side.

"But there was one thing. We asked the students if they would allow us to take home with us letters from the hostages to their families. They said yes, no problem. And before we left, we had 63 letters, sealed and untampered with. I felt then the captors were being honest with us, and I didn't hesitate to say so when the media asked. I thought the world should know.

"I guess I wasn't prepared for the media assault that followed. When I reported that the captives themselves said they were not being mistreated, I sensed a new hostility in the media questions, as if I were a dupe of the Ayatollah. I heard that I was being called 'Dupiper.' That hurt. I just told the truth, but it wasn't what the American public expected. They couldn't or didn't want to believe it. I was overcome with the same feeling as when I was in jail in Recife," Rupiper recalls.

That feeling quickly turned to fear of the CIA again, for good reason.

And Now, Disrespect

"While I was at the Imperial Hotel in Tehran, I got word that an Iranian student friend of mine in Omaha had died in a mental hospital in Lincoln, Nebraska. Somehow I sensed this was the CIA telling me to keep my big mouth shut or else.

"His name was Bijan Ashtiani. His family was from Tehran. I first learned about his being a student in Omaha during my prior December visit to Tehran. Between December and my April visit to Tehran, Bijan and I often talked about the brutal things that had happened in Iran during the Shah's reign.

"He was a student at the University of Nebraska and was housed at a motel near Omaha. I learned later from Bijan's friends what had happened to him while I was in Tehran.

"As an Iranian patriot, Bijan had a picture of the Ayatollah Khomeini hanging on the wall in his rented motel room. The owner of the motel burst in on him one day and told him to remove the picture or move out, although the rent was paid.

"Bijan said no. When Bijan tried to prevent the motel manager from removing the picture, a knife that he had been using as a letter opener was knocked from the desk. The manager grabbed for it, cutting himself on the hand. The ruckus attracted the attention of motel residents, and the cops were called.

"They hauled Bijan off to the mental ward of a hospital, where he died several days later of 'epilepsy.' It was news to me that Bijan suffered from epilepsy. As I found out later, he had a broken wrist, broken ribs, and his body was full of bruises that the hospital staff said were the result of his epileptic convulsions. Apparently, the coroner and police bought the story.

"I was not aware of any of this at the time I got the news, but I just sensed the CIA had something to do with it and that it was a sinister message for me.

"That didn't stop me from visiting Bijan's family while I was in Tehran. The student-captors took me to the Ashtiani family's home. It was a small third-floor apartment in the poor part of town. There was a lot of crying and wailing in the Moslem tradition. I cried too. I explained that I had been a friend of Bijan's and that I, too, was very saddened by the turn of events. They said their son was not epileptic. They were very receptive to me, although they had every reason to be angry with me as an American.

"Through his tears, Bijan's father said to me, 'I know there are many good people in America.'

"After I got back to Omaha, I found out that the Iranian consul had gone to the hospital to see the facilities and to investigate. He told me that as he passed through one ward he overheard a burly patient or orderly with clenched fist ask if this were 'another one' he should take care of.

"To this day," Rupiper says, "I believe Bijan's death was caused by agents of our government who wanted me to shut up. I was telling the world what the US and its CIA operation didn't want to hear: that the hostages were not being mistreated, because they told me they were not being mistreated. I was merely repeating what the hostages themselves told me, face to face. I do not know whether their words flowed from a sense of intimidation. I was trying to be objective and neutral."

Before Rupiper left Tehran, there was the seed of more trouble. One of the hostages had passed him a folded note.

"I tried not to make it obvious. I put it in my shirt pocket, thinking that when I had a private minute I would read it. But a sharp-eyed student-captor had seen what happened. Before I could leave the room, he asked me to give him the note, reminding me of the ground rules that both sides had worked out in advance. Reluctantly, I gave it to him. I don't know to this day what it said or if it caused the writer any grief. I guess I wish I had read it first. I can't even remember the name of the person who gave it to me or the guy who took it. I wish the person who gave it to me would be big enough now, after all these years, to step forward. It would clear up a lot of grief I've suffered.

"I didn't realize until we landed in the US just how angry the State Department was because of my statements about the non-brutal treatment of the hostages. Anyway, a message came through the pilot that the State Department was requesting the three of us to stay on the plane as the other passengers left. So we sat there.

"Then down the aisle comes this stern-faced woman. I figured she was from the State Department. She demanded that we turn over to her immediately all the letters the hostages had written. She showed no credentials. I told her no, that we had promised to deliver them to the families and that the hostages would be disappointed if they didn't receive them.

"She insisted, saying the State Department would take care of the deliveries. So I insisted on calling Norm Forer, who had arranged this trip through the International Conference on the Islamic Revolution. When I was put through to Forer, he simply said, 'The shit has hit the fan at State' and that it was best if we turned over the letters. So I did. Then we were allowed to leave.

"It wasn't long before I learned just how we had been set up to take a fall. In the media after our return and even months later after the hostages were released, all three of us were being called traitors. Word got out that we had letters from the hostages that we hadn't delivered to the families. Nobody believed us when we said the hostages were not being mistreated. "It became obvious to me later that several of the released hostages were trained in what to say when they were debriefed in Wiesbaden, Germany. One was told to say that we were in sympathy with the Iranians rather than with the hostages. Another was told to say that we had no sympathy for the families of the hostages and that we had never bothered to deliver the letters that were entrusted to us.

"You see, the State Department *never* forwarded the letters to any of the families. Their action made us look like we were on the Iranian side, and the hate mail poured in.

"This makes me suspect to this day that the complaints about the mail, which the hostages made, had more to do with CIA and State Department than they did with the Iranians," Rupiper says. "Our side intercepted the mail to make the Iranians look cruel. This whipped up American frenzy.

"As I came to realize later," he adds, "the policy of the US was to try to get rid of the Vietnam syndrome. They wanted the hostage crisis to continue day after day to whip up support from the American public. To beef up support for military action. That's why our government wouldn't communicate. That's why they took the letters. That's why Bijan is no longer alive."

Rupiper said nothing to the media about his offer to become an exchange hostage because he didn't want to look like he was grandstanding. Within days of Rupiper's return from the Easter visit, the pressure from the media became so intolerable that Rupiper took temporary refuge in the home of a friend.

The CIA, the State Department and the Carter Administration secretly benefited from Rupiper's trips. The bustle of activity in and out of the site where meetings with the hostages were held apparently provided some clues to the location of the captives, and indicated that they were all there in one spot. Less than three weeks later, on April 28, 1980, two American aircraft crashed in flames on the Iranian desert in a bungled attempt to forcibly extract the hostages.

"To show you how firmly we had established trust with the hostage holders," Bremer recalls, "Forer and I made telephone calls to the students asking them not to take revenge for the raid by the US; not to harm the hostages. They promised they would not, and they never did. They understood that the raid was something the US government did, not us."

Years later, when Rupiper was asked if any of the letters seized by the State Department might have contained coded messages, he only shrugs his shoulders and wags his head sadly in an I-don't-know gesture.

"Thanks to the State Department, we'll never know what the hostages wrote home," Rupiper says. "By comparison, I doubt my surrender of the little note was anything that would have made any difference, even if I could have got it smuggled out. But those letters could have given 53 American families a ray of hope at that time. As it turned out, they had to endure another year of anxiety just because of the political stupidity of our own government, across two competing political administrations."

Reminded that among the embassy hostages there were CIA operatives clever enough to encode such a message into a simple letter that he might have been carrying, Rupiper says he is reminded of the quote from Sir Walter Scott: "Oh, what a tangled web we weave when first we practice to deceive."

"All we've got to do," Rupiper says, "is follow our own laws and the higher moral laws that say 'Thou shalt not lie,' and 'Thou shalt not kill.'"

Methodist minister Jack Bremer recalls some details that Rupiper cannot. The State Department woman who demanded the letters was actually Mrs. Katherine Keough, a representative of FLAG (Family Liaison Action Group), which was working under the guidance of the State Department for the interests of the hostage families. Bremer says he has no idea why she wanted the letters, which Rupiper was carrying, and, once she had them, why she did not turn them over to the families.

"What I remember most was that she insisted that we should not report to the media that the hostages were being treated favorably. Of course, except for being held against their will, they were treated well — as we learned from one-on-one private interviews.

"One of the first things we did when we got off the plane was to call hostage family members and tell them their relatives were being well treated, that there was no torture and so forth."

Bremer encountered worries of his own. Shortly after his return, his files at his campus church in Lawrence, Kansas, were broken into. And mail — mail which Bremer had mailed to himself from Tehran — containing anti-US banners printed by an Iranian student, had been seized by the FBI in Washington. Bremer was called to Washington by the FBI and confronted with the "evidence." The anti-US banners were laid out across a table in the FBI offices for the confrontation.

Bremer boldly asked the FBI if they had opened his mail. The FBI denied it. Somehow the packages had broken open en route. He asked them if he was under arrest for something. They said no. He asked them if they were then confiscating his property from the mail. They said no. Then he asked them to repackage the material and mail it to him at his Lawrence, Kansas, address. Bremer still has them, although he has since retired and moved to New England.

Whether by coincidence or not, the FBI episode was just a few days before Bremer was invited to the White House to meet with President Carter and Brzezinski. For that occasion, Bremer happened to be in the Capital for a Methodist Church convention and took the occasion, along with ranking Church members, to ask for an audience with Jimmy Carter.

At the White House, Bremer said nothing about the FBI raid on his mail. He and his Methodist bishop and others were courteously received and attentively listened to, Bremer says. They were asked whether the hostages were being mistreated. Bremer restated his previously announced views that they were not mistreated, "except that they were being held against their will."

After revealing the true mood of the hostage holders, the Methodist group was then politely dismissed. They received a non-committal thank-you letter hours later, just before the botched raid attempt in the Iranian desert.

Rupiper and Bremer were not alone in suffering official and secret persecution. Sometime later, according to Rupiper, Fuzzy Thompson had to fight off trumped-up drug charges. "With me, with Forer, with Bremer and Thompson," Rupiper says, "persecution and harassment was the CIA way, our government's way, of getting even. That was the way they treated people in Third World nations, too. That was why they killed my friend Bijan."

When Rupiper went to Iran, it was in the spirit expressed by Professor Norm Forer of Kansas University in a letter to the Ayatollah Khomeini:

We go to Iran not with apologies, nor self-abasement, nor a sense of personal guilt, but simply with the conviction that ordinary Americans can facilitate that process toward peace and reconciliation which our political leaders have so far found to be beyond their capacity.

Forer was one of the few Americans ever to exchange civil correspondence with the regime of the Ayatollah.

When the hostages were finally released and the media furor settled down, Rupiper was left with a bitter condemnation for his lofty efforts. As the *Omaha World-Herald* concluded: "Either he was unbelievably naive or he willingly permitted himself to become a tool of the Iranians."

The newspaper left out the possibility of duplicity by the State Department or CIA, and their deliberate disinformation for the sake of public manipulation.

Rupiper and Bremer both wonder now how naive Carter's military men were, whether they believed they could pull off a helicopter and transport raid from two locations in Iran, and how much the foolhardy venture played into the hands of the Iranians.

Two days after the helicopter crash, the Iranians announced that they were dispersing the hostages to several cities to avoid the prospect of their extraction by military means. Rupiper and his friends had opened a window of opportunity to get them out peacefully; in just three weeks, Carter, the CIA and the State Department had slammed that window shut.

The only window left open was the one followed months later by the Reagan Administration: the secret and illicit trading of guns for hostages in a program that became headlined for history as the Iran-Contra scandal.

"By the time we left, we had gained their trust," Bremer says today. Simply by talking and praying jointly with the student captors in Tehran during two visits to Tehran (December 1979, and April 1980), Bremer quickly discovered that the Iranians took over the US embassy not because of anger at the US people, or a desire to go to war, but because they perceived the embassy itself was a center of the evils visited upon them for decades by the US government and its puppet, the Shah.

"They knew the US was full of good people whom they never had hated. They simply had learned to hate the actions of the US government."

After the hasty Carter action, Bremer was afraid the trust that the trio had built up was destroyed — but a phone call proved that was not the case.

> That was at a time [Rupiper says], when there was every possibility that we might have talked the Iranians into releasing at least some of the hostages peacefully and with none of the gun and drug trading that came to light years later. I am not a man of politics; I am a man of peace. Sad to say, peace still has to come from God through fumbling guys like me. But it comes from God, because mankind does not know how to wage peace.
>
> Eight beautiful lives of loyal Americans were lost in the debris of the helicopters that crashed in the Iranian desert. It didn't have to happen. None of the brutality and terrorism that happened to Iran in the prior 25 years had to happen. None of what happened in Vietnam had to happen, or South and Central America."

A Prophecy, Like Life, Goes On

Rupiper knows about suffering and struggling in other locales as well. After Omaha, he served as pastor of the Precious Blood Parish in Chicago, a remnant of the days when the neighborhood was Polish-Catholic. When Rupiper arrived there it was across the interstate from "the projects", known as Rockwell Gardens, where the violence and poverty equaled that of the infamous Cabrini Greens.

Surrounded by chain link and barbed wire to keep out pillagers, Precious Blood parish appears to be among the poorest Catholic parishes in America. It has no "poor box" because the poor box itself was ripped off the wall. Its stained glass windows were punctured by stray bullets from Rockwell Gardens, where not even cops would enter — unless in group force.

Once again, Rupiper found himself in a poor parish under siege, this time in the heart of a North American urban jungle; but he succeeded in opening the parish's heart, encouraging them to help the poor of the neighborhood over a period of several years. Meanwhile, Rupiper operated a flophouse for the poor (mostly Blacks), who managed, like him and with him, to survive.

Rupiper now lives as a monkish but modern novice-master for priest-recruits atop the limestone bluffs above the Mississippi River near its confluence with the Missouri and Illinois Rivers. Like his life, the locale is a strange confluence of events: here, at the former estate of an Owens Glass millionaire, young men are trained in the vows of poverty, chastity and obedience as they pursue their priestly studies.

Here, the sun seems to set on the upstream end of the Mississippi, creating the illusion that the sun is setting in the north from which the Mississippi flows. The illusion is caused by a huge west-to-east bend in the river above the locks at Alton, Illinois.

Here, below a limestone promontory 200 feet above the river dubbed "the crow's nest", flows the daily commerce of dozens of barges, shipping grain from the heartland of America to New Orleans and hungrier places in the world. Sometimes if you wave and a crewman on the riverboat spies you, you can get a wave of recognition.

Then you get the feeling that, like Ol' Man River, things keep rollin' along — whether for good or bad.

"The river's like a life," Rupiper says. "Parts of it you think you can control and use. Like the locks and dams on the river. Then sometimes, like the flood of '93, you control nothing. This whole confluence a few years ago was a moving lake, submerging everything.

"Submerged. That's how it was in Recife, how it was in Omaha, how it was in Chicago, how it was in Vietnam, how it was in Tehran. Yet, as the song says, it keeps on rollin'. But let me tell you, the human debris, the flotsam of souls on the river of life in this world, is nothing like the romanticized version of the stage show."

Even as Rupiper got off the plane from Tehran on April 10, 1980, in New York, and after his confrontation with the State Department woman, this place of strange confluences came to his mind. For as a novice 40 years ago, he himself had been trained here to cope with life's flow.

When at last the hostages in Tehran were released on January 20, 1981, the very day President Reagan was sworn into office, Rupiper was in Omaha at the New Covenant Justice and Peace Center.

Rupiper and the nation had no way of knowing then that the freedom of the hostages had been purchased at the price of weapons and drugs, arranged by the CIA and LIONSDEN. Rupiper had no way of knowing how desperately the Iranians needed the weapons to fight off the Iraqis, who had waged war against the Iranians in an effort to help America restore a Pahlevi princeling to the throne of Iran.

At that time, Rupiper was busy looking after the street people in Omaha, even as the media and those who hated him began to move in. Among the circling sharks were a few of the very hostages whom he had tried to rescue, without the help of bombs and bullets. Also among the circling sharks were the pernicious conservatives connected to the LIONSDEN system who had maneuvered behind the scenes to make sure of several things:

1. That the efforts of the American-Iranian Crisis Resolution Committee would not succeed in securing the release of the hostages, and thereby embarrass the US State Department and the Carter Administration.

2. That the Carter Administration's bid to rescue the hostages by military means would not succeed, so that Ronald Reagan might assume the hero's role in the Oval Office. (For this, $40 million was secretly paid to Iran in October 1980 by those close to the Reagan campaign. According to Bani-Sadr, then Iranian President, this exchange took place in Paris and included the promise of future arms delivery.) Some sources say former CIA chief George Bush and future CIA chief William Casey coordinated the details.

3. That the conservatives, after winning the election, under the figurehead of Ronald Reagan would get credit for the hostage release and the right wing could once again resume its white-knight drive toward the Cold War conquering of Communism.

None of this was apparent to Rupiper as President Reagan took the oath of office and the hostages boarded flights for home. When Rupiper heard the news of their release, tears came to his eyes. But media interviews with the hostages produced a renewed reaction against him — not the Iranians. Rupiper had become once again the "traitor priest" from Omaha.

Over in Wiesbaden, one of the released hostages, Charles Jones, told the press that Rupiper had betrayed him. He said that, during a little prayer service at which Jones claimed to have made a reading, he had placed a note in the prayer book — allegedly detailing hostage mistreatment. The prayer book was then passed back to Rupiper. According to Jones, Rupiper then took the note from the missal and handed it over to their captors, without even reading the note.

Quite simply [Rupiper says], none of that happened, and I don't know why Jones told such a story unless he was asked by the State

Department to make it up so officials could discredit me. Now that I think about it, the military-CIA helicopter raid was probably already being planned even as I visited with the hostages. But never mind.

The truth is, when I asked Jones as a captive if he wanted to pray with us, he responded that he "didn't go for that stuff." So we just talked about his life as a hostage. He made no complaints. In fact, he told me "They sure are treating us a helluva lot better than I would treat them if we traded places." But Jones did *not* read from any prayer book. He did *not* pass me a note. I understand there is a picture of me sharing an Easter meal with Jones and another man, Gary Persinger. I think it was printed in the *Kansas City Star.*

There was, of course, the *other* note. The only note that I have talked about to the media on other occasions. But I got that note from someone else, not Jones. I remember the distinction well, because Jones was black and the other person was white. (All of the other blacks had been voluntarily released earlier by the Iranians.)

There was no such note from Jones to me. His comments after release were a part of a plan by State and CIA to keep the American public agitated over mistreatment of the hostages and to discredit me. So that my reports to the contrary would seem to be propaganda from the Iranians. So that later efforts to free the hostages under the administration's plan could go forward with popular support for our side and maximum hate for theirs.

I guess all of this was the government's way of saying that if you do things we don't approve of, we'll get even. We (the American-Iranian Crisis Resolution Committee) were doing things that the government couldn't or wouldn't do. They had their own plans, I suppose. And they didn't like us meddling by telling the world that the hostages seemed to be in excellent shape.

As he talks, Rupiper riffles through a thick file of yellowed clippings and dog-eared Xeroxes. There are pictures of him being interviewed in a TV news studio just after he and Pete Grams were kicked out of Brazil in 1968. He laughs at the youthful image.

"Here's proof," he says, "that I used to be good looking. No gray before all this happened."

Would he do any of it differently, given the chance?

Why would I want to change the truth? [he responds, without saying it was a dumb question]. Why would I want to do anything other than to try to make things right for America and for Iran? Maybe I would have read that note before putting it in my pocket. Maybe I would have refused to give up the letters from the hostages. I wish Jimmy Carter had listened to Jack Bremer and canceled his stupid raid. I don't know how I could have gotten those who criticized us to understand that we didn't take sides and that we did tell the truth.

> I remember being on the "Tonight" show and responding to a question about the treatment of the hostages. I was saying that if you took 50 people at random off the streets of any large city and compared their well-being to that of the hostages, the hostages might fare better in terms of physical, psychological and spiritual well-being. At that point, the interview ended abruptly.

Rupiper's comments about the treatment of the hostages are borne out by the notes taken by Rev. Jack Bremer, his Methodist associate on the visit. At the time Rupiper, Bremer and Thompson interviewed the hostages, none of them, including Marine Corporal William Gallegos of Pueblo, Colorado, was critical of their treatment. During his captivity, Gallegos made a publicly televised statement indicating they were being treated well by their captors. Bremer's notes on private interviews indicate that after the first few tense days when the hostages were blindfolded and handcuffed, there was no mistreatment, no brainwashing, no threats. Punishment for disobedient action amounted to being blindfolded, handcuffed and placed in a chair in the corner of the room for less than half an hour. It was something like the dunce stool used by US schoolmasters a century ago.

Hostage comments show that, while forcibly detained, they received books, played chess, were provided health care, were visited by papal and orthodox nuncios, and wrote and received mail freely. Their food was plain but sufficient. Their stress was mainly that of not knowing when they might achieve freedom and why there were being held in the first place. When asked, they acknowledged that they thought the Shah had been abusive to his people and that the US had supported the Shah, according to Bremer.

"That's why I can't understand Gallegos' hostile comments by about me after he was freed," Rupiper says. "Like he wanted to spit in my face or something. I may even have heard his confession during my visit, so I don't know how I earned his bad feelings."

After his release, Gallegos said in a TV interview that his previous comments about not being mistreated should have been interpreted as a signal that just the opposite was true. But a review of the video released by his Iranian captors at that time reveals nothing to hint that Gallegos was sending a hidden message. There were no crossed fingers or eye winking, for example. His change of heart came after debriefing with US officials in Wiesbaden, Germany. After consulting with government agents, Gallegos reversed himself and said abuse had been both "psychological and physical."

It took years for the controversy around Rupiper to subside as he settled back into his ministry in Omaha at the New Covenant Justice and Peace Center, and later, at his ghetto parish in Chicago. Still, he never told anyone about his plan to take the place of at least one hostage (Jerry Miele) and build a bridge between Tehran and Washington during his visit to Tehran.

Even though the furor over the Tehran visit faded, Rupiper's years of activism on behalf of peace and his influence on thousands of others were not over, as his protests in Chicago and Omaha would show.

While Reagan appeared to be the savior of the Iran hostages, other criminal events sanctioned by the CIA and LIONSDEN had been taking place in Central America. These were linked with US complicity in Iran, Iraq, Lebanon, Kuwait and the nuclear arms race in space. It was Iran-Contra.

But nobody knew, until much later.

16. Iran-Contra: The Eichmann Corollary

An estimated 60,000 people in Nicaragua, Guatemala, and El Salvador lost their lives in the '80s to what became known as the death squads of Iran-Contra. The most famous was Archbishop Oscar Romero, killed while saying Mass after preaching a sermon calling for Salvadoran soldiers to stop killing their countrymen.

The Iran-Contra operation, which can be considered a US-backed terrorist program of the CIA, was run in LIONSDEN-fashion out of the Reagan White House basement by Vietnam hero Lt. Col. Oliver North. His operation hid behind the public misnomer of *The Office of Public Diplomacy*.

In Nazi Germany a similar program was called, bluntly, "The Final Solution." One of the SS officers who was finally brought to justice in 1961 for genocidal crimes against European Jewry was Colonel Adolph Eichmann. His case and North's have spine-tingling parallels.

Oliver North, like Eichmann, was a decorated war hero. Both men are connected to the deaths of hundreds of thousands of civilians in wartime; both said they were following orders.

North's responsibility for the deaths of at least 60,000 stems from the business he ran for the CIA: selling drugs into America and guns into Iran. The profits were used to buy more guns, to support the Contra campaign of terrorism by death squads.

A Short, Modern History

The historical background is this. In 1980, Nicaraguan dictator Anastasio Somoza was assassinated, ending the brutal dynasty of the Somoza family (which the US had supported since 1957, when Anastasio's grandfather, Luis, took command). Stepping into the power vacuum after Somoza's death was a political group known as the Sandinistas. The group takes its name from Augusto Sandino, who led a popular peasant revolution in Nicaragua in 1927. (It was eventually put down by the US Marines.)

Daniel Ortega, who headed the Sandinista movement, asserted control after Somoza's death but the US considered him to be a Communist. The CIA therefore organized the supporters of the old Somoza regime to form the *Contras*, whom Reagan called "freedom fighters."

Both sides in the conflict used terrible tactics including the murder of civilians, but the technique of the death squads, trained by the US at the School of the Americas, became the specialty of the Contras. Their style of violence, as they fought to establish right-wing governments, spread throughout Central America to El Salvador, Guatemala, Honduras and Costa Rica, because the Contras and their CIA backers moved the war there by using them as sanctuaries for staging the assault on Nicaragua.

As the contagion spread, so did the killings by death squads. Not even priests, nuns, bishops, or intellectuals were spared. Anyone thought to oppose right-wing dictators was a target. The Sandinista movement, which favored human freedoms and civil rights denied by US-friendly dictators, became an enemy the Reagan administration, which was determined to extirpate all social-political reform before the region turned into another Cuba.

At the same time, Congress feared that aggressive involvement in Central American affairs might produce another Vietnam, and so it passed laws that barred direct intervention by America, particularly in Nicaragua. These series of laws were generally referred to as the Boland Amendment, which made illegal any aid in the form of funds and guns beginning in 1982.

And that is why Oliver North was installed in the basement of the White House, to find covert ways to get military and financial help to the Contras.

This all unfolded against a backdrop of massive unrest in the Middle East. Iran, which had just completed its guns-for-hostage deal with Reaganites in Tehran, was at war with Iraq. Afghanistan, bordering Iran, was at war with the Soviet Union. The Israeli conflict with the Palestinians had moved to Lebanon and almost as soon as the US stepped in as peacemaker, Islamic radicals began bombing embassies and barracks and taking American civilians hostage.

Oliver North and the South, the East and the West

This set the table for North and the whole Iran-Contra plan. A single money-making scheme, managed through the CIA, the National Security Agency and North, could kill several birds with one stone: Iran would get its guns for use against Iraq or for aiding their fellow Moslems in Afghanistan; the Contras would get money to buy guns and conduct warfare to set up regimes desired by the US; the CIA would have the cash flow to fund its secret operations; and the US would have its hostages released. Moreover, if Iraq won the war with Iran, the Ayatollah Khomeini would be dethroned and the US could put the Shah's son on the Peacock Throne. Then America could work out a secure deal for oil, much as it had done with the old Shah.

Most pieces of the scheme actually worked. But it was illegal, even though backed by President Reagan (who seemed to bring with him the notion that whatever he thought and said was law, because he had been elected). He seems not to have been much of a reader, but he acted as if he were quite familiar with Machiavelli's opus, *The Prince:*

> A prince should therefore have no other aim or thought, nor take up any other thing for his study, but war and its organization and discipline. For that is the only art that is necessary to one who commands.

As head of Reagan's Office of Public Diplomacy, North was the non-diplomatic intersection for all the secret hostage negotiations, gun running, and drug running. He knew about all the supply points, drops, secret runways, CIA-owned airlines, and personnel. He knew the purpose of his program and he knew it broke the laws of the land. In this perverse way, North became a hero for supporting the political duplicity of the Reagan camp on two fronts:

1) The announced public policy was: no negotiating with Middle East terrorists, and no support for Iran. But behind the scenes guns became the medium of exchange for political power.

2) The announced public policy was: no direct support for either side in Central America. But behind the scenes, money and guns were supplied

for the Contras and for massive covert intervention.

Perhaps the worst side effect of the double-dealing scheme was the loss of Saddam Hussein as an ally in the Middle East. Angry at being double-crossed, he abandoned the war. The CIA thereafter seduced him into invading Kuwait, and dragged the world into the Desert Storm war, but that story comes later.

This Iran-Contra treachery was hatched even before Reagan was in office. In October 1980, prior to Reagan's election, Campaign Chairman William Casey and (soon to be vice president) George Bush went to Paris. As related in the previous chapter, they paid $40 million for the release of the Tehran hostages, on condition that they continue to be held until the White House was securely in Reagan's hands; and the US would sell weapons to Iran.

The operation was moving quietly along until October 5, 1986, when the C-123 cargo plane filled with munitions was shot down over Nicaragua. The pilot, Eugene Hasenfus, parachuted to safety — but was captured. This blew the lid off the whole scam and prompted a Congressional investigation. When the Congressional hearings were convened, Oliver North, dressed in his army uniform and bedecked with all his medals, told the US Congress, "I assumed that my superiors knew what they were doing and had obtained permission to do it."

This sounded like a fair assumption, since he was operating out of the basement of the White House and his commander-in-chief lived upstairs.

Even Eichmann had been able to use that line of argument to blunt his guilt. Following evil orders is the part of morality and justice that the Nuremberg trials supposedly corrected, at about the time Oliver North was born.

Whether superiors commanded their actions or not, both North and Eichmann were men who knew right from wrong. Certainly, some distinctions can be made: Eichmann had killed millions in Europe by his actions, while North had only killed tens of thousands, in Central America.

When the Congressional maelstrom was over, North emerged as a man who was ultimately rewarded for committing crimes under orders. He received a fine for perjury and for diverting slush funds to his personal use. North, still looking like an oversized boy scout, reacted as if he had just received a merit badge. He is now a man who daily has the ear and admiration of America through his broadcasting job at American Radio Network, another CIA "asset."

News stories from Central America provide some background to the sequence of events. Reagan was inaugurated in January 1981, and the

Tehran hostages were released the same day. By March 1981, the arms shipments to Iran had started. At the same time, efforts to intervene in Central America, which had started in the closing days of the Carter Administration, were stepped up.

March 1981: US sends Green Berets to El Salvador to support the military regime of Jose Napoleon Duarte, whose junta had seized control in 1979. The US already has 54 military advisor in El Salvador and is considering similar action in Nicaragua. After the news announcement, the US embassy was damaged by grenade and machine gun fire. Congress is concerned about the parallel with Vietnam.

May 1981: Six death squad soldiers are arrested for killing three nuns in El Salvador. They had been killed scarcely a year after the assassination of Archbishop Oscar Romero, who had been shot while saying Mass at a convent.

July 1981: Minister Eden Pastora of Nicaragua is forced into exile. In El Salvador, mass slayings of peasants by death squads are reported.

August 1981: In El Salvador, use of toxic gas against rebels and civilians is reported. Two-year death toll reaches 26,000.

December 1981: Reagan signs order broadening powers of CIA to spy domestically.

January 1982: France is to sell arms to Nicaragua and train naval officers and pilots.

March 1982: In El Salvador, US-backed strongman Napoleon Duarte was confirmed in an election that saw four Dutch newsmen killed. In Nicaragua, Sandinista leader Daniel Ortega accuses US of aggression through operations out of Honduras. In Washington, a member of the Sandinistas tells Congress he was not trained in Cuba. In Managua, Sandinistas say they face riots fomented by US. In Guatemala, General Rios Montt seizes power in coup, charging electoral fraud.

December 1982: The Boland Amendment (first of a series), barring any action by US to overthrow the government of Nicaragua, becomes law.

April-May 1983: Reagan admits CIA is giving covert aid to Contra "freedom fighters" in Nicaragua and claims it is legal.

June 1983: Contra terrorists in Nicaragua are found to be in possession of CIA manual instructing them in sabotage, torture and assassination. An attempt by CIA agents to kill Nicaragua's foreign minister comes to light.

July 1983: Iraq complains to UN of weapons flow from US to Iran during Iraq-Iran war.

October 1983: State Department condemns right wing death squads in El Salvador, although perpetrators have been trained by US at Fort Benning, Georgia.

March 1984: US stages military maneuvers in Honduras during elections in El Salvador from its drug profits.

April 1984: Reagan sends military aid to El Salvador without Congressional approval.

May 1984: CIA provides millions of dollars to Duarte's re-election campaign in El Salvador.

May 1984: Five death squad members of El Salvador's National Guard found guilty in murder of four American churchwomen.

September 1984: Israel, nudged by the US, donates $10 million to Nicaragua's Contras. Nicaragua's Marco Colero Portocarrero brags of receiving donations through the CIA from "large, well-known companies" (i.e., laundered drug money.)

May 1985: US bans trade with Nicaragua and mines that country's harbors.

June 1985: Four US Marines are killed in San Salvador.

November 1986: CIA pilot Eugene Hasenfus is shot down over Nicaragua with planeload of munitions, thus exposing the Iran-Contra operation run by Oliver North. The operation includes drugs smuggled to the US for sale by the CIA.

Before Archbishop Oscar Romero died at the hands of the death squads in 1980, he said in a sermon before his Catholic congregation: "Today I have sent a letter to the President of the United States asking him to send no more arms. They are only being used to kill our people."

That letter was never answered, except by the shipment of more guns to Central America, a problem that priest-prophet Kabat had identified years before when he was in Brazil.

The doomed archbishop could not know that Carter's LIONSDEN operatives, pre-empted by Reagan's election-year advance men, were already planning a huge expansion of secret military support to promote terrorism by the Contra death squads in Central America. Romero would be dead before the names of North or Poindexter or Secord or McFarlane or

Abrams or Motley or Shultz or Casey or Bush came to be connected to Iranian arms and South American drug trafficking.

Prophets like the archbishop use simple cause-and-effect reasoning: morally good laws must be followed by everyone, especially by the government agencies that enact and enforce them, while abusive laws invalidate themselves. By the time of the Boland Amendment's passage, its moral backbone was being broken by the Executive branch, via the Iran-Contra and LIONSDEN system.

Which Laws for Which Citizens?

The initiatives of honorable individuals then become a process of breaking the law in order to stop someone else from breaking the law in a more serious manner. But how do you get the public to understand?

The Boland Amendment was a law that came too late. The policy of covertly propping up freedom-repressing regimes in South and Central America had been going on for years. Church representatives protesting the US shipment of arms — such as Archbishop Oscar Romero and many of his priests, nuns and parishioners —had been spectacularly assassinated by the time of the Boland Amendment, thanks to Jimmy Carter's Trilateral policies. Dead were thousands of reform-minded starving peasants, no thanks to a pope in Rome who did not want his clerics to mix theology and politics. (It was as if the aging pope had forgotten the role he had played in dismantling the Communist regime in Poland years earlier.)

Worst of all, the remnants of the Somoza regime in Guatemala were being resurrected by Reaganites as the true freedom fighters, in defiance of the Boland Amendment. This only angered those who had been oppressed by US puppets, and caused the Sandinista fever to spread.

The Hasenfus-CIA-White-House connection, when made public, confirmed for the prophets profiled in this book that the country's leaders had been behaving in an immoral and murderous manner for years. The episode vindicated and encouraged them to continue their protests, to the present day.

Once he was in the White House, Reagan purposely was kept in the dark about the Iran-Contra details so that he could have "plausible deniability", à la LIONSDEN. He didn't ask, and he wasn't told, just what North was up to. While he acknowledged that he knew there was a group working out of his basement (cheek by jowl with the National Security Council) on follow-up matters relating to the release of Iran hostages, and the curbing of communists in Central America, he maintained that he had not been told that the Iran-Contra gang employed drug running in addition to gun dealing in their effort to maximize profits.

Reagan publicly suggested that he believed covert foreign intervention was necessary as a general practice to fight communism; he seemed to disconnect the social harm it produced in Central America from the oil-rich Middle East agenda and the Israeli-Palestinian problems.

Within this fog of official ignorance, courtesy of the LIONSDEN program, the US gradually gained release of the hostages in Beirut as the guns flowed to Iran and cash profits from the fat over-charges flowed secretly to Central America, via Swiss bank accounts, to finance more guns for more war.

Under orders from Admiral John Poindexter and Robert McFarlane in the National Security Agency, North went about his work in the White House. The Contra re-supply operation set up a CIA-owned airline called *Southern Airways*, and established a secret airstrip at Santa Elena, Costa Rica. The airport was carried on the books as a legitimate US foreign aid expense. Southern Airways flew guns to Central America and drugs back to the US. In this way, Costa Rica and other neighbors of Nicaragua enabled the CIA to open up a front for the Contras that avoided the Boland Amendment ban against direct military aid.

Costa Rica's grudging cooperation and silence over the illegal airstrip was bought by the threat of cutting off non-military foreign aid as the airport was built by Project Democracy, a subsidiary of Udall Corporation, S.A., which was a Panamanian company with roots that took sustenance from CIA business connections in the US.

Eventually, the US covert operations even mined Nicaragua's harbor at Managua, disabling several foreign freighters. This was done as a US naval "exercise." (Mining of waters anywhere is considered an act of war under the Geneva Convention.)

Disclosure, If Not Closure

When Eugene Hasenfus was shot down over Nicaragua, he brought crashing down with him Reagan's illegal involvement in Central America, North's CIA drug- and gun-running, and the truth about how the Tehran hostages, and some in Beirut, had been ransomed. Soon after Congress convened its hearings, the world found out that:

- The plane was loaded with 10,000 pounds of ammunition en route from Ilopango, El Salvador, to Nicaragua.

- Hasenfus worked for the CIA under retired Air Force Col. Robert Dutton, who directed the Contra re-supply operation in Costa Rica, Guatemala, El Salvador, Honduras, Panama and Colombia.
- Dutton worked for General Secord and Lt. Colonel North, who reported to the National Security Council.
- Felix Rodriguez (aka Max Gomez) was the El Salvador field director working under Dutton, with reporting relationships to Secord, North and Donald Gregg — all with CIA connections.
- Gregg was Bush's liaison and arranged at least three meetings between Rodriguez (Morales) and the Vice President in the White House to discuss operations.
- Rodriguez was the first to report the downing of Hasenfus's plane, according to records released by the office of Vice President Bush.
- Dutton apologized to Lt. Col. North for the risky action taken by Rodriguez in alerting the Vice President's office directly about the loss of the plane. Dutton suggested that Rodriguez "should be taken out of the net." This soon ended Rodriguez's CIA career, which had hit its peak in 1967 when he captured Che Guevara in Bolivia and had him shot, while Rodriguez watched.

The Hasenfus investigation led to a string of lies being spun by the highest officials in the land, as reported by the Congressionally-hired *Institute for Policy Studies*. The results provide an idea of who were the rulers of the LIONSDEN system at that time, and, thereby, with what level of authority it had been perpetrating atrocities upon the world for so many years.

In fact, as Hasenfus told TV reporter Mike Wallace, his CIA pilot (named Cooper, who was killed on the mission) once explained that the Nicaraguan operation was "the same thing we were doing in Vietnam." (Both Cooper and Hasenfus had CIA assignments in Vietnam.) As for President Reagan, George Bush and Bill Casey, Hasenfus told Wallace: "They would have been delighted if I had been killed," because, in that event, none of the mess would have come to light.

For his part, Oliver North acknowledged to Congressional investigators that what he had been doing in the White House was "in furtherance of the President's policies." North even told his inquisitors that, "I had an indirect connection with that flight (of Hasenfus)." North, in one of his truthful moments, also dropped this bomb under questioning:

"The DC-6 which is being used for runs (to supply the Contras) out of New Orleans is probably being used for drug runs into the US." The pilot involved was identified as George Morales. A memo between North and Robert Owen, a State Department contract employee, reveals that North knew some of his CIA crews were flying drugs and even had criminal records.

All of this suggests that North was involved in just one of many LIONSDEN-style operations connected to the CIA. The cast of characters changed over the years, but the chief executors of such operations are traceable to the White House. It would seem, therefore, that the prophets of this book and their protests against the Trilateral and LIONSDEN policies — which produced direct killings and death by drugs — were justifiable as well as patriotic, and that the imprisonment of these men and women was a miscarriage of justice.

A Whole Cast of Liars

Denials being an integral feature of any LIONSDEN system, there were Iran-Contra denials all around by the highest government figures. Here is a list as extrapolated from the booklet, "*In Contempt of Congress*," published by the *Institute for Policy Studies*. The lies, starting from the top men, were uncovered during the Iran-Contra investigations.

Liar: President Ronald Reagan
Question: Did he know?
> "The Tower Commission was told by the President on January 26, 1987, that he did not know that the National Security Council (NSC) staff was engaged in helping the Contras."
> — From Tower Commission Report.

When NSC Advisor Robert McFarlane was questioned on May 13, 1987, about the President's response, McFarlane said he had given Reagan dozens of reports about NSC efforts to aid the Contras. When Lt. Col. Oliver North, NSC director of Political-Military Affairs, was asked by the Joint Select Committee on July 9, 1997, whether the President's response (lack of knowledge about Contras) surprised him, North's reply was "yes."

Liar: Vice President & Ex-CIA Director George Bush
Question: Did he know?
> "On three occasions when the Vice President met with Mr. Rodriguez, the discussions dealt entirely with the insurgency in

El Salvador and there was no discussion, direct or indirect, of the Contra aid network. . . There was no mention of supply or support operations for the Contras whatsoever."

— Statement by Office of the Vice President on December 15, 1986.

However, an official briefing memorandum shows otherwise. It is dated April 30, 1986, and notes that participants included Vice President Bush, Oliver North, Felix Rodriguez and US Ambassador to El Salvador Edwin Corr. Here it is:

Briefing memorandum from Don Gregg for the Vice President.

Event: Meeting with Felix Rodriguez.

Date: Thursday May 1, 1986.

Time: 11:30-11:45 a.m.

Place: West Wing, White House.

Purpose: Felix Rodriguez, a counter-insurgency expert from El Salvador, will provide a briefing on the status of the war in El Salvador and resupply of the Contras.

Some background is in order. Don Gregg was National Security advisor to Bush, who at one time was director of the CIA. Rodriguez (Max Morales) was a re-supply coordinator for Central America. Rodriguez was first acquainted with Bush as a CIA agent when Bush was its director; but his main claim to fame was that he had captured and killed Che Guevara in Bolivia in 1967.

Rodriguez worked with Hasenfus, the Contras, and the drug contacts within the Medellin Cartel in Colombia and with Manuel Noriega in Panama. Noriega, also on the CIA payroll, was the funnel point of the CIA-Colombia cartel drug flow. Rodriguez also bossed sometimes-pilot George Morales of Miami, whose CIA cover was as a powerboat racing champion. When the lid blew off the CIA's gun and drug running, George Morales was forced to plead guilty to running drugs from Colombia to Florida over a period of several years. His guilty plea came only after Vice President George Bush and Secretary of State George Shultz declined to testify on his behalf at the trial in 1986.

Why would such highly-placed men as Bush and Schultz have knowledge of such tawdry affairs? Because of their mission to raise covert money to support the Contras, at any cost. At a later stage in the drug trials leading to the breakup of the Medellin cartel, convicted drug runner Carlos Lehder Rivas testified at Manuel Noriega's trial that the drug cartel itself had funneled $10 million in contributions to the US-backed Contra rebels in Nicaragua. Despite denials by Bush and Shultz that they had ever been Contra fundraisers, it eventually became necessary for Bush to sever all former ties. The US invaded Panama in December 1989 to capture CIA-hireling Noriega and incarcerate his knowledge of CIA's running of guns and drugs.

The extent of the cover-up and lies became evident as Congress pressed its investigation into the whole Iran-Contra scandal. The questions and conflicting evidence revealed the lies of other top officials:

Liar: Secretary of State George Shultz
Did he pimp other countries for Contra funds?

> "I had no discussion of this matter (contributions to the Contras) with the Sultan or anyone else in Brunei." — George Shultz before the House Foreign Affairs Committee, Dec. 8, 1986.
> "The donation was made at the request of the US Secretary of State, Mr. George Shultz, in the summer of 1986."
> — Statement by Brunei officials, January 16, 1987.

Records show that, at this time, numerous other administration officials were involved in the issue of obtaining Contra funding from US allies. Officials included Elliot Abrams, Assistant Secretary of State for Inter-American Affairs; Richard H. Melton, Director of the Office of Central American Affairs, State Department; Langhorne Motley, Assistant Secretary of State for Inter-American Affairs; and Army general William Singlaub, retired from the Korean command. Countries approached included Israel, South Korea, Taiwan, Brunei, Saudi Arabia, and South Africa. Besides success with Brunei, one memo reports that the Saudis contributed $31 million.

Liar: CIA Director William Casey
Question: Was CIA was responsible for murders?

> "The ultimate distortion. . . speaks of the Agency 'having to be stopped for illegal. . . murders.' This distortion of reality must be corrected."
> — Letter to members of the Senate and House Intelligence Committees from William Casey, October 25, 1984.

CIA manual for Nicaraguan Contras, Fall, 1983: "It is possible to neutralize carefully selected and planned targets, such as court judges, *maesta* judges, police and state security officials. . . Professional criminals will be hired to carry out specific 'jobs'."

"It was standard practice to kill prisoners and suspected Sandinista collaborators. In talking with officers, I frequently heard offhand remarks like, 'Oh, I cut his throat.' The CIA did not discourage such tactics. We were told that the only way to defeat the Sandinistas was to use the tactics that the Agency attributed to 'communist' insurgencies elsewhere: kill, kidnap, rob and torture." — Edgar Chamorro, Contra leader, before the International Court of Justice, September 5, 1985.

Liar: US Attorney General Edwin Meese
Question: Did Meese prevent a criminal investigation?

"So there was at no time any attempt to keep the criminal division out of anything that had criminal implications."

— Edwin Meese, before the Joint Select Committee, July 28, 1987.

"He (Meese) said words to the effect of, 'I just wanted you to know that, with respect to this Iran matter, that the fact that the Criminal Division is not involved is not negligence or sloppiness. . . This is being done that way on purpose.'"

— William Weld, Assistant Attorney General, Criminal Division, in deposition before the Joint Select Committee, July 16, 1987.

Liar: US Secretary of Defense Caspar Weinberger
Question: Did the Defense Department provide the CIA with resources?

"US military exercises have no connection with anti-Sandinistas."

— Quote from *New York Times*

"The Defense Department, according to American officials and documents, has provided the CIA with ships, planes, guns and other equipment at nominal rates as well as free transport for use in the cover war with Nicaragua."

— *New York Times*, May 18, 1984.

In fact, the US conducted military maneuvers in Honduras to disguise their illegal activities while elections were being held in El Salvador; the CIA even mined Nicaragua's harbors, with Pentagon help, in 1985.

The above examples are just a few of the instances where top administration officials lied about involvement in the illegal activities in Central America. Records show that involvement was massive and pervasive even among lesser-than-cabinet-level officials. By the time Bush (senior) became president, he felt compelled to grant Weinberger a presidential pardon, sparing him the embarrassment of a potential indictment for such misuse of public assets.

The officials mentioned, and many others at lower levels, constituted just a part of an ever-changing LIONSDEN modality as it existed during the Reagan Administration. It had many tentacles. The above names alone make it obvious why Congress could not proceed with a Watergate-style investigation. The scandal extended so deeply that to pursue and prosecute would be to destroy the entire Executive Branch, and with it America's prestige. It would have involved the President, the Vice President, the Secretary of State, the US Attorney General, the Secretary of Defense, the National Security Council, the Director of the CIA and dozens of henchmen. All were involved in illegal activities including murder, misappropriation of funds, misfeasance, malfeasance, drug running, undeclared wars, deprivation of human rights, and violation of international law. They were all potentially guilty of having violated the law of the land, and of lying about it or covering up their roles in doing so — just as Nixon had done, not long before, under somewhat more paltry circumstances.

Congress had to let the matter slide; they knew that if Oliver North was guilty, the rest were, too. It was My Lai all over again, but at the highest levels. A serious investigation leading to the whole truth would destroy the nation. It would take years to complete; it would paralyze the nation at a critical juncture in its Cold War efforts; and it would polarize if not anarchize the public. And, at some point, under impeachment proceedings, it would potentially place the then-Democratic Speaker of the House into the White House, with just half a cabinet to work with.

Here is a list, as reported by The Institute for Policy Studies, of laws most likely violated by the Reagan Administration:

1. The Boland Amendment (Thou shalt not mess with Central America.)
2. The International Security and Development Cooperation Act of 1985, Public Law 99-83, Section 722 (d). (Thou shalt not provide funding directly or indirectly against Nicaragua.)
3. The Intelligence Authorization Act for Fiscal Year 1986, Public Law 99-169, Section 101 and 105. (Thou shalt not plan or covet military or paramilitary operations against Nicaragua, directly or indirectly.)

4. The Neutrality Act of 1974, Section 960 Title 18 of the US Code. (Thou shalt not engage in supporting, funding, planning or aiding military adventures against any country with which the US is at peace.)
5. The Arms Export Control Act, US Code Title 22, Section 2778. (Thou shalt not trade in weapons for export without applying for and obtaining a license to do so.)
6. Intelligence Oversight Act. (The CIA shall inform the Congress of intelligence activities regarding foreign countries.)
7. Executive Order 112333. (The US and its agents shall not participate in assassinations.)
8. The Anti-Deficiency Act, US Code Title 31, Sections 1341 and 1350. (Thou shalt not spend money for purposes not specifically authorized.)
9. Misuse of Public Money, Property or Records, US Code Title 18, Section 641. (Thou shalt not use US funds or property of value without legal authority.)
10. Fraud and False Statement, US Code Title 18, Section 1001. (Thou shalt not falsify, conceal or cover up by any scheme, trick or device a material fact or make false, fictitious or fraudulent statements or presentations of same.)
11. Obstruction of Justice, US Code Title 18, Section 1501. (Thou shalt not influence, intimidate or impede the due course of the administration of justice, including criminal investigations.)
12. Conspiracy to Defraud the United States and Commit Other Felonies, US Code Title 18, Section 371. (Thou shalt not plot to violate criminal laws.)
13. Misprison of Felony, US Code Title 18, Section 4. (Thou shalt not fail to report a felony to the proper authorities.)
14. Federal Election Campaign Law, US Code II, Section 43. (Thou shalt not use or "launder" either foreign or federal funds for political purposes.)
15. Misuse of Appropriated Funds for Publicity and Propaganda, Section 501 of Public Law 98-411 under Departments of Commerce, Justice and State, 1985. (Thou shalt not use any appropriation for publicity or propaganda purposes not authorized by the Congress.)
16. War Powers Resolution, Section 4(a). (Thou shalt report to Congress within 48 hours after US forces have been committed to hostilities.)

17. The foreign Assistance Act of 1961, Section 502B(a) (2): (Thou shalt not provide security assistance to any country the government of which engages in a consistent pattern of gross violations of internationally recognized human rights). These rights are defined as: tortures or cruel, inhuman or degrading treatment or prolonged detention without trial or charges, or causing the disappearance of persons by abduction and clandestine detention, or other flagrant denial of the right of life, liberty and security of the person.

None of these 17 violations was ever brought by Congress against the perpetrators, the very leaders of the US government committed by oath to uphold such laws. By contrast, hundreds of citizens were hauled into court over the years for violating other US codes, by stepping across white lines at military bases, for trespassing at nuclear installations, for pounding with hammers on metal and concrete possessions of the military, or for pouring blood on them as symbolic reminders of higher moral law. They were protesting the government's immoral policies, including Iran-Contra.

Most of them spent more time in prison than the felons involved with the Nixonian Watergate burglary. None of them escaped arrest, the way dozens of the Reagan Administration did for breaking oaths of office, misappropriating funds, inciting assassinations, and causing thousands to be killed or be damaged by drugs.

On the international scale, several laws appear to have been broken. These include:

The Charter of the United Nations, Commitment to Non-Aggression. Article 2 (3) and Article 2 (4).

The Charter of the Organization of American States, Commitment to Non-Aggression. Article 18 and Article 20.

On June 27, 1986, the World Court voted AGAINST the United States by a 12-3 vote in the case of the US military and paramilitary activities in and against Nicaragua, saying:

1) That the United States of America by training, arming, equipping, financing and supplying the Contra forces or otherwise encouraging, supporting and aiding military and paramilitary activities in and against Nicaragua, has acted against the Republic of Nicaragua in breach of its obligation under customary international law not to intervene in the affairs of another state... [and]

2) That the United States of America is under a duty immediately to cease and refrain from all such acts against Nicaragua as may constitute breaches of the foregoing legal obligations.

Iran-Contra and Oliver North were America's corollary to Eichmann and were the moral equivalent of the World War II Holocaust; yet no one was punished except those who protested such patriotically disguised immorality.

Plots and Subplots

Within the Iran-Contra plot is a subplot that has to do with the Iranian hostage side of the equation. It shows the subversive and nearly treasonous nature of tactics used by the Reagan Republicans at the time of the Carter-Reagan election campaign.

The subplot involves William Casey and George Herbert Walker Bush. Both men's hands are stained with the kind of corruption that goes with the offices they filled. Those stains came from banking scandals connected to the CIA.

There was the Nugan-Hand Bank in Australia, capitalized out of money the CIA extracted by selling drugs and weapons left over from the Vietnam War. The Nugan-Hand Bank helped to finance, for example, CIA military operations in Angola and the Middle East. CIA director William Colby (1973-1976) was, by virtue of his office, on the bank's board of directors. George Bush assumed Colby's chair when Bush became CIA director from 1976-1977. Immediately after George H.W. Bush left as CIA director, federal bank examiners closed Nugan-Hand. One founder, Frank Nugan, is reported to have committed suicide; the other founder, Michael Jon Hand, disappeared with approximately $20 billion.

While Bush was still CIA director, the Pakistan-based Bank of Commerce & Credit International (BCCI) was capitalized at $20 billion with the help of ex-CIA directors Richard Helms and William Colby. (Years later, Colby was found mysteriously drowned, having gone for a solo canoe ride near his estate.) More than coincidentally, William Casey at this time was president of the Export-Import Bank, and a member of the Foreign Intelligence Advisory Board, having served in Nixon's previous election campaign.

BCCI helped to pump huge volumes of CIA-financed weapons into Saddam Hussein's Iraq. Bush, whose family business was oil, thought it wise to make friends with Hussein to avoid a repeat of the 1973 OPEC oil crisis. Some $20 billion of BCCI's assets have never been accounted for, according to the booklet, *The CIA's Greatest Hits*, by Mark Zepezauer. This was about the same amount that vanished from CIA's Nugan-Hand bank.

Coming from the Ex-Im bank, Casey was named chairman of the Reagan-Bush campaign; he was subsequently named Reagan's CIA director.

George Bush, as vice presidential candidate, did not want a surprise release of the hostages to upset Reagan's chances at the last minute. He put Casey in charge of a cadre of former CIA directors (very likely Helms and Colby) to use their security clearances to snoop on what plans Jimmy Carter might be making to bring home the Tehran hostages. Just as Nixon had thwarted the lame-duck LBJ, where the Vietnam peace negotiations were concerned, the Reagan-Bush team did the same with the Carter Democrats in their day.

As a result, several events coincided, at around Eastertime, 1980. Rupiper and his team had just returned (April 10) from visiting Tehran; the Methodists were having a convention in Washington, DC and Jack Bremer, with his bishop, wangled an invitation to brief President Carter at the White House. They told the President that the Iranians were afraid of provoking a war that would cause great human suffering, and were looking for a negotiated way out of the impasse. Unfortunately, this briefing took place just the day before the rescue attempt by helicopter was to be carried out. Of course, Bremer did not know that at the time. He also did not know (and neither did Jimmy Carter) that the Casey-Bush GOP spy team had a monkey-wrench to throw into the works.

Casey and his CIA big shots knew from purloined White House papers that the rescue plan called for eight troop-carrying helicopters to be sent from the decks of the carrier, *USS Nimitz*, in the Persian Gulf. Tactics dictated that if three of the eight became disabled on the way to the rendezvous site in the Iranian desert, the whole effort was to be aborted.

Somehow, most likely by way of professional courtesies with then-CIA director Stansfield Turner, the Casey-Bush team arranged for a subtle sabotage job by putting CIA Secret Team operatives aboard the *Nimitz*. Such teams were common under CIA-Pentagon strategies. It was their job, in this case, to make sure that by mission-time, there would be only five helicopters left capable of attempting the rescue. If they could make that happen, the mission would have to be aborted.

That's exactly what happened. Although such a failure rate among specially-readied, high-priority military helicopters should have raised suspicions, a sandstorm serendipitously masked the truth.

As events developed, one helicopter never left the Nimitz flight deck, due to a last-minute malfunction. By the time seven arrived at the desert rendezvous with the refueling tanker, another chopper was overheating and a third was leaking oil. Fate and the weather took over from that point. The mission was aborted, but as the choppers attempted their pullout, a sandstorm struck. In the blinding confusion, helicopter blades collided with the tanker plane. Eight loyal, patriotic naval officers died in the ensuing conflagration.

As a backup to the plan, the Casey-Bush team had been prepared to signal CIA agents in Tehran in case the rescue went forward. Poised to spill the beans to the Iranian government, they could have foiled the rescue attempt even as the helicopters were en route to Tehran. As it turned out, that was not necessary, and the Casey-Bush team kept its cover. In all this treachery, eight loyal and patriotic naval officers lost their lives, but Reagan's election was assured.

The bad news made it easier than ever to blame Carter for being militarily too ambitious, which the Congress and the public, prompted from behind the scenes by Reagan publicists, quickly did. Just as quickly, when Bush became vice president, he made sure Casey was put in charge of the CIA, all the better to keep the lid on their treason-lined treachery that won Reagan the White House.

The rest, as they say, is now water over the dam and the world is contending with the flood of events that have resulted. Those who carried out the illegal and immoral activities of Iran-Contra served no time in jail, while those who protested them served many years, some in hard-time solitary.

On a dark night in 1983, squads of Salvadoran soldiers in the foreign barracks at Fort Benning, Georgia, were rudely awakened by the loudspeaker. The Spanish words being blasted from the night sky were from the last sermon ever spoken by Archbishop Oscar Romero of San Salvador, El Salvador. He had been killed by LIONSDEN operatives three years prior, while saying Mass in a convent chapel in El Salvador, shot right through the heart as he approached the sacred ceremony of consecration by a sharpshooter trained at Fort Benning.

"This one's for you, brother (Romero)," said Fr. Roy Bourgeois. But his prayer-like whisper was drowned out by the Spanish words of an assassinated archbishop flowing from the boom box he carried:

> I would like to make an appeal in a special way to the men in the army. Brothers, each one of you is one of us. We are the same people. The farmers and the peasants that you kill are your own brothers and sisters. When you hear the words of a man telling you to kill, think of the words of God: "Thou shalt not kill." No soldier is obliged to carry out an order contrary to the law of God. In His name and in the name of our tormented people who have suffered so much and whose laments cry out to heaven, I implore you . . . I beg you . . . I *order* you to stop the repression.

As the stunned, half-dressed, Spanish-speaking troops stumbled from the barracks into the dark, they looked heavenward, searching for the source of the voice from on high. They soon were joined by US officers and grim-jawed military police with searchlights and combat weapons.

Perched high in a pine tree with the tape player was Fr. Roy Bourgeois, Maryknoll missionary and Vietnam Purple Heart hero, and two other people: Rev. Larry Rosebaugh, an Oblate priest and draft-paper burner who was a seminary friend of Rupiper; and Linda Ventimiglia, a former US Army reserve officer who had once received training at Fort Benning and knew her way around the base.

Of course, their protest was over more than just the death of Archbishop Romero. They knew the Fort Benning death squads had caused thousands of other deaths in Central America. They knew what the Pentagon did not admit until 1996: that US Army intelligence manuals, used from 1982 to 1991 at Fort Benning, contained training techniques including beating, torture and execution methods. They knew what the world did not learn until the United Nations released a report in 1993 on El Salvador's brutal civil war, which America illegally supported by way of commerce in illegal arms and drugs.

The UN report noted that:

- Two School of the Americas graduates were among three officers cited for the assassination of Archbishop Romero.
- Three SOA graduates were among those accused of the rapes and murders of four US Maryknoll nuns.
- Ten SOA graduates were cited as officers who led the massacre of 773 civilians at El Mozote, San Salvador, in 1984.
- Nineteen SOA graduates were involved in the murder of six Jesuit priests and their housekeeper and the rape of her daughter.

It was this kind of terrorist event that prompted Bourgeois, Rosebaugh and Ventimiglia to bring Archbishop Romero's last sermon to Fort Benning in a *Mission Impossible* fashion.

Why Fort Benning? Besides its Death Squad infamy, it had been the focal point of secret military operations against foreign lands for decades. Before its agent-training operations were moved from Panama, it had served as a CIA base for launching the Bay of Pigs attack on Cuba. Fort Benning's vaunted Delta Force detachment was called upon for the Iranian hostage rescue debacle. Clearly, Fort Benning is not an ordinary military base, it is a LIONSDEN operation with ties to the CIA, the National Security Council and the State Department. If protests against immoral operations were to draw public attention, Fort Benning seemed like a good place to do it.

Through the tireless investigative work of SOA Watch staff aide Vicki Imerman, Bourgeois had learned most of the names of Fort Benning graduates and their post-graduate connections with the death squads. They number in the hundreds and include:

- Roberto d'Aubuisson, who was the death squad leader who ordered the execution of Archbishop Romero.
- Panamanian dictator Manuel Noriega, who was captured by the US only after a full-scale military invasion of the Canal Zone. He was a former CIA operative and runner of CIA drugs during the Iran-Contra operation. (LIONSDEN eats its own cripples, whether in Panama or Iraq.)
- Guatemalan Colonel Julio Alpirez, who ordered the extra-judicial assassination of guerrilla leader Efrain Bamaca, the husband of Texas lawyer Jennifer Harbury.

To that list of leaders trained in murder at Fort Benning can now be added the name of Col. Byron Disrael Lima Estrada, mastermind of the assassination in 1998 of Bishop Juan Gerardi of Guatemala.

Roy Bourgeois

Bourgeois was a former US Navy officer who had returned from Vietnam as a Purple Heart hero. And when he first heard that Dan Berrigan was appearing to talk and protest the war, Bourgeois rounded up friends to oppose the priest's appearance. To Bourgeois, Berrigan was a traitor. But eventually, an experience Bourgeois had while in Vietnam with a missionary priest took its effect, and he soon found himself studying to be a priest, a Maryknoll missionary, in fact. In due course and because of his morality, he found himself in confrontation with the forces of evil in the world.

After ordination, Bourgeois served missions in Bolivia, where he was once placed under house arrest. Then he served in El Salvador. As in Bolivia, his preaching of God-given human rights offended the right-wing regime that was backed by the US.

Bourgeois's associate in "crime" at the Fort Benning midnight broadcast was Larry Rosebaugh. Fr. Larry had taught high school and worked among the poor street people in Milwaukee and was one of the

"Milwaukee Fourteen" who burned draft files back in 1968. For that prophetic act, he served two full years in some of the nation's toughest prisons. After his release he worked among the poor in Recife, Brazil.

Fr. Bourgeois tells the story of the trio's infiltration and raid at Fort Benning:

"We could not have done it without Linda Ventimiglia," Bourgeois says. "I got involved at Fort Benning in 1982 after the assassination of Archbishop Romero and then later four churchwomen in El Salvador. Those happened in 1980. There were two Maryknoll nuns, whom I personally knew, one Ursuline nun and a laywoman named Jeanne Donovan from Cleveland.

"A Salvadoran hit squad trained at Fort Benning killed these women and raped them. This was before six Jesuit priests were killed along with their housekeeper and her daughter — all by the same assassins. I was livid (over all this killing). And so I rented a place and started planning for protest. (When I started) I found myself giving a lecture at Auburn University in Alabama.

"Afterward, at the mixer, this outwardly shy 30-ish woman told me she wanted to join my protest. Her name was Linda Ventimiglia. Like me, she was outraged over the killings and rapes perpetrated by Fort Benning foreign graduates. She said she wanted to do what she could to peacefully counteract what was going on at Fort Benning.

"I got really interested when she told me she had trained at Fort Benning and was now in the Army Reserves, and that her stepfather was a lieutenant colonel stationed at Fort Benning.

"I told her," Bourgeois recalls, "that I was having a meeting a few nights later. She accepted my invitation. There were a number of people at that meeting, including Larry Rosebaugh, and two Purple Heart veterans of Vietnam. That's when we found out that Linda lived with her stepfather and mother in the piney woods of Alabama, not far from Auburn University."

Rosebaugh then recounts a series of four incursions onto Fort Benning that led to their arrests.

"There was an army surplus store right near the base," he recalls, "and we equipped ourselves with officers' uniforms. Bourgeois and Ventimiglia had been in the military, so they knew how to play the role. Fort Benning is what they call an open base, with no guard posts, so the three of us walked up to the barracks where the Central American trainees were quartered. They immediately jumped to attention and saluted. Bourgeois spoke excellent Spanish and promptly ordered them to distribute among themselves some folded pamphlets we had prepared. By the time they got circulated to the Salvadoran officers, there were guard dogs and MPs. We got hauled to some building and we were questioned at length. Finally, they drove us out the gate and left us curbside."

Larry is not sure where the next idea came from, but the notion was to go to the base chapel on a Sunday an give an anti-SOA witness at Mass for the mostly-Catholic trainees. Again, they donned their uniforms, and again they got on base. Larry recalls,

We arrived early enough to distribute our leaflets in the pews. Then we stood at the entrance to the chapel and handed out more as the troops filtered in. The chaplain, I don't recall his name, asked us to leave. We explained who we really were, including the fact that we were priests protesting what had happened to Archbishop Romero at the hands of people like those he was about to say Mass for. When he asked us to leave, we simply laid down, blocking the entrance way.

"You should be in Church saying Mass," the chaplain huffed.

"No, you should be lying down here with us."

After a second questioning session and brief detention, the trio were again driven off base and made to walk home.

"It was there we began to lay plans for our most adventurous incursion into Fort Benning," Bourgeois explains. "Free from spying eyes, we tested some pole-climbing spikes in the woods at a farm owned by a relative of Linda's. We tested our boom box there with the tape of the last sermon of Archbishop Romero.

"For a third time, we got into our uniforms with all the appropriate brass and bars," Bourgeois says. "I went in as a lieutenant colonel. Rosebaugh was a major. Linda Ventimiglia was a lieutenant, carrying the duffel bag with our climbing gear and boom box. It was after nightfall.

"So the three of us went on base again. In our uniforms, we got saluted whenever we met soldiers, and were able to penetrate the top security area where the Salvadorans were housed. Using linemen's foot pikes, we scaled these high pine trees right near the barracks. Then we waited for the lights to go out. We whispered a prayer for our fallen friends and flipped the "on" switch of the boombox.

"As Romero's voice boomed into the barracks, it was, uh, one of those... what I would consider a sacred moment," Bourgeois recalls.

"These Salvadoran soldiers were listening to Oscar Romero, the dead archbishop, telling them to lay down their arms. Some of these soldiers coming out of the barracks looked up into the tree, into the sky, hearing the voice of Romero, not being able to see us in the cover of darkness there.

"And, of course, the MPs and the instructors heard it as well, and they came with their lights and arrested us. It took them about 15 minutes to get us down from the tree. We just kept playing and replaying Romero's sermon," Bourgeois says. "After they threatened to shoot us down, that's when we came down.

"Once again, they detained us overnight, questioned us extensively and drove us off the base, leaving us with a long walk back to town."

(It is a subtle point of law that military officials have no authority to arrest civilians, even on base. However, they can detain them until local law enforcement officials can be called; and, in extreme cases, as in wartime, they do have the authority to use deadly force.)

The final excursion onto the base was perhaps somewhat anti-climactic, according to Rosebaugh.

"By that time, we were scratching our heads, trying to figure out what we could do to get arrested, so the public could get our message. So once again, we donned our uniforms and made our way onto the base, this time to the home of the base commander," Rosebaugh says. "We had candles with us, and we were going to stage a vigil outside the General's home. We were taking it to the top, you could say.

"We knocked on the door. It was answered by a young woman who might have been the General's daughter. She told us the General was not at home and shut the door quickly. So we lit our candles and lined the sidewalk with them. Within minutes, a car pulled up with the General. Behind him were a force of MPs. He was pissed off and barking orders. This time, after another round of questioning and detention overnight, they drove us to the city dump and put us out there."

A day later, as the trio once again gathered at the home of Bourgeois for a strategy session, unmarked cars full of suit-and-tie G-men swooped down and arrested all three. The FBI agents took them to county jail where Bourgeois, Rosebaugh and Ventimiglia were booked for criminal trespass and impersonating army officers.

"We got 18 months in prison," Bourgeois says. "That's when I ended up in Sandstone, Minnesota. Larry was sent to La Tuna, Texas, and Linda to Lexington, Kentucky."

Linda Ventimiglia

Bourgeois and Rosebaugh remain priests today. Linda Ventimiglia went on to be a nurse. Not even Bourgeois knows where she is today. But he did have one last contact with her, several years after prison. One night Bourgeois got a call from Linda. After studying for a degree in nursing, she was now being challenged by the examining board because of her past prison record.

Linda's future was jeopardized by Church superiors because of her arrest and prison record. While studying nursing at Auburn, Linda was also teaching Confraternity of Christian Doctrine (catechism classes) as a volunteer under the Vatican's Peace and Justice Program. The nuns, who presided over the CCD classes, were not overly friendly to Linda's concept of Peace and Justice; they fired her.

"I wrote a letter to the mother superior," Bourgeois says. "I said, 'How dare you? You had in your care a prophet who went to prison to protest the rape of nuns and other atrocities and now you want to deny her a vocation to heal?'"

Bourgeois never got any response from that nun, but he's sure Linda got her nursing credentials. As a follow-up, he generated thousands of letters from the *Catholic Worker* community to the board of nursing examiners, which then relented and issued a nursing license for Linda Ventimiglia. Bourgeois says he does not know where she is today.

By the oddest of coincidences, Carl Kabat says he had met Linda before she was involved in the Fort Benning protest. It was in 1980, when Carl was serving a term at Allenwood Federal Prison in Pennsylvania.

"I was walking down a hallway, past an ashen-faced inmate who was unconscious and slabbed on an ambulance gurney. Apparently a guard was refusing to open a locked door so the patient could be wheeled to the ambulance. He must have been waiting for some authorization from the warden's office. This red-haired young lady, the prison's emergency medical technician, was screaming at the guard: 'But he may be dying! I think he's had a heart attack!'" The medical woman was Linda Ventimiglia.

Rosebaugh and Bourgeois Keep the Prophets' Faith

Rosebaugh's imprisonment for the Fort Benning protest, was his third, but not his last. Following release for the Fort Benning protest, he was assigned to the diocese of Santiago de Maria in El Salvador. On March 21, 1988, he was arrested on the streets of San Salvador while walking to a parish meeting. Here is the account given by the Oblate Fathers in their newsletter:

> "While walking down a street at mid-morning in San Salvador, some young army officers asked to see his identification papers. They found in his bag a church calendar that contained some quotations from Archbishop Oscar Romero, who was killed by a right wing faction several years prior. Apparently, it was felt that this was subversive material.
>
> "Larry was taken to a military prison for interrogation. He was not physically abused but he was blindfolded and threatened. He was not allowed to notify either the embassy or the bishop's office of his whereabouts and was never given any reason for his arrest. Of course, his arrests in Brazil and two in the United States were widely known in CIA circles, which by now encircled El Salvador.
>
> "When it was discovered that he was missing, people began to look for him. Finally, at 10 PM that evening, after twelve hours of detention, the vice-consul in El Salvador, Mr. Mark Shaw, located Larry at the Treasury Police Prison and arranged for his release. Larry returned immediately to his mission just outside the capital."

From El Salvador, Larry was transferred to serve the poor in Guatemala, amid a growing respect for him as a priest who works among the poor.

Bourgeois, shortly after his release following the Fort Benning tree climbing, heard about another massacre, this one in El Salvador. Six Jesuits had been killed by death squads trained at Fort Benning's School of the Americas.

"So in 1990, I came back here to Fort Benning to investigate the School of the Americas," Bourgeois explains. "I have since discovered that death squad trainees come here not only from El Salvador but from all over Central and South America, including Colombia, Brazil, Peru, and , Argentina."

In a newspaper interview with the *Texas Observer* in 1997, Bourgeois explained his transformation from a US Naval officer to priest and protester:

"When Vietnam was in the making, I felt it was my responsibility to join the Navy. I became a Naval officer and spent the next four years in the military. The generals, the president, the members of Congress. . . they were saying that we had to go to Vietnam to stop the spread of Communism. And I believed that, and I went.

"In Vietnam, for the first time, I began to look at things with critical eyes and question what was going on there in the midst of all that violence and death and losing friends. I really started looking at my faith more seriously.

"There was this missionary that I met near our base — this Redemptorist priest from Canada, Lucien Olivier, an incredible guy. He was going about his work trying to help the children at an orphanage, about 300 of them, many of them wounded. I saw something in him that touched my life very deeply. I saw him as a healer in the midst of all that violence and death.

"I went to this Army chaplain after a while to ask about doing missionary work, because my year in Vietnam was coming to an end. And he recommended the Maryknoll order. I had never heard of them. So I wrote to Maryknoll and applied and was accepted. And then, after six years in comfortable seminaries, I was ordained.

"But let me say, as a footnote, my life was a struggle. I was not, like Saul of Tarsus, knocked off a horse by a bolt from God. It took me three years after leaving 'Nam to go on my first demonstration with other veterans. I was assigned to a mission in Bolivia, a slum on the outskirts of La Paz. That was home for the next five years. And it was there that I got educated. It was a very radicalizing experience.

"When we as missionaries go to another country, the poor we go to serve become our teachers. There in Bolivia I was taught about their struggle for justice, peace, life itself. It taught me also about my country's foreign policy. We were supporting the dictator, General

Banzer. The CIA was very active there. Multinational companies arrived to exploit the resources of the poor, for profit."

Bourgeois pauses when asked about how the Church views his role as a liberation-theologist. Then he puts it in perspective:

"I was arrested in Bolivia because of my work there. In my fifth year I was forced to leave, *persona non grata*. I went to New York (where the Maryknoll community is based) after hearing about the School of the Americas at Fort Benning. I talked to my community about going to Georgia. There was no problem. For us, as missionaries working in Latin America, it's a simple issue. We are there to relieve the suffering of the poor, trying to be healers as Jesus was a healer.

"So when we learned about the School of the Americas training thousands of soldiers from Latin America, and being responsible for the death of Archbishop Romero, and then the killing of the Maryknoll women by the military, then the killing of the Jesuits by the military and on and on, this became a very clear issue.

"It's an issue of suffering and death. It involves us in a very real way in our work. For example, Father Bill Woods from this Maryknoll community was killed in Guatemala. The military was involved in his murder. He was silenced for trying to help the people, so many others were silenced."

Another Round at Fort Benning

In 1990, Angelo Liteky and his brother Patrick joined Roy Bourgeois at Fort Benning.

"This was right after the Jesuit priests and parishioners had been murdered in El Salvador," Liteky says. "We knew, we just knew, that troops trained here at Fort Benning's School of the Americas had done it. Investigations indicate they did, but the lower-level troops became the scapegoats."

What he means is that Colonel Rene Emilio Ponce, El Salvador's army chief of staff (before becoming minister of defense) defied US officials trying to investigate the murder of the six Jesuits in 1988, 1989, and 1990. In essence, he told US diplomats "to fuck off," as quoted by one unnamed source CIA source in a 1990 article written by Philip Bennett for *Vanity Fair*. It was the CIA, Bennett claims, that first discovered the Jesuit victims, skulls shattered, in the grass outside their campus residences. Ponce was the leader of the Atlacatl Battalion that committed the atrocities against the Jesuit priests.

So back at SOA, one day the trio walked into the public office foyer. No one was at the reception desk. Undeterred, they spilled their own pre-bottled blood on the steps and hallway. Bourgeois held aloft a cross. A major poked his head out of an adjoining office and asked them what the hell they were doing.

> "I told him we were protesting the death squads he had helped train. He just stood there, slack-jawed. We were glad he didn't come at us, because we didn't want to spill any blood on him. That would have ruined our policy of non-violence toward individuals. Blood on anyone would look like a personal assault, and that's not what we're about.

> "After a few exchanged words, we went outside and lay down as if we were dead. We tried to portray the bodies of our dead Jesuit friends and their parishioners in El Salvador," Liteky recalls.

> "We must have been there for 10 minutes before the MPs came. When the arrest and trial for defacing public property and for criminal trespass were all over, the verdict was automatic: six months in the slammer."

This was the start of a series of protests at Fort Benning that involved thousands of people over 10 years.

Bourgeois has no doubt that in subtle ways the military in Central and South America receives the tacit blessing of the Church.

> "Not only in Latin America," Bourgeois says bluntly. "Let's talk about our own backyard. Let's talk about the US Catholic bishops. I think it's shameful. Absolutely shameful. Sinful, really."

Despite his criticism of the Church, which is matched by some of the other prophets, Bourgeois remains a Catholic priest.

> "I guess you could say that I'm a stubborn Cajun. I mean, the way I see it, why should I leave the Church? Why don't *they* leave? I mean,

it's as much my Church as theirs. They (the hierarchy) see it as *their* Church, when it is Christ's church, the church of all the people on earth. What I see is really men, mostly white men, who live a very privileged life, educated in the best universities. All of them hold these big positions of power and privilege. And they get out of touch.

"Rather than being spiritual leaders, they have become corporate executives. They are CEOs. And with few exceptions, they have lost contact with the poor here at home. As far as Latin America is concerned, it's like talking about the moon. I ask them to leave the comfort of the mansions and rectories and take off a few days and go to Latin America, and simply visit the poor.

"Why don't the bishops ask them, 'What's it like for you? Where do your children go to school? If they get sick, what can you do for them?' I tell you, the bishops could be educated in a few days by the poor. But to get that bishop out of his environment of privilege and class, it's not possible. They've reached the heights of power. There's very little hope."

Bourgeois in Latin America

Personally, Bourgeois is not pessimistic when speaking of his crusade.

"Hope may not come from the bishops (except those like Romero), but it does come from the little people, the grassroots people, the people of faith. In this country (US), they hear about the School of the Americas, and they get angry. Why?

"This is what amazes me. When they hear about this issue they say, 'Wait! I remember what happened to the four church women. They were raped and they were killed. I remember Bishop Romero. I remember reading on the front page of my paper about the six Jesuits shot in the head. And you mean to tell me those responsible where trained at this SOA school?'

"Then they get angry. Angry, but not violent. But when the bishops read this in the newspapers, they turn the page. I was in prison for three years for protesting our foreign policy in Latin America, and I would write bishops and ask them to speak out. And I would hear:

"'Well, we shouldn't get involved in politics.'

"Politics?

"And I would write back, and I would simply say, 'You know, bishop, this is first and foremost a moral issue. Giving guns to soldiers who go back to their home countries and kill their own people for speaking out for food and for freedom to live. What is political about that? This is a moral issue. And Jesus would be there speaking out against this clearly and boldly. What about children dying of malnutrition? This is a moral issue. If we can't speak out about this in our churches, where do we do it?'"

Bourgeois's efforts now are directed toward decommissioning the School of Americas. He says it is just a training school for hirelings of the CIA, developing methods of torture and killing. The School of the Americas previously was located in Panama City, in the Canal Zone, but was moved after President Jimmy Carter signed the Panama Canal Treaty.

When Bourgeois was first arrested in Bolivia, he talked to the US ambassador and asked how relations were between Bolivia and the US. He was told they were "very good." He indicated that he had a hard time coming to grips with the realization that the US was really the bad guy.

Bourgeois says that he only began to put it all together when he got to El Salvador. He knew "the military was brutalizing the poor, who were crying for justice." Then he speaks about the rich of El Salvador who have accumulated wealth over the years on the backs of the poor. "They (the rich) need protection for their system. That system keeps them rich and the vast majority poor."

Recently, Bourgeois read a speech by a retired US Army general, who bragged about his 33 years of service as a high-class muscle man for big business. The General said:

> War is just a racket. A racket is best described, I believe, as something that is not what it seems to be to the majority of the people. Only a small inside group knows what it is about. It is conducted for the benefit of the very few at the expense of the masses.
>
> There is no trick in the racketeering bag that the military gang is blind to. It has its "finger men" to point out the enemies; its "muscle men" to destroy the enemies; it "brain men" to plan war, and a "Big Boss": Super-Nationalistic-Capitalism.
>
> I served in all the commissioned ranks, from second lieutenant to major general, and during that time I spent most of my time being a high-class muscle man for Big Business, for Wall Street and the bankers. In short, I was a racketeer, a gangster for capitalism.

Like all the members of the military profession, I never had a thought of my own until I left the service. My mental faculties remained in suspended animation while I obeyed orders of higher-ups. This is typical with anyone in the military service.

I helped make Mexico, especially Tampico, safe for American oil interests in 1914. I helped make Haiti and Cuba a decent place for the National City Bank to collect revenues in. I helped in the raping of half a dozen Central American republics for the benefit of Wall Street. The record of my racketeering is long. I helped purify Nicaragua for the banking house of Brown Brothers in 1901-1912. I brought light to the Dominican Republic for American sugar interests in 1916. In China, I helped to see to it that Standard Oil went its way unmolested.

During those years, I had, as the boys in the backroom would say, a swell racket. Looking back on it, I could have given Al Capone a few hints. The best he could do was operate in three districts. I operated in three continents.

As the dates suggest, the malady of American exploitation in Central America by way of war goes back at least a century. The general who spoke those words was none other than Smedley Butler, the most-decorated officer of the Spanish-American and World War I era.

At least Butler was as bold in his condemnation of the system, in his old age, as he was aggressive in his defense of it in his youth. It is that kind of conversion, away from the racket of war and death squads, that Bourgeois seeks within America's politicians and military people today as he lays siege annually to the gates of Fort Benning.

What have these death squads done besides fight for right-wing causes in what are falsely made to seem like civil wars in pursuit of freedom? They murder unarmed women and children in even more cold-blooded fashion than US troops did at My Lai in Vietnam. Consider this account given by Rev. Daniel Santiago, S.J., in the Jesuit journal, *America*, about a peasant woman in El Salvador:

> She returned home one day to a grisly scene: her mother, sister, and three children had been decapitated. Their bodies had then been arranged around the table as if sitting down to a meal. The head of each person had been placed on the table in front of the bodies, with the hands arranged as if each were holding its own head. Apparently, the assassins from the Salvadoran National Guard could not keep the

hands of the 18-month-old infant in place, so they nailed the tiny hands onto the head. A large bowl filled with blood was placed in the middle of the table.

Father Santiago, in describing other atrocities by the death squads, says it was all done to intimidate leftist rebels or suspected rebel supporters who do not seek to harm the United States. Here are his words:

> People are not just killed by death squads in El Salvador; they are decapitated, and then their heads are placed on pikes and used to dot the landscape. Men are not just disemboweled by the Salvadoran Treasury Police; their severed genitalia are stuffed into their mouths. Salvadoran women are not just raped by the National Guard; their wombs are cut from their bodies and used to cover their faces. It is not enough to kill children; they are dragged over barbed wire until their flesh falls from their bones while parents are forced to watch.

Small wonder that Fr. Rupiper included an account of these atrocities in a letter to President Bill Clinton on September 23, 1999, asking if the President knew the role that School of the Americas graduates play in such crimes. He received no reply.

Small wonder that Archbishop Oscar Romero had lashed out in his sermon against the heinous military, calling for them to lay down their arms and refuse to serve. For that, he was killed.

Small wonder that Bourgeois, Rosebaugh and Ventimiglia accepted jail to bring Romero's message to yet another graduating class of Latin American troops being trained in America to commit atrocities for America, by proxy.

Small wonder that Bourgeois is continuing the fight against the School of the Americas from his tiny office across the street from Fort Benning's entry. And no wonder he continues to be arrested for actions against that base.

What is a wonder is, why more members of the so-called "moral majority" in America are not moral enough to set aside the politics of their conservative religions and back prophets such as Bourgeois in a non-sectarian fight against such immorality. The answer is that the LIONSDEN philosophy has infiltrated the moral majority, just as FBI agents did 30 years ago during the Vietnam War protest. Religious conservatives tend also to be political conservatives. They extend their faith in God to faith in their leaders, so that a little bit of propaganda and misinformation easily cause confusion of moral and political purpose.

Religious prophets have the ability to distinguish the two, when necessary.

Between 1980, when Romero was gunned down, and 1989, more than 60,000 Salvadorans were killed by death squads. Two or three times that number were killed in all of Central America. It is a wonder that the US media, which for so many years worried about 58,000 Americans killed in an unjust Vietnam War, has largely ignored so many US-backed murders south of the border, reporting only when "Americans" were killed.

The media, too, is part of a society imbued by LIONSDEN and Trilateralism. The American way of life is, after all, a comfortable one.

It is a wonder how military heroes like Oliver North and Admiral Secord, operating from President Reagan's White House, got away with defying Congress, the will of the American public and common morality. How could they, for years, sell guns to the Iranians and use the money secretly to supply guns to the Contras in El Salvador? How could White House cabinet-level officials countenance CIA profiteering from drugs? Why did Congress, so openly defied, not bring charges against North or Secord and other agents? Why was the media not more outraged on behalf of the American public and the Constitutional process?

How could they not be sensitive to such outrages when the contingent of Oblate priests noticed it from as far away as Recife? On May 12, 1986, the group of US priests there sent the following letter of protest to President Reagan:

> We, American citizens and missionaries in Brazil, feel bound in conscience to respond to the American government's attack on the people of Libya. We affirm our adherence to the Universal Declaration of Human Rights signed by the United States, and to religious principles of reconciliation and peace based on justice and truth.
>
> We deplore terrorism in all its forms and we believe the use of weapons of violence and terrorism will provoke more violence, more terrorism. We find ourselves shocked and revolted by this action presumptuously taken in our name. We repudiate this action or any future violent action performed in the name of peace.
>
> The people of Brazil with whom we live and work are also shocked, and because of their compassionate stance, question us and the policy of the United States government.
>
> As American citizens committed to non-violence, we believe that other solutions must be sought to the problems of world terrorism.

The letter was never answered, confirming that verbal and written protests are useless in terms of gaining the attention of the public or redress from the nation's leaders. Action and protest at the political level is necessary. That's why Bourgeois began lobbying efforts with Catholic congressmen such as Joseph Kennedy and others who had been educated in Jesuit colleges.

The US House of Representatives, in 1998, nearly passed a resolution calling for the closing of the School of the Americas. Later, US Rep. Joseph Moakley, a Democrat from Massachusetts, took up the same cudgel. Finally, on July 29, 1999, the House passed an amendment to strike — from a bill on foreign operations spending — nearly $20 million for the School of Americas.

Of course, there was "loyal opposition." These elected patriots callously overlooked America's complicity in the murders of several Jesuit priests and Maryknoll nuns and thousands of plain human beings in Central America. Among those defending the funding of the School of the Americas was US Rep. Callahan of Alabama. His strongest sentiment, echoed by House colleagues from Georgia, included the remark, "You can't condemn the school forever for what happened years ago." Callahan added that SOA has "cleaned up its act," as if reform had qualified SOA for continued funding; or as if murder had some expiration time in the Statute of Limitations.

After years of lobbying by Bourgeois and his School of Americas Watch, the proposal was adopted by the House with a vote of 230-197, a significant majority by any political standard.

At last, Bourgeois thought, the prophecies and protests had chalked up a victory. But it was to be short-lived. A House-Senate compromise committee restored the funding with the proviso that the School of the Americas be renamed the Western Hemispheric Institute for Security Cooperation. Accordingly, Bourgeois says, the fight will continue under new resolutions.

The fight against SOA would never have reached the halls of Congress without exceptional campaigning and lobbying by Bourgeois, and the Maryknoll and Jesuit communities. The result is an annual rally in Columbus, Georgia, that draws a crowd of 10,000 peace pilgrims from across the nation — all commemorating the terrorism that has been exported from Fort Benning for decades.

The event draws celebrities such as actor Martin Sheen, folksingers such as Pete Seeger, and world-known protesters such as Daniel Berrigan.

At the rally in 2000, Sheen amused the crowd when he contrasted the unsettled election results in Florida with his own presidential TV role in *West Wing* by saying, from the podium, "As the only duly-elected president, I hereby declare this base closed."

When the laughter settled down, he turned more serious and said, "Everybody knows what I do for a living. This is what I do to *live!*"

Bourgeois says it is prophecy at work when, year after year, offenders are arrested for trespassing and thousands are given "ban and bar" letters, warning them not to set foot on the base again. But they do. And they are not just young people on a lark. There are gray heads and bald heads with protest signs; and Vietnam veterans wearing their old military uniforms — even honorably discharged veterans who took their training at Fort Benning, such as Jeff Moebus, who retired with 28 years of service.

On May 22, 2001, 26 of the 1,700 protesters arrested at the SOAW rally the previous November, stood trial in Columbus, Georgia for trespassing. Most were fined several thousand dollars and given six months in jail by federal judge "Maximum Bob" Elliott, who, decades ago, dealt just as harshly with Rev. Martin Luther King, Jr. Among this group is Richard John Kinane, a red-haired school teacher, who has embraced the Buddhist faith. Kinane's brother, Edward, has already served two terms in jail for similar protests against SOA.

Noting that SOA has changed its acronym to WHISC, Kinane agrees with Bourgeois that it's simply a case of "new name, old shame."

The Bible reports that the prophet Joshua brought down the walls of Jericho by sounding a ram's horn. In today's world, modern prophets such as Carl Kabat are attacking the concrete slabs of nuclear missile silos with jackhammers and trumpeting their message via newspapers.

Among all the anti-nuclear-war prophets, perhaps Carl Kabat has caused the most consternation and stirred the most controversy within the legal establishment. Certainly his prison sentences have been the sternest. Whether Carl was spilling his blood or symbolically sabotaging the instruments of war, something Joshua-like in his style struck sparks.

Carl likes to quote men of peace. "Gandhi once said that you have to *be* the change you want to *see* in the world," he says. "That is pretty Christ-like, I think."

Carl has two other heroes: Franz Jaegerstaetter and Martin Luther King, Jr. Carl assumes everyone knows about King, and he quickly explains Jaegerstaetter: he was a young Austrian farmer who refused induction into Hitler's army, and was beheaded in 1943 for his crime of resisting the state. As for his other heroes, Carl notes that Christ was crucified by the state, and both Gandhi and King were often imprisoned for civil disobedience, before they were killed by those who did not understand peace, justice and freedom.

"All four were killed for the nobility of what they represented," Carl says, "— resistance to evil. But they still won. Now we are beating them (the government) at their own game. When they throw us in jail, others start doing the same things."

Then Carl Kabat laughs happily, bringing a sparkle even to his unseeing right eye.

Kabat was among the first of these prophets to take his protest face-to-face with the President of the United States and the Pentagon. He was arrested in 1976 for picketing Jimmy Carter in Plains, Georgia. In 1978, he poured blood on the portico of the White House and in the mall of the Pentagon with the Berrigan brothers as accomplices.

Carl recalls a funny event that happened while he was in the Washington, DC jail for splattering the White House with blood. Very suddenly one morning, the guards hustled Kabat from his cell, gave him all his personal belongings and some bus tokens, plus a handful of quarters, and literally kicked him out of jail. With no hearing or explanation, the guards simply showed him the sidewalk.

Stranded, it was only after he made some calls to friends, looking for somewhere to stay, that he learned Pope John Paul II was visiting Washington as part of a world tour. Apparently, somebody was worried that the Pope might inquire about America's imprisonment of a fellow Polish priest in the nation's capital.

"I didn't know what was expected of me," Carl recalls with a laugh. "So I just hung out with friends. I wasn't even on the run, and it took the prison cockroaches about a month to find me and put me back in jail."

After his official release, Carl stayed with a peace community known as *Jonah House* in Baltimore, a refuge for activists founded by Philip Berrigan. Within a year, they formed a project-group that became known as the *Plowshares Eight.* They became notorious for hammering on the nose cone of a nuclear missile under manufacture by General Electric in King of Prussia, Pennsylvania, and their trial dragged on until it was finally dismissed in consideration of the time already served by the defendants, who refused to accept bail.

In the years that followed, punctuated by jail terms for various protests, Kabat took a jackhammer to a nuclear missile silo near Kansas City and also disabled a Pershing Missile launcher in Germany — all without doing violence to any person.

These actions prompted one judge to call Carl Kabat "mean and destructive" and "a danger to society." Kabat, of course, maintains that the real danger to society rests in the nuclear missiles he was attacking.

"Mean and destructive" certainly doesn't fit the obedient boy on his father's farm in the largely-Polish community near Scheller, Illinois, or the seminarian who helped equip his seminary building with improved plumbing during remodeling. Whatever the task, Carl was quick to get to the heart of whatever he took on.

"If it's something that needs doing and it's the right thing, then why wait for somebody's permission? Just do it," he remarks at one point in his journals, still on tape. His point of reference at the time was the scolding he received from his religious superiors for purchasing plumbing supplies to get a job done without obtaining advance permission from those who told him to do the job. Carl doesn't like to be micro-managed.

Carl was born in the middle of a family of three brothers and one sister. His father tended a small family acreage while employed as a guard at Menard State Prison in Illinois. His father could be rated as strict in the way he raised his children. His mother, Anna, although devoutly Catholic, was the first woman in her parish to decide not to wear a hat or scarf to Church, as was mandated for all women at the time.

Carl is not so much reckless as he is strong-willed when he knows he's right. By 2001, he had endured nearly 15 years of his life in prison for his dissent. Although he often tends to speak in circles when responding to questions, and although he occasionally stutters from the pressure of wanting to say several things at the same time, in some of his diary tapes he speaks directly of the main purpose of life: to "laugh and dance"; to enjoy life as the Creator intended, but never at the expense of others.

In his recorded recollections, he uses the parable of a kitten that is so playful it seems to exist just for enjoying life, as if it could play forever with a ball of yarn. Then he wonders why that is not possible among humankind. To him, the answer is that:

> Those in power do not play by the same rules as the kitten. They want all the power that a nation can wind onto their ball of yarn. They want all the glory that money brings without sharing with those who help make that money. They want all the fun and enjoyment of life because they think the world is their personal ball of yarn and life is theirs alone to dispose or partake of. They knit from their yarn weapons of mass destruction. They would kill the kitten just to take the ball of yarn.

Prophets like Carl and Paul Kabat learn the hard way that there are no kittens among life's players, only lions, LIONSDEN systems and their prey, and those in power who are willing to lie and exploit and kill, for themselves or the system that sustains them (to protect and serve the bomb, as Frank Cordaro says.)

That's why, when they read about Iran-Contra, a CIA black market in human organs, covert wars and assassinations of bishops, nuns and priests, they are driven by the system to take action. That's why, when they witness the human toll exacted by the system and its leaders, they, like Joshua at Jericho, try to bring down those walls.

Winning his cause is secondary to Kabat. "Success is, in a certain way, unimportant to me," he says. "It is not a matter of fruitfulness but faithfulness. It is not success, in my opinion, that is important. Are we, after all, called to be successful or are we called to be faithful?"

Carl, like many prophets, dreams impossible dreams, just as Colorado's poet laureate, Thomas Hornsby Ferril, did when he mused: "Dare I dream more dreams than I can possibly prove?"

What drives, what fuels prophets like Carl? There is a cause-and-effect chain that leads back to government agencies and policies; what Carl calls "irritants of evil," though until the events of September 11, 2001, most Americans were not prepared to attach any blame to their government.

What caused the Islamic terrorists to protest so violently at the World Trade Center? Clearly, the peaceful nature of the protests by the individuals in this book separates them from the crime of the World Trade Center bombers, but both were provoked by the same evils: the pernicious persistence of violence to humanity as America pursues its gun-slinging cowboy role in world politics; the lies behind the policies that bring death to thousands and misery to millions; America's ability to "get way with it", and convince the world it was right.

To the prophets like Carl, policies such as Star Wars and a trickle-down economy meant just one thing: poverty.

Kabat's tough attitude took root in the '60s with his experience among the Catholic peasants in the Philippines. Sent there to help establish a seminary, he became skinny trying to feed the child-beggars gathered daily around the school. Baptism seemed as futile as burial, because they so often followed each other closely. He preached by his daily actions, helping to build shelters for the people when he wasn't teaching others to help in the same way by their lives. Kabat's superiors sent him back to the States for a rest. But he found he could not rest among those who gave no rest to the poor.

Later, Kabat's concern for the poor grew sharper as, for five years, he watched pitiful, half-starved parishioners disappear and die in Brazil. The oppression came from the brutal hands of Gen. Castillo Branco, whose regime was propped up by US arms and foreign aid money. Knowing where the cause had its roots, yet unable to effect any change, fed a growing, holy rage.

Carl saw profits from the sale of weapons of war in Iran-Iraq being diverted to guns for Central American US-backed dictatorships; profits from drugs peddled by the CIA through puppet regimes to supply more guns for more wars; enslavement to drugs by the peasant growers on one end to victimized users in American ghettos on the other; profits from organs of war victims peddled by CIA ghouls on black markets in the Middle East. Seeing no other way to change society for the better, Carl and others set about their self-appointed task of attacking the central monster: the military, with its nuclear arms and waste of resources.

Translating the words of prophets into action, Carl took on the nuclear dragon.

The Plowshares Eight

On September 9, 1980, Kabat, with the Berrigan brothers and several other protesters entered the General Electric Nuclear Missile Re-entry Division factory at King of Prussia, Pennsylvania. The public doors were open in anticipation of the morning shift of employees. While some of the protesters distracted security personnel, others gained access to the production lines, where nose cones for the Mark 12-A warheads were made. They hammered on nose cones under manufacture, making them ring like church bells. They poured blood on documents and offered prayers for peace.

They were, of course, arrested and received sentences for crimes including burglary, conspiracy, and criminal mischief. Sentences ranged from two to five years for some, and three to ten years for others, including Kabat. The judge denied them a "justification defense" in the interest of national security. "Nuclear warfare is not on trial here," the judge replied at one point, "You are."

Implicit in his words was that the jury would receive no explanation of their motive, an item that is usually at the heart of any trial, when it is known. When Judge Samuel Salus III said citizens have no standing to invoke international law in relation to foreign policy, the accused collectively turned their backs as a sign of protest, expressing their view that justice would not be achieved in that courtroom.

The appeals dragged on until 1990, but in the meantime, the whole group was, as Philip Berrigan describes it, "kicked out of jail" without bond, although they were all still under sentenced time. In short, the sentences were reduced to time served, and they all were placed on parole. The sentence reduction came at a time when GE was under investigation for defrauding the government in its Mark IV contracts, a fulcrum that gave the defendants' attorneys significant leverage against GE's willingness to prosecute.

The group had styled itself "The Plowshares Eight" in the manner of the Biblical passage from Isaiah, 1:13: "They shall beat their swords into plowshares, and their spears into pruning hooks; nation shall not lift up sword against nation, neither shall they learn war any more."

Without realizing it, Kabat became a co-founder with the Berrigan brothers of the so-called Plowshares movement worldwide. Other co-founders included Dean Hammer, of the Covenant Peace Society, New Haven, Ct.; Elmer Maas, musician and teacher from New York City; Sister Anne Montgomery, a Sacred Heart nun and teacher from New York City; Molly Rush, a mother and founder of the Thomas Merton Center, Pittsburgh; and John Schuchardt, an ex-Marine, lawyer, and father.

None of them, to this day, will claim to be a founder of Plowshares, because there was no formal organization, but they became role models for many Plowshares followers who followed their example. As Kabat says,

> We just did something under the biblical mandate that made sense to us and lots of other people. We just kind of turned it loose for the world to meditate on and use if they wanted to. We didn't organize or found anything. But I'm glad we did what we had to do, because it pointed the way for many ordinary people to do what they had to. We are all very ordinary people, after all, fighting an extraordinary evil. We had to use the legal system, the court system, whatever, to give light to the justice of our opposition to war. We all die soon enough at heaven's gate. We don't need to die outside the hinges of some atomic hell.

The technique of the Plowshares Eight worked. Their action inspired numerous other groups to take actions under the Plowshares banner. These included names such as the "Gods of Metal" Plowshares — the Gods of Metal being the missiles and aircraft used for war. These actions, enduring even today, involve the symbolic act of striking the planes or equipment of war with hammers, as if to beat them into plowshares, and also pouring blood upon them to symbolize the taking of life.

The Plowshares Eight action inspired poet Joel Saxe of Greenfield Community College, Massachusetts, to box up a rusty old plowshare and send it to President Reagan at the White House with a letter, which read, in part:

Mr. Reagan:

Enclosed please find a plowshare I'm sending as a reminder of what swords should be beat into.

We have become increasingly concerned about the military buildup that is taking place both here and elsewhere in the world. Talk of "limited nuclear war" and "first strike policy" are frightening enough for an individual to grasp, but all the more horrifying for those with children who must grow into this life. . . We urge you to work for disarmament; to beat swords into plowshares.

There was no response or acknowledgment from the White House, which was still terribly busy with its secret Iran-Contra initiative.

As serious as the intention of the original Plowshares group was, they kept their humor. Schuchardt, a scarred veteran of the law and order system, was heard to remark as the police closed in: "By damn, they won't get away from us this time, Carl, they've got us surrounded!"

The German Plowshares

In Europe, 1983, especially in West Germany, the public gathered by the hundreds of thousands to protest the US emplacement of nuclear-tipped Pershing II missiles. But installation proceeded anyway, under the NATO flag. The Pershings were medium-range mobile missiles that could be operated off wheeled vehicles. Many Europeans felt their presence automatically placed them at ground zero for any military exchange.

To underscore this concern, a trio of Germans invited Carl Kabat (who had been released on bail, pending appeal from his earlier conviction) to help them with a Plowshare protest. Herwig Janzek, Dr. Wolfgang Sternstein and Karin Vly had selected as their "target" the US Army base at Schwaebish-Gmund, West Germany.

Although Carl was multi-lingual, German was not one of his languages, and he admits to being uncomfortable on that score. His German associates had some English skills, "but there was no time to give this Pollack lessons in German," Carl recalls.

"It was 3:30 AM, Sunday, December 4, 1983. That was the time when Doctor Sternstein and I got into the car that had been arranged to pick us up and take us to the base. We loaded our hammers for pounding, and our bolt-cutting tools. The car took us to a point outside Stuttgart. Only the four of us knew the plan.

"We left the car on the outskirts of some small town and walked about a half mile to a children's park. There Wolfgang and I met Karin and Herwig and distributed the tools for the day's effort. Two miles of walking were illuminated by the beautiful starry night. In a patch of forest along the way, we used just a penlight focused on the ground to light our path.

"We arrived at our destination, where two spotlights illuminated the barracks compound. Herwig climbed the berm to see if the Pershing II launchers were still there and to see if there were any sentries.

"At 7:30 A.M., as the sun began to rise, the other three of us climbed the bluff and joined Herwig. Karin was dressed in a white bed sheet with the words, 'Don't shoot, we are non-violent.' She joined Herwig and went up close to the fence. A sentry came by, and they flattened themselves on the ground. After he passed, they ran in a crouch and tumbled over the lip of the berm.

"The Pershing II launchers were there, and Herwig took the wire cutters and slid up to the fence. Ping, ping, ping. You could hear the wire cutters on the fence. Herwig went through the fence followed by Karin, Wolfgang and then me. Hugging the side of the vehicle, I whispered to Wolfgang, 'Where are the Pershings?' He pointed to the vehicle we were hugging. Stupid question.

"My heart started beating faster. Fifteen feet in front of us stood an American soldier in a parka, facing the other way. I climbed up and with the bolt cutter began cutting everything in sight that could be cut. Hoses, tubing, whatever.

"I heard Wolfgang tell the soldier, 'don't be afraid, we are non-violent people.' I chimed in with 'That's all right, brother, nothing to worry about,' as I continued with my bolt cutter. Wolfgang lapsed into German and asked the soldier, 'Can you help us?' He didn't seem to make a move against us, so we kept banging with the hammers and snipping away.

"I didn't hear any alarms, but the soldier must have sent a signal of some kind. Wolfgang used a big sledge hammer, Herwig had a big bolt cutter and Karin had a small sledge. By the time I ran out of things to do, I saw the other three gathering in a small circle in front of the Pershing launch vehicle.

"I climbed down and joined them in a group hug, then we sat down in a circle. We said the Our Father, and began to sing 'All We

Are Saying Is Give Peace a Chance,' as well as 'We Shall Overcome.' When Wolfgang told me that he had asked the soldier to help us, we all had a good laugh. We were surrounded now by several grim, silent soldiers, with their weapons trained on us.

"My voice was getting hoarse and my rear end was getting cold before we were finally put into a German police van, about an hour after we started our action," Kabat says. "I could hear some GI cuss as he surveyed the damage, as we left the scene. For us, it was a very, very good day and I believe God was with us."

In court, Kabat was released on his own recognizance, and the others were held by German authorities. Although Kabat understood he was to return to the court on a certain date, he simply went to the airport, bought a ticket and flew to the US. Nobody challenged him or followed him. He never faced trial.

"I wasn't running away from anything," Kabat explains, "This was just my way of not cooperating with evil."

The three Germans, Kabat learned later, stood trial before a panel of judges and were convicted. The trial judges called their actions "bad prophecy" and characterized their actions as violence. They served 90 days in jail.

"God, if that had happened in the days of the Gestapo, we all would have been killed where we stood," Carl said. "But what's the difference whether a bullet controls you or the metal bars of a cell? What do we have now except a gentler Gestapo?"

Silo Pruning Hooks

Besides plowshares, the other part of Isaiah's prophecy has to do with beating spears into pruning hooks. Pruning hooks, of course, are used to trim useless or harmful or unwanted growths from vines or fruit trees in order to make them more fruitful.

Mindful of that, Kabat's next protest action was a little more forceful, as if to engage in pruning. Joined by his missionary brother Paul and two dedicated friends, he took a jackhammer to the concrete lid of a Minuteman I missile silo at Knob Noster, Missouri, near Kansas City.

On November 12, 1984, even as weapons and drugs were being

secretly exchanged by the CIA's shadowy Iran-Contra three-way trade, the far-less skulking figures of the prophets made their way from an I-70 frontage road through a fence surrounding a missile silo. They ignored signs about possible use of deadly force against trespassers, and cut their way through the fence.

The four were Carl Kabat, his brother Paul, a native American named Larry White-Feather-Cloud Morgan from Minneapolis, and Helen Woodson, mother of numerous adopted children, several with Downs Syndrome. Together, they had rented a jackhammer and air compressor and towed it to the missile site near Whiteman Air Force Base.

Curiously, it took nearly an hour for base police to arrive and make the arrest, so the four had plenty of time to pray and perform other symbolic acts. By the time they were hauled off, the Kabat crew had hammered a pit in the concrete lid, which would not have disabled its ability to open on command but did make it more photogenic. And they'd had plenty of time to take pictures of their actions and deposit them in a pre-designated spot along the roadside for later pickup by non-involved associates. They also held a Eucharistic celebration at the site. Larry Cloud Morgan left behind an indictment by Native Americans of the US government and the institutional Church for their complicity in the pending omnicide of nuclear holocaust.

At trial, they were all declared by Judge D. Brooks Bartlett in Kansas City to be "a threat to the community" and were held in "preventive detention" without bail.

I felt sorry for old D. Brooks Bartlett," Kabat says today. "As the trial progressed, he was under a lot of stress. He had a facial tic that wouldn't go away. I hope we didn't cause it. During a trial recess, he invited us to his chambers to share his birthday cake. But he had legal decisions to make which became huge moral decisions. We all pleaded guilty and basically refused to cooperate with the justice system. I think he felt trapped. I sensed that he was trying to reach out toward justice, but didn't know how. I wonder how he is doing now? He was a decent man charged with making an indecent decision.

Upon conviction for destruction of government property, conspiracy, intent to damage the national defense, and trespass, the judge's gavel fell. On March 27, 1985, they received the most severe sentence of any protest group: Paul Kabat, 10 years; Larry Cloud Morgan 10 years; Carl Kabat 18 years; Helen Woodson, 18 years; all with 3-5 years probation, plus orders to pay restitution of $2,932.80 each, and with 300 hours of community service. The sentences were later reduced on appeal, and Kabat's 18 years became 10.

Helen Woodson refused to appeal. As of 2001, she still is in jail because she believes that nonviolent public resistance to evil action is necessary. And so she took additional felony actions designed by her to prevent parole. Carl was finally released in 1991. Paul had won his release in 1988.

Not long thereafter, the Oblates (OMI) took away Paul's priesthood under Canon Law of the Catholic Church and kicked him out of their community. Cloud Morgan won release from jail in 1989 after additional time for a parole violation. He died soon thereafter.

That wasn't the end of the story, because the immoral activities that drove the protesters were still going on. The US government was still meddling with Iraq, and the sordid details of the Iran-Contra scandal were still steaming. In the White House, President Bush I was telling China that "the US has no political prisoners."

Hundreds of anti-war protesters were making waves at Strategic Air Command and other military installations. Many of the unarmed enemies of the nation had already been assassinated on the domestic and international scene: JFK, RFK, MLK Jr., Archbishop Romero, four Maryknoll nuns, six Jesuit priests, 60,000 Salvadorans. The list of nations and names goes on, documented by official agencies such as the British Parliamentary Human Rights Group and the United Nations.

Refusing to be crushed, prophets like Carl Kabat pressed forward with the cause:

When Good Friday Was April Fool's Day

On several occasions during the late '90s at the Riant Theater, 161 Hudson St., New York City, an unusual off-Broadway theater production played to benefit the anti-war movement. The play was, *A Clown, A Hammer, A Bomb and God*, written by Daniel Kinch, and featuring the acting of Ben Roberts in the role of Carl Kabat.

Sponsored by the Lawyers Committee on Nuclear Policy as part of the *Festival of Hope*," the one-man play is based on Carl's protest action taken in 1994 at a nuclear missile silo near Valley City, North Dakota. Kabat and anti-nuclear friends pounded on the silo lid's iron track with sledgehammers.

The event actually took place on April 1, 1994 (April Fool's Day), which coincided that year with Good Friday. Kabat reckoned it was a doubly symbolic day to protest nuclear arms, and so he dressed in a clown suit for the occasion, so that he could be "a fool for God."

With him were Sam Day, publisher of an anti-nuclear newsletter, *The Progressive*, and Mike Sprong, who has engaged himself in several other anti-nuclear protests that have landed him in jail. It was Sam Day who had told Kabat that if the objective was to protest nuclear missiles, then they should go to where the nuclear missiles were. And so they did. After swinging the hammer against some of the exterior metal pieces at the bomb-proof silo, they broke and shared bread, a symbol of communion. This was another of the "Pruning Hook" prophetic actions.

Either by coincidence or wondrous justice, Day, a lifelong military gadfly and anti-nuclear peace activist, was born in Media, Pennsylvania, in 1926. Media is the location where peace protesters "liberated" FBI files revealing its COINTELPRO operations. Sam Day died January 26, 2001; if he was responsible for the raid on the FBI files in Media, he took that bit of service to the world to the grave with him. Perhaps Nat Henthoff, syndicated columnist for *The Village Voice*, knows for sure, but Kabat does not. (Henthoff was one of the reporters tipped off about COINTELPRO.)

The marvelous thing about prophets like Kabat is their capacity to follow the moral scent without understanding the twists or memorizing the turns in the trail. While this makes documentation of detail difficult, it enhances the result, which is, quite simply, to act, and to run the quarry to ground.

Sprong, too, is such a prophet. By the year 2001, he and others such as Bonnie Urfer were on trial for cutting down the wooden poles that supported the ELF (Extremely Low Frequency) radio antenna in Wisconsin, which sends coded messages to the Trident-armed nuclear submarines. Sprong and Urfer were easily convicted in the Trident case because the government did not allow them to defend themselves by way of motive.

The motive in every protest case has been to stop nuclear suicide and moral cataclysm. That was the mission of Kabat and Day and Sprong on Good Friday (April Fool's Day), 1994, at the missile silo in North Dakota. That is what drives these individuals to sacrifice a comfortable life and go to jail. By Easter Monday, 1994, they were in court. Carl received a five-year sentence.

He would be released in 1998. By that time, Carl's brother, Paul (who, like any older brother, was a hero figure), was dying, near the Kabat family farmhouse at Scheller, Illinois. Carl spent much of his time at his deathbed, until Paul's death in May 1999.

Paul Kabat's death came eleven years after his release from jail for the jackhammer protest, and just a few years after he had been summarily ejected from his missionary order, the Oblates of Mary Immaculate. In 2001, Carl Kabat faces the same possible fate when he gets out of jail (see later chapters).

Even though Carl finds limited sympathy within his own community of priests, he takes solace from what Senator Tom Harkin of Iowa had to say about the immoral and politically offensive affairs of state that Kabat had protested under the Administration of Reagan and Bush. Referring to the Iran-Contra revelations, Harkin said in 1986:

> In his State of the Union address earlier this year, President Reagan heralded the 200th anniversary of our Constitution. He praised the work of our founding fathers and noted that he had read not only our Constitution but the constitutions of other countries.
>
> The President may indeed have read our Constitution, but, as revelations of the Iran-Contra arms sale reveal, he does not understand it.
>
> On foreign policy, the Constitution created an "invitation to struggle" between the President and Congress, but not an invitation to deceive.
>
> The Iran-Contra affair has undermined all conventional notions of executive authority and the foreign policy process. The Reagan Administration — including the President himself — did far more than "wink and nod" at the so-called private efforts to assist the Contras. The White House became the nerve center for shady operations that coordinated the work of a network of ex-generals, old CIA hands and soldiers-of-fortune to keep the Contra war going at a time when such activity was outlawed by Congress.
>
> President Reagan's responsibility in this affair transcends lying and law-breaking. By ignoring the fragile but vital separation of powers between Congress and the Executive, the President demeans the very nature of our form of government.
>
> The secret Contra re-supply operation, organized by the White House to circumvent congressional and public opposition to the President's "dirty little war" in Central America, bypassed and denied Congress its two greatest constitutional powers — the sole authority to appropriate funds and the power to declare war.

Perhaps we should not be surprised. The use of ex-generals and sultans to spearhead a foreign policy apparatus is a logical extension of the Reagan Doctrine: this policy of Soviet rollback through worldwide sponsorship of counterrevolution has been advanced in Angola, Cambodia, and Nicaragua. Its principal instrument is the CIA and covert operations.

In its zealous pursuit of this doctrine, the Reagan Administration has written assassination manuals, mined ports, and created an armed band better at killing innocent peasants than government soldiers. Ronald Reagan has waged is own "holy war" against the alleged Soviet menace, in the process adopting the methods of our enemies. Whoever "wins," if that is possible, America stands to lose its most precious possession: our rule of law.

Americans should have learned a decade ago, with the revelations of Watergate and the Church Committee, that covert operations and the American constitutional system are incompatible. In Nicaragua today, as in Chile and Vietnam a generation ago, those involved in US policy operate in secret, behind a bodyguard of lies, and in violation of international as well as domestic law.

I can think of no better way for Americans to celebrate the Bicentennial than to restore constitutionalism and the rule of law to foreign policy.

Harkin, of course, has a political duty to criticize the morality of government policies. Prophets like Carl Kabat have a moral duty to criticize the politics of government policies.

"God's law comes first," Kabat says simply. "That's where the latitude of life and how we control it as a peaceful people comes from in the first place."

Fr. Carl suggests that we might ask ourselves just when trying to save lives in the face of nuclear disaster became a felony instead of a heroic act.

Meanwhile, tough-minded as he is, Carl Kabat looks back with optimism, from behind bars, on his seven decades of life. He still has his clown suit; he still has his hammer; he still opposes the bomb; and he still has his God. As for his nation and his world of parishioners, Kabat has only to recall the closing line from the *Pledge of Allegiance*: "One nation, indivisible, under God, with liberty and justice for all." He focuses on the "liberty and justice for all" and "under God"; for if this nation does, indeed, proceed under God towards liberty and justice for all, its government does not.

The Gulf War and Desert Storm were not, as is popularly believed, the direct result of unilateral aggression by the "madman" of Iraq against tiny Kuwait. It was part of a LIONSDEN plan, a spinoff from the Iran-Iraq war for the sake of US oil supplies.

Not commonly known is that, as part of LIONSDEN's war mongering over oil, the CIA apparently developed a black market in organs for transplant. These were obtained by vivisection from orphans and from other Central American casualties during the Iran-Contra wars.

In fact, this black market discovery proved to be key to winning support from Saudi Arabia in the Middle East oil market for the future, and to neutralizing Saddam Hussein's power, granted earlier and recklessly by the CIA when Bush was its chief. By the second year of the Iran-Iraq war, US plans proved to be self-defeating when Hussein learned that Iran was receiving weapons from the US.

It seems that once the US lost its oil supply from Iran, it tried to gain this back by siccing Iraq on Iran in an effort to restore the Shah. That plan was doomed once Saddam Hussein learned how the US had double-crossed him. Too late, desperate LIONSDEN planners realized that Iraq, a major oil supplier was now so angered it could cut off oil to the US and perhaps lead OPEC, including Saudi Arabia, toward another 1973-style embargo.

The priority in LIONSDEN planning, therefore, became how to neutralize hostility from mightily-armed Iraq and the demonized Saddam Hussein. To unseat him in any frontal manner was sure to stir the anger of other Arab oil states, especially Saudi Arabia and cost the US half its oil supply. The CIA master plan called for getting Saudi Arabia to go along with a covert plan to oust Saddam without divulging the means: warfare.

As in the Tonkin Gulf deception, the technique was to provoke a war that would appear to be just, even to the Arabs. In any case, the US would need a base for its troops, and it could not use Israel because it was the common enemy of all Arab states. And given its Israeli ties, the US did not have the strong relationship necessary to place troops on Saudi soil.

That's where the organ transplant scheme came into play.

It seems several members of prominent Saudi families were afflicted with medical disorders requiring organ transplants. The US had the medical technology to perform the transplants, but the "spare parts", so to speak, were in short supply and, for the most part, were dedicated to cases in America.

The CIA logic was as gruesome as it was cold: there were lots of spare parts available from countless victims of war in Central America, including those from wounded or tortured rebels and children who had become orphaned and would die anyway. Why not use them, the LIONSDEN planners reasoned, and make America the hero of their Saudi friends?

The notion is not as unworkable as it may seem. Anybody who knew the general character of the Saudis knew it tended to be flawed toward magnanimity, pride and ego; and thus one might have understood how the plan could succeed, if its inner workings were kept secret.

The Saudi character flaw is described in an anecdote by Ray Vicker in his 1974 book, *The Kingdom of Oil.* (Vicker is former chief of the London office of the *Wall Street Journal*):

> Two oil-rich Saudi sheiks are passing by a Cadillac dealership after lunch together. One expresses an interest in buying one of the new models.
>
> "Oh, no," says the friend. "Let me get it. You got the sandwiches."

A Favor They Could Not Resist

In other words, Saudi pride never lets them forget a favor. It was this kind of character trait that gave the CIA the opening it needed to implement Desert Storm and the intended downfall of Saddam Hussein. As the LIONSDEN planners looked around for a chance to do the Saudis a favor they could not resist and would feel bound to repay, the transplant organ scheme seemed most opportune.

The other part of the plan, goading Iraq into waging war over oil, would be easy once the shooting with Iran stopped, because Hussein would be looking for revenge. It would be an easy thing for LIONSDEN double agents to whisper in Saddam's ear that his impertinent little neighbor, Kuwait, was stealing his oil by use of slant wells and reselling it to the US. In fact, there were such directionally drilled oil wells violating, underground, the geological border between Kuwait and Iraq. Value of such oil, by then already furtively extracted, was estimated at $17-$18 billion by knowledgeable industry sources.

As a result of this LIONSDEN scenario, Iraq could be expected to invade Kuwait. Then the US could ride to the rescue from Saudi soil. Saudi Arabia would have three strong reasons to allow the US military to risk defiling Moslem soil territory: 1) A threat from an Arab neighbor to its own resources and turf. 2) An ally and trading partner with the military strength to push Iraq back at minimal risk to Saudi lives. 3) A democratic power which had done the royal family a life-saving favor by providing special access to organ transplants.

To begin the plan's implementation, a LIONSDEN type network would be established in Central America to harvest organs from the very war victims the CIA was creating via Iran-Contra.

Activity began in the early '80s, before the US Congress passed the National Organ Transplant Act in October 1984. That act, sponsored by then-Senator Al Gore, forbids the establishment of organ-transplant businesses for profit. The ethical decency represented by Gore's action did not stop the CIA; it merely made their plans illegal. More daunting were the logistics. It would be difficult to hire transplant experts on the Q.T.; but specialists were certainly needed, to handle all the problems of matching tissue types and organ size, never mind the surgery itself. Even so, it didn't matter if unqualified doctors made mistakes, the organs would simply be discarded if necessary.

Laws have since been enacted to monitor the organ transplant chain of source and possession, but the CIA found a way to use the organ bank system to its advantage. It was also able to bribe officials in the country of origin, and enrich medical people who worked at the ethical fringes of their profession.

It wasn't until January 1987 that the first inklings of the butchering of living orphans for their transplantable organs began to emerge from Central America. By that time, the favors for the Saudis had been completed. Here is a sketch of what seems to have happened:

Peasants on the brink of starvation in places such as Guatemala frequently turned over their youngest children to "feeding centers", supported, like orphanages, by the state. The parents were given to believe that their children would be adopted, and given a better life — which sure beat watching them starve to death in their own arms. Some parents even sold their younger children for a few dollars into "adoption" to support other family members. Moreover, the civil wars were creating many orphans (and critically injured adults) at the same time.

Some orphans actually were adopted, for a price, and taken to decent homes. But these feeding centers, *alimentarios*, became a primary source for trafficking in organs. For the ailing and unadoptable kids, falsified adoption papers were readily drawn up to cover the surgical extractions and death. Local police and judges were on the payroll. When accusations arose, the CIA simply claimed it was anti-US communist propaganda. Certainly, that was more believable than the truth.

Of course, proper removal of organs requires medical expertise. In one known instance, the CIA hired a doctor from Miami who was facing charges of medical malpractice and potential loss of his license. The CIA provided Dr. Robert G. with an alibi to save his license. It seems the doctor had neglected his US patients, the CIA told the Florida medical board, because he was working in the jungles of El Salvador and Nicaragua for the CIA, caring for injured rebels and soldiers backed by the US.

This was a rare example of the CIA's testifying to save one of its own, something it would not have done if they hadn't needed him so badly. Whether Dr. G. was hired for the medical purposes stated by the CIA or for organ removal may never be known for certain.

Coincidentally, in 1985, a "computer entrepreneur" in McLean, Virginia, tried to establish a company that would guarantee insured individuals a priority for transplant organs to be bought in an open-market environment. McLean, of course, is the headquarters for the CIA. There were no laws against such commerce in 1985.

The plan was to use a Denver group, Transplant Technologies, Ltd, which had been set up with the financial backing of politically active millionaires including brewer Joseph Coors (a big contributor to Reagan's election campaign.) The network would use Denver General Hospital as a manager for the system and a potential source for organs. DGH at that time was not a center for transplant expertise but served many uninsured and indigent patients. By the time the US Department of Justice investigated the company, it appeared to be violating the new law against trafficking in organs. So the CIA folded its scheme and took the rest of its organ transplant program underground.

Using this mode, the CIA managed to set up a method for using the existing organ supply system. The organs needed by Saudi clients were drawn from the existing legitimate supply in the US hospitals. At the same time, those organs were numerically replaced in the system by organs whose medical legitimacy was forged out of Central America. With its private fleet of airplanes and access through customs, transportation of illegal cargoes was no problem for the CIA.

In this way, LIONSDEN operatives gained preferential medical treatment status for the Saudi clients of the US. Uninterrupted commerce in oil, as well as calming political Mideast water, became part of the bargain.

As for practical considerations go, when adult-sized organs were needed, agents used kidnapped suspected rebels whose organ types could be determined before harvest. This may account for some of the known instances of evisceration found among wartime cadavers, many dumped into jungle rivers near where CIA agents were operating in Central America. Beyond politics, there was money to be made by the CIA through their human junkyard program.

Payments for the intercession necessary to obtain hearts, livers and kidneys amounted to as much as $30,000 each, according to newspaper reports and rumor on the streets of Central America. The money from organs, like money from drugs and guns, helped to fund the CIA's banned activities.

For their part, the Saudis who paid these pittances assumed, correctly, that the organs going into their bodies came through legitimate donors. The only thing they never were told was how the implanted organs were replaced at the other end of the supply line. Also kept in the dark were the surgeons and hospitals who may have been innocently involved. Eventually, regulations and oversight of the organ transplant process eliminated the chances for the kind of abuse that LIONSDEN/CIA agents were able to get away with.

Sadly, those who made the arrangement came to be thought of as benefactors by the Saudis. This was of central importance to advancing the CIA's oil-war plans in the Middle East as the first Bush regime set up Saddam Hussein for a fall in the Desert Storm war. It is a point of irony that another Bush president now commands the CIA on the basis of having stolen the election from Al Gore, who pioneered laws against organ transplant trading just before the Desert Storm war conducted by the first Bush president.

Throughout history, the indigent have been forced to "sell their bodies" to stave off death. This is perhaps the first time that they have been lured into selling their body parts, and actually hastening their death. By "donating" these precious organs, Central American victims of the US-backed death squads became part of the gambit to induce the Saudis to allow the US to build military bases in Saudi Arabia and engage Saddam Hussein in Desert Storm. When President Bush (the First) said the war was "not about oil," he lied about more than one awful reality.

The existence of the grisly organ program has been universally denied by US officials. Although the gruesome activity has never been absolutely proven to be connected to the CIA as a prelude to Desert Storm, the Latin American media were flooded with reports of the organ transplant activity. Articles about the black market in body parts appeared in the February 1987 *OSGUA Newsletter*, the stateside communications medium for the Organization in Solidarity with the People of Guatemala. Other articles and news reports circulated in dozens of Spanish publications including the newspaper *Excelsior* of Mexico City. Most of these reports seemed to come after the fact.

Rupiper tried to draw the attention of the US media to the scandal, including contact with independent newscaster Bill Kurtis who was with WGN in Chicago at the time. The Associated Press in America ran an article on the subject, but its sources labeled the story as "rumor." Here is an English translation by Fr. Carl Kabat of the 1987 report from the newspaper, *Excelsior*:

A NET OF CENTERS OF CONCENTRATION DISCOVERED
GUATEMALAN CHILDREN SOLD IN US AS RAW MATERIAL FOR ORGAN TRANSPLANTS
Guatemala, March 4, 1987 (Cerigua) — Local press media revealed today the discovery of a clandestine network of centers of concentration of children less than 16 years of age, whose ages vary between a month and two years, who would be exported illegally to be used as raw material for organ transplants.

The newspaper, *Prensa Libre*, said that 12 boys and 4 girls would be distributed in three known locales in this capital, where the implicated were holding them, in order to feed them until the illegal documentation was resolved so they could be exported; they would be sold at prices going from 20 to 30 thousand dollars per infant.

About a month ago, 14 children (8 girls and 6 boys) of which 11 were recently born, were found. Some of them were declared lost by their family members.

The newspapers also published that many of those children are sold to the USA to be used in transplanting of organs to children of millionaires that suffer from birth defects.

According to the *Prensa Libre*, an important element in the case against one of the persons implicated in the "business" is that the police persecution against the bands of traffickers of children have as their objective to see to it that high-ranking government officials can hold onto the "business."

Newspapers affirm that the said network implicates judges, immigration officials and members of the Foreign Relations of the Democratic Christian Government who smooth out the red tape so that the children's travel documents are apparently legal.

According to informed sources, from the first of October of 1985 to March 31 of 1986, 166 minors were "exported" in this way: 79 to the United States, 21 to Belgium, 16 to Italy, 13 to Canada, 12 to Norway, 8 to Switzerland, 5 to France and 12 to various other countries.

Because so many documents were forged to make such trafficking in children possible, no one knows for certain whether these youngsters were adopted into loving families or were merely diverted by CIA Secret Teams to human abattoirs. In the United States, the press reports were discarded as left-wing propaganda.

News of this human butchery naturally brought investigations — especially after the practice spread to Honduras and neighboring countries. But the agents had developed an official smokescreen through collusion with local officials, who looked the other way while bureaucrats forged adoption and travel papers.

In Guatemala, one such helpful person was Ofelia Rosal de Gama, the sister-in-law of ex-President Oscar Mejia Victores, a US puppet. According to newspaper reports, at one time Rosal de Gama was the "owner" of 24 youngsters in feeding centers in Guatemala City. She directed a group of six nurses in the nefarious activity. No charges were ever brought against her by the administration of Vinicio Cerezo, the hand-appointed successor to Victores.

In Honduras, investigations were conducted by Leonardo Villeda, General Secretary of the National Board of Well Being, and by Mirian de Azcona, wife of the Honduran president. The probes yielded clues that children were being used as organ donors and that each child brought a $5,000 profit to the traffickers. The system reportedly used a network of nurses and lawyers, but no one was ever prosecuted.

In the United States, reports in the media easily dismissed as Communist lies; but the stories and fears kept circulating, even years after the collapse of the Soviet Union.

Other Organs of War

Other aspects of the CIA game were not going as smoothly. The Iran-Contra gun trading had been exposed. The US now had on its hands an oil-greedy dictatorial bully in Iraq, where once there had been a compliant ally. Hussein had to be unseated without incurring the wrath of the oil-rich Moslem world. Because of its support for Israel, US relationships with the Moslems were shaky at best. After all, the Israelis had bombed Iraq's first nuclear reactor in June 1981; Israel's war with the PLO had spread to Beirut along with the Iranian-style taking of hostages; and Egypt's Anwar Sadat had been assassinated, as had been several of Khomeini's top aides.

Control had to be imposed again.

Now that Saudi cooperation in the establishment of US bases was virtually assured, and the Iran-Iraq war had come to a draw, CIA agents set the trap for Saddam Hussein. US contacts implied that he could take over Kuwait without objection from the US. This was the American way of apologizing for sending guns to Iran; and it would make up for the broken promise that Saddam could take over Iran's oil along their common border.

Hussein did not need much prodding, because he also had learned from CIA agents that Kuwait and its US friends had been using directional drilling and had been pumping and selling oil from under Iraqi territory.

To lend credibility to its assurances that the US would turn a blind eye, the CIA showed Saddam genuine satellite photos of his Iraqi troops poised along Kuwait's border. By showing him how the US was spying against him, the double agents seem to have won his confidence that they were on his side. Already burned once, Saddam wanted official reassurances. The agents then suggested that Saddam himself meet with the US ambassador to Iraq, April Glaspie, for further confirmation.

Just five days before Iraq invaded Kuwait, Glaspie told Hussein in a face-to-face meeting that the "US takes no position" in the threatened confrontation. Then she told Washington, as prompted by CIA officials, that Hussein would not invade Kuwait — because that was the information she had been given by the CIA LIONSDEN agents.

To achieve its ends, the CIA would say anything, to anyone, even the US ambassador.

Confident that he had the green light, Saddam Hussein set out to take Kuwait. The Bush Administration responded by launching a counter-invasion from Saudi territory.

But Bush did not go all the way to Baghdad; he said Saddam Hussein was not the target; and he loudly proclaimed that "this is not about oil." Was he, for the sake of deniability, not fully briefed? As former CIA Director, how much briefing would he have needed? To the extent that it was not about oil, what US interest in the Middle East *was* it about?

Days after Desert Storm ended, in a four-day rout of Iraq's troops, Bush issued what appears to be a sloppily thought-out call for Saddam Hussein's ouster by internal revolt, seeking to encourage a military coup in Iraq. What followed, instead, was a disorganized uprising by the Kurds in the north and by the Shiites in the south.

The Bush-incited revolutions appeared to be heading toward success, but Bush withheld the *coup de grace*. He was reminded by State Department professionals that if the two factional revolutions succeeded, Iraq would likely be fragmented into three parts; and if that happened, it would be well nigh impossible to shape the political outcome, and regain control of the Iraqi oil. Worse, it would upset the stability of the pro-NATO Turkish regime that shared borders with Iraq and the Soviet Union.

As history shows, having enticed the rebels, Bush then left them to suffer the consequences, putting in place only a "no fly" zone over the most prized parts of Iraq's oil territories — under the guise of protecting the restive Kurds from Hussein. This gave the US the excuse to bomb Iraq at will, and it did so with great frequency.

In spite of all the orphans made at the World Trade Center and the Pentagon on September 11, 2001, the US continues its own orphan-making policies: it maintains its bases in Saudi Arabia; it maintains illegal no-fly bombing zones over Iraq; and it doesn't force Israel to make peace with the Palestinians.

While the US has won control over its oil supplies for the time being, within its tactics of war it lost something more vital to its long-range interests: the respect for its principles among people so terrorized and so angered that they sacrificed themselves to hurl airplanes at America's commercial and military centers.

In 1987, then-Senator George McGovern wrote a preface for part of the Iran-Contra report. He closed with a prophetic thought from the past, applicable to America today:

"If we are to persevere as a republic, we must place regard for our own institutions at the very top of our priority list and pay close attention to the real conservatives in American life and history. One of them, President John Quincy Adams, offered words of wisdom to all those who would claim conservative heritage:

> 'The true American goes not abroad in search of monsters to destroy.... [America] well knows that by once enlisting under other banners than her own, were they even banners of foreign independence, she would involve herself beyond the power of extraction, in all wars of interest and intrigue, of individual avarice, envy and ambition. Though she might become the dictatress of the world, she would no longer be the ruler of her own spirit.'"

Any examination of the revolutionary protests of America's founding fathers reveals the nobility of their patriotism against despotism. Any examination of the founding documents of America shows the motives of their authors were based on high moral principles. For Americans, the revolutionary period was the unrecognized beginning of moral patriotism, even as Church and State matters were to be held as separate but coexistent within the lives of the citizens who lived dually in each domain.

Today, our jailed prophets are living proof that America's original moral patriotism has been murdered. Killed also in the process have been thousands of innocent men, women and children to whom the prophets ministered.

Whether in the Balkans, in Africa, in the Americas, in Ireland, in Indonesia or Afghanistan, the issues are the same: war, violence, suppression of independence, and lust for political, military and economic dominance. These are all consequences of long-standing American policies. The results include social injustice, poverty, starvation, disease, and repression of personal human freedoms. From the priest-prophet point of view, these all lead to the stunting of humanity's spiritual development.

These are not just the idle opinions of disgruntled and radical clerics. Oscar Arias, former president of Costa Rica and a Nobel Peace Prize winner, had this to say at a "Peacejam" rally at the Jesuit Regis University in Denver on February 26, 2000:

You [the United States] sell arms to countries which are not democratic, which violate human rights. Eventually both the people of those countries and even American soldiers are killed by American arms. They were killed in Central America, Haiti, Panama, Somalia and in the Persian Gulf war.

In other words, *they*, within the system, are killing us, the people who are supposed to be the system.

In his *Power of Myth*, Joseph Campbell notes that centuries ago in most cultures, the highest structure in any human settlement always was the temple; or the steepled church; or the mosque with its lofty minarets. The visual prominence of things religious reflected the deference given, by the society in question, to the most revered and most domineering aspect of their lives.

Over time, as Campbell points out, the highest structures within these societies became the palaces, the capitol buildings or city hall, as government asserted its dominance over the lives of people. The final societal change came with the towers of commerce. The buildings cast a pall over the importance of whatever was previously highest, especially temple, church and mosque. The result is the antithesis of individual moral patriotism.

The industrial-military complex that Eisenhower warned his nation about in 1960 has come to be. Thanks to the critical massing of technology and politics with economics, the world society has a condition that sociologists someday might call "socio-mili-techno-polinomics," or SOMTEP. By its nature, the SOMTEP way of life, engendered by government obsession with national military and economic security, destroys the values it was meant to propagate for society.

That explains how THEY, the system, are killing us, the people.

We, the SOMTEP system, evolved from the exigencies of the Cold War despite Eisenhower's alarm about the military-industrial complex. That complex was already in the process of becoming inextricably tied to the economic, technical, and military (nuclear and space) substrates of the system. The Cold War, or something to replace it, became an economic necessity. A neo-Cold War, involving military aggression and political repression of the type that goes back to Iran-Contra days, fills the need. The Neo-Cold War and SOMTEP together explain the Iran-Iraq war, Desert Storm, Asian political and monetary unrest, the Balkan and Iraq bombings, Middle East mini-wars, and plans for US conquest of the world through "Son of Star Wars."

They also explain our protests and our fears for the effects of SOMTEP on the Third World, and they also explain the anger behind the attack of September 11.

There is a folk story about a frog that did not jump out of a kettle because the heat of the water was raised so gradually the frog didn't notice the change until it was too late. America today, armed and prepared to accept war and killing for the sake of SOMTEP's economic and technological way of life, is such an unsuspecting frog. The military is gratified by the "democratic" results this process of moral murder has delivered for the fatherland in countries previously hostile to, but now subdued by, US policy. Just one example proves it:

On November 17, 2000, as a rally against the School of the Americas was forming outside the gates of Fort Benning, Army Colonel Glenn Weidner presented for the news media a series of graphs which showed how deaths from civil unrest in Central America had subsided ever since SOA had trained an increasing number of foreign officers in the ways of American military democracy.

The best way to explain what the graphs really showed would be to say that once death squads kill enough people over a sufficiently long period, they win. Then the death rate drops because there are fewer targets left to shoot at. The drop in death rates is interpreted as a movement toward democracy. Then democracy, of the SOA-export brand, is said to bloom. But Weidner did not allow time for such criticism.

While he was indoctrinating the media, a display was being assembled in the lobby of the headquarters building of Fort Benning. At the center of the exhibit was the motto, *Pro Deo et Patria* — the motto of the US Army's Chaplain's Corps — "For God and Country."

The Fort Benning display, according to Chaplain-Captain Jett, was designed with the Thanksgiving holiday in mind. However, its timing also coincided with the protests just outside the fort's gates in commemoration of the six Jesuits murdered in 1988 by El Salvador's Atlacatl Battalion. Officers of that battalion, such as Colonel Rene Emilio Ponce, were trained by School of the Americas in the '80s.

Ironically, the motto of the Atlacatl Battalion is, "For the Fatherland, with God.".

Besides the venal and gratuitous use of God's name, the Atlacatl Battalion uses on its coat of arms a human skull juxtaposed above a lightning bolt. All the Jesuit priests the battalion killed in 1988 were shot through the skull.

Question: Where did the Atlacatl Battalion get its motto and its lust for skulls, if not from the SOA at Fort Benning? There *is* a moral link between the death squads and the SOA, even down to the fine point of committing murder in El Salvador under shared mottos.

Using God's name in vain at Fort Benning goes further. The motto of Fort Benning itself is a sword on a shield with the words, "Follow me." This would seem to make a mockery of the exhortation that Christ gave to his apostles, "Come, follow me." However, Christ also told St. Peter, "Put up thy sword," something that the Fort Benning shield also mocks.

These contrasts show that the military has no scruples about using moral exhortations that are sacred to the public to gain acceptance for SOA's immoral training, which exists for supposedly patriotic reasons.

They Are Still Killing

In 1998, the world media was too preoccupied with the Clinton White House sex scandal to give much notice to the April 26 death squad that struck at the home of Bishop Juan Gerardi, of Guatemala City, and beat him to death while a military jeep waited.

Why? Because this bishop, like Archbishop Romero 18 years before, in El Salvador, had accused the US-supported military of past human rights abuses. Gerardi had pointed his bishop's finger at the military for the death and disappearance of 200,000 Guatemalans during the 36-year civil war covertly supported by the United States through the CIA and School of the Americas. Such internecine strife and such assassinations had supposedly ended in 1996 with a peace accord.

Two years into this uneasy peace and two days before Bishop Gerardi's brutal assassination, he released a report, *Guatemala: Never Again.* The report placed the blame for the Central American holocaust at the feet of the US-supported military.

On January 21, 2000, after several deliberately false explanations, the murder suspects were arrested: Col. Byron Disrael Lima Estrada and his son. According to a declassified US Defense Intelligence Agency record, Col. Lima Estrada was trained both at Fort Benning and at the US Army School of the Americas (SOA), at that time located at Fort Gulick, Panama.

A soldier who was with the army band at Fort Gulick in the '50s notes that the base was then known as USARCARIB (US Army Caribbean) School of Infantry. The soldier, John C. Strabala, Jr., said, "It was set up to train Latin-country infantry officers. When they graduated, they left with their US-issued M1 rifles. This was common knowledge." He said none of the GIs knew how this training was put to use, just that the base was giving military police training to foreign infantry officers. The training mission was later moved to Fort Benning.

Before they brought in Estrada, in early 1999, an Associated Press dispatch reported that the FBI had been engaged to examine blood DNA evidence supposedly linking the Bishop Gerardi killers to the crime. Very quickly, a suspect was named: Father Mario Orantes.

When Orantes was released for lack of evidence — after eight months in jail — the prosecutor, Otto Ardon resigned, according to the *National Catholic Reporter*. His replacement, Celvin Galindo, who was beginning to point the case toward the military, fled from Guatemala with his family because of death threats. Father Orantes also fled the country for his own safety.

The office of School of the Americas Watch, headed by Bourgeois, issued the following news release about the arrest:

> According to a declassified US Defense Intelligence Agency biographic sketch, Lima Estrada took military police training at the US Army School of the Americas at Fort Benning, Georgia. Lima Estrada went on to head the infamous D-2 military intelligence agency at the height of the genocide campaign in Guatemala's civil war.
>
> Bishop Gerardi was bludgeoned to death in his home two days after he released a human rights report that implicated the D-2 for atrocities committed during the war. The report is based on thousands of testimonies collected by the bishop's office. In a chapter entitled *The Very Name of Fear*, the report severely criticizes the military intelligence agency headed by Lima Estrada from 1983-1985. It cited the D-2 for playing a central role "in the conduct of military operations, in massacre, extrajudicial executions, forced disappearances, and torture."

With Lima Estrada arrested and charged in Guatemala, the criminal-political smokescreen has been penetrated. Clearly, the US-supported system are still killing poor people and priests, and human justice and morality in the process.

Meanwhile, like the tide on a beach, time launders its flotsam and jetsam as items of political interest float ashore. In 1999, headlines about repression of the vote for independence in East Timor, Indonesia, grew large. But nearly four years before, three women had protested repression in East Timor in a "Plowshares" action. They had entered the British Aerospace facility at Warton, England, and hammered on the radar cone and control panel of a HAWK 200 plane. It was one of 24 aircraft Great Britain has since sold to Indonesia, which even in 1996 was conducting a genocidal war against the people of East Timor.

The women prophets, Jo Wilson, Lotta Kronlid and Andrea Needham, were arrested and jailed. So a system called *they* is still killing, and those who protest are locked up.

Another headline, on August 29, 1999, reads, BRAZILIAN ARCHBISHOP CALLED THE 'BROTHER OF THE POOR' DEAD AT 90.

When Archbishop Dom Helder Camara died, so did a chunk of the lives of several of the prophets portrayed in this book. Those prophets shared Camara's dream to free some of the poorest people on earth from the misery inflicted by the *Norte Americanos* and their banking and military-industrial trusts that have dominated the region for 100 years. As Archbishop Camara pointed out in his book, *Spiral of Violence,* the US invests in Latin America about $3.8 billion a year and receives back about $11.3 billion (under the economics of several years ago).

It was Archbishop Camara who gave Fr. Rupiper a pat on the back after securing his release from a jail in Recife in 1968, and told him to "Tell the American people what they are doing to us." Rupiper tried, and was scorned and jailed for doing so; and the CIA killed his Iranian friend, Bijan.

Like Rupiper and others who engaged in protests to carry that message, Dom Helder Camara was criticized and threatened. Like those he took under his spiritual wing, the archbishop was alternately called a saint and a communist. His house came under gunfire, at times. He watched thousands of the faithful in his diocese disappear and heard horrid descriptions of their murders.

Four times Dom Helder Camara was nominated for the Nobel Peace Prize. Four times he lost, to world leaders who had merely paused in their war-making.

"If I gave food to the poor," Camara once said, "they called me a saint. If I asked why the poor do not have food, and they called me a communist." Pope John Paul II, from the opulence of the Vatican, called Archbishop Camara "a brother of the poor." Years before, the Polish pope had forbidden bishops such as Camara to get involved with "liberation theology."

Where does this leave the priests and nuns and prophets who try to emulate Camara? What does that make of Archbishop Oscar Romero, scolded by the same Pope for his efforts to help the poor, just weeks before he was sent without sympathy from the Vatican to his assassination?

In 1996, Archbishop Camara said, "The passage of time has demonstrated that Communism was not the monster some authorities thought. It was so fragile that it collapsed overnight. The real monsters were poverty and misery. They still are."

"If that is the case," Rupiper says, "if the years of repression of freedom were necessary for the sake of defeating Communism; if Communism is no longer a threat; then why are bishops such as Gerardi still being killed in Central America? Why are US nuclear missiles still pointed at targets where no enemies reside or threaten?"

The violence will continue because violence is still the response of choice by world leaders in settling disputes. Governments will still use lies to carry out their killings to avoid blame. The rich will still own the assets and rob the poor of a living.

In this way, *they* are still killing.

On November 1, 1999, 140 nations of the United Nations General Assembly voted for the resolution entitled "Prevention of an Arms Race in Outer Space." Two nations abstained: the United States and Israel. Why? The US reasons are outlined in a 1996 report of the US Space Command. That report, "Vision for 2020," has a color cover that depicts a weapon shooting a beam from space and zapping a target on earth below.

The report proclaims, "US Space Command — Dominating the Space Dimension of Military Operations to Protect US Interests and Investment," and "Integrating Space Forces into Warfighting Capabilities Across the Full Spectrum of Conflict." On page three, it says, "The medium of space is the fourth medium of warfare — along with land, sea, and air. The emerging synergy of space superiority with land, sea and air superiority will lead to Full Spectrum Dominance."

Who gave the US title to all of space?

This attitude puts the US directly in conflict with UN objectives and with basic human morality. In opening the 1999 UN conference on space militarization, in Vienna, UN Secretary-General Kofi Annan said,

> We must not allow this century, so plagued with war and suffering, to pass on its legacy when the technology at our disposal will be even more awesome. We cannot view the expanse of space as another battleground for our earthly conflicts.

Among the military brass, the former SAC commander General Lee Butler is a rarity because he agrees with the UN position and has voiced thoughts worthy of the heroes of this book. A longtime Air Force Academy professor of political science, Butler told the National Press Club on February 2, 1998:

> Our present policies, plans and postures governing nuclear weapons make us prisoner to an age of intolerable danger. We cannot at once keep sacred the miracle of existence and hold sacrosanct the capacity to destroy it. It is time to reassert the primacy of individual conscience, the voice of reason and the rightful interests of humanity.

The opposite view is held General Joseph W. Ashy. In 1996, the former commander-in-chief of the US Space Command told *Aviation Week and Space Technology*, "We're going to fight from space, and we're going to fight into space. That's why the US had development programs in directed energy and hit-to-kill mechanisms. We will engage terrestrial targets someday — ships, airplanes, land targets — from space."

Gen. Richard Rogers, as head of Space Command, said in a 1997 MacArthur-like speech to the National Space Club, "With regard to space dominance, we have it, we like it, and we're going to keep it. Space is in the nation's economic interest."

For perhaps the first time, the military confirms what prophets like Kabat have been saying for decades: that there *is* linkage between the politics of economics, technology and the military, and that the linkage is immoral by intent and result. Now that we know the immorality of that system is going to be extended into space, we can assume that it will aggravate the conditions of war, poverty and lack of human freedom that the prophets decry.

This means *they* are still killing, and will go on killing.

Who or what is behind this pressure for the military to build space-age killing machines at a time when the US is supposedly at peace? Wall Street and the Trilateral Commission come to mind.

Take, for example, the Wall Street investment firm known as Carlyle Group. Its senior counselor is none other than James A. Baker III, the secretary of state under President G.H. Bush. The elder President Bush is also a member of the Trilateral Commission and recently became a principal of the Carlyle Group. It was Baker who helped save the political bacon of George W. Bush in the presidential election.

So what?

At a time when young Bush was running for election, the Carlyle Group, with all its connections, acquired significant investment interests in space and aeronautical companies such as Grumman, Vought and Northrop — all deeply embedded in the military-industrial complex. After Baker defended the election interests of George W. in Florida, young Bush forged a political team with three former defense-connected cronies of his father: Cheney, Powell and Rumsfeld. All of them are in strategic positions to heat up the Pentagon and its space warfare program, ensuring the Wall Street success of the military-industrial part of Carlyle's portfolio. Military contracts will ensure their bottom lines and that of Carlyle's principals.

That shows how *they* are still killing.

And then there was the scene described by an American businessman named Kerry Appel, who, while trying to establish a coffee marketing business among the Tzotzil Indians of Chiapas, Mexico, had to enter this bloody report in his diary:

> December 22, 1997, Acteal, Chiapas. A Tzotzil Indian village where the coffee for the "Human Bean Company" is grown. As women and children fled down from the steep mountain path towards the valley, armed men shot them from behind. Some who reached the underbrush by the river below were discovered by the assassins when the cries of their babies gave them away. The assassins cut open the stomach of a young pregnant woman, tore her unborn baby out and cut it up. A baby less than one year old survived because her mother covered her with her own body and received all the bullets. One baby was shot in the head at close range. It was not possible to identify the bodies torn to pieces by the machetes. The Red Cross found many bodies hacked into pieces and thrown in the underbrush in an attempt to hide the immensity of the crime.
>
> The massacre went on for almost five hours, while dozens of armed civil guards stood on the road above and did nothing.

These troops, either directly or indirectly, were under the command of SOA graduate Gen. Manuel Garcia, who had military responsibility for all of Chiapas. The slaughter of the Tlotzil villagers was reminiscent of what had happened in 1981 to the village of El Mozote in San Salvador, when 773 men, women and children were massacred by SOA-trained death squads.

The trigger for the war between the Mexican Indian rebels — the Zapatistas, and the one-party Mexican government of Carlos Salinas, was the NAFTA treaty.

Its terms, under agricultural imports from North America, threatened the already-impoverished "corn people" and independent coffee farmers of the region who had been robbed of their best land by *ganaderos*, the establishment ranchers backed by death squads supported by the Mexican military. This land grab was ratified by the passage of legislation that undermined Article 27 of the Mexican constitution.

"NAFTA is a death sentence." These are the words of Zapatista leader Subcommandante Marcos, as reported by *Vanity Fair* magazine in its March 1994 issue. "Look at this land," he said then. "How can we compete with the farms in California and Canada?" Indeed, this is just one more form of death by foreign exploitation.

To emphasize his point, Marcos timed the Zapatista rebellion in Chiapas to coincide with the effective date of NAFTA: January 1, 1994. The Chiapas massacre in 1997 followed three years of stalled negotiations with the Mexican government and isolated killings sporadically exchanged between the rebellious Tlotzil Zapatistas and the "white guard" security forces of the *ganaderos*, who were given free rein under the patronage of the US-supported Mexican government. (The Clinton Administration, with its Trilateral ties, was prepared to prop up Salinas' political regime with a $40 billion package to rescue the falling peso and salvage the Mexican portion of NAFTA.)

Indeed, something called *they* are still killing.

At just about the same time, back in Washington, D.C., a famous author was celebrating the publication of a book that made her perhaps millions of dollars. The book, *It Takes a Village*, is a privileged person's look at how to raise children in this world. The premise, which no one in the slaughtered village of Chiapas ever read before dying, is that it takes a village to raise a child. It says nothing of what it takes to kill a village of children.

Appel, having witnessed the slaying of a whole village by brutes with arms and economic purpose supplied out of Washington, is the kind of man who can disagree effectively without raising his voice. Like the prophets, he has had his taste of jail in Mexico for objecting, and in Denver for trying to get politicians to do something about such abuse. Appel is now identified as a suspect in a special file of the Denver Police Department's list of terrorists.

Whether victim, witness or prophet, those most closely involved would say it does not necessarily take a village to raise children unless they are orphaned by the system. It takes simply a mother and a father in a home, albeit a hut of sticks and mud, living in a village where economic and political life is sustainable and independent of outside forces that occupy by proxy. In other words, a family among other such families, free to think and act and do what is necessary to survive. . . . A family from which mom and dad are not hauled away in the middle of the night for political-cleansing purposes, never to return.

What's really needed is a place where the leaders of that village, not assassinated by clones of the CIA Secret Team, can direct their people in peace pursued by a simple life; a village without the domination of poverty imposed by a military regime that kills to retain power for foreigners with economic agendas made by Wall Street; a place where the citizens of that village can function without being smothered by the dollared structure of a multinational corporation. What's needed to raise a child is a village where the corrupting influence of outsiders do not disrupt the process of raising a family so each member may experience in freedom the basic civilization of Sartre's "Noble Savage."

Mrs. Clinton's book misses the point of the society she and her Trilateral husband and his colluding predecessors have helped to create: The world is becoming a globalized collection of savage civilizations. The American-led globalization has wrecked civilizations that are inherently nobler than ours, on a human scale. Deliberately or not, it has ravaged villages the world over.

If, indeed, it takes a whole village to raise a child, then the Prophets Without Honor are forced to ask wherein lies the wisdom and moral justification, under global dominance goals, for destroying any of those villages — whether in Vietnam, Lebanon, Iran, Iraq, El Salvador, Guatemala, Yugoslavia, or Mexico?

Working without any official backing from the Church in Rome, prophets such as Cordaro and his friends are still conducting protests at STRATCOM's Offutt Air Force Base near Omaha every anniversary of the bombing of Hiroshima. Nearby is an Air Force military chapel where a chapel window sanctifies nuclear mushroom clouds in Japan. He wonders if a stained glass window that glorifies space lasers zapping other Asian countries could be far behind.

Bourgeois still is staging rallies at the gates of School of the Americas at Fort Benning, Georgia, and people still are being arrested, tried and jailed for their efforts.

In the wake of the September 11, 2001, events, the city of Columbus has limited the parade permit: protesters cannot go within one mile of the Fort Benning gate without risking arrest. An "open" base for years, it now has chain link entry gates with guards.

Even before September 11, dozens of activists in the United Kingdom and across NATO-dominated Europe continue to be arrested, tried and convicted for *Plowshares* protests against the reign of terror imposed by nuclear weapons. They join in spirit the growing family of prophets who speak their minds and their hearts on behalf of humanity though they remain without honor in their own lands.

As if showing the burden of its age, the Catholic Church still hesitates to take a leadership role in the effort to resist oppression. If its sacred heart were in the right place, the Church would more openly support the civil defiance of its activist priests and laymen. Instead, it has used its moral force to outlaw so-called liberation theology of the type created independently by Rev. Martin Luther King, Jr., and Archbishop Oscar Romero, both killed for their prophecy.

Perhaps liberation theology is too Protestant-sounding to receive a sympathetic ear in the Gregorian confines of the Vatican. But it is Catholic enough for Prophets Without Honor such as Bourgeois, because it has brought the martyrdom of so many fellow Christians and people of all faiths who defy an immoral secular system.

Theologian Jack Nelson-Pallmeyer, author of the book, *School of Assassins — Guns, Greed and Globalization,* gives this view of liberation theology:

> Building on Vatican II (1962-65), which had called on the Church to be a living sign of God's loving presence in the world, the Latin American bishops, meeting in Medellin, Colombia, affirmed in 1968 a theology of liberation in response to their world of poverty and misery. Liberation theology clashed sharply with traditional theology. It stressed that poverty reflected unjust systems and not God's will. It affirmed the dignity of the human person and said that in order for political, economic, and social structures to reflect God's intent, they had to be organized to make dignified living possible.
>
> Liberation theology named concentrated land ownership, the huge gap separating the rich and poor, and other structural problems as examples of social sin and institutional violence. It spoke of a spiral of violence in which oppression of the poor sparked rebellion that, in turn, was met with repressive violence. [Liberation theology says] the spiral could be broken only if the Church worked to end oppression and broke its cozy relationship with the powerful military, economic and political forces that controlled the oppressive social order. Liberation theology transformed Jesus from simply an object of faith to an example of a subversive who, like faithful Christians today, challenge oppressive groups and systems.

In 1998, only 75 US bishops and no cardinals of the Church signed a pastoral letter instructing the faithful against the evil of nuclear weapons. The Church pays millions of dollars to salvage its reputation in the tort cases of priests gone morally wrong, but not a penny for the defense of those priests who fight for the principles of the Church: peace and justice.

For what the rhetoric is worth, some US Catholic bishops have managed to utter the following pronouncement:

Fifteen years ago, we stated that, because of the massive, indiscriminate destruction that nuclear weapons would inflict, their use would not be morally justified. We spoke in harmony with the conscience of the world in that judgment. We reaffirm that judgment now. Nuclear weapons must never be used, no matter what the provocation, no matter what the military deterrence.

Fifteen years ago (1983) we concurred with Pope John Paul II in acknowledging that, given the context of that time, possession of these weapons as a deterrent against the use of nuclear weapons by others could be morally acceptable, but acceptable only as an interim measure and only if deterrence were combined with clear steps toward progressive disarmament.

In 1998, the global context is significantly different from what it was a few years ago. . . Today the Soviet Union no longer exists. . . Yet the Cold War weapons amassed throughout that struggle have survived the struggle itself and are today in search of new justifications and new missions to fulfill.

We note the dramatic public statement of December, 1996, in which 61 retired generals and admirals, many of whom held the highest positions in the nuclear establishment of this country, said that these weapons are unnecessary, destabilizing and must be outlawed. We also note the historic International Court of Justice opinion of July, 1996, that "The threat or use of nuclear weapons would generally be contrary to the rules of international law applicable to armed conflict, and in particular the principles and rules of humanitarian law."

Unfortunately, the monumental political changes that have occurred in the wake of the Cold War have not been accompanied by similar changes in the military planning for development and deployment of nuclear weapons. . . Rather, nuclear weapons policy has been expanded in the post-Cold War period to include new missions well beyond their previous role as a deterrent to nuclear attack.

The United States today maintains a commitment to use nuclear weapons first, including pre-emptive nuclear attacks on nations that do not possess nuclear weapons. "Flexible targeting strategies" are aimed at Third World nations, and a new commitment exists to use nuclear weapons either preemptively or in response to chemical and biological weapons or other threats to US national interests. This expanded role of the US nuclear deterrent is unacceptable.

In order to maintain the necessary credibility required by a continued reliance on nuclear deterrence, the United States is today embarking on an expansion of its nuclear weapons complex. [It is] an effort at modernizing the nuclear weapons complex to provide for the continued research, development and testing of nuclear weapons well into the next century. The cost of this Stockpile Stewardship Program is currently estimated at $60 billion over the next dozen years.

Instead of progressive nuclear disarmament, we are witnessing the institutionalization of nuclear deterrence. The recent presidential decision directive on nuclear weapons policy, partially made known to the public in December, 1997, makes this point clear. The directive indicates that the US will continue to rely on nuclear weapons as the cornerstone of the nation's strategic defense; that the role of these weapons has been increased to include deterring Third World non-nuclear-weapons states and deterring chemical and biological weapons.

The Department of Energy's timetable for the Stockpile Stewardship Program indicates that the US will continue to develop, test and rely upon a nuclear deterrent through the year 2065. This is clearly not the interim policy to which we grudgingly gave our moral approval in 1983.

The vast majority of the world's nations have forsworn nuclear weapons under the Nonproliferation Treaty. In exchange, the nuclear weapons states agreed to eliminate their nuclear arsenals. As the nuclear weapons states embark on their current modernization programs, they send a clear message to the rest of the Treaty's signatories that not only do they not intend to uphold the agreement, they believe that nuclear weapons are indispensable to their national security. . . It may not be long before other nations who feel threatened renounce their pledge not to develop nuclear weapons.

The policy of nuclear deterrence has always included the intention to use the weapons if deterrence should fail. Since the end of the Cold War this deterrent has been expanded to include any number of aggressors, proliferators and so-called 'rogue nations.' The inherent instability in a world constrained by the great-power standoff present throughout the Cold War leads us to conclude that the danger of deterrence failing has been increased.

The former Soviet Union has in recent years eliminated some of its huge, superfluous stockpiles of nuclear weapons. Our country has no intention or policy position of eliminating these weapons entirely. Rather, the US intends to retain its nuclear deterrent into the indefinite future.

As bishops of the Church in the United States, it is incumbent on us to speak directly to the policies and actions of our nation: We recall the words of another Vatican message to the United Nations. . . that these weapons "by their cost alone, kill the poor by causing them to starve." . . . We call for an end to the reliance on nuclear deterrence and instead call upon the United States and other nuclear weapons states to enter into a process leading to the complete elimination of these morally offensive weapons.

Nuclear weapons are incompatible with the peace we seek for the 21st century. They cannot be justified. They deserve condemnation. . . This is a moral challenge, a legal challenge and a political challenge.

We are painfully aware that many of our policymakers sincerely believe that possessing nuclear weapons is vital for our national security. We are convinced, though, that it is not. Instead, they make the world a more dangerous place. They provide a rationale for other nations to build a nuclear arsenal, thereby increasing the possibility that they will be used by someone.

Not only are they not vital for national security, but we believe they actually contribute to national insecurity. No nation can be truly secure until the community of nations is secure. We are mindful of Pope John Paul II's warning that "violence of whatever form cannot decide conflicts between individuals or between nations, because violence generates more violence."

Nuclear deterrence as a national policy must be condemned as morally abhorrent because it is the excuse and justification for the continued possession and further development of these horrendous weapons. We urge all to join in taking up the challenge to begin the effort to eliminate nuclear weapons now.

To what, specifically, is the bishops' criticism directed? What is the Stockpile Stewardship Program all about? In simplest terms, it means that the US will keep spending billions of dollars to technologically refresh its stockpile of nuclear weapons.

An article in the *Wall Street Journal* of August 2, 2000, describes how Los Alamos scientists are trying to perfect nuclear testing of atomic explosions by computer. The fear is that as atomic physicists age, the knowledge of how to make and enhance nuclear weapons will fade because there will be no military projects with enough just cause to attract younger experts into the field of atomic physics. After all, scientists have consciences, too, and are aware of the dire social consequences of nuclear war that their science has engendered

Conscience is why Albert Einstein, Bertrand Russell, Linus Pauling and seven other men of science signed the Russell-Einstein Manifesto in London, July 9, 1955, at a time when the nuclear arms race and the Cold War and the prospect of global destruction had just begun to shatter mankind's complacency. Every year since then, scientists opposed to the use of nuclear weapons, and, indeed, war itself, still meet to re-ratify that manifesto which said, in part:

> We are speaking on this occasion, not as members of this or that nation, continent, or creed, but as human beings, members of the specie, Man, whose continued existence is in doubt. The world is full of conflicts; . . . .
>
> We have to learn to think in a new way. We have to learn to ask ourselves, not what steps can be taken to give military victory to whatever group we prefer, for there no longer are such steps; the question we have to ask ourselves is: what steps can be taken to prevent a military contest of which the issue must be disastrous to all parties? . . .
>
> The best authorities are unanimous in saying that a war with H-bombs might possibly put an end to the human race. It is feared that if many H-bombs are used there will be universal death, sudden only for a minority, but for the majority a slow torture of disease and disintegration.
>
> Many warnings have been uttered by eminent men of science and by authorities in military strategy. None of them will say that the worst results are certain. What they do say is that these results are possible, and no one can be sure that they will not be realized. We have not yet found that the views of experts on this question depend in any degree upon their politics or prejudices. They depend only, so far as our researches have revealed, upon the extent of the particular expert's knowledge. We have found that the men who know most are the most gloomy.
>
> Here, then, is the problem which we present to you, stark and dreadful and inescapable: Shall we put an end to the human race; or

shall mankind renounce war? People will not face this alternative because it is so difficult to abolish war.

The abolition of war will demand distasteful limitations of national sovereignty. But what perhaps impedes understanding of the situation more than anything else is that the term "mankind" feels vague and abstract. . . . the danger is to *humanity*. [People] can scarcely bring themselves to grasp that they, individually, and those whom they love are in imminent danger of perishing agonizingly. And so they hope that war may be allowed to continue, provided modern weapons are prohibited.

This hope is illusory. Whatever agreements not to use H-bombs had been reached in time of peace, they would no longer be considered binding in time of war, and both sides would set to work to manufacture H-bombs as soon as war broke out, for, if one side manufactured the bombs and the other did not, the side that manufactured them would inevitably be victorious.

Although an agreement to renounce nuclear weapons as part of a general reduction of armaments would not afford an ultimate solution, it would serve certain important purposes. First: any agreement between East and West is to the good in so far as it tends to diminish tension. Second: the abolition of thermonuclear weapons, if each side believed that the other has carried it out sincerely, would lessen the fear of a sudden attack in the style of Pearl Harbor, which at present keeps both sides in a state of nervous apprehension. We should, therefore, welcome such an agreement though only as a first step. Most of us are not neutral in feeling, but, as human beings, we have to remember that, if the issues between East and West are to be decided in any manner that can give any possible satisfaction to anybody, whether Communist or anti-Communist, whether Asian or European or American, whether White or Black, then these issues must not be decided by war. We should wish this to be understood, both in the East and in the West.

There lies before us, if we choose, continued progress in happiness, knowledge, and wisdom. Shall we, instead, choose death, because we cannot forget our quarrels? We appeal, as human beings, to human beings: Remember your humanity and forget the rest. If you can do so, the way lies open to a new paradise; if you cannot, there lies before you the risk of universal death.

RESOLUTION:

We invite this Congress, and through it the scientists of the world and the general public, to subscribe to the following resolution:

"In view of the fact that in any future world war nuclear weapons will certainly be employed, and that such weapons threaten the continued existence of mankind, we urge the governments of the world to realize, and to acknowledge publicly, that their purpose cannot be furthered by a world war, and we urge them, consequently, to find peaceful means for settlement of all matters of dispute between them."

Einstein and his peers have not been heeded. The pastoral letter signed by 75 Catholic bishops has not been heeded. Former New York Governor Mario Cuomo said of nuclear freeze proposals in 1973: "If our government doesn't do more to control the spread of nuclear arms, then we have to do more to control our government." He has not been heeded.

The world is still in as much imminent danger of universal death from progressively more powerful and efficient nuclear weapons as it was in 1955. Since the World Trade Center disaster, new enemies have been created to replace the old as an excuse for not abandoning the nuclear path. The US now proposes a missile shield against them, whoever "they" may be, at a time when they are attacking us with puny box cutters.

How can those possessing the nuclear key to global power be expected to give up or throw away the secret to such power?

What the United States now is doing is to verbally affirm the need for peace, while continuing to use force, abandon treaties, and computerize the development of new nuclear weapons. That is exactly what Fr. Frank Cordaro is driving at when he says society has obligated itself "to protect the bomb."

Not much has changed within the institutional Church, either. Even if priests continue to spill their blood symbolically, the Church will never grant them sanctuary — either literal or symbolic — in spite of all its moral sermons.

That's because the Church, like the world's political system, within which it functions, cannot abandon the instruments of war; that's because the instruments of war such as politics, economics, exploitation and technology are the pillars which support the Church's own dwelling place. In this context, Church and State are separated only in the sense of being two sides of the same coin.

As a sign of how tied the Church is to the world's political centers of power, the Vatican granted sanctuary in the case of Panama's Manuel Noriega when he fled the search-and-destroy mission of the United States military in December of 1989. While the Church shelters a member of the US LIONSDEN system such as Noriega, it denies sanctuary for its own prophets of morality and peace such as Palecek.

The Vatican was willing to protect Noriega because he represented power and secular stability for the Church. Consistent with its support for "stability", the Church opposes what is called liberation theology, a movement of radical Church clerics that would use religious philosophy to motivate the enslaved peasants to overthrow their oppressors. The conservative Church apparently prefers to save souls for heaven rather than rescue them from the hellholes of life. It abandons its faithful to secure as best they can in the face of violence and immoral laws a way to secure decency of life and the justice of freedom and peace.

That suggests the Vatican has never been willing in atomic times to protect its prophets when they protested immoral policies promulgated by CIA-paid leaders such as Noriega and their death squads. The Church does not want to turn its moral force into political force and risk the wrath of national regimes where the Church needs its own institutional freedom to operate.

Much of the same soiled-principle approach prevailed in the Catholic Church's more recent defense of Chile's dictator-killer, Pinochet.

These examples show that the Church hierarchy does not practice what it preaches. It has been, even in the days of Hitler, a moral chameleon. It camouflages its moral spots for the sake of political expediency, especially where fascism is concerned. It rejects the so-called liberation theology of the morally-correct left, but grants a form of "salvation theology" to the morally-corrupt right because that is where the political, military and economic power abides.

In his Christmas message for the third Christian millennium, the pope decried the use of arms and war. The message falls, because of its countervailing hypocrisy, on deaf ears of Catholics and other Christians in nations where atomic armament and military suppression by US puppets occupy the pulpit of life on weekdays.

The Church's mainstream clerics will continue to turn the protesters over to the FBI, given a choice. It happened in Omaha, in the case of McGuire and Palecek. It happened again in Omaha when the bishop himself supported charges against Sister Marylyn Felion. The public seems to approve, and the Church coffers cannot afford public disapproval. The public, no matter of what religious faith, will cast its own stones if clerics do not knuckle under to the secular world's way of doing things. Is this moral leadership on the part of the Church?

It is happening even among Carl Kabat's own religious community of Oblate priests, whose superiors have threatened to kick him out for his activism.

On another Church level, Bishop Francis X. Roque, prelate of the territorially amorphous US military archdiocese, says America should "feel good about" the School of the Americas, according to a report in the *National Catholic Reporter.*

Such conservatism comes from the Holy See itself, which is surprising, given the Polish pope's own form of activism against Poland's immoral communist rulers decades ago. The pope's refusal to support Archbishop Oscar Romero's resistance to the government of El Salvador is linked to the death of that prelate. Ironically, the nation's Spanish name means, "The Savior."

In 1980, Pope John Paul II recalled Archbishop Romero to the Vatican after several activist church people in El Salvador had been killed. Instead of offering sympathy, the pope first made Romero wait two days for the audience, then he lectured Romero against the dangers of supporting the communist agenda, and finally he ordered Romero to make an arrangement with El Salvador's government.

The archbishop was shattered, according to aides, and felt abandoned by his Church; yet he tried to comply out of obedience. The more Romero sought reconciliation with the military in El Salvador, the less they respected him.

Within a month of that Vatican visit, Archbishop Romero was shot and killed while consecrating bread and wine at Mass for a community of nuns in their convent. Even at his funeral, several of the faithful were shot and killed in the streets in the presence of political and religious dignitaries from across the world. The shootings were blamed on an unruly mob of mourners.

The pope's error became a death warrant for anyone at whom the godless oppressors chose to point their M-16s, made in the USA. The pope's public outcries thereafter over assassinations rang a cracked bell, because the perpetrators knew they could kill priests and bishops without the Church of Rome doing anything except to wring its hands and pray. Such events set a precedent for Mexican drug lords later to kill a cardinal of the Church.

Even after Romero's assassination, the pope continued to be critical of regional Church support in Central and South America for liberation theology. In 1983, three years after Archbishop Romero's death and two years after the attempt on his own life, the pope visited Nicaragua. There, he was angered by signs thanking both God and the revolution. Fearing the seeds of schism fomented by the blending of politics and religion, the pope lectured against "liberation theology" and gave private tongue lashings to the cardinals and bishops there for taking sides with the leftists among the faithful being killed.

The pope's idea of freedom was to rely on faith and prayer to weather any storms raised by US-backed military governments. Clearly, he thought the hierarchy in Central America had somehow strayed to the side of Communism, a mortal sin in America's politics, if not first on the anathema list at the Vatican.

In response to cries for peace and freedom from his audience at the public mass in Nicaragua, the pope shouted angrily *"silencio! silencio!"* The crowd, as television showed, seemed shocked to hear the representative of Christ tell them to shut up. When he got silence, the pope went on to say that "the Church is the first to want peace."

For those old enough to remember, the words were shockingly similar to those of British Prime Minister Neville Chamberlain, who talked about "peace in our time," after signing a pact with Hitler conceding the Sudetenland (Austrian Czechoslovakia) in 1938. Unfortunately, four decades later the pope seems to have concluded that Communism, the political opposite of fascism (although, carried to an extreme, its effect on people's lives is similar), was the worst of what was happening to the people of his world.

Roberto Suro of the *Washington Post*, as recorded for TV's *Frontline* program, discloses that when the pope got back to Rome, he shut down several Central American seminaries, reassigned their personnel, and installed bishops of his own conservative thinking. The clergy got the message: to leave the repressive regimes alone and tend to the business of baptizing, marrying and burying so that the Church might survive, by dint of its no-birth-control numbers.

In the moral vacuum left by the Church on political matters, the blood baths of the death squads continued unabated, keeping the clergy busy with requiems.

With this lesson in mind, the Catholic bishops of the United States are not about to bless prophetic actions stronger than prayer and sermons in confronting the military or political excesses of any state. The shooting death in 1993 of Cardinal Juan Jesus Posadas Ocampo of Guadalajara,

Mexico, only underscored the message. It is theorized that he was caught in a deadly crossfire (at point-blank range) between two rival drug gangs. Obviously, the Cardinal knew too much.

Was this an object lesson for the Church to keep its moral mouth shut about drug trafficking that had been stimulated by the CIA and the Iran-Contra program? After all, his murder followed closely the conviction in the United States of Panama's Manuel Noriega. Noriega's arrest and conviction, after a brief sanctuary in the Vatican's Panamanian embassy, virtually created war among the Mexican drug lords and threatened to draw attention to the CIA and its LIONSDEN links with the Mexican drug lords.

Except for individuals bold enough to risk all, moral law and faith itself find no practical sanctuary within the Church. Similarly, the moral base of patriotism, wherein people struggle to be free of the sin of despotism, has no safe harbor because the policies of secretive US agencies back the despots.

The Church's prophets have been left to lead their causes at their own risk, because the moral crusades of the prophets are politically too adventurous in the direction of truth for Church or State to countenance.

As far as the Vatican is concerned, the sanctuary is no place for moral patriotism. By contrast, where the brave men and women portrayed in this book are concerned, moral patriotism is *required* in this world today if the souls of the people are to be touched by Christian or even humanistic principles.

In this standoff, the immoral militarists and the politically corrupt have cowed the Church, so there is no liberation cause or moral justification to rescue even the prophets from their imprisonment.

Like Daniel, the prophets stand alone in the LIONSDEN. That is how *they* are still killing.

Without the backing of the Church, the prophets must deal on their own with several questions: How is anything systemically immoral to be practically opposed or made right? Why did Rome ask the elected Jesuit priest, Father Drinan, to withdraw from the US House of Representatives? Is the role of the Church and clergy limited to forgiving sins, or should it try to prevent evil? Does not even the Lord's Prayer ask, "... lead us not into temptation"?

The solution of the freelance prophets has been protest directed at winning moral reform in both Church and State, because the people of the prophets live in both worlds at the same time. The Church seems to dismiss this consideration as secular humanism. Nevertheless, British politician-philosopher Edmund Burke made a sound suggestion 200 years ago when he said: "When bad men combine, the good must associate; else they will fall, one by one, an unpitied sacrifice in a contemptible struggle." It is sad to note that the Catholic Church does not associate itself in that struggle other than by sermons and holy pronouncements.

Reformers who do not adopt Burke's advice know they and their Church will wither like good theological seed on the political wayside. The prophets are not about to let that happen.

Thanks to a campaign led by Roy Bourgeois and the Maryknoll and Jesuit orders of priests, federal funding for the notorious School of the Americas was deleted briefly in 1999. But a way around that moral correction was quickly found, so that it would seem that those who are in charge of such immorality have the approval of the highest officials. These cadres of foreign troops continue like hit-men to support repressive dictatorships backed by the US, suppressing the legitimate desire of Latin

Americans for true freedom they should have under the banners of State, Church and common humanity.

Several years ago, US Secretary of State Madeleine Albright was asked by a reporter about the death toll among children in Iraq being starved by the US embargo and bombing of that country. Her response, carried on the airwaves of CBS's *60 Minutes* May 12, 1996, was "I think this was a very hard choice, but the price. . . we think the price was worth it." Ironically, that program segment was tagged *Punishing Saddam.*

Albright's response, taken to heart as it was viewed by Rupiper, sums up the terrorism of US government policy in foreign affairs.

Albright's comments, advocating an immoral policy, afforded a good specific opportunity for the Church to speak up. More than preaching should be done about that kind of immorality, Rupiper says. Church representatives have a moral obligation to the members of that Church to condemn without reservation the leaders of the offending nations.

That is why Carl Kabat still is struggling in his post-prison world to right the world's cascade of continuing wrongs. That is why Paul Kabat lived among Indians and was defrocked for disobedience by the Church, before he died. That is why Larry Rosebaugh volunteered to work in the barrios of Central America. That is why Darrell Rupiper is training yet another generation of young men to work among the downtrodden — perhaps someday to render more prophetic lessons to the world's morally obtuse leaders.

That is why Frank Cordaro took a leave of absence and then sought reconciliation with his bishop. That is why Charlie Liteky gave up his Congressional Medal of Honor and joined the anti-SOA army of prophets. That is what drove Mike Palecek to the verge of insanity. That is why people such as Dan and Phil Berrigan still suffer for passing along their prophetic message of peace.

Yet none of these men, even in the absence of support from the Catholic Church, will utter a condemning word against their pope, because the pope still represents the ramparts from which they fight their lonely war. Even the excommunicated Phil Berrigan cites the encyclicals of various popes in his autobiography. He still follows their theological lead in matters of human justice and peace, although he has been excommunicated for marrying and having children.

As Philip is fond of reminding himself, he "is a Catholic learning to be a Christian."

The situation is more than parable. It is life-and-death for the after-life. As Rupiper recalls an incident in Recife, when a woman dying in poverty posed a prophetic question: Would things would be better after she died? All he could do, he says, was nod — to avoid letting her hear his voice break, if he spoke.

In that case, the recurrent thought crossed his mind: *they* are still killing.

The United States could not have killed any more people in Central America even if it had used atomic bombs, although it could have done it more quickly. It could not have killed any more people in Iran or Iraq if it had pressed the nuclear button. It would simply have done it faster.

Instead, it used indirect means and covert, double-cross maneuvers that served ends usually quite different from their stated purposes. The National Security Agency is an expert at such methods, including that of spying on its own citizens and allies. The NSA has had in place for several years a military-based, super-computer system called *Echelon* to monitor every message transmitted worldwide via cell phone, microwave and satellite link, to eavesdrop on American and European citizens by tapping their e-mail or voice communications that are not land-based.

The CIA, through Director George Tenet, took pains to deny the spying at a Congressional hearing. At about the same time he was denying, the FBI stepped forward and sought permission from Congress to use a similar communications spy system of space satellites called *Carnivore*. Both *Echelon* and *Carnivore* are based on the technology of spy satellites used by the Pentagon.

A story in the *New York Times* indicates that the Clinton Administration developed a plan for an extensive computer monitoring system, overseen by the FBI, on the pretext of protecting the nation's crucial data networks from intruders or saboteurs:

> The plan, an outgrowth of the administration's anti-terrorism program, already has raised concerns from civil liberties groups.
>
> A draft of the plan . . . calls for a sophisticated software system to monitor activities on nonmilitary government networks and a separate system to track networks used in the banking, telecommunications and transportation industries.
>
> The effort . . . is intended to alert law enforcement officials to attacks that might cripple governmental operations or the nation's economy.
>
> But because of the increasing power of the nation's computers

and their emerging role as a backbone of the nation's commerce, politics and culture, critics of the proposed system say it could become a building block for a surveillance infrastructure with great potential for misuse. . . .

As part of the plan, networks of thousands of software monitoring programs would constantly track computer activities. The draft report, which has been circulated widely within the executive branch, has generated concern among some officials over its privacy implications.

This means that the FBI and CIA would now be given the most powerful computer tools to perfect their control. *Echelon* and *Carnivore* are software systems capable of snatching from the airwaves "packets" of any microwave or Internet communication at will. This wireless phone tap would require no court supervision or permission, only voluntary adherence to laws prohibiting interception of messages without cause. Obviously, the systems give the FBI, the CIA the NSA and ultimately the White House the means to violate the Constitutional right to privacy of every citizen.

According to recent testimony before the House Judiciary Committee's Constitution Panel, Dan Kerr, director of the FBI's Laboratory Division, admitted that information has been shared between the National Security Agency and FBI through the overlapping *Carnivore* and *Echelon* systems. According to the testimony of a panel of government electronic experts, *Carnivore* is a "non-passive" system for "trapping and tracing" suspect messages on the Internet. As reported on a PBS television program, *Big Brother*, the system can instantly track, by use of "key word" entries, any name or topic programmed into it. Using a net of super-computers, *Echelon* can determine the location of any given caller going through an up-link anywhere in the world within an instant. It can pinpoint the geographic address of the caller and the one being called.

In 1996, *Echelon* was secretly put on loan to Russia's Boris Yeltsin during the Chechnya revolution. It easily pinpointed the location of the rebel headquarters through a cell phone call made from the rebel site. The ensuing Russian missiles, guided to the coordinates thus provided, killed a Chechen rebel leader and members of his staff.

The Chechnya example is not an isolated one. Although the National Security Agency neither confirms nor denies the existence of Echelon, Wayne Madsen, a retired NSA agent, has told news outlets that, "Anybody who is politically active will eventually wind up on the NSA's radar screen." Associated Press reports out of London, Washington and Brussels in February 2000 say that spy agencies in Great Britain, Canada, Australia, New Zealand and the US have spied on Princess Diana, two British cabinet members, the son of the former British Prime Minister, at least one American senator, Amnesty International, Christian Aid, Greenpeace, the Pope John Paul II, and Mother Teresa.

As an example of how this process can go wrong and become a violation of human rights, a Canadian intelligence agent, Michael Frost, noted that an American woman wound up in Echelon files because she told a friend in a casual telephone conversation that her son "had bombed" in a school play.

The prophetic question thus becomes, how are peace and justice ever going to be brought to such a world?

Carl Kabat has always had the answer, which he credits to Christ: "Resist what is evil."

It's a long way from Des Moines, Iowa, in the heartland of the United States, to Nuremberg, Germany. In fact, it's a long time since the Nazi War Crimes Tribunal, when the US government of occupation set the following precedent in international law:

> Individuals have international duties which transcend the national obligations of obedience . . . . Therefore (individual citizens) have the duty to violate domestic laws to prevent crimes against peace and humanity from occurring.

Taken as a whole, the rulings of the Nuremberg Tribunal mean that military officers and, indeed, citizens of any country can be held criminally liable for performing acts ordered by their country when those persons know such acts to be crimes. At issue in the Nuremberg war crimes trials was the killing of millions of people in what became known as "the Holocaust."

The defendants were being tried for having known about or actively participated in the crimes; they claimed as a defense that they were just following orders. The tribunal threw out that defense, establishing a duty to refuse. They were found guilty and sentenced, some of them to death. For the same reason, Adolph Eichmann was tried in 1961 and later executed.

Michael Sprong

The inverse happened in Des Moines, Iowa, on June 5, 2000, when a jury from this bucolic state charged Michael Sprong with violating the law of the land for protesting actions by the United States which he knew to be criminally wrong. He was accused of trespassing at the Iowa Air National Guard base in order to protest the sending of warplanes to Iraq to enforce the so-called "no-fly zone." In his words, he was "trying to prevent a crime."

In a classic Catch-22 situation, Sprong found himself damned by national law if he did protest and damned by international law if he didn't. The legal implications are part and parcel of the moral conclusion that if Sprong did not protest the US bombing of Iraqi civilians in a war action (that does not even have the approval of the United Nations) then, like an accomplice, he would be as guilty as those who were about to drop the bombs and commit murder.

Sprong defended himself on the basis of international law. Assistant Polk County attorney Fred Gay and District Associate Judge Matthew McEniry set a legal precedent for allowing an international law expert, Prof. Richard Falk of Princeton, to testify as an expert witness. This precedent is paralleled only by the milestone trial of John Peter Zenger in colonial times, in which the judge allowed testimony that had the potential of jury nullification of guilt. That is, while the defendant admits guilt as to the facts, the nobler purpose of conscience as to motive is allowed by the judge to be pertinent for jury consideration. In Zenger's case, it was for printing pamphlets found to be seditious by the King of England, yet determined by the colonial jury to be patriotically justified. And so Zenger was set free.

In 1969, the famous defense attorney William Kunstler tried in vain to use the Zenger precedent to free the defendants in the Milwaukee Fourteen case, which included Rev. Larry Rosebaugh. The judge would not allow it because he feared to set a new precedent for jury nullification by way of conscience; but that was in a federal court.

In Sprong's state court case, where the chance for jury nullification was allowed, the offense was simple trespass on government property. Yet the jury found this minor and peaceable offense to be punishable because they chose to make no connection between the misdemeanor and the larger crime of killing innocent civilians for political purpose. If the jury had exonerated Sprong, they would have been implicating the US.

And so, the United States is free to order its citizen-soldiers to commit the crimes associated with the bombing and the economic embargo of a foreign nation, thereby starving children — as is occurring in Iraq. Tragically, what the Sprong verdict tells the American people is this: the Nuremberg verdicts were wrong and the defendants should have been set free — even the Nazi State was right. The Sprong verdict says you can be punished for trying to stop the nation's leaders from committing a crime. That is a conflict in the law that all Prophets Without Honor have experienced the hard way: The law of the State is being made to supersede the morality of the Church and the individual.

While Sprong himself would eschew the label of prophet, he has worked alongside Rev. Frank Cordaro at the Catholic Worker House in Des Moines and shared his inspirational fire. Sprong also assaulted the concrete of a missile silo with Rev. Carl Kabat.

Frank Cordaro

On his own account, in other times and places, Cordaro has earned the wrath of both Church and government and has served several years in jail as a result. His actions included scattering ashes at the feet of President Carter and pouring blood on planes of the type that dropped bombs on Iraq and Yugoslavia. For similar reasons, then, Sprong joins Cordaro and the others as a convict for his national conscience against killing as an extension of politics.

Sprong's sentence in the Des Moines case was paltry: 40 hours of community service. Of course, he thought he *was* serving the community when he landed himself in court. The Sprong case may seem trivial, but, by dint of its historic and legal repercussions, it is not. If the Zenger precedent or the international law defense were allowed, then none of our prophets would have been sentenced. Then, by implication, the nation's leaders and all who knowingly followed their orders would now be guilty of war crimes, whatever the political rationale.

Sprong was also tried in Wisconsin for cutting down radio poles needed to communicate with Trident submarines. The federal judge would not allow any defense related to international law, leaving Sprong with no defense at all to explain his actions. In effect, the judge turned it into a "show trial" in which Sprong was stripped of any Constitutional defense and virtually declared guilty by orders of the judge.

As *Des Moines Register* columnist Rekha Basu noted in Sprong's Des Moines case, "The day's testimony segued from the post-World War II Nuremberg trials to France's invasion of Rwanda, grazed collateral damage in Kosovo and came to rest on the legality of the ongoing US-led military operation in Iraq." Pretty good. As Falk said, in defense of Sprong: "If the members share the knowledge that it's illegal, then they would be subject by the Nuremberg standard to being engaged in criminal activity." In earlier statements, Falk declared that actions taken under orders by the Iowa Air National Guard are "without Security Council authorization and therefore violate the United Nations charter."

Even so, the jury seemed to realize that to exonerate Sprong was to implicate the Air National Guard of any state, and its supreme commander, the President of the United States, in international murder. Accordingly, all the jury needed was to hear the prosecutor say that "Sprong crossed the line". Falk testified that the military incursion of Iraq has caused civilian casualties, the ruin of religious shrines and the destruction of electrical and water infrastructures. He implied, by the Nuremberg corollary, that these actions all result in a Hitler-like pogrom of death for non-combatants. At the same time, he said, the economic embargo, enforced by the US without Security Council authorization, "violates the United Nations Charter." In this manner, Falk charged that the Iowa Air National Guard plays an illegal role when it flies such missions, even if ordered to do so by the US government. At least, Sprong's point was made.

As Des Moines columnist Basu said in her summary, "Something else was on trial in Room 113 besides trespassing and the legality of our Iraq policy: what it means to be a responsible citizen."

Meanwhile, a trial of another sort was taking place behind the scenes: a modern version of the Inquisition by the Catholic Church against one of its priests, Frank Cordaro.

Having been warned of possible excommunication, and having taken a year's leave of absence to assess his outspoken views for reform within the institutional Church, Frank Cordaro has reached a written accommodation with his bishop. While some of Cordaro's followers liken it to the medieval request to recant, as Galileo did 500 years ago to save his life, Cordaro does not.

"It's more a question of my protest style," he says. "I'm willing to accept that rebuke."

To regain his status as a priest, which Cordaro values highly, Cordaro has agreed to tone down his rhetoric on controversial issues such as birth control, ordination of women and Church reform, and to check with his bishop about protests he plans to make, especially if they might land him in jail.

"Does this now settle all the issues?" Cordaro asks. "Probably not. The diocese and I are going to need to live with this arrangement."

These are the words of a still-feisty prophet backed into a corner by his Church, by his government and by his personal sense of mission to the world. Clearly, he intends to continue that mission even as he chooses his words more carefully.

Cordaro's situation cannot help but intrigue Catholics and non-Catholics alike for the insight it provides on how the Catholic Church operates its mind control program alongside its soul control — even as it accommodates excesses and evils by the political and economic systems within which it operates.

Whatever the case, most prophets are so ingenuous they don't care about choosing their words carefully, the way the most disingenuous politicians do. Obviously, the Church itself is more political than ingenuous, as its history shows, even into the present.

In the end, the pressure on the prophets comes not only from the hierarchy of the Church; it comes from the political and economic connections that the Church has consolidated through time. Like a Spanish-moss epiphyte, the Church drapes itself from the limbs of its political, military, economic and governmental hosts. By this spineless process, the Church has let many of its prophets and faithful suffer imprisonment, excommunication, torture and even murder just for living the Gospel in the manner of a man named Jesus Christ.

To the prophets it must seem ironic that Drake College Law Professor Gregory Sisk's argument for the prosecution against Sprong prevailed with the jury, when he said: "I believe in democratic principles and the rule of law." Even Agnew and Nixon took that position.

Sisk subsequently argued that it sets a dangerous precedent for individuals to place themselves above the law, to be arbiters of right and wrong. Is he suggesting that individuals are not masters of their own moral behavior and should have no conscience that is not dictated by federal law?

Sisk has got law-and-order all wrong. States are creatures of the people. Laws come from the people, who decide what is right and what is wrong. If Sisk has his way with the courts, who, then, besides lawyers paid by politicians, will define the law in moral areas? Do they thereby claim that the institution of the Church and its clergy or laity have no special knowledge of right and wrong after centuries of studying the morality, theology and philosophy that formed out society?

The lesson of Des Moines is this: that, socially speaking, there can be no separation of Church and State in this world as long as politics, backed by the rule of law of militarism and economic exploitation, is an inescapable part of the social and moral equation.

As the prophets know, every government poses for its citizens, on a daily basis, moral questions for which each person must find answers in the religious or spiritual corners of their lives.

American educator John Dewey once said: "The only way to abolish war is to make peace heroic."

Ostensibly, that is what the Nobel Peace Prize is all about. However, too often the prize rewards those who first engaged in war and then decided to make peace. These include Theodore Roosevelt, hero of the Spanish-American war; Gen. George C. Marshall, chief of staff during World War II; Henry Kissinger, architect of the Vietnam War; Anwar Sadat and Menachim Begin, adversaries in the Middle East; Mikhail Gorbachev, involved in the Afghan war; Yasir Arafat, Shimon Peres and Yitzhak Rabin, the Palestinian-Israeli foes.

Somewhat similarly, Philip Berrigan (World War II), and Roy Bourgeois and Charlie "Angelo" Liteky (Vietnam) served their country in wartimes, in the interest of restoring peace, as they thought at the time. All were ordained as Catholic priests and each has been on both sides of the peace-and-war fence. All have been in prison more recently for their non-violent modes of advocating peace. All three received medals.

Of the three, Liteky is the most militarily famous. Now 70, a former army chaplain who was awarded the Congressional Medal of Honor, he has relinquished his priesthood and the nation's highest honor in favor of federal prison for peacefully protesting the death squad crimes of the army's School of the Americas. He was most recently released from jail in the summer of 2001.

Although all three once were proud to serve in the military because they thought they were fighting for America's freedom, they now believe that America has been leading its people and the world away from peace. They see American policy producing only poverty, exploitation and death.

In his latest peace effort, Philip Berrigan and several compatriots were arrested just before Christmas 1999 for pouring blood on A-10 Thunderbolt warplanes and hammering on their fuselages at a Maryland Air National Guard base. They were protesting the use of depleted uranium as armored cladding for weapons delivered by such planes in Desert Storm and Yugoslavia.

The Pentagon finds depleted uranium useful because of its extreme hardness and ability to penetrate armor, but "depleted" is a misleading tag because the metal, with most of its radioactive isotopes scavenged for atomic bombs, is still radioactive. Only the "bang" has been removed. The lower-level radioactivity in the metallic residue poses environmental hazards and causes slow but long-lasting health damage. Data is coming in from the Balkans and from Iraq, indicating the devastating effects on civilians. British and European troops who were stationed in Yugoslavia during the recent war are also showing high rates of cancer.

While Berrigan was in jail for protesting the use of depleted uranium, *The New York Times* syndicated an article January 7, 2001, about post-war bombing inspection results in the Balkans. It validated Berrigan's concerns. "We found some radiation in the middle of villages where children were playing," says Pekka Haavisto, who headed the UN inquiry over the NATO bombing of Kosovo.

The findings came a year and half after the halt of bombing. The *New York Times* report also says:

> The discovery by Haavisto and his team at eight of the 11 sites sampled seems certain to fan a sense of fury and panic across Europe about the well-being of soldiers sent to serve in the Balkans, more than a dozen of whom have since died of leukemia.
>
> Residents of Bosnia, Kosovo, Serbia and Montenegro may also resent that they were unaware until now of the need to clean up the low-level uranium dispersed by American weapons dropped over Bosnia in 1995 and Yugoslavia during the war in Kosovo.

European newspapers are describing what they call the "Balkan Syndrome" among people who had collected ammunition shards as souvenirs or who live in the midst of the contamination. Symptoms among soldiers and civilians alike include chronic fatigue, hair loss and various types of cancer, symptoms most frequently caused by exposure to plutonium radiation.

Carl Schoettler of the *Baltimore Sun* hit the nail on the head when he wrote, on January 14, 2001:

> The biblical observation about the prophet without honor in his own country has taken a sadly ironic turn for Philip F. Berrigan, Baltimore's immutable peace activist.
> Berrigan remains locked in a Maryland prison for protesting the use of depleted uranium ammunition by American and NATO troops during the war in Kosovo.

Just before Thanksgiving 1999, Fr. Roy Bourgeois Roy mobilized about 12,000 people for a protest at the gates of Fort Benning, for the tenth year running. Daniel Berrigan joined him, arthritic back and all. With them was popular actor Martin Sheen. Before the day was over, 10 people were to be charged with criminal trespass for stepping across a white line drawn at one of the entrances to this "open" base. (An open base means the public normally can access the base without a pass or checkpoint.)

One of those arrested was even more special than TV star Sheen: Charles "Angelo" Liteky.

Charles "Angelo" Liteky

When he served as a Catholic chaplain in Vietnam, Liteky was known for his ability to combine the sacred and the secular in his military ministry. Scuttlebutt had it that Liteky, on occasion, heard the confessions of soldiers while sharing a can of beer with the penitents, who appreciated the outcome, spiritual, physical and psychological.

Liteky was ordained in 1960 within the order of priests known as the Missionary Servants of the Most Holy Trinity, so designated by the initials M.S.SS.T., after its lengthy title in Latin. At his ordination, Liteky took the religious name of Angelo. Liteky was born in Washington, D.C. By virtue of his place of birth in the nation's capital, his Vietnam heroism was especially symbolic. He became the whole nation's hometown hero.

For what?

In the course of a battle in which he killed no one, Liteky dragged 23 wounded men to safety at Bien Hoa, even while wounded in his foot and neck. He still carries a piece of shrapnel in his foot, which doesn't seem to impede his mobility even at age 70.

When the smoke cleared at Bien Hoa, his soldier-parishioners of the 199th Infantry Brigade believed "he could walk on water." His company commander commented, "The hand of God must have been on his shoulder" as he somehow dodged machine gun bullets.

In 1968, Liteky's shoulders received the Medal of Honor from President Lyndon Johnson at the White House. LBJ is reported to have said, "Son, I'd rather have one of these babies [medals] than be president."

Ironically, it was Johnson's lie about the Gulf of Tonkin ruse that drew Liteky and those he rescued into Vietnam on a full-scale war footing. That lie, which has cost hundreds of thousands of lives, including more than 58,000 US dead, set the scene on December 6, 1967, in the jungles near Bien Hoa, as reported in *USA Today:*

> During his first 11 months in Vietnam, Chaplain Liteky went along on 20 patrols, carrying only a chaplain's bag (containing a Bible, prayer books, confessional stoles, and holy oils for last rites). He never had seen the enemy.
>
> The brigade's base camp had come under mortar fire the previous night, Dec. 5. On Wednesday morning, Liteky volunteered to accompany a patrol assigned to find the mortars. He was with the lead 30-man platoon, cautiously moving toward a thick line of trees, when two figures in black pajamas darted across the patrol's path.
>
> The Americans fired and advanced into the tree line. Suddenly the jungle exploded with enemy fire. Machine guns seared the elephant grass. Rockets thundered. The platoon had stumbled onto a well-entrenched NVA battalion. The Americans hugged the ground. No one moved. No one returned fire. Several soldiers in the lead had fallen, and the rest of the unit was in danger of being wiped out.

The official wording of Liteky's Medal of Honor citation continues to tell the drama which followed:

> Observing two men wounded, Chaplain Liteky moved to within 15 meters of an enemy machine gun position to reach them, placing himself between the enemy and the wounded men. When there was a brief respite in the fighting, he managed to drag them to the relative safety of the landing zone.
>
> Inspired by his courageous actions, the company rallied and began placing a heavy volume of fire upon the enemy's positions. In a magnificent display of courage and leadership, Chaplain Liteky began moving upright through the enemy fire, administering last rites to the dying and evacuating the wounded.

Noticing another trapped and seriously wounded man, Chaplain Liteky crawled to his aid. Realizing that the wounded man was too heavy to carry, he rolled on his back, placed the man on his chest and through sheer determination and fortitude crawled back to the landing zone using his elbows and heels to push himself along.

Pausing for breath momentarily, he returned to the action and came upon a man entangled in the dense, thorny underbrush. Once more, intense enemy fire was directed at him, but Chaplain Liteky stood his ground and calmly broke the vines and carried the man to the landing zone for evacuation.

On several occasions when the landing zone was under small arms and rocket fire, Chaplain Liteky stood up in the face of hostile fire and personally directed the medevac helicopters into and out of the area. With the wounded safely evacuated, Chaplain Liteky returned to the perimeter, constantly encouraging and inspiring the men. Upon the unit's relief on the morning of December 7, it was discovered that despite painful wounds in the neck and foot, Chaplain Liteky had personally carried over 20 men to the landing zone for evacuation during the savage fighting.

Through his indomitable inspiration and heroic actions, Chaplain Liteky saved the lives of a number of his comrades and enabled the company to repulse the enemy. Chaplain Liteky's actions reflect great credit upon himself and were in keeping with the highest traditions of the US Army.

Now, 35 years later, Liteky is doubly famous. He is the only Medal of Honor winner ever to be jailed for his moral patriotism, and just the second man ever to surrender the medal out of religious or moral conviction — and foregoing the medal's associated pension rights of $600 per month.

He did so in July 1986, by placing the medal at the Vietnam Veterans Memorial Wall in Washington along with a letter to President Reagan. As few other men in history can claim, Liteky represents the moral patriotism of the prophets.

"I was 100 percent behind going over there and putting those communists in their place," says Liteky, who responded to a call among priests in 1966 for Vietnam army chaplains. "I thought I was going there to do God's work." His conversion from that point of view was gradual but dramatic.

After he received his medal, Liteky "re-upped" for another tour of duty. By this time, Defense Secretary Robert McNamara's infamous penchant for body counts had become an order. The way the Army chose to implement it raised the first voice of moral dissent from any chaplain in Vietnam. That voice was Liteky's:

"I saw this soldier dressed in battle fatigues shining his boots," Liteky says. "So I said to him, 'Looks like you are going on R & R (Rest and Relaxation).'"

"'Yes, sir,' the solider said. 'It's for three days at Vung Tau, on the beach. It was easy. Just three VC kills.'"

Seething with anger, Liteky says he immediately did an about face and all but ran to the battalion commander's bunker.

"I didn't even bother to knock before interrupting the colonel's privacy. 'What do you know about the policy of granting three days of R & R at Vung Tau for three VC kills?' I asked. (I breached military protocol for addressing a superior officer.)

"The colonel told me the policy was not his. It came down from 'brigade'. 'Then I'm going to see the General, I replied.'

"'Good luck, Chaplain,' the colonel said."

The brigadier general's headquarters were at Long Binh. Despite the danger of ambush while traveling dirt roads at night, Liteky and his driver arrived safely at the rear base camp.

"I spent a restless night thinking about my unscheduled, unannounced encounter with the General in the morning," Liteky says. "When the aide ushered me into the General's office, I'm not sure I even returned his greeting. I just remember telling him why I was there and what I was prepared to do if the three-day, three-kill R & R policy was not abrogated.

"I told him that if this policy was not changed immediately, I would tender my resignation. And, if my resignation was not accepted, I would send a copy of it to every newspaper in the US, along with the reasons behind it," Liteky says.

"This brought the General to his feet in anger. He said, 'I'll be goddammed if I will stand here and let you threaten me.' I remember saying that I was not threatening anyone, but merely pointing out, as strongly as I could, that the policy was an open and immoral invitation for bounty hunters to commit murder and atrocity; that it could lead to killing of the wounded or prisoners, for example, or even civilians.

"I concluded by saying that I hadn't come to Vietnam to support bounty hunters; that I had volunteered for Vietnam to join in a struggle for peace," Liteky says.

"Privately, I think the General knew I was right; that men at the front might do anything to remove themselves from the danger of death, even for a few days of fun and safety. Anyway, by nightfall, the whole policy had been canceled after a meeting with most of the brigade's officers.

"When I reflect on my own reaction now," Liteky says, "I realized it was this bounty-hunting attitude, applied against a whole race of people, that was to trigger the My Lai massacre in November 1969. The main question asked by military commanders after any action at that time was not about American losses, but about the enemy body count. I heard and observed this and knew it was wrong. At this time, and for a while after I left the Army, I hung onto notions that as long as war was necessary, there was no clean way to conduct it. I was wrong about its necessity."

Liteky's confrontation with the one-star general resulted in an invitation to share supper with General Creighton Abrams, then in overall command of Vietnam operations. Liteky recalls that the HQ building in Saigon, being a quonset hut, was not imposing from the outside, but was quite luxurious in its interior decor. The meeting was one-on-one, except for the presence of the chief chaplain for the Vietnam theater, a Catholic colonel who had little to say. He was there, Liteky believes, at the behest of the chief chaplain of the US Army, Colonel Sampson.

Abrams was very much like an uncle [Liteky says], gracious and relaxed. He asked me what kind of music I'd like with dinner. I wish I had said Gregorian chant, but I offered something classical. After a cocktail and chit-chat, Abrams referred to my bounty-hunter objection by saying, "All of us have someone to answer to." Then he told me that he had nothing to do with the three-kill bounty policy and said he found it as abhorrent as I did. He said he had already ordered any field commanders who might have been offering such incentives to rescind them.

The bounty-hunting incident proved to be yet another turning point in Liteky's life. In 1971, he left the Army, seeking "another way to do God's work," as he puts it.

God's work led him on a period of soul-searching. He had grown disillusioned with America's role in the war and with his personal support of the killing his service represented. He left the priesthood, working first at a service station. Then he lived in a wooden hut on a Florida beach and later counseled ex-soldiers for the Veterans Administration in San Francisco.

There he met and married Judy Balch, a teacher and former nun of the Immaculate Heart of Mary order, who was sympathetic to the plight of Salvadoran refugees pouring into the San Francisco area. Through Judy, Liteky applied to the El Salvador refugees the same concern about human life that had made him a hero in Vietnam, and also had put him on the carpet with General Abrams.

"Judy introduced me to a young woman named Gloria, from El Salvador," Liteky says. "Gloria was just a teenager. Her father had been abducted by one of the military death squads and tortured, then briefly released. Gloria could hardly bear to talk about her father's injuries and pain. He had told his daughter that, as he was being tortured and questioned while blindfolded, he definitely discerned the accent of a 'gringo'. In other words, he believed that US agents were connected with his abduction and were present and directing the torture.

"Under house arrest, Gloria's father urged his children to flee. They came to America. They haven't heard from him since," Liteky says. "At first, I didn't believe the stories, but as I went to more and more of these meetings, it became clear these people spoke the truth. And it was sad. And it made me angry. I needed to do something about it, just like at Bien Hoa."

Within months, Liteky visited El Salvador and met with a group of women, all widowed by the unknown fate of their spouses, and most of them mothers of children who had disappeared.

"These women had been presented by military squads with pictures of their dead husbands, their bodies so horribly disfigured that identification was tenuous at best and became a torture of its own. This was in 1986. I saw some of the pictures that had been left with the women, just to intimidate them.

"All these images," Liteky said, "flashed me back to Bien Hoa. I knew I needed to do something to change things. I didn't know exactly what, but I knew whatever I did, I had to be led by a spirit of love. And so I prayed for that leadership."

That spirit led Liteky to the Vietnam War Memorial in Washington in July 1986, where he publicly placed his Medal of Honor, along with a letter to the reigning president, Ronald Reagan.

Liteky recalls that the last line of the letter contained words to this effect: "I hope someday you will open the windows of the White House when the wind is blowing from the south so that you will hear the cries of the people coming from Central America."

The president never responded, but the medal and the letter were collected from the Memorial Wall by the National Park Service. Both are now on display at the National Museum of American History in Washington.

Shortly thereafter, Liteky told members of the media asking for interviews, "I find it ironic that conscience calls me to renounce the Congressional Medal of Honor for the same basic reason that I received it — trying to save lives."

Later, at his pretrial hearing in Georgia for trespassing at Fort Benning, Liteky told the court, "I have only one thing in life that I am really proud of, and that's the fact that I returned, I renounced, the highest medal that the Army gives to someone in combat. I renounced it, and I'm happy about that."

Within a month of the medal's renunciation, Liteky staged, with three other veterans, a 47-day, water-only fast on the steps of the nation's Capitol. It had little effect, except the near-death of a companion, George Mizo. At that point, Liteky and his other two friends, Duncan Murphy and Brian Willson ended their fast. (Years later, Willson lost both his legs trying to halt a train carrying nuclear waste out of Concord Naval Weapons Station in California. The train, at slow speed, deliberately drove over Willson as he lay on the tracks.)

Eventually, Liteky heard about the School of the Americas at Fort Benning, Georgia, and he took up vigil there and began protests alongside Roy Bourgeois and others. Some of the troops there occasionally stop to shake his hand and talk about the issues that divide or, perhaps, unite them. As a further sign of respect, the Fort Benning commander, Maj. Gen. John LeMoyne, invited Liteky to an annual symposium on human rights, sponsored by the School of the Americas, which, in 1999, was under the command of Col. Glenn Weidner.

Featured speaker at the event, held in December 1999, was former Lt. Hugh Thompson, the helicopter pilot in Vietnam who ordered a stop to the massacre of the civilians at My Lai as it was occurring in 1969. Thompson, risking mutiny, had to threaten Lt. William Calley at the point of his helicopter gunship in order to curtail the massacre he saw unfolding on the ground below him. Years later, Calley was court-martialed at Fort Benning and convicted, but after presidential review he was pardoned on the grounds that he could not receive a fair trial because of the publicity surrounding the case. Capt. Ernest Medina, who commanded Calley, was implicated but never charged. As a result, Fort Benning was once again involved in a massacre of civilians in a military setting that went unpunished.

"School of the Americas staged this human rights discussion in an effort to improve its image," Liteky says. "They said, 'See what just one man can do?' They used Thompson to claim that military training still allowed for such independent action where human rights are concerned. "How can the US military arrogate the right to teach anyone about human rights when their very purpose is to instruct military men in the methods of suppression of those rights by use of intimidation, violence, torture and death, right out of their own field manuals?

"Because I had given my word not to disrupt the seminar, as a condition of being able to attend, I had to bite my tongue. But I wondered inside myself how many people there are in the world who had the balls of a Hugh Thompson to confront superior authority at the point of a gun in order to stop an immoral pageant of war being played out at its worst.

"There was no Hugh Thompson at El Mozote when 773 freedom-seeking peasants were massacred by death squads trained at Fort Benning. Why was Thompson, two decades after his rare action, held up as a hero by the very military that intended, the day after the seminar, to resume teaching hundreds of foreign troops to do just the opposite of what Thompson had stood for?

"I know there are not enough Hugh Thompsons in the world to stop such murders in all the places where freedom is needed; where those needing it are killed almost daily, all because of a militaristic US policy supporting economic exploitation of poor countries.

"The reason I'm protesting against School of the Americas," says Liteky, "is to stop the training of the military dragoons from the Third World. These trained brutes are shown the power of weapons, how to use them, how to act like guerrillas against their own people, and take the training back and employ it in the oppression of their people. They have no human rights conscience. It's a job that lifts them for the first time above the poverty they've had to endure, so they don't care what they have to do.

"When you think about it, El Salvador and Central America are just other Vietnams without combat troops. We've been using foreign troops, trained at Fort Benning, to do the dirty work. We're not getting our hands dirty like we did in Vietnam, but the results are the same and just as deadly.

"Now we're into what the military calls low-intensity conflict (indirect involvement), but it comes with high-intensity killing of the poor at the hands of others who are involved.

"Our diplomacy across the years has slipped from the traditional statesman-to-statesman format into a military-to-military protocol. That is the desired effect and function of the School of the Americas. The generals in the Pentagon love the latitude it gives them. SOA becomes the alma mater (nursing mother) of killer-graduates whose troops are at the Pentagon's beck and call.

"If I can avert such a final effect by resigning my Medal of Honor, then my protest is worthwhile. If I cannot turn the focus of the White House or State Department or Congress on this issue, then the Congressional Medal of Honor means nothing, and the process by which I earned it demeans my life, the lives of my fellow citizens, and even the lives I saved." Liteky heaves a sigh.

"I guess I have the faith to embrace the idea that non-violence may someday find its proper place within our system, but that may be centuries away."

The tone of Liteky's voice reveals that he doesn't like the prospect of seeing such a bright outlook postponed for so long.

Even among his fellows, honored with the Congressional Medal, Liteky is making an impact.

"I have respect for the courage of his views," says Paul Bucha, ex-president of the Congressional Medal of Honor Society, as quoted by the *San Francisco Chronicle*. "It's difficult to be an iconoclast. It's much easier to go along," Bucha says. "Men like Liteky make us stop and think. They should not be ostracized or criticized for this. They are entitled to their views, and maybe we'd be better off it we listened."

The protests eventually caught the attention of the US Congress and brought economic censure for SOA under bills proposed in those hallowed halls. The withdrawal of funds for SOA was later reversed by the Senate.

Over the years from 1990 to 2000, Liteky, Bourgeois and many others were arrested for protests at Fort Benning. They would stage, on the grounds of the base, mock funerals for the death squad victims. These events included commemoration of the assassination of El Salvador Archbishop Oscar Romero, as well as the murders of six Jesuits.

Liteky was arrested for trespass in 1996 and 1997, but not prosecuted. His wife, Judy, has crossed the line at Fort Benning, but not arrested. However, she had been arrested previously in Washington and jailed overnight for praying, after hours, in the Capitol rotunda. She had to be removed.

Liteky's brother, Patrick, was arrested in 1998 for splattering red dye at the Pentagon and also at Fort Benning. He has served more than a year in prison.

Willa Elam and the Challenge of Making a Challenge

Another protester for whom Liteky has high praise is Willa Elam, a black woman lawyer from Washington, D.C. During holiday standdown on Thanksgiving Day 1998, Elam spray painted anti-SOA messages on the office and hallway walls in the SOA building at Fort Benning. Then, from the office chair of the SOA commander, Col. Weidner, she called for the MPs to arrest her. Weidner, having just taken over the SOA command, was said to be personally furious. Despite Elam's extensive defacing of the building, the military decided not to prosecute her, Liteky says, most likely, because her case might have stirred more public sympathy to the cause.

Liteky also found that Justice Department officials were reluctant to prosecute him.

"This (non-prosecution) worried me," he admits. "I thought they were taking it easy on me because of the medal. I wanted them to treat me like everybody else who was protesting. But maybe they were afraid of the publicity I might bring to the cause. Maybe they wanted to hide my public profile. If I had any clout because of my medal, I wanted the world to know about the heinous nature of the military and economic US policy in El Salvador, and what similar policy was doing to the poor people everywhere in the Third World.

"Hell, all any of those peasants wanted was the same freedom we brag about in the US, the kind of freedom and patriotism for which our guys in Nam were wounded and killed. I sent a lot of their souls to heaven from there with God's blessing. And for what?

"Sometimes I think I was brainwashed, and that we all have been brainwashed. We all follow our subcultures too closely, and we do things that we shouldn't, if we were humanely enlightened."

Part of Liteky's subculture came from his upbringing. His father was a career Navy man for 32 years, a survivor-hero of the *USS Hornet,* the carrier that launched the Doolittle bombing raid on Tokyo in World War II. Liteky's education, readings and passions have directed him toward nobler outcomes in life. One of his favorite thoughts is from the pre-communist-era Russian author, Leo Tolstoy:

Patriotism is the cruel condition which exists. . . because governments and the ruling classes are aware that not only their power but their very existence depends upon it. [And so] they persistently maintain it among the people by violence and cunning.

"That pretty well summarizes the ongoing policy of our own government in regard to Third World nations," Liteky says. "It explains how the Vietnam War could happen; how the Iran-Contra outrages could happen with the approval of the American public; and it explains the basic intent of the School of the Americas to commit murder in the name of our political and economic system.

"What's worse, it's difficult for First-World beneficiaries (such as Americans) to understand that poverty itself is a form of violence," Liteky says.

North American blindness to the "violence of poverty" is eloquently expressed in the words of an unidentified Salvadoran peasant Liteky is fond of quoting:

You gringos are always focused on violence done with machine guns and machetes, but there is another kind of violence you must be aware of, too. I used to work on the hacienda. My job was to take care of the dueno's dogs. I gave them meat and milk, food I couldn't give to my own family. When the dogs were sick, I took them to the veterinarian in Suchitoto or San Salvador. When my children were sick, the dueno gave me his sympathy, but no medicine as they died. To watch your children die of sickness and hunger, while you can do nothing is a violence to the spirit. We have suffered that silently for too many years. Why aren't you gringos concerned about that kind of violence?

Obviously, Liteky and his counterparts are concerned about both forms of violence. As recently as November 1999, those thoughts led Liteky and 12,000 other Americans, including Daniel Berrigan and Roy Bourgeois, to protest peacefully outside the gates of Fort Benning. Just 23 were arrested. Ten were charged, and found guilty.

As soon as the 10 were declared guilty, six others who had been arrested but passed over for trial objected by staging an additional protest. They marched back to the base, dug a hole, and buried a baby's empty coffin in the ground to commemorate the innocents killed in the El Salvador carnage. These protesters were promptly arrested and eventually served jail time.

When Liteky came before the court, he represented himself. While acknowledging he had violated the law, he did not plead guilty but insisted that his actions did not constitute a crime. The following partial transcripts reveal the depths of Liteky's beliefs and the eloquence of his rationale on behalf of moral patriotism:

> On November 21 and December 12 of 1999, I was fully aware that I was breaking the law. However, I did not consider my actions as crimes against the US Army at Fort Benning or the federal government.
>
> On the contrary, I regarded my civil disobedience to be in keeping with the historical spirit and moral significance of calling attention to laws that violate respect for human life or to the absence of laws that would foster respect for human life.
>
> Historically and currently, what has been taking place at the School of the Americas, Fort Benning, Georgia, cries out for laws that would prohibit the US military training of third-world militaries that oppress the poor and support the rich. Training in state-of-the-art methods of counter-revolutionary warfare given to Latin America militaries with decades-old records of human rights abuses should not only be stopped, but should be outlawed by a country that claims to have championed human rights.
>
> November 21 and December 12 are the dates (we used) to call to mind the brutal killing of six priests, a mother and a child, the massacre of a thousand Salvadoran peasants, the assassination of an archbishop, and the murder and rape of four US religious women by graduates of the School of the Americas.
>
> I did not simply walk over the bright-white boundary line that

separates the property of Fort Benning from the property of Columbus, Georgia. I was part of a mock funeral procession to keep alive the memory of these and other victims of atrocities committed by graduates of the School of the Americas.

The gross crimes against humanity committed by the graduates of the School of the Americas need exposure more than the School of the Americas needs protection from public demonstrations calling for its closure.

Civil disobedience that results in the trial and incarceration of an offender is one of many methods used by informed citizens to awaken their fellow citizens to the injustices that may need to be addressed and rectified. I am in no way trying to avoid the legal consequences of my civil disobedience. I simply cannot plead guilty to a crime. That verdict must be rendered by an officer of the law, like yourself, Your Honor, who looks upon my intention to break the law as a criminal act rather than an act of community service directed toward the exposure of crimes, the evil of which cannot be compared to simple trespass.

My state of mind, conditioned by years of studying the US foreign policy implemented by institutions like the School of the Americas, tells me that I have performed a community service rather than the commission of a crime.

While Liteky awaited sentencing, he began work on a project larger than the Vietnam War Memorial. He calls it the Latin American Wall Memorial. He hopes to gather all the names of the victims of US-inspired violence in Central and South America into a portable diorama to be erected near the entrance to Fort Benning.

"The object is to shame the School of Americas in front of the American public," Liteky says, "just as the Vietnam War Memorial in Washington vividly reminds viewers of the horrors of the Vietnam War and the never-ending pain of its survivors."

Another line from Tolstoy propels Liteky toward his memorial wall project: "The strongest of all warriors are these two — time and patience."

As Tolstoy suggests, Liteky, the Medal of Honor priest-warrior-prophet, patiently is gathering around himself the support of like-minded people. In time, given Liteky's record of performance, there is little doubt that he will be able to gather the names of the victims from the thousands of unjust little wars in Guatemala, Nicaragua, El Salvador, Honduras, Costa Rica, Panama, Colombia, Bolivia, Brazil and Chile.

Liteky will gather them just as he did the shattered bodies of 23 warriors in Vietnam. He hopes the number of supporters who can help him in his cause will grow far beyond the 12,000 who gathered at the gates of Fort Benning in 1999; far beyond the thousands who have protested at Offutt over the years; far beyond the 500,000 who protested at the Hague in 1983 over the deployment of nuclear missiles in Europe under NATO action; far beyond the millions who privately and publicly protested the Vietnam War in which Liteky earned his Medal of Honor.

On June 8, 2000, Liteky and nine others received their sentences. Liteky received one year in jail and a $10,000 fine. Before his sentencing, Liteky read the following statement to the court:

> I consider it an honor to be going to prison as a result of an act of conscience in response to a moral imperative that impelled and obligated me to speak for voices silenced by graduates of the School of the Americas, a military institution that has brought shame to our country and the US Army. I dedicate my time in prison to the victims, living and dead, of the graduates of the School of Americas. The dead number in the thousands, the living in the millions. They are the spouses, sons, daughters and mothers who live with the sad, horrible memory of their victimized loved ones.
>
> One living victim in particular has touched me deeply. Her name is Rufina Amaya, the sole survivor of the El Mozote massacre, December 11, 1981. El Mozote was a small village in the mountains of El Salvador. She is one in a thousand. For what she has suffered over the last 20 years, I'm sure she would have preferred to die along with her husband, children and fellow villagers. She witnessed the decapitation of her husband, Domingo Claros, and listened to the terrorized cries of her children as they were about to be shot or macheted to death. Rufina Amaya lives to tell her story to anyone willing to listen.
>
> When I enter prison, it will be as a prisoner of war, the war against the poor who have little hope of carrying out a legitimate revolution against counter-revolutionaries equipped and trained in military institutions like the School of the Americas. The SOA and schools like it are now in the service of First World economies that want to keep the First World first and the Third World third.
>
> May God have mercy on us, for we know exactly what we are doing.

As US District Judge Hugh Lawson pronounced sentence, he told

Liteky he did not understand "the connection between what is going on at the School of the Americas and this court."

Liteky, aware that Congress had recently approved a name change for School of the Americas, responded out of court that he intends to write Judge Lawson from prison "because I want him to understand that connection." School of the Americas was recently renamed the Western Hemisphere Institute for Security Cooperation.

"Our system is afraid of the sound and sight of truth," says Liteky, who finished his jail term in August 2001. He remembers the judge as being "a poor man struggling with the abundance of truth he heard repeatedly."

The nine people sentenced with Liteky included two retired ministers, a child therapist, a graphic artist, an environmental chemist, a pharmacist, a teacher, a therapist, and a nun.   These people are typical of the demographics of protesters. No matter where in the world they are arrested, all are highly intelligent, in socially beneficial jobs, many college trained. Examination of police files shows they come from all walks of life; all protesting those who make war with the blood of their children.

The point is, there are among the prophets and protesters no "bums" as a cynical and arrogant Nixon called them, in the wake of the Kent State massacre of four students.

There are thousands like them, men and women, blacks, whites and others, religious and atheists, who have protested on campus, at Omaha, Recife, Fort Benning, and at more than 50 bases and military contractor sites worldwide. They form a cross-section of American and world society. They are all Prophets Without Honor, just like the Berrigans, the Kabats,. the Cordaros, Rupiper, Rosebaugh, Palecek, Bourgeois and Liteky.

They are all using the bitter lessons of history in their struggle to make the world right for the future. In that sense, they are all Medal of Honor heroes, just like Liteky.

Yet, in the mind of most governments and many unseeing citizens, they have all been stripped of their honor just for turning away from the dishonor of military and economic predation.

The prophets can only hope that the third millennium's heroes will be known not for their prowess in war, or their ability to stop wars, but for their bravery on behalf of peace in the face of politics and systems that penalize and abuse them as well as those they seek to save. They hope that the honors bestowed upon the new era's heroes will be not for action on the battlefield but for service to mankind, and for the cause of peace, human justice and morality — the peaceful morality of Jesus, when he said, "Jerusalem! Jerusalem! Thou hast killed thy prophets and stoned those sent to thee. I might have gathered thy children. . ."

Maybe then, this Jerusalem-world will realize the protests of the prophets have been as necessary as they were radical and heroic.

A prophecy dies, it is said, only when it is disbelieved, but it rises from the grave of its disbelief when it comes true. This requiem-resurrection process in the case of Carl Kabat's prophecy may have already started.

Like the flow of history and the events which feed it, prophecy does not stand still like some immutable truth. By its nature, prophecy has a changing dynamic because it wrestles with ever-changing power as it corrupts. This has been the case with Father Carl Kabat and his priest-brother, Paul.

What happens, besides jail, to prophets like the Kabats?

Carl Kabat's own religious community, the Oblates of Mary Immaculate, to which he has belonged for nearly 50 years, has warned him he might be expelled from its company. Carl's superiors say it's a question of the vow of obedience; Carl thinks he is obedient to what his conscience tells him is right: resist evil.

Because of his own Quixotic correctness and energy, it seems Kabat not only has been turned into a pariah in his own country, now he has been turned away by his own religious family.

Carl Kabat: Nine Strikes, You're Out

Here's how this happened:

On August 6, 2000, Carl Kabat committed his ninth prophecy, if episodes of protest and jail are the measure. He staged a protest at a missile silo. It was timed to coincide with the 55th anniversary of Hiroshima's atomic bomb. The protest took place at a Minuteman III nuclear missile silo near New Raymer, Colorado, in a field lapping across three states where the US Air Force had control.

In 1998, on the 53rd anniversary of Hiroshima, this same missile silo, known to the Air Force as N-7, became the target of a sledgehammer protest. Swinging the hammers at that time were Daniel Sicken, an Air Force veteran and tax dissenter, and Sachio Yo-Kin, a nursery school teacher. The men bent several bolts that fasten the silo lid track to the concrete and spray-painted on the silo lid the silhouettes of a tombstone and a broken rifle to emphasize their objections to instruments of genocide. Two years later, they still were in prison.

In 2000, Kabat's own prophecy at silo N-7 was both non-violent and non-destructive, although in the past he, too, had wielded hammers. This time he damaged nothing, not even the chain link and barbed wire fence, which he bridged with a ladder. Kabat, witnessed by a small group of supporters, dressed himself in a clown suit for the occasion. Then he placed unconsecrated bread and wine on the missile silo lid, along with a small hammer and prayed for the Hiroshima victims.

At the same time, Kabat made prophetic sense of his clown outfit with these words:

> We are fools and clowns for God and humanity's sake. We bring bread and wine and a hammer as symbols of life in this damnable place of death. The bomb dropped on Hiroshima by the Enola Gay killed more than 100,000 people. If we calculate what 147 bombs could do, each 20 times as powerful as that original bomb, we come up with a number of dead approaching a billion people. All this, just from the small portion of the nuclear arsenal housed in Colorado.

Bill Sulzman of Colorado Springs, Kabat's protest companion, made this statement at the New Raymer silo:

> I have chosen to hold a banner and risk arrest at silo N-7 today to express my personal outrage and opposition to Colorado's 49 Minuteman III missiles, each with three hideous nuclear bombs attached. I reached my final decision to act today during my recent visit to the Buchenwald concentration camp in Germany.
>
> When evil reaches a certain level and one is aware of it, it is impossible to be an innocent bystander. There is no moral or legal

code anywhere in the world that justifies the use or threatened use of these monstrous weapons. And yet, more than 30 years after their insertion into Colorado soil, they remain on alert, directing their cargo of mayhem and death at some distant point on our planet.

Even before these words were uttered and Kabat staged his protest in Colorado, his religious superior, Father David Kalert, OMI, provincial of the Oblate missionaries in the US, was making plans to kick Kabat out of the Oblate community. This is not surprising because Paul Kabat, another peace radical, had been kicked out unjustly in 1988.

In late August of 2000, an advisory letter written by Kalert finally caught up with Carl Kabat long after he had been arrested and arraigned in Federal District Court in Denver. That letter was dated August 2, four days before Kabat had acted at N-7. It was accompanied by a cover letter dated August 22.

In its most pertinent parts Kalert's letter of August 2 said:

> This letter is to officially notify you that you do not have permission to participate in any action of civil disobedience and that you do not have permission to reside outside your designated Oblate community.
>
> Because you are illegitimately absent from the community and in light of the province policy on civil disobedience that was carefully explained to you. . . I must remind you that this new action on your part constitutes cause for dismissal from the congregation.

In explaining the August 2 letter which had gone errant because of Kabat's move to Colorado, Kalert's catch-up letter of August 22 repeated, "I am pursuing your dismissal from the congregation." Attempts by Kabat's friends both inside and outside the Oblate community have failed to dissuade Kalert from this drastic course of action. Kalert is waiting until Kabat gets out of prison to make a final decision.

Had Kabat, after years of being allowed by the Oblates to deliver prophecy against the evils of war and nuclear weapons, become a public embarrassment, in Kalert's mind? Was his clown motif too non-clerical and eccentric? Had the off-Broadway staging of the play, *A Clown, A Hammer, A Bomb and God*, placed Kabat in the limelight too brightly? Is that why he was denied permission to travel to New York to be honored at its opening? Or was his notoriety beginning to affect donations to the Oblate's top money-maker, the Shrine of Our Lady of the Snows, at Belleville, Illinois (the city where Kabat was assigned to stay)?

Nobody is sure of the answers and Kalert is tight-lipped, except to cite Kabat for disobedience. Over the years, the shrine raked in hundreds of millions of dollars in donations, but none of the money was ever used to defend Kabat in court. Back in the '80s, during one prison stint, Kabat received some money from his community to make commissary purchases.

Waiting for trial, Kabat would have faced the Colorado weather without winter clothes in 2001 except for a friend who delved into his own closet. Left by the Oblates for many years to look after himself, Kabat had nothing but the clothes on his back to call his own. After a failed cataract surgery on Kabat's right eye, years ago, the Oblates omitted to provide money for corneal surgery, so he sees the world with one eye.

"I think I see the world better with one eye than most people do with two," says Carl, always self-deprecating.

Carl now walks with a limp because of an injury suffered on a prison basketball court; a ruptured Achilles tendon. More resilient than the semi-god Achilles, Kabat views it as a trophy for being on the championship team of the prison seniors.

In the wake of this record of neglect for one of their own, Kabat's boss, David Kalert, tells news reporters that the Oblates "will not abandon" Kabat. In spite of the dismissal letters Kalert has written to Kabat, he speaks to the media as if nothing is certain. But those who know say he is "determined."

Officially, Kalert's beef about Kabat is disobedience to his authority, as provincial. In the Church, obedience is a serious matter for priests like Kabat, who have made lifetime vows of poverty, chastity and obedience. Usually, care is taken by superiors not to order any priest to perform unreasonable duties in giving obediences (assignments). But Kalert found a way to turn a reasonable assignment into a prison.

In December 1998, Kabat was out of prison on probation. Kalert wrote a letter, dated December 16, ordering Kabat to live in the Oblate house at St. Henry's, the former Oblate seminary in Belleville. Further, Kabat was told he could not leave the premises overnight without Kalert's permission. Kalert told him that these orders, which did not include any priestly duties, were part of his official obedience. To Kabat, this was the Church equivalent of prison.

Prior to these orders, Kabat had been allowed to live with his brother's family at DuBois, Illinois, where his defrocked brother, Paul, had died. His only restriction, where the court was concerned, was that he could not leave the state of Illinois without permission from his probation officer. Kabat felt this was like cooperating with an evil system, and so he chafed.

While Kabat had been in prison for his clown caper at the North Dakota missile silo, the priest who served the prison on a monthly basis offered him the opportunity to say weekly Mass for the inmates. However, the prison chaplain was informed by Kalert, over the phone, that Kabat no longer had priestly faculties. When these were lifted, and by whom, Kabat was never notified. In effect, Kabat was a priest with no more powers than a layman.

However, once at St. Henry's he was allowed to concelebrate Mass in private with other priests, most of whom were retired. Once, when Kabat was the main celebrant at this Mass, he was criticized for changing some of the wording of the liturgy and gospel passages to make them sound non-sexist. This offended the traditionalists, who took him out of the rotation for leading the concelebrated Mass. He says this form of shunning hurt him more than anything that happened in prison, but he had no friendly ears in his community to hear his thinking or complaints.

Carl works from a kind of logic that hopscotches from one half-sentence to another, as if expecting the listener to follow the unspoken thoughts in between. Sometimes he rambles to his point. . . all signs of a mind assembling thoughts faster than the mouth can speak them.

"They were unchristian," he says of his community. Then he stops, as if to stifle an unchristian thought of his own. "But they didn't even know it."

In trying to explain how he thinks he got into trouble with his superiors, he will wander onto other subjects such as how to help the poor. It is almost a separate conversation. But he is certain of one thing: "I felt freer in prison than I ever did at St. Henry's. In prison I was free to follow Jesus according to my conscience."

At another point in a rambling conversation, he recalls that Kalert once asked him what he wanted to do, now that he was out of prison.

"I told him, 'I just want to BE'. And I knew from his blank look that he didn't understand, and that I could never make him understand."

The restrictions at St. Henry's chafed at Kabat's spirit. The only requests that Kabat made for being absent from St. Henry's and which Kalert considered to be "reasonable" were to visit his terminally ill older brother, Paul, who had been tossed out of the Oblate order, and his dying mother.

Kabat went from feeling frustrated to desperate. And so he planned another protest, this one in Colorado. After first giving notice for a three-week vacation, he left a note for his local superior indicating he was about to stage another protest; but he didn't say where. He said he could not involve anyone else in his plans because he feared they might be arrested as conspirators. This is what prompted Kalert to notify Kabat he was to be kicked out of the Oblates.

It didn't seem to matter to Kalert that Kabat's dismissal was to come after 49 years with the Oblates as a student, a teacher, a parish priest, a foreign missionary, and a protester of nuclear evil for which even the Pope and America's Catholic bishops had prescribed resistance.

It didn't seem to matter to Kalert that this dismissal threat was being heaped like scorn upon Kabat at a time when he faced further sanctions from the legal system. . . a system which had already placed more than 14 years of Kabat's life behind bars.

To judge from Kabat's outward reaction, dismissal doesn't seem to matter to him, either, although he says he does not want to leave the Oblates. So what things do matter to Kabat?

Among the things that matter most to Carl, he mentions his protest actions, especially the one at the GE plant in 1980, later dubbed the "Plowshares Eight," which spurred the formation of the so-called "Plowshares Movement" across the world.

About that movement, in his autobiography, Philip Berrigan writes:

> The Plowshares Eight (Daniel Berrigan, Philip Berrigan, Dean Hammer, Elmer Maas, Carl Kabat, Anne Montgomery, Molly Rush and John Schuchardt) have no illusions about the warfare state. Congressmen and women won't visit us in jail, the Pentagon isn't going to invite us over for a chat, the President will never call to ascertain our motives for invading G.E.'s plant.
>
> Nothing of that matters; we aren't attempting to reform or overthrow the government, we don't care who sits in the White House, or who walks the hallowed halls of Congress. . . We pour our blood in order to proclaim the sin of mass destruction. We are confronting the spiritually insane. . . The authorities react to us with apprehension, even hatred.

Because of these things which matter most, Kabat does not try to convince those in authority of anything against their will or the force of law. Although he prefers to stay with the Oblates, Kabat refuses to argue his case with Kalert, but he did try once. The result, as he describes it, was "a monologue, not a dialogue."

Kabat considers that the matter of his dismissal is already beyond his power to control by one-on-one discussion.

"If the Oblates are not proud of who I am and what I've done and don't want me to carry the OMI name, I certainly don't want to force myself on them," Kabat says. "I can't and won't force my views on anyone. That's what non-violence in the face of violence is all about. That was the way of Jesus and Gandhi and Martin Luther King. All I can do is point to what I think is wrong and let others make whatever decision they must. That is my conscience in action. It's the only way I can BE and let others be. That's what I meant when I told Kalert I just want to BE."

Paul Kabat

Carl says his brother Paul, also an Oblate, had the same philosophy. In 1988, Paul Kabat was coerced by his Oblate superiors to sign papers rescinding his priesthood because of his peace activist style. That process also started as a "discussion" that ended in "laicizing," a canonical term. In blunt terms, his ordination was nullified. He was defrocked.

Therein lies the story of a prophecy betrayed by those whom Paul Kabat had tried to help, and by officials of the Church who were more connected to the system than they were to one of their own brothers in Christ.

At the heart of Paul Kabat's troubles was his literal interpretation of a general order given by the founder of the Oblate Order, St. Eugene Demazenod: "to serve the poorest of the poor," and never to be "a smoldering wick." Fr. Paul's ministerial inspiration conflicted with that desired by his superiors, who refuse to divulge the official reason for his dismissal.

Kabat family sources say his first scrape came early in his assignment as chaplain for the Newman Center on the Bemidji State campus around 1970. Apparently he allowed a non-Catholic groom as a mixed marriage to receive the Sacrament of Eucharist. This scandal put Paul on what is called (in secular circles) "the shit list."

Fr. Paul's duties in Minnesota weren't confined to the tame life of a campus ministry. He often helped at Mesabi Iron Range parishes on weekends, and he even opened a house for the homeless in downtown Bemidji. The area was also was refuge to many Indians and social castaways, replete with alcoholics and mental cases expelled by the hospitals into the streets...what both Kabats called "broken people."

It took Fr. Paul a while to figure out how the people had come to be broken; but, just as elsewhere in the world, it turned out to be the exploitative system. The iron ore that produced the wealth also produced the poverty, which produced the human hopelessness that produced the mental, psychological and spiritual derangement. The nation's steel mills at this time, 1971-1983, were losing steam, and taking down with them the lives and pride of once-proud-but-poor Iron Range people. "Hardscrabble" is the mining town description of such conditions. Ironically, this was also the place where the Berrigans were born.

At some point in this period, Fr. Paul figured he could best serve the poor by opening a shelter in a region that had never quite got over the Great Depression. To do so, and in order to gain funding from local assistance programs, he had to own the property from which he would serve the down-and-outers. He didn't think this really was a violation of his vow of poverty because the property was for the use of others, not for himself. Moreover, he didn't think this was a violation of his vow of obedience which — strictly construed — meant that his superiors had to approve of such ownership and be the proprietor. His Oblate superiors, unwilling to accept the associated liabilities, refused to take that role.

In the end, Fr. Paul, while not censured for bending the rules, was left to his own devices. Gradually, his basic humanism (a philosophy which has been listed on the Vatican's Syllabus of Errors for centuries) took over. He took into his community home anyone in need. Not surprisingly, most who came to Fr. Paul's "Home of Community" were mentally unstable or social misfits.

Fr. Paul's "broken people" were allowed to come and go as they wished. There were virtually no rules to choke their personal freedom except for each to assist the community in whatever way he or she could, as long as they chose to live there. If someone came with welfare funds or social security checks, the funds were pooled along with Fr. Paul's own funds and used to support community operations, and were doled out according to personal need.

When people wanted to leave, they left with whatever was in their account, or whatever could be spared, if that had been depleted. Many of the more permanently scarred and marginal residents were mentored by Fr. Paul. In some cases, he was their official guardian.

One such person was Ms. X, an on-again, off-again schizophrenic whose parents had provided a small trust fund for her care. As her guardian, Fr. Paul helped to develop her basic skills for coping with life. As she responded and gained some balance in her personal life, he turned over some of the community's operations to her. She became his trusted assistant, freeing Paul to expand his activist horizons.

Frustrated after years of a ministry given mostly Sunday-style lip service by his Oblate superiors, Paul traveled to Omaha where he joined fellow Oblate, Darrell Rupiper, to protest against nuclear weapons at Offutt Air Force Base. He did this in 1982, and again in 1983. As anticipated, he served time in prison and enjoyed the spiritual release that only unjust punishment can deliver. Out of jail, he returned to Minnesota.

At some point while Fr. Paul was in jail, Ms. X had been operating the Community House, but she had allowed herself to become pregnant. The father was an itinerant Iranian student, who had taken flight at first word of paternity. On Fr. Paul's return, he took pity on her and continued to support her and the baby after the child was born. Together they struggled to keep the Community House operative.

In 1984, Paul joined his brother Carl in the jackhammer raid on a missile silo at Whiteman Air Force Base near Kansas City. With the Kabat brothers were Larry White Cloud and Helen Woodson, an activist despite being the single mother of several foster children. The care of the Woodson children was underwritten in advance by a Hollywood persona as part of the advance planning for the missile silo raid, because it was assumed that Woodson and the others would all have to serve jail time.

Paul received a 10-year sentence for his part in the missile silo protest, an outcome much more severe than anyone had anticipated. Leaderless, the Bemidji Community House was orphaned and fell prey to budget cutting by social agencies. Because it lacked the official support of the Oblates as well, there was no money to support the sad mélange of damaged people gathered under its leaky roof.

In a moment of panic, Ms. X took a desperate gamble to save the only home she had. She claimed Fr. Paul was her child's father and tried to extort support money from the Oblates. This claim would have been easy enough to refute, but the Oblate priests were more interested in suppressing scandal than in determining truth. They feared that even a just defense would look like another Church smokescreen.

Once Paul got out of prison in 1988, his Oblate superiors called him on their rubric-red carpet and, without investigation, coerced him into signing away his priesthood. Thereby did the Oblates rid themselves of a potential embarrassment that had to do more with economics and public relations than with truth and justice. Laicized (stripped of his priesthood) Fr. Paul Kabat was kicked out with nothing but a small monthly stipend to provide for his barest needs. After 30 years with the Oblates, Paul turned his steps back to the Kabat family farmhouse in Scheller, Illinois.

At Paul's instigation, that farmhouse soon became the national headquarters for the North American Farm Alliance, a group concerned with preserving the family farm as a part of the American scene. That activity drew Paul to Memphis, briefly, but his health began to fail him.

It was at this time that Paul first learned that he had been born with just one functioning kidney. With a failing heart and after a series of strokes, he returned to the Kabat farmhouse. He died May 31, 1999, where he had been born, but not without a measure of personal vindication.

Some time after Fr. Paul's disgrace, Ms. X wrote him a letter of apology for her lie. Paul's sister, Mary Ann, burned that letter out of bitterness, after Paul's funeral.

Before Paul died, he told his brother Carl a story about another protégé of the Bemidji Community House. The man, a long-time street person, had been diagnosed as some sort of mental case, but had been cast off by the system. The hospitals didn't want him; the social system ignored him. He and his mentally retarded wife lived under Fr. Paul's roof because, as Paul told Carl, "it seemed like there was no other place on earth for them."

As the story goes, Paul was in jail when the man's wife died. Without his mentor, the man did not know what to do with his wife's body. And so he took her out into the woods of Minnesota and placed her under a tree. Because of his strange actions, the man was subsequently charged by state officials with murder, which was never proven. Because the man was also using a fake social security card, Fr. Paul's Oblate superiors had not been pleased to be associated, through Paul, with yet another scandal.

Paul Kabat's fate at the hands of his Oblate brethren for caring too much for his Indian friends have taken an ironic turn since his death. A *New York Times* headline dated November 2, 2000, reads: "Indian Lawsuits on School Abuse May Bankrupt Canada Churches." Included among those being sued is the Canadian branch of the Oblates of Mary Immaculate. The charges are for cultural abuse of Indians in the dozens of schools the Oblates had operated for decades in the Canadian provinces. (The American Oblates worked among the Indians in Minnesota and South Dakota.)

The article says, in part: "In Manitoba the Missionary Oblates of Mary Immaculate, a Roman Catholic order, want to hand over to the federal government virtually all their property in the province in return for about 2,000 claims against the order. The Oblates fear that legal bills will eat up their assets before any money can flow to legitimate claimants."

A big part of the Indian grievance is the fact that for decades the

Indians were not allowed to speak their language or pass along the customs of their ancestors in the schools where they learned the white man's ways and religion.

By contrast, Paul Kabat, and for a time his brother, Carl, had worked in free-lance fashion among the Indians around Bemidji, Minnesota — but with more compassion than their Oblate superiors thought wise.

Carl Kabat is still privately upset with his order for the shabby treatment of his brother. It is even possible that Paul's experience has brought continued wrath upon Carl from the same Oblate brethren, but Carl says he doesn't reflect on that. However, fearing treatment similar to what Paul Kabat received, Carl refuses to engage in discussion about his future with his Oblate superiors, and seems to be more comfortable with his peace-and-jail ministry.

Fr. Carl's refusal to argue his own case is typical of his battles with the US and world legal system. He has always preferred to fight from behind bars as a form of protest. He refuses "to cooperate with what is evil," even to the point of signing papers that might release him on personal recognizance.

Until the protest in Colorado, Carl Kabat never took the option of personal recognizance bond when offered. He did so in the Denver court only because his pro-bono attorney, Walter Gerash, tried the case on the basis of international law. Kabat saw in this course of action the possibility of vindication for the efforts of all anti-war and anti-nuclear protesters from the Berrigan brothers to the present.

In the meantime Philip Berrigan, from his prison cell in Maryland, urges Kabat to "fight tooth and nail" to defend himself against his Oblate persecutors. About his friend Carl, Berrigan has this to say to Fr. David Kalert, OMI, Carl's superior:

> Friends tell me that Rev. Carl Kabat, OMI, faces exclusion from the Oblates of Mary Immaculate for alleged disobedience. If such is the fact, I denounce such a provision on the grounds of Christian freedom of conscience, and obedience to the Gospel of Jesus Christ.
>
> For twenty years Carl has been an international symbol of non-violent resistance to the nuclear gamesmanship of the nuclear club, led by the US In that time, he has endured more unjust imprisonment (approx. 14 years) than any other nuclear resistor in the world. And, you'll pardon me, if the truth were known, this faithful priest has been the glory of the OMIs and the American Church. For we American Catholics are more notable for complicity with doomsday

weaponry than we are for resistance to it.

Re conscience: Carl has habitually followed the highest law of God — "Thou shalt not kill," rather than taking notice of the strictures of superiors who tend to be woefully ignorant of the fierce idolatry of the national security state and its nuclear arsenal.

Re the gospel: As the gospel tells us, the supreme law of love taught by Christ was love of enemies. All the love that Jesus professed and lived was encapsulated in love of enemies. As we know, He prayed from the cross for his enemies, pleading with God to forgive them. Carl personifies love of enemies, risking his life and his freedom to protect and encourage the victims of his government's nuclear lunacy.

Now, considerations are afoot to eject Carl from an order that has been his home and dedication for 50 years. Please reflect on the sheer injustice of that.

Despite Berrigan's eloquent plea, Fr. Kalert remains, like a stony Sphinx, silent about the prophet who continues to inspire Plowshares protests. His latest letter to Fr. Carl, dated January 15, 2002, says in part, "I am assuming that about the middle of the year you will be released from prison. At that time, I ask you to report to Fr. Allen Maes, and we can proceed with determining what your future will look like. "

Within a month of Kabat's Colorado protest, five nuns engaged in a protest during an air show at Peterson Air Force Base in Colorado Springs. One of them, Sister Anne Montgomery, is one of the "Plowshares Eight."

The base lies in the shadow of the North American Air Defense Command Headquarters tunneled into Cheyenne Mountain. As it turned out, Carl Kabat and co-protester Bill Sulzman (both out on bond) were living near enough to encourage the nuns. On September 9, the nuns poured blood on a military fighter and pounded on nearby equipment with hammers.

The nuns were arrested and charged with criminal mischief and destruction of government property. Within a week, while the nuns refused bail, the charges were dropped, partly because of the Air Force fear of publicity but mostly because damage to government property was negligible.

The nuns were described in *The Denver Post* as "graying and wrinkled" and ranging in age from 52 to 73. Their collective action, dubbed "Sacred Earth and Space Plowshares," was staged to coincide with the 20th anniversary of the first Plowshares protest at a missile factory in King of Prussia, Pennsylvania.

With Sister Montgomery in Colorado Springs was Sister Elizabeth Walters of the Immaculate Heart of Mary; and Sisters Jackie Hudson, Ardeth Platte and Carol Gilbert, all of the Dominican order. Sisters Gilbert and Platte reside at the Jonah House in Baltimore, a community founded by

Philip Berrigan and his wife, Liz McAlister, for non-violent anti-nuclear activists. All the nuns are well known to Kabat, who was on hand (while awaiting his own trial), to attend their court hearings.

The target of the nuns' wrath was the US Space Command and its document called *Vision 2020*, which the nuns say sets forth plans for US military control of space by that date. The cover of that document features an illustration that shows a death ray emanating from a space satellite toward some target on earth.   By the time of the nuns' protest, the brochure had been changed to show only peaceful artistic renderings about Air Force Space Command. Now called *Almanac 2020*, the booklet uses the same subject mottos: *Strength and Preparedness; Mastery of Space; Poised for Peace; Space Warfare Center*. There is no lack of Latin mottos: *Pax Orbis per Arma Aeria* (Peace on earth through aerial war) and *Impavide*, (Fearlessly).

If these mottos seem contradictory or confusing, the words of the leaders at Space Command are not.

In 1996, General Joseph W. Ashy, the former commander-in-chief of the US Space Command told *Aviation Week and Space Technology*, "We're going to fight from space, and we're going to fight into space. That's why the US has development programs in directed-energy and hit-to-kill mechanisms. We will engage terrestrial targets someday — ships, airplanes, land targets — from space."

His words are not hollow, as headlines in the *Rocky Mountain News* show on January 26, 2001:

AIR FORCE CONDUCTS VIRTUAL SPACE WAR
At Warfare Center, Experts in Simulated Battle Set in 2017
"This is a look into the future, at what a potential adversary might have in space and what we might have."
— Brig. Gen. Doug Richardson, Commander of the Space Warfare Center

Such is the vision the Pentagon has for the year 2020: war from space waged upon people confined to earth.

Gen. Richard Rogers, as head of Space Command, said in a 1997 speech to the National Space Club, "With regard to space dominance, we have it, we like it, and we're going to keep it. Space is in the nation's economic interest."

In other words, the Pentagon's plans show that the United States of America is going to expand war from the earth into space, at a time when

Janus-headed diplomats are trying to convince Russia to change the Anti Ballistic Missile Treaty to allow for America's Son-of-Star-Wars concept.

From space, what big eyes America will have — all the better to see with, in order to kill people and destroy nations — and we can make money doing it, if the words of General Rogers are to be believed. And as of 2001, the Air Space Command is already practicing to deliver these wonders from space.

"This is not defensive weaponry," says Colorado Springs activist Bill Sulzman, "It is first strike capability, because no other nation, including Russia or any of the so-called rogue states, have a first strike capability from space, or even from earth. From what, then, do we pretend to defend ourselves?"

As somebody said, years ago: There is no such thing as war games. If it's war, it can't be a game. If it's a game, it can't be war.

That is why the nuns, and other prophets before them, have spilled blood at missile manufacturing plants and other sites and have gone to jail for it.

"We believe that under law, certainly under God's law, but under international law, we are not guilty," says Sister Gilbert. "We came to Colorado Springs because it's the center. . . the whole Star Wars technology is based here. It seems like the perfect place for us to come and shed light on what the government is trying to keep in the dark."

The nuns explained to the media at the time of their arrest that they are part of a worldwide Plowshares peace movement, which they helped to co-found and spread, and which adheres to the Bible verses found in Isaiah and Micah:

"They shall hammer their swords into plowshares and beat their spears into pruning hooks. . . Nations shall not lift up their swords to other nations, nor should they train for war anymore."

There have been between 70 and 100 Plowshares actions worldwide since the first one staged by the Berrigans, Carl Kabat and Sister Montgomery. As of 2000, more than a dozen participants are now in jail, including Philip Berrigan for an action taken in December 1999 at a Maryland military base.

Prison is not new to the five nuns who protested in Colorado Springs. They say they have been in jail more times than they can remember. When asked why, they respond unanimously that the US should not spend billions of dollars of destruction when there is poverty worldwide. And so their mission is a religious one.

It's a very spiritual act [says Sister Platte of her spilling of her own blood]. It's a very non-violent, loving act. We use our blood as a symbol of life. It sort of unmasks what the government does not show us. They do not show us the bodies of hundreds of thousands of people who were just murdered in Iraq or killed in Kosovo. They will not show the bloodshed, so we pour out our own blood. Then we hammer.

Her words, like the sensitive tapping of a mallet, sum up what all the prophets have been saying for decades. When asked if such actions are sanctioned by the Catholic Church, Sister Gilbert, a Dominican, says, "We are all in good standing with our congregations."

Her words stand in stark contrast to Kabat's situation, and cast further shame on his congregation for seeking to dishonor him by ejecting him from his spiritual home.

Carl Kabat truly is a Prophet Without Honor. Nevertheless, he holds his head high because, despite betrayal, he believes his ideals someday will be honored by the billions who have been spared nuclear oblivion as a result of his actions and those of his friends.

"How did life become all about killing?" the woman asked softly, as if to herself. "And when?"

Unsure of her point, I withheld my answer and let her talk.

"We give our emotions and our wombs and our lives and the milk of our breasts to recreating life, sustaining life, and what do we get? War. Killing. Lies to hide the deeper lies that do the killing with unseen bullets. Where is the love we lovers and mothers made from the beauty of being peaceful, blissful in bed or honest and giving, mate to mate, in life? It's all about. . . about killing, ever since the war. What kind of ugly thing is that to share with your kids or mine? What does that say about the world and those in America who presume to control it with deceit and with bombs and bullets?"

A vegetarian, she stabbed savagely with her fork at the Swiss chard leaf in her salad and crunched with requited vengeance its molared vulnerability. She chewed silently, well aware of the grenade-like impact of the thought she had exploded. I wanted to say something about all of our kids and grandkids being in the same boat, but she had beat me to the punch.

The war she was talking about was most likely Vietnam, I wasn't sure. She could hardly have been more than a knee-scabbed child when World War II tore millions of older lives apart nearly everywhere in the world and gave rise to the mushroom cloud. Now she was in a lovingly controlled kind of rage, the kind that only a giver of life is capable of.

Her name was Andy, short for Andromeda. She said she used to be embarrassed about explaining her unusual name. But now Andy seemed as natural as the long-gone scabs on the knees of her childhood. She claimed she could point in the night sky to where Andromeda glittered, but tonight was too overcast and misty.

When she had got on the shuttle bus, she gave the impression of a nun-like person, shy and reserved, but poised enough to defend, however weaponless, whatever she confronted. In life, gradually, she had become a teacher, become a wife and mother, and finally divorced — as much by the vicissitudes of life by force of changing personal realizations.

We had met on an airport shuttle bus, headed to Columbus, Georgia, from Atlanta. There was a kind of rain as if the day seemed to require the seep of its gentle tears for no apparent purpose. Initial conversation was tenuous until the subject came to the anti-SOA rally. A brochure protruding from her carry-on bag gave me that clue and my conversational entree. Newspaper reporters, even retired ones, always follow a lead.

The result of my inquiry was a shared supper of no culinary note, and a lot of conversation. She spoke about the hard realities of the world, but was not bitter. As we talked, streaks of gray showed at her temples where the pulse of thought flexed with each word. Even in conversation, she managed a lulling smile, betraying a soothing inner grace. She was here, like me, at an anti-military rally at the gates of a huge military base, Fort Benning, protesting the inhumanities inflicted for years by what that base represented to other humans in distant lands via the School of the Americas. The same base, the same school whose brutal mission for training Salvadoran soldiers Roy Bourgeois and Linda Ventimiglia and Larry Rosebaugh had protested years ago.

With a mouthful of pizza, I said, "Peace is left to bury and excuse what war kills."

She nodded.

"It seems like medals bestow honor on the process. If there were no medals to be claimed, perhaps there would be no war, no burials but those for natural cause."

I waited as she swallowed.

"Then I would say that kind of peace kills with hollow-point honor. Peace derived from war is not true peace. It still crushes humanity by lack of its ability to stop what is evil."

"Where then," I asked, "lies the reconciliation of one against the remedy of the other, peace not prevailing?"

"In us," she proclaimed. "Once you break the chain of war, the war-

and-peace cycle in the hearts and minds and souls of each person."

"And how is that accomplished?"

"By dying deep within, before the bullet strikes. It makes you kind of bullet proof — not outside, but inside."

"You are killing yourself?"

"No. I'm trying to survive and helping others to survive."

"Why did you come here? The protest, of course, but...?"

"It is a question," she replied, "not so much of protesting the way the world is, but of what it is not, or might have been."

We walked such avenues of thought until, dinner over, we then strolled through an occasional pesky mist on a sadly glistening avenue of asphalt.

"Do you know that pursuit of peace can kill you?" I asked.

"It has killed millions," she said quietly. There was mist upon her cheeks and mine as well from accumulated raindrops.

"I sense in you a great intellect, or insight." It sounded patronizing even as I said it.

"Intellect, talent, or insight — whatever your terms. They have no power of their own on my part or yours until they are endowed back to the people by those holding power."

"And how," I asked, "does one gain control of power or the attention of those who hold power?"

"Politically, I don't know, except through rallies like this. But it takes millions of us. Philosophically the course of misdirected power is hard to change because it has a fixed rudder. They stay the course. I suppose it's gained in the first place by subverting intellect, talent, and insight and even one's own purpose in life to selfish purpose."

"And so you hint at treason, as if the people like us, who bestow their power, have been betrayed by our leaders?" She didn't miss the opening I gave her.

"If this be treason, we should make the most of it. Because treason against the people is what happens behind the gates of Fort Benning, and the portals of the Pentagon, and the steps of the White House. But they disguise it as patriotism and national security." Andy said.

As I posed another question, it was matched by rumbles from the dark unseen horizon, hinting that it might rain again.

"Iran-Contra?"

She spoke of such sinful matters in mauve tones, as Eve might have in Eden. Yet with each word, her facial expressions seemed to kaleidoscope through all the emotions and hues of humanity. Her eyes changed from mosaics of milky blue through hazel, before narrowing into piercing arrows of marbled light summoned to reflect the pupils of an uncertain black infinity.

If there was anger, there was also the flicker of hope that somewhere, on the unseen horizon of where those eyes probed, might lie the resolution of her anxiety — and humanity's fate.

The impression of anyone gazing into them might have been divided: whether to call 911 to lobotomize her unexpressed feeling of stifled desperation, or to continue on an after-dinner walk under a mottled night sky in the mist. Her eyes contained, in all, a vision of hopelessness about what was unachievable, yet still had to be. From somewhere else came a glimmer of hope. Then the perspective was washed away by the commercial pulse of some nearby neon light, reflected. My point seemed blunted in a flash.

"You asked why life must always be all about killing? What do you mean? Who is being killed? I mean, I know about the six Jesuits, and Archbishop Romero. That's what this protest is all about."

"You and I are being killed," she said. "Our children. Our future. The whole damned earth. That's why I am here. All the way from Alaska. Otherwise, what's the point?"

"Alaska? That's a long way to make a point."

"It's more a part of the world than the rest seems to be."

"You mean the world that used to be?"

"I guess so. A long time ago. Someone said you can't go home again. Was it Thomas Wolfe? Someone else said you can't stand in the same river twice. A Greek philosopher?"

"I suppose that's because the river from moment to moment never contains the same water or fish?"

"No," she said, "More like we ourselves are not the same as when we first waded. We've lost the innocence of our first wading. The river of the world has dissolved it without our permission. The world that used to be doesn't exist anymore. Not even in our own lifetime. Not any more than the starlight you see up there scattered between the clouds. By the time the twinkling message gets from there to here, the reason of its instance, the reason it was sent is gone, evaporated by time and distance and maybe even the cloud of the moment. Gauging by the 'now' that exists on earth, the star has already moved from where we now observe it, having done so before we were born. Andromeda sends us its starworld blink, but between the moment of dispatch and the moment we can blink back, what is true in the exchange has already changed. The same thing is true for us here as we struggle to respond to events. We respond not to life, but to what is already dead about it."

From nowhere special, the conundrum of the tree falling in the forest crashed into my mind.

"So why does Andromeda still shine?" I asked.

"So that we can be reminded."

"Of what? Reminded of what?"

"Of everything that is sacred about each present and passing moment. Each life that winks, however briefly, like Andromeda. So that we can shine and be reminded of where we are letting ourselves be led whenever someone else holds the light. Each of us holds the light and should not let go. I am reminded of the past, from which we seem to have been pushed into the present reality by moments not nearly as brilliant as our leaders might think."

"You've gone Einsteinian and relative, uh, cosmic on me. Help me out, here."

"Of course cosmic. Where else do we live if not in the cosmos? The question is, what do we do about it in our lifetime on earth, our little bit of the cosmos. Or, as Hawking put it, in our cone of time. . . the present moment in an eternity we don't understand."

"You speak of Hawking and Einstein. Common people do not understand. What is the question? That we are letting ourselves be led by fate like common sheep into some pen for shearing?"

"More or less, yes. But more like for slaughtering, for which they give us medals if we survive."

"Can we lose the allegory? Explain what you mean."

"Look, to get real, the problem is what the atom bomb did to all of us. We learned to accept the power it gives. We learned to need war. Fission, fusion, they are the fire, the power of the cosmos. Perfectly acceptable, fully needed. Having stolen this power, we now lead Promethean lives, chained to our fiery discovery. So we live in an era where technology runs the military that runs the economy that runs the political power of the people."

"It's a process from which we can't escape, then, except by peace?"

"Most of us are innocent trusting people who don't see these connections. We live among villainous politicians and economists who do, but wish to profit from their power and so they exploit our trust in their knowledge. But most of all, I'm telling you the problem is now about space, where nature left alone, lets fission and fusion happen so it can give life. But then there's earth, where those who tinker with such starlife processes choose to extinguish its presence among us. And I don't like that. We're all made of star matter, you know."

"Yes, the universe is alive. Everything is stardust to stardust. But what's your point?"

"You know. You already know. The living, intelligent part of our universe is dying all around us. Smothered by what we do and think and support until it must explode in some critical mass of evil. The universe is not being extinguished, we are. Our universe, as we know it or knew it, was injured at Hiroshima, Nagasaki, Bikini Atoll, on the Steppes and in the Nevada tests. Injured perhaps irreparably from a moral or philosophical point of view. We are nothing but the shreds of today testing tomorrow. A tomorrow that never comes until today is dead and shredded into atomic dust for analysis by anthropologists from Andromeda, perhaps."

"Well, isn't that the answer to your dilemma? Isn't tomorrow always here?"

There was a long pause. Footsteps ricocheted like echoes from the pavement.

"Sure," she said. "That's it, but only if there is peace. Tomorrow's always here. You just have to know its arrival and departure time. It's just that the Pentagon seems to be holding the White House stopwatch."

Her intuitive logic never quavered; her delivery was never tenuous. Truth spilled out in a monotone of certainty as if born of sad fact. Still, I didn't understand her.

We were both at a Catholic-organized rally to commemorate six Jesuits and their housekeeper and her daughter who were killed in El Salvador in 1988. The bullets were all made by factory workers in arsenals such as Rock Island, who only sought to live by the sweat of their brows for the sake of their families.

Her demeanor told the story: peace always follows the dead when the smoke clears. Yet she was a Mennonite, plainly dressed and coifed in pragmatic braids, all tied with the kind of indecorous strings a child might use in play, or a butcher might use for a rolled roast. Her former husband was Jewish. Her only son was dead, I gathered, but from what war I wasn't sure.

I questioned further.

"Vietnam," she said, "was the prototype for me. I should have seen it coming. Fifty-eight thousand grieving mothers, just on our side, if sides of the wounded mothers must be delineated. And for what? The vainglorious lies of a Texas president who pisses off the edge of his own ranch porch one day and launches squadrons of B-52s the next? There should have been no sides. And yet, oh shit, there still is. . . there still are sides. Raging all around us. None of them makes any sense. The sides, I mean. It's all about killing. Smart bombs. What is so smart about killing? How to kill more. How to kill quicker, better, faster. Then how to stop killing by bombs and go back to bullets. The issue in the end is how our leaders control life as we are forced to live it. It's all about accepting killing as an option, a way of life. But that's not all.

"Not all? What else is there to it?"

"Hiding the reason for dying is an obligatory fact of life, given the way they present the options now for society. They have to disguise the reasons, the real intended and selfish results. The system makes us live for the profit of big companies. They call it progress and globalization. They make us live for the benefit of government, which presumably benefits us who are globalized without our consent. And so, we are taxed in life to support a way of death — not a way of life — for us and our children. Some may call it democracy, but they deliver it now in lethal doses."

Her words stunned me. "We'll all die soon enough, so what's the difference. . . is that what you say they are telling us?"

"Exactly. That IS what they are saying and want us to think. The way it is, we won't be able to live before we die. They won't let us. If we can't live long enough to understand life here, how are we ever going to get from here to wherever it is we belong and deserve to be when we die?"

"Ah! So we must find the solution to suffering and poverty?"

"No, no, no! You talk like a priest. To *get* the bastards who cause this mess so we can have peace in our lives here, then peace hereafter."

"Whoa. So why do you want to *get* them? What does that mean? Surely not violence?"

"I mean, to identify them for the public, which nobody has done. The Johnsons, the Nixons, the Reagans, the Bushes, the Clintons, the unelected Rockefellers. To make the public see what's happening so we can force change, never again to have to use force. Or maybe just to be able to avoid the bastards or work around them politically. Like using this whole SOA thing. The military bastards deny everything, wash their hands of the blood they spill.

"Are you sure you are a Mennonite?" She ignored my question.

"You know how I cope? It's my favorite expression I thought up one morning in the garden: 'The person who endures the trying moment thwarts the bastard who caused it.'"

Again I was stunned by the impact of her thoughts. She sounded a bit like Dorothy Day, so I said, "I like that. Yes, it's neatly sardonic. So the bastards will fall when their power system decays of its own corrupt nature?"

"With a nudge from us. Even so, the innocent will get hurt; but I guess they are already suffering. The eventual result has to be peace, when peace is used to confront. Don't you think so? I think war, if it's a constant part of life, leaves nobody alive who knows how to wage peace. That's why I came here, to act out something peaceful. I cannot do that screaming and shouting hysterically, because nobody will listen unless I am, in my own way, silent and calm and peaceful when they are not. I think about our presence on earth. I think about the beauty of life. Why can't I make that be my shout so that I can live and die in peace? I want my life to be my eternity, and they, these warmongers are standing in my way."

"Like who? What warmongers did you have in mind?"

"Like Colonel Weidner and General LeMoyne and every FBI agent and every CIA spook and the attorney general and every damnable federal court judge, and all the Trilateralites and everyone who thinks like Dulles, and most of the people of this miserably misled gilt-edge nation."

"So you are willing to go to jail at their hands?"

"In principle, yes, but in practice, no. If they put me in jail, nobody can hear my thoughts or observe my witness. Out of sight, out of mind. That's how they plug even the ears of those I wish to fill with thoughts of peace. With people like me out of the way, they can then fill those ears instead with the sounds of gunshots and screams of the dying and call it necessary for our national security or global economy or whatever."

She paused, as if to evaluate her own thoughts.

"They don't want people to hear ideas like abolishing the CIA and establishing a Secretary of Peace instead of a Secretary of War, as the defense establishment used to be called. Maybe make an army of government service out of the Peace Corps. That's how to wage peace. Demobilize. Show the world you mean peace, not just mouth it. Then you wouldn't need the military version of the School of the Americas. You could convert it to a real school for freedom and democracy and justice based on peace without weapons."

I wanted to tell her that she reminded me of Helen Woodson and Linda Ventimiglia and Anne Montgomery and Liz McAlister and Ardeth Platte and Ruth Liteky and Willa Elam and dozens of other women prophets, but my after-dinner walk with Andromeda was over as easily as it had begun, in a pizza diner in the drizzle.

Nobody but me knows Andy's name and address, yet everyone knows where she lives. She lives where it's peaceful. Somewhere in the universe between Alaska and Andromeda.

Fr. Larry Rosebaugh, who turned 65 as the new millennium dawned, left his parish work among the poor in Guatemala and placed himself on retreat to reflect on his life and to meditate in the company of other Oblates from across the globe. Just before he left Guatemala, he began writing a letter to a friend. It starts at a place called Eden.

Christmas, 2000
Dear Friend,

How will I be able to put down all, if any, of what the Jubilee Year, a year of grace, has brought my way?

Some Lightness: At 6:30 a.m. this Saturday morning, I heard a voice below my window on the second floor saying, "*Buenos dias, padre, buenos dias.*" Since there are two other *padres* living below me on the first floor, I waited hopefully for one of them to respond to whomever it was greeting us and stirring us from our early morning slumber.

Ruben heard the call and went to attend our visitor. But two minutes later I heard him say, "Lorenzo, you have a visitor."

With this, I arose and made my way down to the front door. There sat a youth holding a duck in his lap and saying, "Padre Lorenzo, here is the duck Maria Elizabeth sent you for your *despedido* (departure) from Guatemala."

[The duck was given to him a few days before, by a woman in a rural village who had learned that he was about to leave. Since, at that time, he had to travel on foot for two more days, there was no way he could take it in his backpack. This young man was making personal delivery of the gift.]

It's true [Larry's letter continues], that earlier this year I was brought to a certain clarity about my life and stay in Guatemala. I have passed the 65 year mark. Our parish will continue advancing and bringing to our indigenous community opportunities to observe, to judge and to act in front of the difficult circumstances of social injustices and violence that surface everywhere — if not more so — since the signing of the Peace Accords in December, 1996.

Part of that clarity occurred on the occasion when I was celebrating a Eucharist in one of the small villages. So this woman brought me this beautiful duck. Then a *campesino* came with a bright yellow towel wrapped in a black plastic bag, while still another man slipped me 20 quetzals saying, "For you, padre."

Before I knew what was happening, I saw several women uncovering baskets filled with hot tamales and then passing them out to all those present. The word had slipped out about my departure and they wished to express their sentiments.

Arriving in another village, a woman came to the sacristy where I was hearing confessions. She knelt down and said, "Padre, I've come to bestow my blessing upon you. I want to thank you for the years you have spent trekking through the mud and the rain and over the treacherous hillsides to baptize our babies and witness our marriages. May God bless you every step into the future." All I could say to myself was WOW.

"And now, for the *tinieblas*, the dark side of things: On September 25 I went to a community to celebrate the Eucharist. It was about 3:15 PM. when I was passing through a small village called Eden.

The rain was pouring down. I looked out my side window and noticed a rather large number of people standing under the shelter of a small store and thought perhaps they were on their way to the Mass in the adjoining village of Cari. I went on my way, not giving it a second thought. The rain came down through most of the celebration. At the end of Mass everyone was in a joyful mood as we parted company.

It was about 6:30 PM. when I entered Eden once again, only to be met by the military police, accompanied by several soldiers in uniform. "Padre, don't go any farther. There is a demonstration going on up ahead. It's best you return to Cari until things calm down."

It was pitch dark outside. I pulled the Toyota to the side of the road behind what seemed to be 10 or 12 other trucks and cars stopped for the same reason. I got out of the car as if to rest for a few moments. The police and soldiers disappeared into the darkness.

Out of curiosity, I made my way up the road to where I saw a crowd of what I guessed to be two or three hundred people standing in a huge circle. As I drew near I began to hear shouts and distinguish the word "gasolina," which brought me to my senses. I was caught up in the midst of a lynching, a word which has its own meaning in Guatemala. A lynching here means the taking of the law into one's own hands and killing those caught robbing or found guilty (by the mob) of a serious crime.

In this case, five young women walking on a path to a nearby village were stopped by four men with their faces painted in various colors. The men managed to take two of the young teenagers into custody and rape them. Three of the women were able to break away, return to Eden, inform their parents and name the men responsible, since the men were from the same pueblo.

In Eden, the parents united and notified the national police, who in turn informed the soldiers at the military base close by. Arriving in Eden, the soldiers, accompanied by the National Police, were directed to the houses of the assailants, who by this time had returned.

Capturing three of the four men, the police put them into their vehicles and proceeded to leave the village, only to be stopped in their tracks by an angry mob waiting for them. With the overpowering force of the mob and the threats to the life of the local judge accompanying the police, the three men were released to the crowd and the lynching began.

When I arrived on the scene, an hour and a half later, the three men were bound with ropes tied around their ankles. One of the men was still kneeling with his arms outstretched, pleading for his life. The other two, in exhaustion, had fallen to the ground. For some God-unknown reason, I instinctively pushed my way through the crowd to within a foot or two of the kneeling man. Looking directly into his eyes, with the shouts of the crowd bearing down on us, this allowed me, if only for a moment, to feel the anguish of the man before me.

After that, I remember only turning and pushing my way to the outskirts of the crowd. In numbed condition I began to focus on the faces of those present. I felt a hundred sensations all at once. Disbelief that this really could be happening. Fear of the totally uncontrolled emotions of the crowd about me.

I managed to begin a conversation with a catechist in charge of the liturgy of the local community. Slowly the pieces began to fit into place: ever since the war ended four years ago, organized crime in the form of armed robberies, shootings, bombings, raping of women had spread throughout the countryside. In our diocese of Quiche, the reaction to these crimes committed began to take the form of lynchings.

I learned that the word "justice" was without meaning in this country. That if one was arrested for a criminal act, even for murder, he or she needed only to pay a bribe to be released and put back on the streets in no time. The argument of these people carried with it much truth.

Looking back at the history of Guatemala within the last 36 years of civil war, it is not hard to imagine the effects on the human psyche and consciousness of its people. With little difficulty, it is easy now to understand how this wave of lynchings has swept across Guatemala and countries the world over, who have been through similar experiences of war.

As I stood there in the middle of the crowd, I sensed the atmosphere of a sports spectacle. Cheers and whistling and hissing sounds could be heard from the crowd with the landing of each stone thrown, or a crashing blow of a 2-by-4. Finally, around 11 PM the word *agonia* was heard passing from one to another. . . a word used to describe a person in his or her last stages before dying.

Death, in fact, had taken its toll. Then a father with a young child in hand approached one of the bodies, as if it were the natural thing to do. . . the correct manner to introduce death to an innocent child. Not until 4 AM would those of us driving cars or trucks be allowed to leave. I walked back to the car and decided to pull up alongside the small Catholic Church.

Sitting, numb, alone in the darkness of the night, I spontaneously began to pray. I began to recite the rosary. The Sorrowful Mysteries. Never in my life had I come to grips with what Jesus's death was all about as I did that night in Eden.

Jesus, too, was lynched by a mob gone mad. And yet Jesus's death was followed by his resurrection, and that, too, is our hope for the people of Eden and throughout Guatemala. Reconciliation, not only in Eden, but throughout Guatemala is what we all must be about. How and where to begin is and has been the question, especially within the Church, ever since the signing of the Peace Accords.

Rosebaugh's letter, written years after the assassination of Bishop Juan Gerardi, suggests what he is thinking about on his retreat. He is likely thinking about the moral erosion of whole societies as a result of the Iran Contra treatment, and the anarchy that now flows from the lack of a free and just system. The sin of the knowledge of evil, which Larry Rosebaugh witnessed helplessly on a rainy day in Guatemala, has happened before . . . also at a place called Eden.

Carl and the Next Generation

Larry Rosebaugh left the deathbed of his 98-year-old mother in Belleville, Illinois, to witness the trial of his friend, Carl Kabat. The trial started April 30, 2001, in Denver. He saw what I saw. He heard what I heard. While his perceptions may be subjectively different than mine, I must add this description of Larry. His emaciated face, unkempt beard and rag-like clothes give him the image of a park bench bum. Yet he radiates inner comfort. His Eminence, the Cardinal Archbishop Francis George of Chicago, once described Larry in a phone conversation as "a saint."

Typically, Rosebaugh just shrugs off such comments. The point is, when the trial began, there were two prophets in court: Fr. Larry, the one in the gallery, and Fr. Carl, who was in the defendant's docket. Naturally, I expected to hear prophecy, and I did.

· "We have already won," Fr. Carl Kabat told me in the hallway outside. This was day three of his trial for trespass, but his real crime was placing bread, wine and a toy hammer atop a 350-kiloton nuclear warhead at a missile silo in northeast Colorado on Hiroshima Day.

"Is that a prediction of the verdict?" I asked, "Or a prophecy?"

"It's just that we've already won," he said with a smile. He left to get a drink of water.

After dozens of interviews with Carl, I still couldn't figure him out. In my newspaper career I had interviewed thousands of people including several cabinet members, one-on-one. I had interviewed the rich and the poor; the powerful and pitiful; the ordinary and the uncommon; the blunt and the evasive. Even though this was a man I had known since 1958; even though he had eaten at my table; even though I had asked him hundreds of questions, Carl Kabat was the toughest interview I ever had, in terms of completely understanding why he said what he said about what he had done.

His speech pattern was cobbled and thoughts sometimes seemed to be arranged illogically, as in a stream of consciousness. Occasionally he stammered; but obviously, the thoughts were flowing through his mind faster than he could speak them. And so he often switched in the middle of a sentence to the conclusion which seemed like it might be related to a different topic.

Then lightning struck the rod. For months I had been thinking of him symbolically as a prophet. When I reflected on his speech pattern, I realized Carl Kabat literally had the Biblical "gift of tongues," uttering Pentecostal words whose notions were never directly comprehensible. We were indeed approaching the Pentecostal season of the Catholic Church liturgy.

I thought perhaps I was stretching the analogy until I remembered his story about the kitten playing with the ball and how he compared that to what we should all be doing even in life's serious moments. The man speaks in parables. My own thought astonished me. No wonder he seldom answered yes or no to a question whenever I interviewed him. He always spoke, looking at a larger picture than the focus of the question. Of course, he was logical, he just couldn't fit his thoughts into my language, my perception.

My thought-language was binary: right and wrong, day and night, off or on, up or down, yes or no.

It was then I knew he would be his own worst witness on the stand, because prosecutors insist on yes or no answers to prove guilt.

The next day, under cross-examination by Prosecutor George Gill, the agony began. I had previously given character witness that Fr. Carl "was not capable of telling a lie." I had dozens of instances in mind to conclude he was that honest.

"Did you know it was wrong to go over that fence?" Gill asked Kabat pointedly.

It is impossible, even using a tape recorder, to put together a single complete sentence in his answer. He began to speak of higher moral law, and how, when he first came to Mississippi he should have taken a drink from the "Colored Only" water fountain in the bus station. Gill stopped him.

"Simple yes or no," he demanded. "Did you break the law at the fence?"

Again, an explanatory answer. Again an interruption by Gill and an insistence on a one-word answer. Carl looked pleadingly at the judge.

"You are instructed to answer the question as directed by counsel," Magistrate Boyd Boland said.

"I can't . . . I mean . . . the truth is, I wanted to show how evil that missile is."

"Mr. Kabat," Gill said, deliberately refusing to use Kabat's priestly title of *Father*, "You have people here who have testified that you tell the truth. Tell me the truth, yes or no,"

Even Kabat's supporters were squirming in their seats, wanting to put words into Carl's mouth. They knew the jury would think he was being evasive. They couldn't know, in fact, that his stammering, largely overcome by homiletic practice, got worse under pressure. Out of false kindness, defense counsel had not disclosed Kabat's tendency to stutter. Finally, the truthful word came out.

"No. Not God's law."

This did not satisfy Gill, who thought he had Kabat's guilt pinned down, because all he had to do to get a conviction was to establish that Carl knew he was breaking the law when he went over the fence.

"That is a qualified answer," he said. "I want to know, yes or no, whether you knew.

"Objection!" shouted his attorney, Walter Gerash. "Witness has answered the question with the word no."

Magistrate Boland again ordered Kabat to respond more directly. More explanatory words came out of Kabat's mouth; then he repeated his answer.

After a few more attempts, Gill moved on, satisfied that the jury would think of Kabat's hesitancy as an effort to avoid the truth.

Of course, Kabat knew that crossing the fence broke a law; but in his mind it was no more a legitimate law than the Jim Crow laws of the South in days of segregation. After all, the warning posted on the silo fence protected something that he knew to be illegal and a crime of war.

At some point, Gill brought up the issue of responsibility and why Fr. Carl Kabat thought it was his responsibility to tell the world what he thought about nuclear missiles; after all, he didn't even have the permission of his religious superior to be at the missile silo.

"If we are not responsible, who is?" Carl responded. Relieved to have the chance to respond in something more than a monosyllable, the words shot like bullets from Kabat's mouth. Gill changed his attack to another point.

"You left Illinois without permission from your probation officer, didn't you?"

"Yes."

"You left your place of residence, the Oblate House, without permission from your superior, Father Kalert, didn't you?

"He lives in Washington, D.C.," Kabat responded. "My superior, Urban Figge, was gone, so I left a note for him and discussed it with whoever was in charge."

I held my breath. Was Gill going to take on Kabat on the matter of the vow of obedience? He would never get that untangled, and the jury might begin to sympathize with Carl. They already knew from a previous question that Carl had written a letter to Kalert which objected to being treated like a 13-year old. Kalert had, in fact, placed Carl under a virtual house arrest. Kalert had subsequently waffled on his mandate, and besides, I knew that Carl had been scheduled for vacation at that time and could spring that fact, if he had the presence of mind.

Sensing a morass, Gill moved on, and concluded his cross-examination with a series of less hostile questions.

During a recess, Kabat's supporters agreed that he had sounded evasive and were worried. They knew he was not afraid to face jail. He had done so on numerous other occasions for a total nearing 15 years. But in this case, where no vandalism or damage had occurred, they sensed that maybe there was hope for an acquittal. Even so, I knew he faced the possibility of three to five more years for breaking his Illinois probation.

The closing statements were spiced with oratory biased on both sides. Gill told the jury, "Free speech ends at the wire." Later Gerash said, "I'd be ashamed to prosecute this case."

The hardest fight came with the jury out of the courtroom, as the judge, the prosecutor and the defense struggled with the instructions for the jury. The biggest bone of contention was the distinction between 'intent" of Carl (what was in his mind when he went over the fence) and his "motive" which had to do with why he did what he did.

As things turned out, even though Kabat had been allowed to "tell why he did what he did," the jury was instructed to ignore it in their deliberations; they could reach a not-guilty verdict only if they felt the motives influenced the intent of going over the fence.

Although I had been the most optimistic for Carl, not even I was surprised when the verdict came back "guilty." Even so, Carl's courthouse prophecy about winning was yet to come true and I remained puzzled.

Naturally, all kinds of related questions flashed through my mind as Fr. Carl Kabat, a prophet of what is to become of us all, was declared guilty in federal court in Denver. As he told the judge, he was tired of cooperating with an unjust system, even under the freedom of personal recognizance, and wanted to be sentenced immediately. For Carl Kabat, jail for a just man has become his only way to offer proof of injustice done by the system.

"As long as the world is held prisoner to missiles, I must be held hostage," Kabat once told me in an interview.

"Aha!" I thought to myself, "That is what Carl meant when he said, 'we have already won.' He knew he was going to ask for immediate sentencing, even if he had been declared not guilty. This would fluster the judge and the prosecutor and make him seem victorious."

But my early conclusions were wrong. It took a while for the prophecy to become obvious.

When Carl was judged guilty, I cried, and he smiled. It was a triumphant smile as I hugged him and watched him hug his attorneys, Walter Gerash and Sue Tyburski, and then all of his friends. Gerash kept insisting that Carl should change his mind; that the case could be won in appeal; that he should take bail. It was to no avail.

Among Kabat's courtroom friends on hand to receive a goodbye hug was a denim-clad man from Colorado Springs with three children. The man, with his family, worked as a volunteer at a hospitality center for people who were down and out. Kabat had been staying at this hospitality center ever since he was released on bond.

The children, who had restlessly observed the day's proceedings under their father's watchful eye, understood the verdict. I know, because they were crying and hugging Carl just before FBI agent, Janet Hukill, an advisory witness in court for Prosecutor George Gill, took him away. In removing bits of the defendant's evidentiary material from the courtroom, the father of the three children claimed the banner that Kabat had used for his protest at missile silo N-7. It was then that I remembered Kabat telling me a folksy yarn about entertaining some children on Easter Sunday in a clown costume like the one he had used in several of his protests.

Outside the courtroom building, I saw these three children take that banner joyfully into the cold spring rain and unfurl it. Gerash, who doesn't like to lose a case and seldom does, said as he observed the children, "Well, maybe we have won a victory that we will not live to see, but they will."

Then I finally understood Carl Kabat's courtroom prophecy. The action by the children and Gerash's final words turned out to be the fulfillment of Carl's prophecy, "we have already won."

An hour later, sitting at my computer terminal, I wrote the following email message to a network of Kabat supporters to apprise them of the trial results.

"We have already won," Carl Kabat said the day before a Denver jury declared him guilty of trespass in less time than it took him to climb over the silo fence and be arrested last August. Like a prophet, he was right, because just minutes after his conviction, three teary-eyed children whom he had entertained on Easter Sunday in a clown outfit were outside the federal courthouse holding an adult-sized banner reading NO MORE HIROSHIMAS. It was the same banner used at the missile silo site, now being shown to the world on 19th Street — this time by a new generation touched by Kabat's actions.

Before the jury left, Kabat thanked them for their efforts and asked God's blessing on them. As the jury filed out of the courtroom, one male juror respectfully and silently saluted Kabat, seated at the defense table. This was taken as a signal that at least one juror had been forced to act against his conscience because of the strict instruction of Magistrate Boyd Boland. As soon as the jury left, Kabat asked for immediate sentencing, but the judge said he was unable to do that because of the requirements for pre-sentencing hearing. Carl's pro-bono attorney, Walter Gerash, offered to appeal his case, but Kabat could not be dissuaded.

"I'm through cooperating with an evil system," Kabat told the magistrate. "I ask you to revoke my bond and have someone put me in jail. Otherwise, I leave here and make myself available for arrest at the home where you know I am staying." He flourished a hand-written note on which he had scribbled his demands. After the flustered judge consulted with the prosecutor and his companion FBI agent, Janet Hukill, Boland revoked bond and Carl was taken by Hukill to jail (the Federal Correctional Institution). Before leaving, he was given a chance to embrace and thank his friends and supporters in the cause of nuclear weapons protest.

WOW! Just as I was typing this report, I got a call from Vicki Makings, one of the jurors. She called to try to get a message to Fr. Carl. "Just let him know we felt very constrained by the instructions. I want him to know how much he touched us and we all went home every night thinking about him. We felt the passion and message he conveyed and we were looking for a way out for him." She added that the speed of the verdict (about an hour) was the result of the very narrow consideration the court mandated. (That is, whether or not Carl intentionally broke a law by going over the silo fence.)

Friends, obviously there is more at work here than just Carl Kabat! But then, I guess we knew that . . . this just confirms it. Once again, Carl's prophecy is right, "We have already won."

Without knowing how, but only sensing that he and his fellow prophets have won, Carl Kabat is known to pass out to some of his friends a T-shirt featuring the figures of such contemporary figures of protest as Mohandas Gandhi, Rosa Parks, Cesar Chavez, Bishop Tutu, Nelson Mandela and Martin Luther King, Jr. The legend on the T-shirt is a quote from anthropologist Margaret Mead. It says: "Never doubt that a small group of thoughtful, committed individuals can change the world. Indeed, it's the only thing that ever has."

In consideration of 83 days spent in jail while awaiting sentencing, Carl Kabat was set free by Judge Boyd Boland on Friday, July 13, 2001. But not before the US District attorney's office in Denver had extolled the military's "unending instruments of death" as the means of achieving peace.

Citing the need for war and weapons of war in order to make peace, US Assistant Attorney Jim Allison asked the judge to impose the maximum sentence for Father Kabat's crime of crossing a fence to pray. Allison was substituting for US Prosecutor George Gill, the man who invented the federal imperative, "Free speech ends at the wire". Gill had asked to be excused from the final step in the trial "for personal reasons."

Allison argued that laws give our country its strength. He claimed that laws and weapons of war are more important than man and prayer are to our society. Here is an account of Allison's monologue by Mike McPhee of *The Denver Post*:

> "We are a nation of laws, not men. Because we respect these laws, we remain free.
>
> "It was not prayers that ended wars. It was an unending supply of instruments of death that stopped the horrors of Nazism and Fascism. It was our overwhelming military might and the sacrifice made by our soldiers," Allison said.
>
> "This is the eleventh time [Kabat has broken the law]. This smacks more of narcissism than commitment. He was dressed as a clown."

Defense attorney Walter Gerash compared Kabat's actions to those of Nelson Mandela, Gandhi and Rev. Martin Luther King, Jr., all men of peace who went to jail or were killed for their civil disobedience on behalf of peace and justice. "Even though they broke the law, history shows they were on the right side," Gerash said. "They enabled us to have a better society (of laws).

"Why do billions of dollars go to missiles in the ground, in the sea and now in space, each one 20 times more powerful than the bombs dropped on Hiroshima and Nagasaki? Instead of jail, Father Kabat should be honored. His protest (of prayer) was entirely symbolic and protected."

If Gill, by his absence, was stricken with conscience, Judge Boland seemed suddenly stricken with a form of Solomonic wisdom, given his anti-Kabat rulings during the trial. In effect, he divided in half the baby of victory in the case, giving a conviction to the government and release to Kabat.

"This is the case of a defendant acting on his conscience," Boland said, "and this is a government of the majority; a majority that elects representatives; a majority that enacts laws. Not everybody agrees with the majority," Boland said, addressing Kabat. "But you, like Thoreau, are confident you know true justice, the natural law.

"You are free to see yourself as Thoreau's one honest man who will resist the perceived evil of these weapons. You knew when you threw that ladder over the fence that the government would react by putting you in jail. That's why you did it.

"I would be foolish to think I can lock up your ideas or the power of your acts. I believe that as a result of long sentences, you have changed. No more jackhammers, no more damage (to facilities). You merely crossed a fence and waited to be arrested. I don't think you're a danger to the community."

The judge's conclusion brought to mind Kabat's prophecy during the trial, "We have already won."

Prior to the judge's words, Kabat delivered a statement spelling out his understanding of the moral implications that are present wherever weapons of mass destruction are found; the view that, out of fear and indifference, complacency and busyness, Americans have become hostage to their own leaders; and the distinction we must make between personal responsibility, moral law and humanitarian law on the one hand and obedience to government on the other.

In conclusion he said, "To you (Boland and Gill) and to all prosecutors, magistrates and judges, I hope that if you have another opportunity that you would stretch yourselves a bit and take a little risk for God and humanity's sake. You have the examples of the judges in Germany who blocked the transport of Pershing II nuclear tipped missiles, which are gone now. I presume you have enough confidence in yourselves to at times be a fool or a clown for humanity's and God's sake.

"As Gandhi, a lawyer, said, 'It is not in the courts, or the halls of justice or the assemblies of power that justice and truth are to be won, but in the jails and sometimes on the gallows.'"

By limiting Carl's sentence to the time already served, Boland appeared to send a discretionary signal that a protest involving trespass without property damage deserves more consideration under the law than peaceful protests where damage is done.

In Carl's case there was still the matter of the Illinois probation violation. Even the attorneys were confused as the hearing closed. They expected, because of a prior warrant from Illinois, that the US marshals would take Kabat into immediate custody once the Colorado sentencing was consummated.

However, the federal marshals in Boland's court told Kabat's attorneys that if someone would provide Father Carl with a set of street clothes, he could be released immediately. Kabat saw enough free time to visit his relatives in Illinois. Federal agents rearrested Kabat a month later, at the Shrine of Our Lady of the Snows at Belleville, Illinois.

On August 14, 2001, the federal court in East St. Louis, Illinois, sentenced Carl to 1 year and 1 day for violating parole and probation terms in connection with his Colorado protest.

Behind bars, Kabat's mind still is on the missiles, but he doesn't think of himself as being alone.

"In or out of jail, we're all still being held hostage," he says.

"Unless we harness war's wasted billions, mankind is doomed."

These are the frightening words of renowned architect and thinker Buckminster Fuller in a 1970 essay entitled *"The Earthians' Critical Moment."* The essay was a ponderous examination of the predicament of the world as its wealthy and technologically endowed segments were spending billions of dollars on politically-sparked warfare — to the abuse and neglect of its "have-nots."

To a large extent, Fuller's prediction about the world is as true today as it was in 1970, and it matches recent statements by personages as diverse as Mikhail Gorbachev and Daniel Berrigan.

But, is there a way out?

Perhaps, but only if we understand the way we got in.

The way out still lies with the people whom the heroes of this book have always defended: the deprived, the exploited, the impoverished. They should be the ones to decide how they shall be governed. To do this they need to be free to protest when they are not governed equitably. To be in that situation, they need America, champion of freedom, to cease and desist in its efforts to dominate and globalize everything, just as Gorbachev has suggested.

Natural law, which validates the system of laws that we sustain today, contains a principle which is expressed in Latin: *cessante ratione legis, cessat ipsa lex*: an irrational law (such as, that which sanctions the "just war" policy, or the nuclear threat policy) cancels itself. It means such a bad law is no law at all and need not be followed.

This means that we are not guilty of breaking a law when we object to such unjust laws; indeed, we and the people of the world actually are obliged to object.

Our present laws, our present attitudes, our present policies are blocking the way out of the trap. We have laws that protect the nuclear weapons; laws that protect the ways of war; laws that punish those who say they are evil.

If the laws and justice are ever to arrive at any connubial conclusion with truth, the parable of Pontius Pilate must be applied. As Pontius Pilate pondered a life-and-death matter still pertinent today, his question was: "What is truth?"

It took the silence of Christ and nearly two millennia for today's prophets to answer that question: The truth, Mr. Pontius Pilate, is that evil persists so that good may endure. The final hopeful prophecy, then, is that truth itself is good because it has the power to endure.

Prophetic Postscript: Towers of Babel

Pride goeth before destruction, and a haughty spirit before a fall.
— Proverbs 16:18

The whole earth used the same language and the same speech. While men were migrating eastward, they discovered a valley in the land of Senaar (Babylon) and settled there. They said to one another, "Come, let us make bricks and bake them." They used bricks for stone and bitumen for mortar. Then they said, "Let us build ourselves a city and a tower with its top to the heavens; let us make a name for ourselves lest we be scattered all over the earth."

The Lord came down to see the city and the tower which men had built. And the Lord said, "Truly, they are one people and they all have the same language. This is the beginning of what they will do. Hereafter they will not be restrained from anything which they determine to do. Let us go down, and there confuse their language so that they will not understand one another's speech." The Lord scattered them from that place all over the earth; and they stopped building the city. For this reason it was called Babel, because there

the Lord confused the speech of all the earth. From there the Lord
scattered them all over the earth.
— Genesis, Chapter 11

The dozens of protests discussed in these pages were staged against
the policy of nuclear war. More than being *against*, they were *for*
something . . . for peace. And we should have known, the minute the
prophets were put in jail for peace, that war was coming.

Indeed, as our leaders tell us, war came to America on the island of
Manhattan on September 11, 2001. Was it war, or was it murder? A huge,
horrendous, unthinkable mass murder, invited by those same leaders
through their war-mongering policies? Was it, in fact a protest in its own
right, albeit appallingly far from the standard of nonviolence profiled in
these pages?

For decades, moral individuals have prophesied, have protested, have
sought to draw Americans' attention to the consequences of their immoral
policies and the violation of international law. The prophets served years in
jail and created headlines as a way of warning and predicting disaster for
America and the world.

In 2001, their prophecies came true, not with war as had been feared,
but with mass murder. You cannot get even with murder, because
execution of the perpetrator is not assured. But politicians and their
plebeian constituents think you can get even if you go to war; at least, you
can get revenge. The problem is, we don't know where unjustified murder
leaves off and what is called justifiable war begins.

And so the world, led by America and seduced by the spectacular
nature of the tragedy, has gone to war once again. As a target, Osama bin
Laden was selected. The motivation was to do away with his anarchistic
idea, Al-Qaeda. How do you annihilate an idea with bombs? How do you
murder a cause? Not even the leaders of the war know, because they admit
it is a war without end, Amen.

If achieving "Enduring Justice" is the goal, then both war and murder
as a reaction are as wrong as the way the perpetrators chose to settle their
score with America. Enduring justice would simply mean for the US to quit
doing what it has been doing to the rest of the world.

On September 11, Americans acted as if they never had been warned;
as if they never had done anything to provoke such an outrageous action.
As the preceding chapters show, they *were* warned and they *did* provoke the
attack by the continuous exercise of pride that comes before destruction.

Like the ancient tower of Babel, the modern towers of the World Trade Center were brought down, and a people's haughty self-absorption was shattered. Deceived by incomplete impressions of the past and fueled by their own anger, most of America refuses to understand the anger and hatred that stoked their suicidal adversaries to do what they did. The disastrous result is not a failure of airport security, although by superficial proximity of cause, it was.

Everyone ignored the prophecies, paying them no honor because the prophets, in their zeal to overcome apathy, seemed to be "too critical" of their own country. In a facile conflation of ideas, anyone critical of his country in its present extremity is deemed a traitor, an enemy.

Until scattered and shaken by the attack, America's systems, like the people of Biblical Babylon, were too busy speaking in one tongue, one language, to see how the language of economic globalization was pridefully setting up a nation and a world for the fall that the prophets feared.

In that context, the examination of the actions of the prophets in this book shows how the events of the last half-century — many staged secretly and with evil effect by the United States — have triggered this latest catastrophe.

Such analysis suggests that, within the expired Cold War itself, that a kind of Silent War of hatred existed; a Silent War that hardly anybody realized they had spawned in the distant lands they chose to exploit. There were warnings aplenty, from peaceful prophets and from others whose patience was gone: those who bombed the World Trade Center in 1993; bombed the US barracks in Saudi Arabia; bombed the African embassies in 1996; and bombed the USS Cole in Yemen's harbor. The prophecies, like the bombings, were received with arrogant disdain.

Why does so much of the Third World and Moslem population seem to hate the US?

President George W. Bush offered a disingenuous answer when he said, "They hate our freedoms." In fact, the opposite is true: They hate us for the way we *abuse* our vaunted freedom to hurt them.

Afghanistan's Mullah Mohammed Omar, the Taliban's leader, offers a more correct answer to Americans: "You should know whatever incidents and sorrow you suffer . . . are a result of the erroneous policies of your government."

That is exactly the conclusion reached years ago by the heroes of this book. When they drew that conclusion, it may have sounded like defiance; but it is a prophecy that has now come true all too horribly.

To what policies does the mullah refer? In an article on September 27,

2001, *The Christian Science Monitor* cites some of the same ones discussed in this book, along with some others:

1. The injustice done to the Palestinians by the US-supported Israelis;
2. The cruelty of continued sanctions against Iraq, especially the endless bombings;
3. The presence of US troops on Saudi Arabian soil, which Osama bin Laden and others have always considered a sacrilege in the heart of Islam;
4. The support, and then abandonment, of troubled regimes (as in Afghanistan during their war with the Soviets);
5. The repressive and corrupt nature of most US-supported governments in the Middle East, such as Iran under the Shah.

It is through such captive states that the US exercises a "double standard" in doling out peace, justice and freedom; it is the only nation strong enough to do whatever it wants with such human rights commodities.

When the Iranian students took over the US embassy in Tehran in 1980 and held 52 hostages for 444 days, they did not ask for weapons of war, they asked four simple, peaceful things:

1. An admission that the US had exploited the Iranian people, with an apology.
2. A pledge that the US would refrain from such exploitation in the future.
3. The return of the Shah Mohammed Reza Pahlevi to Iran to stand trial.
4. No reprisals, including war.

What did they get from the US? The kind of silence that precedes war; then guns. In itself, the reaction was not only a prophecy, but a reflection of the Ugly American countenance.

In other words the US, no matter how kindly-intentioned are its people, is a sometimes-benign bully whose economic and military power delivers plunder by way of technological dominance. Its hypocrisy has been evident for years in the repressive way it has mishandled peaceful domestic dissent, as in the civil rights demonstrations of the '60s; as in the police suppression of dissension in the streets over Vietnam; as in the murderous meddling in the internal affairs of other nations, including Iran, Iraq, Egypt, Syria, Jordan, Lebanon, and Afghanistan, among many others.

Its hypocrisy is evident as well in its penchant for breaking treaties and temporary alliances at will. All of this means the world feels the US cannot be trusted to do the noble things that it claims to stand for. And those parts of the world with which it has the least in common culturally feel particularly targeted.

These points of resentment, building over the years, led to the hatred or abhorrence that finally exploded in Manhattan and the Pentagon. As the *Guardian of London* noted in an article September 27, 2001:

> Failure to read these signs would be the grossest irresponsibility. Those who insist that the attacks had nothing to do with the US role in the Middle East — but were instead the product of existential angst about Western freedom and identity — not only demonstrate their ignorance of the area, they also weaken the pressure to address the long-standing grievances fueling this rage.

The article identifies that rage as coming from "not only Western indulgence of Israeli military occupation, but decades of oil-lubricated support for despots from Iran to Oman (and) Egypt to Saudia Arabia" where there have been "routine military interventions to maintain US control."

The hatred for the US comes not only from the string of military humiliations the Middle East people have felt at the hands of Israel and its almighty patron, the United States, but also from a sense of betrayal by the US of those nations which, at times, it had succeeded in befriending.

This was the case with Pakistan, for example, in its 1965 war with India and later its entanglement with Afghanistan. Moreover, every time Israel retaliates against the Palestinians there is a feeling that the US allows the Jewish nation to "get away with murder," as one-on-one interviews in *The Christian Science Monitor* reveal.

If these observations are correct, it means that the United States, through those agency leaders responsible for its economic, military and intelligence policies, has created enemies where there were none, and invited its own punishment. History indicates this is something it has done repeatedly throughout the world.

For example, the US supported and armed oil-rich Libya, making a friendly and then an adversarial dictator out of Khadafy. (At one time the brother of President Carter was Khadafy's public relations man.) The US supported and armed the Shah of Iran, whose cruel tyranny produced the reactionary Ayatollah Khomeini. Yet again, the US supported and armed

Iraq and sicced Saddam on post-revolutionary Iran. Then Hussein turned against his CIA masters, when he found out the US was arming Iran against him. The irony is that President Bush (as CIA director) armed Saddam Hussein as an ally, and now President Bush (II) has to deal with him as an enemy.

The bad thing about history is you don't see it coming, unless you are a prophet; and when you do, it's too much like the future to believe.

Through such a wormhole on earth there now comes Osama bin Laden, the current object in a war of revenge instead of a target for justice. He, too, was supported by the CIA. At one time he was brought into Afghanistan to fight with the Mujahideen against the Soviet-backed regime; now the world is fighting the evolved form of the Mujahideen, allied with a conservative Moslem group, the Taliban.

In the '80s, the US poured billions of dollars into helping to arm and train the Mujahideen in Afghanistan against the Soviet Bear; then, when the Soviets left, America did too, leaving a nation with no resources to clean up the mess the superpowers had left. The Taliban, with only bin Laden and his CIA-inspired Al-Quaeda training bases for a patron, stepped into the power vacuum.

For those who are tracking cause-and-effect, it is from these American terrorist roots that the terrorists who executed the September 11 assault sprang.

All of these explanations support the central theme of this book: that the US and its shadow government have conspired over time to exploit the world by use of military and economic power — overtly and all too often covertly.

The prophets of this book identified this moral defect nearly everywhere as they worked among the poor of the world. For their vision and criticism, they were kicked out of countries by US puppet regimes. Peacefully protesting the policies in the United States, they were arrested, convicted and jailed.

Their point has always been that our multinational corporations, protected by the US government and its proxies abroad, are exploiting people in the Americas, in the Middle East, in Asia (and most assuredly, in Africa, too). The prophets consistently maintained that the corporate rich were making the unincorporated poor even poorer, while making themselves and our nation richer and more powerful. Wherever oppressed people protested or formed governments that the US didn't like, the US has created coups, and bombed, jailed or murdered the protesters. It remains to be seen what lies behind the brief ouster of Hugo Chavez, originally elected by a huge majority of the "ordinary" people of Venezuela — to the dismay of the wealthy class — and rather tidily re-instated after just a few days, on a rather general promise of "reform". Chavez is a friend of Cuba and Iraq, and appears to be a thorn in the side of Washington. "Business" (Venezuela is the world's fourth-largest oil producer) says it doesn't like him.

Prophets, What Say You, Now?

The US decided to seek revenge through a war to wipe out the terrorism its own policies incited. Here is the result of a poll taken among the Prophets Without Honor. Their responses illustrate their continuing determination to resist even this kind of war in favor of non-murderous, peaceful means of restoring justice.

Rev. Darrell Rupiper, showing his farmboy background, says sadly, "The chickens always come home to roost, don't they?" With those few words, he understates his moral outrage, not so much at the current war as at its underlying cause. He reports that members of a parish in Illinois that he serves on a weekend basis "are donning the red, white and blue," and don't want to hear him preach anything like peace.

"In the end, I asked them to exercise their citizenship by asking our leaders if theirs was a voice for revenge or for justice. At the same time, I asked them to keep in mind the one they had come to worship: the non-violent Jesus."

Before the bombs started to fall in Afghanistan, Rupiper had volunteered to go with Rev. Jesse Jackson on an unsanctioned people-to-people mission to that tormented land. However, the opportunity faded because the US by its attitude had rendered such an option inherently futile, if not dangerous.

Rev. Frank Cordaro, who once spilled ashes at Jimmy Carter's feet in the White House while calling the SALT Treaty a lie, says sadly: "All the talk of war and revenge is most disheartening." Within days of September 11, Cordaro suffered a heart attack, from which he recovered in time to be jailed for yet another protest.

Former Vietnam chaplain Charlie Liteky, who relinquished his Congressional Medal of Honor 15 years ago to join the ranks of peace activists, said it all in 1999 at his sentencing for protesting the training of death squads at Fort Benning: "It doesn't take a genius to recognize that poverty is a seed bed for violence. But it is difficult for First World beneficiaries to understand that poverty, of itself, is a form of violence we have inflicted."

Rev. Larry "Lorenzo" Rosebaugh, one of the "Milwaukee Fourteen" who burned draft files with homemade napalm made from a Green Beret recipe, stands by a statement he made when he burned those files: "For a growing number of us, the problem is no longer that of grasping what is happening. We know it by heart. Ours is rather a problem of courage, one of offering our lives and future to absorb and transform the violence and madness which our society has come to personify."

Onetime FBI fugitive *Rev. Daniel Berrigan, S.J.*, reminds an America that forgets its past: "We are captive of our future." Berrigan led the FBI on a year-long chase following his trial for protesting the Vietnam War. His protest consisted of burning draft files, an action that ignited similar protests among draft-age men nationwide.

Maryknoll priest and Vietnam veteran *Rev. Roy Bourgeois*, nemesis of the School of the Americas, said years ago: "Reaction from the Third World is a case of the poor teaching us about the consequences of poverty and death brought to them by the multinationals." Today he says, "If the president wants to destroy all the terrorist training camps, he should start at home with the School of the Americas."

From his federal prison cell, *Rev. Carl Kabat* repeats a question he asked at his Denver trial convened for a missile silo trespass: "If we are not responsible, who is?" He constantly reflects on the statistic that somewhere between "19,000 and 40,000 children die of starvation every day, worldwide." These include hundreds in Iraq, which the US is still bombing and embargoing. "We have much more to mourn," says Kabat, who thinks every life is sacred, "than those killed on September 11."

From his federal prison cell, excommunicated *Josephite priest Philip Berrigan*, writes: "Glossed over totally in the official screams for vengeance was the default of our multi-billion-dollar 'society' and the blindness and stupidity of our peerless leaders. Warnings had been issued, for example, to resolve the Palestinian tragedy, and after the bombing of the World Trade Center in 1993, to 'understand' Arab grievances or risk both towers. Our greed and arrogance created a self-fulfilling prophecy. [There are] stirrings abroad for non-retaliation, and I rejoice in them. The media and official claim of unanimity is a lie, of course."

Even though these views identify the same faults in the US that Osama bin Laden has indicated, the prophets are 100% opposed to what bin Laden said (and did, by proxy) regarding the September 11 atrocities. The difference is simple: The prophets have peace in their souls for people of both sides and all faiths, regardless of the circumstance; bin Laden, purportedly a devout man, finds murder not only justifiable, but something to thank his god for.

The priests profiled here do not view the confrontation as a crusade. They do not think there is such a thing as a "just war" or a "holy war." They hope this will not turn out to be a Christian-Moslem conflict reflective of history. They prefer to see the application of international law. They do not wonder who is the infidel; they ask only who, among the leaders of Church and State, has broken the faith and hearts of mankind.

That said, what Osama bin Laden is doing through his terrorist training camps is exactly what America has been doing — with Latin America's death squad training at Fort Benning — to the people of Central America and elsewhere. To the chagrin of America, bin Laden is simply applying, on behalf of his own part of the world, the lessons he learned from the CIA.

Not surprisingly, on October 8, 2001, US newspaper headlines use the word, "retaliation," and President Bush ends his speech of the previous day with the prayer, "May God bless America." That same day, in a TV video release, Osama bin Laden also called on God, saying: "America was hit by God in one of its softest spots. America is full of fear . . . thank God for that."

Both men are mistaken, and it takes the words of a fiercely peaceful man, Philip Berrigan, speaking from his jail cell, to set both Bush and bin Laden straight. Berrigan says in his autobiography: "God is non-violent. He allows his sun to shine upon the wicked and the good; allows the rain to fall upon the just and unjust. He is benign, loving, and compassionate, never retaliatory, never revengeful. He never punishes us; we punish ourselves. When we sin, are unjust, and exploit one another, we punish ourselves."

It is possible to find thoughts about how to smite the enemy in both the Bible and the Koran, but it is not possible to find such thinking in the prophet Berrigan. This suggests a truer meaning for what the shallow-thinking Pentagon brass called "infinite justice" before changing the code name to "enduring freedom."

Clearly, America's leaders are not listening to its prophets of peace. They do not want to understand the "why" of September 11 because they know the cause is rooted in America's own insolence and greed. And so, America's leaders shall never resolve the coefficient of evil they have set forth in the world, yet claim to be conquering.

In a CNN interview, on October 8, 2001, Sen. Evan Bayh of Indiana repeated the spurious notion that the attack on the World Trade Center and the Pentagon were "unprovoked." Did he not hear bin Laden explain the reasons? Did no one in America know that the US bases in Saudi Arabia, previously bombed, were an insult to conservative Moslems? Was no one aware, even as America instituted a cabinet-level office for Homeland Security, that the Palestinian homeland issue remained unresolved after more than 50 years?

Self-criticism and inward reflection are not the exclusive domain of Christian priests. San Francisco Rabbi Michael Lerner, who is editor of the magazine *Tikkun*, identifies some of the same causes of the September 11 events as does Osama bin Laden, but he comes to a totally different conclusion. For his honest appraisal, Lerner has received numerous threats, including death threats. Here are some of Lerner's thoughts:

> There is never any justification for the acts of terror against innocent civilians — it is the quintessential act of dehumanization and not recognizing the sanctity of others, and a visible symbol of a world increasingly irrational and out of control. The perpetrators deserve to be punished . . . imprisoned for the rest of their lives.
>
> We need to ask ourselves, "What is it in the way we are living, organizing our societies, and treating each other, that makes violence seem plausible to so many people?" The willingness of people to hurt each other to advance their own interests has become a global problem, and it is only the dramatic level of this particular attack which distinguishes it from the violence and insensitivity to each other that is part of our daily lives.
>
> We may reassure ourselves [that] the hoarding of the world's resources by the richest society in world history, and our frantic attempts to accelerate globalization with its attendant inequalities of wealth, has nothing to do with the resentment that others feel toward us. . . . The inability to feel the pain of others is the pathology that shapes the mind of these terrorists.
>
> I see this in Israel, where Israelis have taken to dismissing the entire Palestinian people as "terrorists", but never ask themselves "What have we done to make this seem to Palestinians to be a reasonable path of action?"
>
> Similarly, if the US turns its back on global agreements to preserve the environment; unilaterally cancels its treaties to not build a missile defense; accelerates the processes by which a global economy has made some people in the Third World richer but many

poorer; shows that it cares nothing for the fate of refugees who have been homeless for decades; and otherwise turns its back on ethical norms; [then] it becomes far easier for the haters and the fundamentalists to recruit people who are willing to kill themselves in strikes against what they perceive to be an evil American empire represented by the Pentagon and the World Trade Center.

Most Americans will feel puzzled by any reference to this "larger picture." It seems baffling to imagine that somehow we are part of a world system which is . . . quickly transferring the wealth of the world into our own pockets . . . Most of us lead perfectly reasonable lives within the options that we have available to us — so why should others be angry, much less strike out against us?

The truth is, our own anger is also understandable; the striking out by others in acts of terror against us is just as irrational as the world-system that is seeks to confront. Yet our acts of counter-terror will also be counter-productive. We should have learned from the current phase of Israeli-Palestinian struggles that responding to terror with more violence . . . will only assure more violence in the future.

This is a world [Lerner concludes] that is out of touch with itself, filled with people who have forgotten how to recognize and respond to what is sacred in each other.

In other words, Americans, and those in the world who have been Americanized, live in a strangely privileged world now tortured and punished by its own excesses.

At Christmastime 2000, no less a world figure than Mikhail Gorbachev told the recently and dubiously-elected George W. Bush, "Mr. Bush, the world does not want to be America." Gorbachev spoke from the pages of the *International Herald-Tribune.*

Yet the Trilateralized push for a globalized economy continues. Much of the world views this process as a threat to its cultural way of life, because of the economic, political and military baggage that globalization brings with it. That baggage is part and parcel of America's security blanket in the Post-Cold-War world.

Who is resisting such unwanted changes and who taught the resistance fighters? Educator Noam Chomsky, in a recent radio interview in Belgrade, suggests an answer: "He (bin Laden) was one of the many religious fundamentalist-extremists recruited, armed and financed by the CIA and their allies in Pakistani intelligence to cause maximum damage to the Russians. . . . Not surprisingly, the CIA preferred the most fanatic and cruel fighters they could mobilize."

Once the Russians left Afghanistan, the CIA-trained Moslem extremists, including bin Laden, fought on the side of the Bosnian Moslems and even joined the rebel efforts in Chechnya, Chomsky claims. By then, President Clinton, perhaps on the defensive due to the heavy criticism stemming of his personal life, opted not to have the US interfere with such subversive actions.

In that vacuum, Al-Qaeda was propagated.

As for America's anti-terrorist war, Arundhati Roy of the *London Guardian* wrote on September 29, 2001:

> The trouble is that once America goes off to war, it can't very well return without having fought one. If it doesn't find its enemy, for the sake of the enraged back home, it will have to manufacture one. Once war begins, it will develop a momentum of its own, a logic and justification of its own, and we'll lose sight of why it's being fought in the first place.
>
> As deterrence, its arsenal of nuclear bombs is no longer worth the weight in scrap. Box cutters, penknives and cold anger are the weapons with which the wars of the new century will be waged. Anger is the lock-pick. It slips through customs unnoticed. Doesn't show up in baggage checks.

It is the fear among many leaders of peace groups in America that war in such an elusive context will prevail over peaceful means for resolving the issues.

For example, Bill Sulzman, who leads the *Citizens for Peace in Space* from his Colorado Springs home, says: "The initial reaction of the public to the acts of mass murder at the Pentagon and the World Trade Center has caused a shrinking of the space for political discussion and dissent." Sulzman, a former priest whose peace activism got him in trouble with the Catholic Church, was arrested with Carl Kabat in August 2000 for a protest staged at a Colorado missile silo.

Another friend of Kabat is Bob Kinsey of Arvada, Colorado, who heads the Peace and Justice Task Force, Rocky Mountain Conference, United Church of Christ. Kinsey, who also leads the Colorado Coalition to Prevent Nuclear War, has grave doubts about the war option Bush has chosen:

"It raises questions about why the concept of international law is not a part of the discussion for solutions to the September 11 event." The long-term concern is "that the USA is following policies of dominance rather than cooperation in its foreign policy," he says.

If the progress of globalization is an indicator, Kinsey is right. He also identifies another failure within the Euro-American community.

> The Christians are not expressing outrage at the revenge and retaliation language that abounds. But then, the overwhelming majority of Christians haven't objected to the ideas of collateral damage ever since World War II.

Kinsey's concerns match those of Francis Boyle, professor of international law at the University of Illinois. It was Boyle who helped to resolve the dispute between the US, Britain and Libya over the handling of the Libyan suspects in the Lockerbie bombing case. Boyle's position for the rule of international law, and not war, prevailed.

In the World Trade Center case, Boyle contends that the 1971 Montreal Sabotage Convention, which was applied in the Lockerbie case, is directly applicable to the current crisis. His point is that the Bush administration should not be presenting the September 11 event as an act of war but as a crime against humanity.

Boyle tried to use a similar argument for international law in Kabat's case in Denver, but never was allowed to testify.

To support the position against war, Kinsey also points to a conclusion reached by Walden Bello, executive director of *Focus on the Global South*, and professor at the University of the Philippines. Bello says:

> It is for the United States to reexamine and substantially change its policies in the Middle East and the Third World, supporting for a change arrangements that will not stand in the way of the achievement of equity, justice and genuine national sovereignty for currently marginalized peoples.

Another friend of Kabat is Mike Palecek of Sheldon, Iowa. Mike, who also has served time in prison for anti-war protests, is co-author of this book. As a Democratic Party candidate in 2000 for the Congressional seat in Iowa's fifth district, he won his place on the ballot by petition; his peace platform cost him the election. Here is Mike's take on the recent horrible events:

If the bombing of the World Trade Center and the Pentagon was an act of war, it certainly was not the first salvo. At the same time, it certainly should not have to be said that the bombing was evil. It never is right to kill.

But we have to ask what kind of suffering must a person go through to make them capable of committing such an insane act?

There really is no violence as jolting as a quiet Iowa neighborhood street when children in other parts of the world are dying for lack of life's basic necessities. What if it were my children suffering and the world was paying no attention? What would I be capable of doing? Plenty, I'm afraid.

On September 11, we saw the reality of the rest of the world coming at us from our TV screens. The awful reality of the violence hit home, it jarred. These airline hijackers do not have a wickedness gene. They are just like us, minus the running water and 3-car garage.

About ten years ago, I was working for a weekly newspaper in the sandhills of Nebraska. The Gulf War happened, and I wrote a column saying I did not support the war. That was when yellow ribbons were our national ornaments. We held parades while in Baghdad tearful mothers and fathers carried their dead children home in their arms.

This time, there are parades elsewhere, and the dying was done by us, and we got an idea of how terrible it all is. This, of course, is NOT right or moral or fair. People should not be killing people. There is no good war. There never was, never will be, even now.

Some say we should "take care of business" by hitting back. Inevitably, we will send our own terrorists in F-16s to kill other men, women and children to avenge our own men, women and children.

A proper response would be to really take care of business; correct the injustice in the world, the lack of health care, housing and food. Why must we push people to the breaking point and then act surprised and victimized when they react one morning, when they have no way out but desperate, violent acts?

Palecek, who once studied to be a priest, speaks with the authority of every prophet who has spent time in jail for the cause of peace. Even though he and the others predicted disaster years ago, none of them takes an "*I told you so*" attitude about the World Trade Center attack. They understand that all of America was on the airliners that were hijacked.

The larger question, raised in the death, desolation, dust and smoke in Manhattan and at the Pentagon is this: by whom have we been hijacked?

The answer is provided by the defunct comic strip character, Pogo, who puckishly said years ago, "I have seen the enemy, and he is us."

That is why these prophets want to eliminate *all* nuclear weapons, and that is why they have spent so much of their lives in jail. After all, most of the atom bombs are in the US, which is the only nation that has ever used the atomic bomb. It is the United States, along with the USSR, which threatened, like terrorists, to use them throughout the Cold War.

That is why the prophets say that, if the trillions of dollars spent on nuclear armament alone had been directed toward programs for eliminating world poverty, then September 11, 2001, would have been just another blue-sky day over Manhattan. This is true because crucial policies, social governance and intra-national attitudes would have changed the world. As it is, we continue the process, carried on for decades, to eliminate by war terrorism at its source, without recognizing that the source is the First World, led by America the Beautiful.

As a consequence, alongside the ashes of the World Trade Center, there lies buried the ashes of whatever budding peace people like Kabat and Palecek have sought to nurture. Prophecies aside, no matter how the war against terrorism turns out, it will not be a question of who won, but who was wrong in the first place.

This book, in all the sad history of terrorism that it has analyzed, suggests that the bombings of US embassies and military installations and offices were all, one way or another, aimed at Wall Street and the Pentagon, because that is where the longstanding provocation is centered.

This is not to excuse the murderous deeds of the attackers; it is not to say that the attacks were justified or even mitigated by the symbolism of the targets. It is to convey an honest understanding to Americans of why they have enemies who would attack in this way. Perhaps then Americans finally can formulate a means outside of war to establish peace and justice.

While war may satisfy the primal lust for revenge, it does not create peace. People do; even people who have been hurt, as they have been in Manhattan. They share an equal hurt with mothers and fathers and spouses in places like Iraq, Iran and Palestine.

Is the US continuing to hurt them by dropping bombs in the "no-fly" zones of Iraq? How does that create peace and not make enemies? In that zone ordinary men women and children, pitifully poor, still are being killed. That too, has been an outrage that prophets of protest, jailed by the US, tried to warn against and bring to an end.

That the nation's people at large were, and still are, ignorant of these underlying causes goes without saying, because the government, under the guise of national security, wants it that way. That the nation's people at large have allowed their misgivings about their government's actions to be swept under the rug of patriotism and national security, over the years, is just as certain.

On that basis, almost no one can claim to be the innocently wronged victim of this latest exchange of volleys in the silent war waged by the United States.

Because of the Cold War, millions of decent people on both sides were distracted from the moral issues in the struggle for supremacy and national security. Yet all of them should have known that they were trying to raise their countries to a level of supremacy that no nation has sole right to claim.

Those who deny that the US in any way provoked this historic moment of angst are people who look at life's daily events as if each happens in isolation. When people fail to see the sequential or causal links in the everyday stream of events, they never see how their own government deceives them about the consequences of policies followed out of blind loyalty.

British politician Lord Acton, in his essay on *History of Freedom*, provided the best answer: "It was from America that the plain ideas came that the nation is responsible to Heaven for the acts of the state. . . That a nation can never abandon its fate to an authority it cannot control."

It is not fate, but exploitation instead, that leaves many nations poor when one neighbor is full-bellied and powerful. Neither is it destiny, but the booty of exploitation instead, that enables one to be rich when all around are poor and powerless. Sadly, the world much sooner is what its political predators say it is than what its prophets say the world can be or should be.

Nobody except the Prophets Without Honor dreams such things, or ask why things are not the way things should be. If their vision had been honored instead of jailed, the World Trade Center Towers would still be standing.

APPENDIX:
THE LIVES AND "CRIMES" OF THE PROPHETS

The following is a brief listing of major events in the lives of those profiled in this book.

Rev. Darrell Rupiper, O.M.I. (Oblates of Mary Immaculate):

Born 1937, farming community, near Carroll, Iowa.

Ordained Oblate priest, 1963, Pass Christian, Mississippi.

1964-1968: Served the Oblate mission in Recife, Brazil.

1968: Jailed in Brazil and deported for inciting to revolution (by preaching human dignity and civil rights).

1970-1972: Newman Club chaplain, University of Illinois, Champaign.

1972-1977: Oblate House of Studies, Omaha, Nebraska.

1977-1985: New Covenant Justice & Peace Center, Omaha, Nebraska, where he established a shelter for the homeless.

1979: Jailed in Chicago for protesting sale of weapons to Brazilian generals who had oppressed his parish in Recife. Convicted, with Carl Kabat, of disobeying police. Served several days.

1980: Selected by the Iranian Crisis Resolution Committee to negotiate for release of US hostages in Iran without official US government approval.

1983-85: Jailed in Omaha on three occasions for trespass at Strategic Air Command while attempting to keep appointment with base commander to discuss nuclear arms. (He stepped across a line drawn at public entrance.) Sentenced to one month, three months and six months respectively on the three charges over a period of three years.

1985-1995: Ministry at Precious Blood Parish, Chicago, Illinois, where he established a community offering shelter for street people.

1995 forward: Priest-novice formation, Godfrey, Illinois.

Rev. Lawrence Rosebaugh, O.M.I. :
> Born 1935, Appleton, Wisconsin.
>
> Ordained Oblate priest, 1963, Pass Christian, Mississippi.
>
> 1963-1964: St. Casimir's Parish, St. Paul, Minnesota.
>
> 1964-1967: Cathedral High School, Duluth, Minnesota.
>
> 1967-1968: St. Benedict's High School, Chicago, Illinois. Also founded Casa Maria, Milwaukee, Wisconsin.
>
> 1968: Arrested and jailed in Milwaukee as part of "Milwaukee Fourteen" group that burned A-1 draft files to protest Vietnam war. Served two years in federal prisons.
>
> 1975-1981: Oblate mission in Recife, Brazil.
>
> 1977: Arrested and held without charge in Recife.
>
> 1981-1982: Chicago, Illinois.
>
> 1981: Arrested for trespass at Pantex nuclear processing plant, Amarillo, Texas. Six month sentence.
>
> 1982-1986: Catholic Worker House, New York City.
>
> 1983: Arrested and jailed in Georgia for unlawful entry and impersonation of an officer. (He and an associate played last recorded sermon of archbishop slain in El Salvador. The broadcast was directed as protest against El Salvador death squads being trained in School of the Americas at Fort Benning, Georgia.) He served 18 months in prison.
>
> 1986-1993: Christian Volunteer Ministries, El Salvador.
>
> 1988: Arrested in San Salvador for possession of a church calendar imprinted with the sermon of an assassinated archbishop. Released after brief detention.
>
> 1993-present, Guatemala street ministry.

Rev. Paul Kabat, O.M.I.:
> Born 1932, Scheller, Illinois (brother to Carl Kabat).
>
> Ordained Oblate priest, 1958, Pass Christian, Mississippi.
>
> 1959-1960: Pastoral House, St. Paul, Minnesota.
>
> 1960-1964: Shrine/Our Lady of the Snows, Belleville, Ill.
>
> 1964-1966: St. Casimir's Parish, St. Paul, Minnesota.
>
> 1966-1967: Northome, Minnesota.
>
> 1967-1968: International Falls, Minnesota.
>
> 1968-1969: Green Bay, Wisconsin.
>
> 1969-1970: Grand Forks, North Dakota.
>
> 1971-1983: Bemidji, Minnesota, Indian ministry.

1982: Arrested Dec. 28, 1982, for trespass, Offutt Air Force Base, (Strategic Air Command), Omaha. Rearrested March 15, 1983, for unlawful re-entry of base. Jailed several days.

1983-1984: Indian ministry, Minneapolis, Minnesota.

1984: Arrested Nov. 12, Whiteman Air Force Base, near Kansas City, for destruction of government property, conspiracy, intent to damage the national defense and criminal trespass. Held without bail. Convicted. (For attempting to disable missile launch silo lid with jackhammer.) He was sentenced to 10 years, later reduced to 40 months with 4 year's probation. All appeals denied. Released in 1988.

1988: Expelled from Oblate Order, returned to family farm.

1999: Died of a stroke, May 31, 1999.

Rev. Carl Kabat, O.M.I.:

Born 1933, Scheller, Illinois (brother to Paul Kabat).

Ordained Oblate priest, 1959, Pass Christian, Mississippi.

1960-1961: St. Henry's Seminary, Belleville, Illinois.

1961-1962: Pastoral House, St. Paul, Minnesota.

1962-1964: International Falls, Minnesota.

1964-1965: Cathedral High School, Duluth, Minnesota.

1965-1968: Oblate mission, Philippines.

1968-1969: Richfield, Minnesota.

1969-1973: Oblate mission, Recife, Brazil.

1973: Fled arrest warrant in Brazil for inciting to revolution by conducting church socials and preaching that the kingdom of God starts here on earth with human dignity.

1973-1977: Bemidji, Minnesota, Indian mission.

1976: Arrested in Plains, Georgia, for parading without permit (nuclear arms picket). Jailed and released.

1977-1980: Baltimore, Maryland at Philip Berrigan's Jonah House.

1978: Arrested twice for spilling blood at Pentagon. Sentenced to two six-month terms in jail.

1979: Arrested and jailed in Chicago for protesting sale of weapons to Brazilian generals who had oppressed his parishioners in Recife. Convicted with Darrell Rupiper of disobeying a police officer. Served several days in jail.

1979-1980: Arrested in Washington, D.C., for pouring blood on the White House steps. After release, arrested and jailed for pouring blood at Pentagon. Served 11 months for both offenses.

1980-82: Arrested with Berrigans and others at GE nuclear missile plant, King of Prussia, PA, charged with several misdemeanor and felony counts, including conspiracy, burglary, and criminal mischief (pouring blood on Mark 12A warheads and hammering on them). Served 14 months in prison while case was appealed. (Settled, 1990)

1983: Arrested Dec. 4 at US Army base at Schwaebish, West Germany, for destruction of government property, criminal trespass. (Used bolt cutter to disable Pershing II Missile launcher.) Fled German prosecution to US.

1984-1991: Arrested Nov. 12, Whiteman Air Force Base, near Kansas City, for destruction of government property, conspiracy, intent to damage the national defense and criminal trespass. Held without bail. Convicted (for disabling missile launch silo lid with jackhammer). Sentenced to 18 years (later reduced). Served time in several federal prisons. Released on parole in 1991.

1991: on detached service with Oblate Order.

1992-93: Arrested for unlawful entry to silo at Kansas City. Received six months in jail.

1994: Arrested April 1 at missile silo in North Dakota for destruction of government property, conspiracy, intent to damage the national defense and criminal trespass (broke some external components with hammer). Convicted and sentenced for five years (served half of that time.)

1996: Arrested in Oklahoma City for violation of parole (traveling without permission). Served out balance of previous sentence. Released in July 1998.

Rev. Frank Cordaro (diocesan priest):

Born 1951, Des Moines, Iowa

1976: Discontinued priestly studies to found the Des Moines Catholic Worker house of hospitality for homeless.

1977: Arrested with Philip Berrigan for spilling blood at Pentagon.

1978: Arrested and released in five-day protest at Rocky Flats nuclear weapons plant, Colorado. Blockage of railroad tracks.

1979: Arrested at White House press conference about Strategic Arms Limitation Treaty. Spilled ashes at feet of Jimmy Carter as protest to all nuclear arms. Publicly called treaty "a lie." Arrested and jailed numerous times for protests at Strategic Air Command, (SAC) Omaha. Served jail terms totaling 10 months.

1983: Resumed priestly studies.

1985: ordained Diocesan priest.

1985-1992: Parish priest, Logan, Iowa. Arrested more than 15 times for non-violent acts at SAC. Served three different six-month terms in prison.

1992-1995: Parish priest, Council Bluffs, Iowa. Arrested for "crossing the line" at SAC. Served another six-month sentence.

1995-1998: Parish priest, Milo, Iowa. Arrested for protests at the Pentagon, and in New York City. Arrested in Des Moines at governor's speech for protesting policy to reinstate death penalty in Iowa.

1998-1999: Arrested for protest at Andrews Air Force Base. Spilled blood on B-52 bomber and hit it with hammer. Served 6-month sentence for destruction of government property.

Rev. Roy Bourgeois, M.M. (Maryknoll):

Born: 1938, Lutcher, Louisiana.

1962: graduate of Louisiana State University.

1963-1967: US Navy, serving as officer in Vietnam. Received Order of the Purple Heart.

1968: Entered Maryknoll seminary.

1971: Arrested at White House protest staged by Vietnam veterans. Jailed overnight.

1972: Ordained Catholic priest, Maryknoll missionaries.

1972-1977: Bolivian Maryknoll mission.

1977: Placed under house arrest in Bolivia for subversion; kicked out as "*persona non grata*" by military regime.

1979: Arrested at arms bazaar in Chicago for failing to obey a police officer. Served several days in jail.

1980-1982: El Salvador mission.

1983: Arrested and jailed in Georgia for unlawful entry and impersonation of an officer. (He and associates played last recorded sermon of archbishop slain in El Salvador. The broadcast was directed as protest against El Salvador death squads being trained in School of the Americas at Fort Benning, Georgia.) Served 18 months in prison.

1984-forward: Placed on special assignment by Maryknolls for "SOA Watch" near Fort Benning, Georgia.

1990: Arrested in Georgia for trespassing, destruction of government property at "Hall of Fame" at School of the Americas at Fort

Benning (on the first anniversary of the killing of six Jesuit priests and two coworkers in El Salvador by death squads trained at Fort Benning). Served 14 months of 16-month sentence.

1996: Arrested for criminal trespass at Fort Benning. Served six months.

1998-forward: Arrested for criminal trespass at Fort Benning. Served six months. (Occasion was "funeral" for all those killed in Central/South America by Fort Benning's death squad graduates.)

Rev. Charles J. "Angelo" Liteky, M.S.SS.T. (Missionary Servants of the Most Holy Trinity):

Born: 1931, Washington, D.C.

Ordained: 1960, Holy Trinity, Alabama.

1960-1963: Retreat preacher, Shrine of Saint Joseph, Sterling, N.J.

1963-1966: Rural mission parishes, northern Virginia.

1966: Joined US Army as chaplain with rank of captain for service in Vietnam.

1967: Rescued 23 wounded men in face of enemy fire at Bien Hoa while wounded, administering last rites.

1968: Received Congressional Medal of Honor, and Purple Heart, at White House.

1971-75: Resigned commission from US Army, served as counselor to veterans through Veterans Administration.

1975: Left priesthood, and continued counseling of Vietnam veterans at VA hospital in San Francisco.

1983: Married.

1986: Surrendered his Medal of Honor at the Vietnam War Memorial in Washington, D.C. as personal protest of US involvement in Central America. Participated in a 47-day fast on Capitol steps, Washington, D.C.

1990: Arrested at Fort Benning, Georgia, for defacing government property with blood. Sentenced to six months.

1996: Arrested at Fort Benning, Georgia, for trespass.

1997: Arrested at Fort Benning, for trespass.

1998: Arrested at Fort Benning, for trespass, destruction of government property, resisting arrest. Not prosecuted.

1999: Arrested at Fort Benning, for trespass. Found guilty.

Michael Palecek, former seminarian:

> Born: 1955, Norfolk, Nebraska
>
> 1978: Graduated from Wayne State College, Wayne, Nebraska.
>
> 1979: Attended St. John Vianney seminary, St. Paul, Minnesota.
>
> 1979: Assisted at protest rallies in Chicago, at the White House and at the Pentagon. These variously involved the Berrigans, Carl Kabat, Darrell Rupiper.
>
> 1980: Staffer at New York Catholic Worker and worked among homeless.
>
> 1981-1982: Finished college, earned teaching certificate, married.
>
> 1982: First arrest for crossing property line at SAC.
>
> 1983-1986: Taught at high school. Founded Norfolk, NE, Catholic Worker Community and served in soup kitchen. Crossed line at SAC 15 times. Arrested and jailed several times. Served sentences of 10 days; 30 days; 50 days; 6 months; 6 months. Suffered mental breakdown in federal prison.
>
> 1989: Released from prison; graduated Wayne State College.
>
> 1989-1998: Worked as columnist, editor at several weekly newspapers in Iowa, Nebraska and Minnesota.
>
> 1999: Crossed line again at Offutt Air Force Base. Not charged.

Rev. Daniel Berrigan, S.J. (Society of Jesus):

> Born: 1921, Minnesota Iron Range near Bemidji.
>
> Ordained: 1952. Became Jesuit teacher.
>
> 1965: "Exiled" to Latin America by Cardinal Spellman for justifying Roger LaPorte's self-immolation over Viet war. LaPorte's action as a war protester was thought by Spellman to be a mortal sin of suicide. Berrigan disagreed in print. (La Porte worked for the "radical" publication, *The Catholic Worker.*)
>
> 1966: Returned to US to edit Jesuit Mission magazine.
>
> 1967: Joined faculty of Cornell University.
>
> 1967: Marched on Pentagon, arrested for failure to obey an order to move. Spent five days in jail.
>
> 1968: Criticized for his trip in February to Hanoi to help return three captured American pilots.
>
> 1968: Burned draft files in May at Catonsville, MD, in company of eight others including his brother, Philip Berrigan, S.S.J. Collectively the group became known as the "Catonsville Nine." Convicted of destruction of US property; destruction of Selective Service records; and interference with Selective Service Act of

1967. Sentenced to three years in prison, released on bail pending appeal.

1970: Became fugitive when appeals failed. Captured after several months and returned to prison.

1971: Named unindicted co-conspirator by J. Edgar Hoover and Harrisburg grand jury while in prison. Charged with plotting to kidnap Henry Kissinger and blow up the utility tunnels of nation's Capitol buildings. Acquitted.

1972: Paroled. Back to teaching, organizing and lecturing.

1980: Pouring blood, hammering on nosecones of Mark 12A warheads at GE nuclear missile plant, King of Prussia, PA. Charged with conspiracy, burglary, and criminal mischief. Convicted and given 3-10 year sentence. Appeals lasted 10 years. Sentence reduced to time served. This was the founding act of dissenters known as Plowshares.

To the present: Teaching, organizing and lecturing.

Rev. Philip Berrigan, S.S.J. (Society of St. Joseph):

Born: 1923, Minnesota Iron Range, near Bemidji.

1943-1945: Served in WWII, artillery officer, Europe

1955: Ordained in the Josephite Order, specializing in ministry and education among poor blacks.

1956-1963: taught at St. Augustine's high school, New Orleans, an all-black school.

1963-1965: Taught at Josephite seminary, Newburgh, New York.

1965: Arrested for crossing line at Fort Meyers, Virginia, during meeting of Joint Chiefs of Staff.

1966: Served at St. Peter Claver parish (mostly black) in Baltimore.

1967: Poured blood on draft files in Baltimore in company of three others. Collectively they became known as the "Baltimore Four." Bailed out in 1968.

1968: Burned draft files in Catonsville, Maryland, with help of eight others including his brother, Fr. Daniel Berrigan, S.J. Collectively they became known as the "Catonsville Nine." Convicted of destruction of US property; destruction of Selective Service records; interference with the Selective Service Act of 1967. Sentenced to six years for the Baltimore action plus three years and six months concurrent for Catonsville. Released for 2 years during appeals.

1970: Married secretly to Elizabeth McAlister, an activist nun, Order of the Sacred Heart. (Marriage formalized in 1972 while in prison.)

1970: Became fugitive when appeals failed. Captured and returned to prison.

1971: Named co-conspirator by J. Edgar Hoover and Harrisburg grand jury while in prison. Charged with plotting to kidnap Henry Kissinger and blow up the utility tunnels of nation's Capitol buildings. (His wife, Liz McAlister, was also indicted.) Convicted only of violating prison rules for smuggling out letters.

1973: Excommunicated from Catholic Church for marriage.

1973: Paroled (effective December, 1972)

1974: Cofounded Jonah House community of war resisters in Baltimore.

1975-76-77: Pouring of blood, digging of "graves" at White House and Pentagon on numerous occasions, resulting in several jail terms ranging up to six months.

1980: Pouring blood, hammering on nose cones of Mark 12A warheads at GE nuclear missile plant, King of Prussia, PA. Charged with conspiracy, burglary, and criminal mischief. Convicted and given 3-10 year sentence. Appeals lasted 10 years. Sentence reduced to time served. Action became known as "Plowshares Eight."

1983: Philip's wife and six others pour blood on B52s at Griffiss Air Force Base, Rome, NY, and hammer on planes. She receives three-year sentence, serves 25 months in prison.

1999: Pouring blood on A-10 Thunderbolt warplanes and hammering on fuselage at Maryland Air National Guard Base. Awaiting trial. Protest was against use of depleted uranium in weapons delivered by such planes in Desert Storm and Yugoslavia. Sentenced and jailed.

Printed in the United States
717900002B